COMPANION CD-ROM INCLUDED

The Professional Bar & Beverage Manager's Handbook

How to Open and Operate a Financially Successful Bar, Tavern, and Nightclub

Atlantic Publishing

THE PROFESSIONAL BAR & BEVERAGE MANAGER'S HANDBOOK: HOW TO OPEN AND OPERATE A FINANCIALLY SUCCESSFUL BAR, TAVERN, AND NIGHTCLUB

DOUGLAS ROBERT BROWN

Copyright © 2006 by Atlantic Publishing Group, Inc.

1210 SW 23rd Place • Ocala, Florida 34474 • 800-814-1132 • 352-622-5836–Fax

Web site: www.atlantic-pub.com • E-mail: sales@atlantic-pub.com

SAN Number :268-1250 • Member American Library Association

ISBN-13: 978-0-910627-59-7 • ISBN-10: 0-910627-59-2

Library of Congress Cataloging-in-Publication Data

Miron, Amanda.

The professional bar & beverage manager's handbook : how to open and operate a financially successful bar, tavern, and nightclub / Amanda Miron.

    p. cm.

  Includes index.

  ISBN-13: 978-0-910627-59-7 (alk. paper)

  1. Bars (Drinking establishments)--Management. 2. Taverns (Inns)--Management. I. Title.

TX950.7.M57 2005

647.95068--dc22

2005032247

10 9 8 7 6 5 4 3 2

Printed in the United States

EDITOR: Jackie Ness • jackie_ness@charter.net

ART DIRECTION & INTERIOR DESIGN: Meg Buchner • megadesn@mchsi.com

BOOK PRODUCTION DESIGN: Laura Siitari of Siitari by Design • www.siitaribydesign.com

"If you are thinking of opening your own bar, make sure you read this handbook first. It may even save you thousands of dollars by avoiding costly mistakes in areas you may have overlooked."

> — Mike Snyder
> MrGoodbeer.com

"This is an excellent book, providing a thorough examination of the bar business. Anyone considering the bar business, whether as a new start-up or purchasing an existing one, would do well to read this book. For the beginner, it poses some important aspects of the business and points out the work involved with operating successfully versus the "romantic" idea of what being a bar owner is.

It covers the essentials like legal issues, permitting, and determining customer base and appeal in detail for the beginner. For the seasoned bar owner or manager, it gives good advice on assessing customers, cost issues, and dealing with problems. As someone who has professionally consulted with prospective and present bar owners about their businesses, this book will be a welcome addition to my job.

There is no one who wouldn't be able to apply knowledge from this book to their business and improve the business."

> — Jeff Uher
> Co-founder, Uher Hospitality, LLC

"The Professional Bar & Beverage Manager's Handbook is a necessity and your ultimate guideline to success!"

> — Gilles Bensabeur

Table of Contents

CHAPTER 4　Bar Layout (Nuts and Bolts)

CHAPTER 5　Advertising and Marketing

CHAPTER 6　Types of Beverages

CHAPTER 7　Preparing and Serving Beverages

CHAPTER 8   Food & Sanitation

CHAPTER 9   Bar Controls

CHAPTER 10   Money

CHAPTER 11   Customers

CHAPTER 12   Tips to Making Your Bar a Success

CHAPTER 13   Your Bar's Personality

CHAPTER 14   Dealing with Problems

CHAPTER 15   Myths About Managing a Bar That Could Hurt Your Business

CHAPTER 16   Nightclubs

CHAPTER 17   Additional Equipment

CHAPTER 18   Laws by State

CHAPTER 19   Forms and Charts

Conclusion

Glossary

Manufacturers Reference

Index

Introduction

Many reports have circulated suggesting that most new bars that are opened last less than a year before closing. This leads many would-be bar owners to give up their dreams of owning a bar long before they ever establish their premises. However, you should not let doom-sayers talk you out of owning a bar if that is your dream. In fact, studies have consistently shown that even in bad economic times, bars tend to do well, and bars are often the most profitable part of a dance club or restaurant.

So how can you make your bar a success? The secrets to creating a well-managed bar that makes a profit and creates genuine pleasure for customers is described here in this book. After reading these pages, you will be ready to successfully manage every aspect of your bar business, whether you are new to the bar business or looking to improve your current establishment.

This book is organized to help you find the information you need—fast. You can use this book in two ways. First, read the entire book, front to back, to get plenty of information about management, and then refer to this book as needed to help you resolve the inevitable day-to-day quandaries that will occur as you run your business.

In these pages, you will find it all:

Chapter 1 will cover the basics about opening a bar. Here you will learn about conducting market research, examine the competition, tips on location, zoning information, permits and licenses, and much more. Even better, you will learn the basics of building a business and financial plan that can get your bar off the ground and making profits. You will learn how to open correctly so that patrons seek out your bar.

Chapter 2 will cover the hiring and training of employees. Your employees will be your most important asset—they are the ones who will ultimately determine whether your customers are happy and whether your bar delivers high-quality service. Don't make costly mistakes that can affect how customers see your bar—learn the right ways to find out whether your staff is reliable and trustworthy. Also, discover the best ways to train your staff.

Chapter 3 will cover all you need to know about inventory, including the basics of storage and dealing with vendors. Here, you will also learn which supplies you need in order to be a success.

Chapter 4 will cover the nuts and bolts of bar layout. You will learn how to set up a bar to ensure maximum productivity and high profit. Don't let poor design drive away your customers; find out how to set up your bar so that customers will love visiting your establishment.

Chapter 5 will cover the basics of advertising and marketing. You will learn how to use word-of-mouth advertising, press releases, and other professional marketing tools to entice customers and ensure that your bar is a success. You can spend less money than you imagined and still create plenty of buzz about your bar—find out how in this chapter!

Chapter 6 describes the various types of liquor and other alcoholic beverages with which the restaurant manager must become familiar. Consider all the types of liquor before ordering a bottle for your bar!

Chapter 7 covers the basics of preparing and serving the beverages—one of the fundamentals of running a successful bar. In this chapter, you will find tips for serving and mixing drinks. You will also find a no-nonsense guide to drink recipes. You will also learn about flair bartending, one of the more controversial aspects of bartending out there.

Chapter 8 describes the food that is an essential component of every bar. Find out why your bar should serve at least some food and what types of food you should serve to really attract patrons to your establishment. It also deals with HACCP and sanitation, which are critical to any establishment that serves food.

Chapter 9 covers the bar controls that you need to enforce in order to make a profit and to keep your bar running smoothly.

Chapter 10 covers money. Here, you will learn all you need to know to manage money for your bar. You will also learn the biggest money losers for a bar and how successful bar managers make money less of a hassle.

Chapter 11 outlines the backbone of your business: your customers. You will learn how to attract the customers who will make your bar the most talked-about establishment in town. You will also learn the successful bar manager's secrets to making each customer a raving fan of your establishment.

Chapter 12 describes the extras that can make your bar a success. Here, you will consider the sound systems, themes, and additional expansions that often make or break a bar.

Chapter 13 considers the personality of your bar and the ways you can project a certain image that can lure specific clientele and attention.

Chapter 14 is a troubleshooting guide to the common problems that bars face. With this guide, you will be able to deal with problems quickly and effectively—before they hurt your business. You will find the common problems that can sink a bar, as well as the solutions that can ensure that these problems don't even faze you.

Chapter 15 outlines the myths that bar managers sometimes hear. You need to learn the truth about these misconceptions before inaccurate information hurts your business.

Chapter 16 deals exclusively with nightclubs. It details the different types of nightclubs as well as discussing expanding into the nightclub business.

Chapter 17 focuses on the equipment needed to make your bar run smoothly.

Chapter 18 is a comprehensive listing off each state's alcohol laws.

Chapter 19 has over 50 pages of charts and forms that can be easily implemented to streamline the running of your bar and increase profits.

There is also a complete alcohol-related glossary of terms.

Whether you are a bar owner or owner/bartender, running your own bar can be a very rewarding prospect. Consider the fact that bars are a big part of our social history. In Europe, bars have been part of the social scene for hundreds of years. In North America, they are often depicted as key social centers in movies. Where would the characters in the classic film *Casablanca* be if it were not for "Rick's," the perfect bar in the middle of a desert metropolis? Today, bars are where people go to get away from their lives and where they go to seek time with friends. People celebrate life's biggest milestones in bars.

If you are running a bar, you make a bigger impact on people's lives than you might imagine. Patrons will turn to your bar for entertainment and good times with friends. Providing a pleasant place to eat, drink, and celebrate will not only ensure business success for your bar, but will also allow your bar to become a place patrons look forward to visiting. With the ideas and tips in this book, you will be able to run a bar that is satisfying to yourself and your customers.

Foreword

The on-premise beverage alcohol industry makes a substantial contribution to the state's economy. According to a recent study, the economic impact was $10.5 billion yearly in total business activity, $4.7 billion in annual wages generated, $676 million each year in state and local taxes, and 327,790 jobs created in New York state alone. While working with the Empire State Restaurant and Tavern Association, I have had many members join the association who needed a lot of guidance in gaining profit. We are the spokesperson for the industry dealing with the local, state, and federal governments. We work on programs such as credit card processing, disability insurance, health insurance, package insurance policies, payroll processing, and workers' compensation insurance.

The Professional Bar & Beverage Manager's Handbook is a solid, practical guide for someone in the business or someone considering getting into the business. It not only goes into detail about how to start fresh, it also goes into detail about ways to improve once the establishment is running. This book is for novices and veterans alike. With very friendly style writing, it is organized so that it can be used as both a primer and a reference. Running a bar or tavern is not simple, and tons of minute details become very important. Without a reference, it is extremely difficult to survive.

Having a reference such as *The Professional Bar & Beverage Manager's Handbook* will help you succeed as a bar or tavern owner. It is said that the best information on a topic comes from someone who has already accomplished it. With true case studies of real bars and taverns, you can read what other people have done to make their establishment different and more profitable.

— *Scott Wexler, Executive Director, ESRTA*

CHAPTER ONE

Opening a Bar—An Overview

If you do not currently run your own bar, then you are probably reading this to learn how to start your business. Opening a bar is a daunting prospect, and one that should not be taken lightly. You will have to plan and pay for the initial outlay of supplies and drinks, arrange the legal aspects of opening, and hire new employees, all time-consuming and potentially expensive tasks. On the other hand, if you are opening a new bar, there are a few advantages you can look forward to:

- The opening of a new bar is likely to generate new interest and publicity on its own, especially in a place where no bar has been before. Newspapers may report on the opening of a new bar on their own volition, and customers are likely to drift in even with little advertising, merely to "try the new place."

- Since you will be dealing with new employees, you will also be dealing with employees who will likely still be excited with their jobs and still working hard to make a good impression on you, the employer. This may propel them to work harder than average to be nice to customers. This can help ensure repeat business—at least in the beginning.

Before opening a bar, you will want to consider whether you make a good bar manager. While the movies may make managing a bar seem simple, in real life, successful bar owners and managers require a few specific traits:

- **Are you personable?** Bar management is largely about the people, not the drinks per se. If you want to operate a successful bar, you will do much better if you either genuinely enjoy spending time with people (employees and patrons alike) or are willing to hire someone who will perform this function for you in the bar.

- **Can you get the startup money?** In addition to renting or buying a space for your establishment, you will need to budget for purchasing supplies and hiring your employees. You may also need to pay for a liquor license, advertising, and legal costs of starting a bar business. If you have the savings for this, great. If not, you will need to find a partner who can help you fund your business or a lender willing to give you a business loan that can help you get started.

- **Do you know what it will take to set up a bar in your area?** You should spend some time looking at bars in your area with a critical eye. Talk to friends and family about their favorite establishments to get a sense of why people go to bars and what sorts of bars will be successful. Well before you establish and run your own bar, you need to have an idea of what will work. In general, this is based on a good understanding of the current bar scene in the area where you will be opening. To have this understanding, you must do your research about what bars are doing in your area to be successful—and what needs that have yet to be filled by a bar or establishment in the area.

- **Can you take care of the legal and business aspects of running a bar?** Most governments closely control the running of a bar, but exact legalities differ from area to area. Contact your local municipality to find out which forms and licenses you need to open an establishment. Your local library will likely not only have a full account of local laws, but also books about running a business successfully. These make excellent reading as you work to open your new bar. In addition, the advice of an attorney who specializes in these matters is crucial.

JACK D. KEANE IS THE OWNER OF **NEVADA SMITHS**, A BAR IN NEW YORK CITY THAT WAS STARTED AS A PLACE TO WATCH FOOTBALL AND GREW INTO MUCH MORE. JACK FEELS THAT AS LONG AS HE HAS SOMETHING DIFFERENT THAN EVERYBODY ELSE, HE IS DOING SOMETHING RIGHT.

It all began a decade ago. New York is the center of the universe but doesn't have a place to come worship the beautiful game of football. So it began with a satellite dish and a couple of customers, and now a decade later it has become famous the world over. We have daily, year-round coverage of all the best European football from England, Spain, Italy, France, and Germany. We also have complete UEFA Champions League, UEFA Cup, World Cup, and European Championship coverage with up to fifty live games a week. All the U.S. MNT games and Metrostars matches are also included. We are the home of the HARDCORE FOOTBALL FAN. Over a dozen supporter clubs are based here, the rich and famous mingle with the working class, and it's a football stadium within a NYC bar. We don't have any martinis or fancy food here, mate! It is impossible to categorize this place. Countless TV crews have recorded and uplinked live from here, and our staff is trained in the belief that FOOTBALL IS RELIGION.

Market Research

In market research, you will learn about your customers (or potential customers, if you have not yet opened for business) and your competition.

Basically, you are trying to find out the answer to one question: What do my customers want?

The bars that answer this successfully usually prosper because they are able to offer the services and products that customers want more effectively than the competition. They also know who their customers are and can focus their efforts in marketing and advertising on the people who are most likely to provide a steady profit.

Before you can determine what your customers want, you need to know who your customers are. How you decorate your bar, how you market, what drinks and foods you sell—most aspects of your bar, in fact, will be guided by who your customers are. Obviously, if you are catering to the college crowd, you will want a very different bar than if you are mainly visited by business types who want to do business at your establishment.

If you already have a client base and are happy with it, knowing your customers is as simple as looking around and stopping by a few tables of regulars to ask how things are. Regular customers will often be happy to give you a sense of the sorts of changes you can implement in order to increase customer satisfaction.

If you have not yet opened a bar or have not been open for long, you may have a harder time gauging your customer base. If you have not opened yet, you may spend some time thinking about who you want to attract. You should base this not on who you think would make the best clients but on who you would genuinely enjoy seeing at your bar each day. You may also consider the location of your bar. If you are near a factory or college, your bar may attract those workers or students who are closest. If your building was previously a bar, look at the type of bar and clientele that was involved. You may attract the same type of clientele as before, as former regulars drop by to take a look at what has been done to the "old place." If you want to attract a different clientele than the location suggests, then you will have to work hard in your décor and managerial decisions to create an atmosphere that would appeal to the clients you wish to have. However, if you are lucky enough to attract particular clients already, you may not want to snub your customers and may wish to cater to them instead rather than gamble on attracting enough of the patrons that you would prefer to have.

If you have opened a bar but get clients that you find undesirable for some reason, you may also have to work hard to overcome your current reputation and style. Often a too-eccentric or vague bar style confuses customers. A specific theme or ambience usually works best. You may also want to begin having a specific theme night for the clients you want to attract. Organizing one night is often easier than trying overhaul an entire bar's structure. If the clients that you are trying to attract like the service and drinks that they get at your bar, they may simply return on other nights without any effort from you.

Ways to Conduct Market Research

Hire a Market Research Company

In your local phone book, you will easily be able to find companies that are willing to help you—for a price, of course. The big advantage of hiring a market research and analysis group is that you will be able to get professional market research results in a short amount of time. These companies use strategies such as customer polls, focus groups, online and in-person surveys, telephone surveys, and product testing, among others, to help you decide who your customers are (or who they could be) and what these customers want. The companies will even interpret the results for you in a way that is perfectly clear and understandable.

The major disadvantage, of course, is cost. These companies do charge money for their services, and if you are just starting out, this outlay of funds can seem very large. If you are able to afford a market research company, by all means hire one. If you cannot, though, do consider saving up to hire one after you have been open for a while—the insight you can gain from a professional market analysis can be a big help in maximizing profits.

Do Your Own Customer Market Research

If you cannot afford to hire professionals, you will simply have to invest your own time and effort into learning about your customers. You cannot skip this stage of planning a business, even if you are feeling overwhelmed. Without knowing your customer base, you simply will not have the information you need to make the right decisions about pricing, marketing, bar décor, and almost every other aspect of opening a bar. What you learn in your market research will literally affect every aspect of your business and will make all parts of your business more profitable.

You can do your own customer market research by asking customers or potential customers some questions. The easiest way to do this is to arrange some volunteers to ask acquaintances or coworkers a few questions. Have questionnaires printed so that volunteers can record the answers. Keep questionnaires short and to the point. If you have not yet opened, ask questions such as the following:

- **When traveling, what was the best bar you visited like?** (This question will help you establish what people like and what they might like to see in their own hometown.)

- **When do you go to bars and pubs?**

- **How often do you go to bars and pubs?**

- **What do you like about bars and pubs?** (The answers here will give you a sense of what customers are looking for.)

- **What types of bars or pubs do you visit?**

- **What do you wish were different about bars and pubs?** (Listen closely to the answers to this question—the answers will give you some ideas about what the competition is missing.)

- **What sort of bar would you like to see open in the city?** (The answer to this question will give you ideas about niches that your bar could fill—and what the customer response might be.)

- **What is the best drink you ever had at a bar?**

- **Describe your best customer service experience at a bar.** (The answer will give you a sense of what your staff should be like to create enthusiastic customers.)

- **How much do you usually spend per drink and what sorts of drinks do you order on a night out?** (This will give you an idea of what you need to offer and what prices you need to set to draw in customers.)

- **Name your three favorite bars.** How did you find out about each? (This will give you an idea of how you need to advertise in order to attract customers to the bar.)

- **Tell me a few things about you** (You can also ask volunteers to note the sex and general age of each respondent. The idea is you want to know the basic demographics about each person so that when you analyze your market research, you can see whether many respondents who visit bars or who seem like good potential clients are easily reached in a particular way. If most of your potential clients are middle-aged men who like sports, then you may want to rethink your original idea about a feminine bar, complete with fashion magazines at each table.)

If you already have a bar established, you still need to do some market research. This is much easier, however. All you need to do is offer your customers the chance to take a survey. Offer this as an option while the customers are waiting for their drinks or as an option before they pay their bill. You will get the best results if you offer customers a chance to win a prize in exchange for their participation. Just have customers leave their first name and phone number on the survey and place each completed survey into a drawing for a nice prize. As an added bonus, you can also give customers the choice of providing their e-mail addresses to be provided with details of upcoming events at your bar. For those customers who want this service, e-mail ads are a great and inexpensive way to promote your bar.

You will want to do this type of market research at least occasionally once you are in business. Although going through the surveys is time consuming, it can tell you exactly what customers want and need. Better yet, regular surveys will let you know whether your customers (or their needs) are changing and whether you need to make changes in order to keep up.

On questionnaires for your existing customers, you will want to ask some similar questions as you would ask potential customers, but with a few differences:

- **Demographic information.** (Asking customers to tell you where they live, their age range, and their occupation lets you see who comes to your bar the most and who you need to target in ads and in the bar's appeal.)

- **What was your server like?** Were you satisfied with the service? What did you like/dislike about the way your server handled your order? (This lets you know how your employees are doing in making customers happy.)

- **Where did you first hear about us?** (This lets you know which of your marketing strategies are actually working.)

- **Would you come to this bar again?** (This lets you gauge customer satisfaction.)

- **How often do you come to this bar?** (This question lets you see who your regulars are.)

- **How often do you visit establishments like this one?** (This lets you see how often the competition is getting business that could be yours.)

- **What would you like to see changed at this bar?** What would you like to see offered? (Here you can get useful suggestions for changes or expansions.)

- **Are the hours of business convenient?** (If they are not—or if you are not staying open late enough—you may well be losing business.)

You simply cannot be shy about talking to others about bars. You do not need to announce that you are the owner of a new (or upcoming) bar. Simply ask others—ask anyone you can—about their bar experiences. Many people enjoy talking about themselves and will be glad to offer feedback. Talk to others, even to your competition's customers. You never know what you will find.

There are other ways besides asking questions to find out who your potential customers might be, including the following:

- **What is around your bar?** If you are close to a college, you can expect college students to pop in, and you can likely build a respectable business by creating a student-friendly atmosphere that will draw in students eager to unwind after a long day. If your bar will be located near a factory, find out about the drinking and eating habits of the workers there—many may be interested in dropping in after work for a pint. If there are businesses near your bar or pub, consider who might come into your establishment for a business lunch. Your bar's location can be an important clue as to who your potential clients may be.

- **What other establishments are in your area?** Chances are if there are other establishments in your area, they cater to a specific set of people. These same clients may be willing to come to your establishment—if you've made it attractive enough for them. For example, if your bar is located near boutiques that cater to women, setting up a cozy place where "the girls" can meet for a chat after shopping may be a savvy business strategy. If your bar is located near strip malls that sell auto parts to car enthusiasts and car mechanics, consider that these same clients may be willing to drop by your place for a quick drink and snack before heading home. If your bar will be located by several tourist traps, then a bar with plenty of local flavor may appeal to visitors eager to relax after sightseeing. The idea is that the stores and businesses near your bar's location are already marketing and drawing regular customers—you can attract these same clients (who are, after all, in your area regularly) simply by making your bar appealing to them. It's a very simple idea with a big profit potential.

- **How many bars are in the city and what are they like?** Researching your competitors is covered in detail in the next section of this book, but as you are researching your customers (or potential customers), be aware that they do not live in a vacuum. If they already have a sports bar that they frequent (and that sports bar has a stellar reputation), you may need to offer something different or better in order to draw loyalties away from the competition. Your customers are looking at other bars—and visiting them. Have an idea of where your customers are going and why they are going there to get a sense of why they might come to your bar instead.

- **What was in your previous location and who frequented it?** If your establishment was a bar before (or a restaurant or other shop), find out who frequented it. You may find that the same groups of people are still willing to eat and drink at the "new" place.

- **What isn't in your area?** Consider what types of bars are missing in your city or town. Is there no quiet bar that appeals to the artsy crowd? Is there no jazz bar? Is there no loud bar that is also a great place to dance? Research your customers well to make sure that there is a need, but if you do see a need that is not met, do not be afraid to jump at the chance. Being able to fill a need is a great way to ensure your bar's success.

- **Try asking people for recommendations to bars.** This can be as simple as walking down the street, stopping a passerby, and asking, "Excuse me, what is the best bar near here?" You will learn useful things about what is considered "the best" in an area.

- **Don't be afraid to ask people you know.** Acquaintances, friends, and family all have their own ideas about bars. Ask them where they go and tag along on a trip to the bar. Ask them what they like about their favorite bars and what they don't like.

Bar managers who care little about marketing research are unlikely to succeed. They may not seem to care about their customers or may fritter away their marketing money on potential customers who simply do not visit the bar.

Once you have done your market research, you will want to analyze your findings. It is a mistake to ignore the market research you have done because you have a different idea about the customers you want to attract. It's very nice to have an image of a fancy bar with celebrity clientele. If your market shows that most of your paying customers are going to be blue-collar workers, it is best for you and your business to follow the market research rather than your own ideas of what will work.

At the same time, you should not strive to implement every change that customers want. Not only will it be a very expensive venture, it may make the bar too hectic to introduce many new things. Instead, when you are looking at your market research, look for patterns:

- **Who are your customers?** What are their ages, sex, and occupation? Do you have a different crowd at lunch, a different one in the early afternoon, and a different one in the evening? If so, divide the surveys into these crowds so that you can see what you need to do at each "peak" hour.

- **What do your customers want?** Again, look for patterns. You may hear about everything from jukeboxes to bands. What your customers may be saying is more entertainment. Try to provide some of what customers want, and always try to provide those things that do not cost extra (friendlier atmosphere or waitstaff, for example, often is highly demanded by customers but costs the bar manager only effort rather than large amounts of money).

- Ask yourself **what small changes could meet the most customers' demands**—and then implement your changes. A few small changes can have as much influence as a larger, more expensive change but at a smaller cost.

The Competition

Your competition is the other bars and restaurants with bars. Ignore your competition at your own peril, because as savvy bar managers know, what the competition is doing may have a big impact on your business. There are several things you will want to know about your competition:

- **Who are they?** Look in your phone directory at the bars and pubs in your area. Review ads to determine which bars are your most direct competitors (either because they are close to your establishment or because they seem to be appealing to the same customers who will be visiting your bar.)

- **What are they like?** Try to get a sense of the selection, quality, service, and atmosphere of each competitor (or each direct competitor, if there are very many bars in your area). Getting a sense of the competition will give you a chance to see what you need to do better or what you need to offer in order to lure customers.

- **Who visits them?** Which customers does your competition attract? College students? Businesspeople? Blue-collar workers?

- **How do they advertise?** Look at the ads your competition runs and really analyze them. To whom are they meant to appeal? How effective are they? Where does the competition seem to advertise the most? Often bars that are successful have already done the market research that tells them which ads bring in the largest profits. You can learn a lot about a successful ad campaign by looking at a successful competing bar.

- **What do they offer?** Which drinks does your competition overlook? Which drinks are hot sellers at competing bars? What sort of menu or extras (gambling, live acts, jukeboxes) does the competition offer? Knowing what your competition offers lets you know what you need to offer. For example, if every competitor offers draft local beer because it is a hot seller, then you need to offer it as well. From what the competition offers, you can also get a sense of what is missing. Do no bars in your area offer specialty coffees even though your market suggests some customers want it? Offering what your competition does not—and advertising exclusive availability at your bar—is often a good way to draw customers. You will know what to offer if you research both your customers and your competition.

- **What are they doing right?** Bars that have been in business for a while that draw plenty of customers are doing something right. If you can pinpoint what that something is, you will have learned a key lesson about what it is that your bar needs to offer in order to draw customers. Is the competition able to offer many specialty drinks? A great atmosphere? Super service? A wonderful location? A view? Special events? You can learn a lot from a successful bar—and then tailor what you have learned to your own bar.

- **What are they doing wrong?** Try to figure out what the competition is not doing correctly—and then do it right at your bar. Is the hot bar in the city a beautiful place to drink but offers slow service? Offer speedy and friendly service as well as an attractive atmosphere and you will get plenty of customers to your bar. If you notice something wrong at a competing bar, chances are that customers notice too. They will generally be glad to visit a bar that offers a better experience. Don't forget to look into bars that seem to be doing plenty wrong—the bars that seem to be empty every night. You can often learn as much from these bars as from the successful ones. If you can pinpoint what the failing bars are doing wrong, you may be able to avoid their fate.

- **What are their busy nights?** What are the slow nights? Figure out what the "hot" nights are for the major competitors in your area. You may want to hold your own big nights on other evenings to avoid the well-established competition. You may want to hold smaller specials on the big nights to draw those customers who cannot get into the crowded bars.

- **What are the prices?** Look at your competitors' prices; they are what they are for a specific reason. Can you under-price them (and if you can, will that draw customers)? Can you offer something more? Your prices should not be very much higher or lower, but slight differences (up or down, depending who you are selling to and what prices you can offer) can make your bar successful.

There are several ways you can learn more about your competition:

- **Visit them.** The very best way to see what your competitors are like is to visit them as a customer. Sit down at a competing bar, order a drink, and look around you. What is the bar like? How are customers treated? Who is in the bar and how content do they look? What is the quality of the food and drink? What is the quality of the service like? Often the best research you can do on a competing bar is the research you can do with your own senses. Try to visit as many bars as you can before you actually start to set up your own. There is nothing like being a customer to actually let you see what works and what does not in nearby bars.

- **Talk to their customers.** Do not be afraid to strike up conversations with your competition's customers. Talk to them about the bar and ask them what they like about it, where they heard about it, and what they think of it in general. Do not try to sound like an interrogator; simply try to strike up a conversation to find out how other customers see a particular bar.

- **Read their ads and press.** The competition spends plenty of time marketing and advertising. Read what they have to say about themselves; you will be able to gauge what they offer and who they are trying to entice. You will likely find that some bars use very good marketing strategies that you can incorporate into your own marketing and advertising. You will also likely see some costly advertising mistakes that you can avoid.

- **Read guidebooks and reviews.** Reviews online and in newspapers and guidebooks can give you a good sense of what others have to say about the competition. You can easily get another perspective on what a competitor is doing right or wrong. You can then use this information to do the same things right while avoiding the same mistakes. Reviews can also be a great way to tell what is missing. If your top three competitors get poor reviews for service and great reviews for atmosphere, then you can provide excellent service (and fill a need). Even if you cannot hire the same expensive decorators, offering something that the competition does not can help ensure your bar's success.

Your Business Plan and Financing

Before you open a bar, you will need to develop a business and financing plan. A business plan can help you get financing, so it makes sense to tackle this part of the business first. Business plans are written for every type of business, and this plan basically is the road map to the future of your bar. It outlines where your bar is today, what you plan for your bar in the future, and the exact steps that you plan to take in order to accomplish success. If you will be applying for financing or loans or if you are planning on operating a business with another owner or partner, a business plan is essential. Others will determine whether to support your business or not depending on what you have written. Plus, a business plan is also useful for yourself. It lets you see on paper whether your bar plan will work or not—well before you invest time and money in a project that may have serious problems. A business plan also acts as an action plan, telling you what you need to do in order to make your bar a success.

To begin your business plan, you will need to gather all the research you have done in terms of marketing, about bars, and about the competition. Look at this information closely—where is the evidence that a bar with your idea will be successful? Remember, anyone reading your business plan will be looking for a detailed idea of what your business is like, but they will also want to see evidence that you have done the footwork to prove that your idea can work. Your business plan should convince readers that your bar has a good chance of success.

Before you begin writing your plan, you will need to have a purpose and a general plan. What do you hope to accomplish with your business? What needs do you see your bar fulfilling? Who will your customers be? What will your bar be like? What do you expect profits to be like? What steps will you need, exactly, in order to reach this ideal version of your bar? Work on paper, jotting down notes to yourself on where the bar project is now, what still needs to be done, and your final vision of the bar. Write down what you know about your company, the products you will be offering (drinks, entertainment, food), the competition, the potential market, and the possible risks of the business.

Once you have gathered your ideas and research, you can start putting together your business plan. Begin with an executive summary of your bar. This entails writing approximately two pages about the bar itself—what it is, what the purpose is, and what skills and resources you have for making the business work. Once you have explained your business, offer a detailed explanation of the products and services you are offering. Obviously, much of your plan will focus on drinks, but don't forget to mention food or any entertainment you will be offering to patrons as well. In this section of your business plan, you will need to detail where you will get your supplies (vendors and suppliers) and the costs that you expect to incur in getting your initial inventory. List your suppliers and carefully note the costs of getting food, drink, and entertainment for your bar.

Next, you will need to discuss the market you are entering. This means you will have to talk about the state of the bar industry overall and in your particular area. You will also have to provide details on your potential customers—who they are, why you are targeting these specific customers, why they are likely to spend, and what their spending habits at the bar are like. You need to prove in this section that there is room for another bar in your area and that there are enough spending customers in your area to support your business. You can contact your local government to get statistics for your area that are pertinent—someone in the statistics department of your local or state government will be able to help you find information about businesses similar to yours and statistics about the local economy. In this section, you will also have to provide an analysis of your competition—who they are and where there is a space for your bar among these competitors.

Next, you will have to include a marketing plan in your business plan. This part of your business plan will detail where and how much you plan to advertise. List any advertising or marketing resources you already have and estimate how much advertising will cost (conservative estimates are best). Do not overlook word-of-mouth advertising, print ads, and any other ways you have spread the word about your business. It is important in this section to include specific information about why you think your projected advertising will work: Does it target the potential patrons? Does it offer something that advertising for the competition does not? Remember that your business plan (and the marketing plan inside it) are an argument for your business. Using your plan, you are trying to show readers why your bar is destined to work. This means that you need to show evidence that suggests that each part of your business plan is well thought out and likely to succeed.

Finally, you will want to detail your financial plan and estimates. You will need to list your expenses and your projected yearly profits. You will also have to show readers how you arrived at your numbers. Again, you must be convincing and you must show in your business plan that you have carefully researched your business and have a clear and reasonable idea of what to expect from a bar. Note where you expect to get your initial financing and how much of your initial financing you have taken care of already.

Before you have your business plan printed and submitted to companies, investors, and the like, make sure that you take the time to read it over and polish it. While you are eager to open your doors to business, you need to develop a workable business plan first. Consider the following checklist before printing your business plan to make sure that you have a plan that will get results:

- **Keep your plan under fifty pages.** Most of the readers of your plan will get many business plans each day. Most readers will spend only a few minutes browsing your plan. Based on this initial browse, they will decide whether to keep reading or not. Your plan needs to be long enough to give details about your bar, but it cannot be so long that no one will be able to get through it.

- **Make it clear and logical.** Use complete sentences and follow a logical outline or argument. The business plan should be easy to understand and should answer the basics about your business—what it is, who it is for, where it is located, why it is a good idea, and when your specific ideas are going to be implemented. Readers should not have to read through your entire report to get a sense of what your business is.

- **Make it well organized.** Use headings to guide readers around your business plan. Make sure to follow the basic guideline of a business plan. Start with a summary of your business, move on to a complete description of your business, detail the products you are offering, discuss your market, delineate your market and then wrap up with financial information. Good organization will make your report flow and will make it easy for your readers to find the information they need.

- **Make it professional.** The report should be well-written and nicely formatted. It should look like a document that is important and has been worked on extensively. That means it should use a professional tone of writing and should be printed on high-quality paper.

- **Make it appealing.** First impressions count, so make sure that your business plan makes a good initial impact. Use bullets and lists as well as paragraphs. Use enough white space on your pages to avoid making pages look "crowded." Use graphs and charts that let readers see what you mean quickly and effectively. Color graphs are especially good.

- **Make it current.** You will need to update your business plan regularly so that it always includes the latest market information and the most current information about your business. It may be a pain to update your business plan, but it is essential in order to ensure that your business works well. With time and practice, drafting a business plan will become easier.

Need more help? If you need in-depth help writing your business plan, consider *How to Write a Great Business Plan for Your Small Business in 60 Minutes or Less: With Companion CD-ROM.* This manual covers every element of a business plan step by step in an easy-to-understand manner. The CD-ROM has a sample business plan in Microsoft Word as well as sample financial documents. To order, call Atlantic Publishing at 1-800-814-1132 or visit **www.atlantic-pub.com** (Item # GBP-01, $39.95).

Once you have your business plan, you will be able to see exactly what your initial expenses and your financial status is. You will also be able to use your business plan in order to get financing for your bar.

While many bar managers are excited by the bar concept, they are likely in bar management, at least partly, as a way to make a living. This fact makes money an important part of managing a bar. Unfortunately, it can also be one of the most confusing parts of bar management. As a bar manager, you need to consider:

- Costs of renting or owning the establishment

- Costs of hiring employees

- Starting costs—including costs of decorating and buying equipment

- Costs of licensing and services (such as consulting services, legal services, cleaning services, contractors, etc.)

- Costs of special events

- Utilities

- Insurance costs

- Prices and profits from drinks and food

When you first open a bar, you will have many initial expenses to consider all at once, and these expenses will come well before you make your first profit. Luckily, you do not have to take on the entire burden yourself. There are many places where you can find help for financing your business:

- **Loans.** Whether from a private lender or a financial institution, business loans are widely available for new business—including for your bar. Business loans need to be paid back—with interest—no matter how successful or problem-ridden your bar is, so it is important to do your research before applying for a loan. Make sure that you choose a lender offering good terms and a good rate. Also, make sure that you go over your financial forecasts and expenses again and a again so that you borrow the correct amount. In general, you want to borrow enough to get the business going but not so much that repaying the loan will be a burden.

- **Partners or investors.** You may be able to get financing from someone who has money to invest in an idea. These people advertise in financial and entrepreneurial publications all the time. On the plus side, you will be able to get the money you need—often in exchange for a share of the profits rather than for an interest rate. However, you may also have to relinquish some control, as many investors will want to have some say in the running of the bar. If you decide to take on a partner, you will also be taking a risk, especially if you know nothing about the person. To make sure that you are not taken advantage of, carefully research any potential investors or partners and have your lawyer draw up a contract that will protect your interests and those of the bar.

- **Small business grants and programs.** Most local and state governments want to encourage new businesses. New business creates jobs and essential services and helps ensure prosperity. For this reason, most governments have programs and incentives to help new businesses succeed. You can find out what your local and state governments can do to help your business by contacting your local and state chamber of commerce and asking about assistance available to new businesses, especially new bars. Even some programs that do not offer money directly can help your initial finances by reducing the amount of money you need to spend on specific items; such as employee training, for example.

- **Savings and assets/personal finances.** Many people opening a new business will use personal money such as savings or assets in order to get the business going. This tends to ensure that you will get into less debt and can help so that you do not have to pay as much interest. On the other hand, when you use your own money, you do risk your own wealth. If you are beginning a business with someone else, you must take steps to ensure that your own personal investment is well protected through a legal contract or other legal document.

Your Bar's Location

Now that you have a sense of your bar's customers and competition, you can start actually putting together the details of opening a bar. Hopefully, you have done your research well and have file folders of information that tell you who you are selling to and the things you need to do in order to draw customers. If you do not, go back and do more market research and research about competing bars carefully. The rest of this chapter will have you make decisions that will rely upon what you have learned in your research.

Real estate agents are famous for saying that the three secrets to a sale are "location, location, location." If you have been doing your research about bars in your area, you have likely noted this phenomenon. In almost every town there is a bar that does well despite terrible service and low-quality drinks. Usually, they can get away with it because their location gives them a "captive audience" or an audience that does not have a choice. The bar may be located near a hotel, where a transient population ensures that someone will always peek in. The bar may also be the only one within a particular area, making it the obvious choice. In contrast, in your research you will likely find great bars that are half-deserted. Their location in out-of-the way spots likely dooms them, even if they have great business plans and super service and offers.

You can learn a lot from this; namely, that you need a great location in order to succeed. Before you buy a location for your bar, consider some traits of a great bar location:

- **Pedestrian traffic.** A bar location that sees plenty of pedestrian traffic, such as downtown areas or theater districts, is great, since passersby are more likely to peek into an establishment, while drivers are likely to speed by, intent on their destination. Walkers are more easily turned into customers than drivers.

- **Near other businesses and places of work.** People may want to drop in after work for a quick drink. If your bar is in the middle of nowhere, people will need to work much harder to find it—and so are more likely to go elsewhere. A location on a well-traveled route is ideal; a main road from a big factory, for example.

- **Near other entertainment.** People will often drop in for a drink either before or after some other entertainment. If your bar is near a stadium, theater, or some other place where people go to enjoy themselves, it is more likely that your establishment may become a place to meet before a night out or a place to enjoy a nightcap. This is exactly what you want, as it means that your location itself is generating customers.

- **Visible.** Tiny bars in alleyways may sometimes get business, but most people looking for a spot to have a beer or glass of wine are more likely to be curious about the attractive bar that they see. Face it, most of us are visual creatures. A visible bar advertises itself, especially if it is also on a route that sees plenty of traffic.

- **Evening traffic.** If your bar's location is very busy in the morning but less busy in the afternoons and evenings, you may be setting yourself up for trouble. You want a location that is lively during the hours that you expect most of your business. Not only will this help ensure a steady flow of people who will enter your bar, but a lively evening place is simply more inviting to many customers than a single bar open among closed stores and businesses.

- **Parking.** If your customers will be traveling to get to your bar, then you will need to provide them with some place to park their cars.

- **Affordable.** You need to be able to pay for your location and still make a profit. Unfortunately, many prime areas for business are very expensive (precisely because they are prime). However, you do need to keep price in mind. If your operating expenses are larger than your profits, you will find yourself in financial trouble.

- **Available.** In most cities and towns, there are specific rules about where alcohol can and cannot be sold. Before you purchase or lease any place for your bar, check zoning regulations at your local city hall to ensure that you can operate a bar business at the location.

Choose your location carefully, as it can help ensure a successful bar—or it can make running a successful bar more frustrating and difficult. If you have a choice, try to make your location work for you, not against you.

Of course, this is all assuming that you have some choice about your location. What if you have no choice about location because you have already purchased or leased a spot? You can try to make the most of your location by advertising and marketing more heavily. In an era when most people have cars, you may be able to lure customers, but if your location is truly terrible, you may need to offer incentives in order to attract customers. You may also need to change your strategy and start targeting the customers who are available in your area.

In the end, though, a bad location will work against you. If your location seems to be costing you profits, you have to seriously think about moving. You may also want to either set up a different business, one that caters to the location. Whatever you decide to do, make sure that the bar and the bar's location are working together for the best profit.

Zoning, Permits, and Licenses

There are millions of words written each year about the laws and regulations concerning the sale of liquor. No matter how small your town is, there are likely many rules and regulations that will affect your bar. What can be more frustrating is that these rules are not only difficult to understand but also change frequently. They are also different for each location, so even if you have owned a bar in one location, you will still need to re-learn the rules and get new permits and licenses for a new location.

Frustrating as they are, the permits, licenses, and zoning laws that can make opening a new bar so difficult are actually meant to protect both the bar patrons and the bar owners and managers. Rules and laws make sure that each bar is operated according to certain procedures. If anything bad does happen at your bar, having the right permits protects you by showing others that you followed all the right procedures concerning the running of your bar. Customers feel better going to bars that they know meet certain minimum requirements for safety and cleanliness.

Even though permits, licenses, and laws may actually give everyone peace of mind, they can easily drive you to distraction when you are trying to start up a business. Bars, especially, have many regulations ruling them since alcohol is closely controlled. It is normal to feel overwhelmed by the sheer number of laws you need to read and by the sheer number of permits and licenses you need to obtain. Luckily, the process is somewhat streamlined for you.

Before you invest money into your bar, you will want to contact your local town hall to find out whether you can get a liquor license and whether your bar can meet current zoning laws. Liquor licenses may be difficult or expensive to get in some cases, especially if there are many bars in your area already. Getting a liquor license in your area can depend on many things, including your history, the type of bar you want to open, the type of license you are applying for, and zoning laws in your area. Zoning laws regulate what types of property can be established where. These laws regulate how large buildings in certain areas can be and what types of businesses can operate in those areas. For example, when you apply for a liquor license, you may learn that your area does not permit bars within a certain distance from schools. Your local county or municipal government will have a branch that deals with liquor control and a branch that deals with zoning. You will need to contact both branches (check your phone book for local contact information) for the most up-to-date information.

If you are purchasing an existing bar, the licenses may not be transferable. Before you sign all the papers, make sure that you get the licensing you need. Without the right licensing, you will not be able to open your bar.

Check your local phone book and start contacting the organizations that you need to contact to get the licensing information you need:

- **State bar/restaurant association.** Most states have these organizations. These groups offer "startup" kits for business owners that detail the specific state laws and licensing regulations in clear language. You will need to go over these kits several times and understand the information before starting your business.

- **State chamber of commerce.** Your state's chamber of commerce can tell you about state requirements for opening various types of business and can send you the forms you need in order to set up your business in the state.

- **Local chamber of commerce.** Your local chamber of commerce will have easy-to-read instruction books and starter kits for new businesses. These will detail all the information you need to know about zoning laws and licenses in order to open your business. Your local chamber of commerce can also send you the forms you need to fill out in order to operate a business at the local level.

- **State department of alcohol.** These are called different things in different states, but whichever body regulates the sale of liquor in your state is the body you need to apply to for your liquor license.

- **Local trade associations.** Local trade groups are gatherings of business owners and managers who exchange information about business. This is a great resource for finding out about upcoming legislation that will affect your business. It is also a great source of information about local regulations and expectations for a new bar.

- **Internal Revenue Service.** You will need to start paying taxes as a business. You will also need to get federal SS-4 Form Application of Employer Identification Number. This form, when filed, will allow you to open a corporate bank account and will also allow you to pay your bar staff. The IRS can also tell you about any special taxes you will need to pay on liquor in your area.

This obviously represents a lot of reading and plenty of forms to fill out. However, keeping track of all the information and forms you get (as well as actually reading the information) is key. Your local and state governments will have the information you need about licensing. Make sure that you order the newest kits, information packages, and forms for your local area and state, as the information is changed very often. Once you have read the information sent to you, you will likely realize that you are in need of an attorney.

Legal Advice

Legal issues will affect your business right from the start; bars are simply more closely regulated than other types of businesses. As a bar manager/owner, there are several types of laws with which you will need to concern yourself:

- Bylaws regarding signs and advertising
- Zoning bylaws
- Employee regulations and laws
- Fire regulations
- Safety regulations

Most bar owners worry about lawsuits the most—and with good reason. There have been many cases in recent years of bar owners and managers being sued as a result of a drunk patron's actions. Bar managers and owners can also be sued by employees if work conditions are unsafe. Lawsuits are everywhere, and to legally protect your business, there are a few things you can do:

1. Hire a good lawyer.

2. Do all you can to make your bar a safe place.

3. Get the very best insurance that you can.

A good lawyer can be helpful if you find yourself in legal trouble. He or she can represent you in case of court action and in some cases can help avoid court action in the first place. Your lawyer can also ensure that everything in your bar is legal and that you feel peace of mind. You will want to do your research for a good business lawyer well before you ever need one. Meet for consultations and choose a lawyer or law firm that you are confident will be able to help you. You might require a lawyer to witness some of the forms you need to start your bar in the first place. This is an excellent opportunity to ensure that you start a business relationship with a lawyer who can help you.

Secondly, you will want to make sure that your bar is as safe as possible. This will help ensure that any problems are avoided in the first place. Even if you do find yourself involved in a lawsuit, being able to prove that you did all you could in order to make your bar safe can go a long way in protecting you legally.

One of the most important ways to keep your bar safe is to make sure that your bar staff know the signs of intoxication and are prepared for the legal responsibilities of alcohol. Intoxication is the largest concern for a bar. Intoxicated customers can create legal problems through their actions. For this reason, long before you open your bar's doors, you and your staff need to be prepared to deal with intoxication:

- **Develop an alcohol sales policy.** This type of policy generally includes a description of federal, state, and local laws that govern the sale of alcohol in your area. Ideally, this information should be clearly and briefly written to make sure that your servers can understand and remember it. Your state department of alcohol and local chamber of commerce will generally have easy-to-understand legal information about alcohol sales. Your alcohol sales policy should also include the bar's own rules for servers. Basics such as not selling to minors and not selling to intoxicated customers should be part of these rules, but you also need to make these rules are more specific so that your servers know exactly when limits are reached. For example, you may want to put a policy into place that requires a server to notify the manager about any customer who has had more than four drinks (or three, or six, depending on the policy). The manager can look at the situation and determine what to do. This ensures that staff do not have to take full responsibility for making decisions that affect the legal life of the bar and the customer's safety. You may also want to set up a relationship with a local cab company in case you need to suggest a cab for a customer.

- **Make sure servers are aware of alcohol laws.** Each server should have a complete guide to local and state alcohol sales laws. Test each server on their knowledge. Your state's department of alcohol regulation will generally have informational guides and even testing materials you can use with your servers so that you do not have to come up with your own.

- **Train your servers to serve alcohol responsibly.** You should have a documented alcohol service training program in place that covers the effects of alcohol, blood alcohol concentration levels, and alcohol's effects on the body. *The Responsible Serving of Alcoholic Beverages: A Complete Staff Training Course for Bars, Restaurants, and Caterers* is an excellent manual that covers all aspects of alcohol service in depth and has a comprehensive in-house training program that is easy to set up, customize, and implement. It comes with a CD-ROM that contains all forms and training materials discussed in the book. To order, contact Atlantic Publishing at 1-800-814-1132 or order online at **www .atlantic-pub.com** (Item # RSA-01, $49.95).

- **Make sure your rules are clear and check to make sure those rules are followed.** Make your employees fill out forms that keep track of customers' alcohol intake if there appears to be a potential problem. Have servers offer a menu to any customer who is only drinking or offer a free appetizer to a customer who has had a few drinks. Ensure that servers are checking IDs and that the amount of alcohol poured into each drink is measured.

- **Make sure your server gets management involved** in any incident involving an intoxicated customer. Document everything that occurs.

The best way to ensure that you and your staff can handle an intoxicated customer is to make sure that everyone working at the bar knows what to do with an intoxicated customer.

Many people think that alcohol stimulates. Certainly ads suggest that alcohol creates a fun time. In fact, alcohol alters moods and affects how the body functions, but it does these things as a depressant. As the bloodstream absorbs the alcohol that has been consumed, the body is affected. It is only when the liver removes the alcohol from the bloodstream by oxidizing it that the body returns to normal. It takes time for this process to take place. Folk remedies such as strong coffee or cool water will not help. A person needs to stop drinking alcohol entirely and allow the body to cope with the substance already in the system.

Problems occur when someone drinks excessive amounts of alcohol or more than the liver can comfortably deal with. The alcohol amount in the bloodstream increases, and as it does, the moods of the person affected—as well as the behavior and motor function—change. The more alcohol that is present in the bloodstream, the more a person is affected.

It is not always easy to tell when a person has over-indulged. In many cases, a person will sit quietly and keep drinking so that servers will not see visible signs of too much alcohol consumption, such as swaying or slurred speech. Also, each person can drink different amounts before being negatively affected. Larger men and those who drink frequently will often have a higher tolerance, and their bodies will be able to handle larger amounts of alcohol. Patrons who drink slowly and drink on a full stomach may also take longer to experience the ill effects of alcohol than patrons who drink quickly and on an empty stomach. Some patrons will be able to drink four drinks or more without any ill effects while some will become unruly after only two drinks.

Clearly, you do not want to "cut off" someone who is not intoxicated and who is simply having a nice time. However, it is your legal responsibility to cut off any patron who is drunk. There are several ways that you and your staff can tell when a patron has had too much alcohol:

- Patron will get louder and may become more friendly, possibly accosting staff or other patrons with familiarity (this usually is thought of as the first stage of intoxication).

- Patron may have motor skills affected by alcohol, meaning speech will become slurred, walking will become unsteady, and may have a difficult time picking up change or a coaster. At this stage, usually called the second stage of intoxication, the patron may become more difficult, even aggressive. Patrons at this stage may also start swearing, complaining, or may become withdrawn. They will usually wish to drink more at a faster pace and become careless with their money and about their surroundings; dropping change or bumping into others, for example.

If you see the above signs, you need to stop serving the patron. This can become difficult, especially if the patron wishes to continue drinking and becomes aggressive or argumentative. An intoxicated patron who makes a scene when not served can be nuisance and a distraction to other customers. There are several ways to ensure that dealing with an intoxicated customer is less of a hassle:

- Try to prevent a customer from becoming out of control in the first place by having the establishment's alcohol serving policies firmly in place. This means that your staff should always check patron IDs where there is any question about a patron's age. In fact, staff should check the ID of any person who appears to be under thirty. Identification should be a photo ID with a current expiration date. The ID should show no marks of tampering (cuts, fonts that do not match, lack of holograms). A bar may be held responsible for serving alcohol to a minor, even if the minor uses a fake ID, so staff need to be alert. Staff should be especially careful about patrons who arrive together and have the oldest member of the group purchase alcohol. Everyone who is drinking needs to have their ID checked. Staff should also refuse to serve any patron more than one drink at a time. Patrons should be offered a menu if they are drinking, as food in the stomach can slow down the speed in which alcohol is absorbed. Remember, prevention is your best bet in avoiding problems associated with an intoxicated patron. Impairment (or being affected by alcohol) begins with the first drink, and the savvy bar staff will work hard to ensure that impairment does not turn into intoxication.

- If a patron does get intoxicated, it is important that staff react while the patron is still at the first stage or early in the second stages of intoxication. At this stage, the patron's drinks should be slowed down and the patron should be offered a menu.

- Try to avoid direct confrontation with an intoxicated patron. Staff who notice someone who has consumed too much should alert the manager and slow down service to that patron. This can be as simple as being suddenly busy and by not asking the patron whether they want anything else. This can help give the patron time to metabolize the alcohol that is already in his or her system.

- Staff and the manager should start paperwork as soon as they notice that a patron has had too much. This paperwork should include a quick inventory of the date, a description of the patron, a listing of when the patron was served, a list of the drinks served, and a description of any events or conflicts which occurred. This will help ensure that in case of legal trouble or a patron complaint, staff will have the information needed to show that the bar acted properly.

- If avoiding serving the intoxicated patron does not help, the manager should be called. The manager should treat the complaint as a regular service complaint, apologizing for the inconvenience but quietly and firmly noting that the bar cannot legally serve the patron. Many bar staff members shy away from this sort of direct confrontation, as they fear how such a conversation will look to other patrons. When handled firmly but politely, this sort of chat with a customer can help make other patrons more comfortable with the bar, as it shows other guests that the bar is serious about keeping customers safe.

- Where appropriate, intoxicated patrons who have been refused service should be offered something else, such as a free nonalcoholic beverage or a free snack, in order to keep the customer happy and to allow the customer time to "sober up."

- The patron may continue to argue loudly. If the patron becomes a problem or starts to distract other customers, he or she should be asked to leave. In general, the manager will want to offer the patron a taxi cab, as it is important that the patron arrive home safely. There have been lawsuits in North America filed against bars who ejected a customer who then did not make it home safely. You are certainly not responsible for paying for a patron's fare, but you should offer to call a taxi.

- Do not worry if the patron threatens to never come back or threatens to patronize another bar. Be secure in the knowledge that you are protecting the patron, other customers at the bar, and your own business by refusing to serve someone who has had too much to drink. Even though how much is "too much" is a relative concept, it is better to err on the side of caution and risk offending someone rather than continue serving someone who will be in an accident as a result of their intoxication or who will be a threat to themselves and others. Most patrons will respect a bar more for being firm with an intoxicated customer. These customers will continue to come to your bar, even if the upset patron does not.

SYMPTOMS *of* INTOXICATION

Know the symptoms of intoxication! Intoxication is a legal term defining the level of alcohol in the blood.

Drinking Very Fast

Ordering More Than One Drink At A Time

Overly Friendly

Loud Behavior

Buying Drinks For Others

Lighting The Wrong End Of A Cigarette

Careless With Money

Use Of Foul Language

Concentration Problems

Mood Swings

Enhance your décor and help employees serve alcohol responsibly with posters. Atlantic Publishing offers a series of ten posters that deal with alcohol awareness. Pictured above is the Symptoms of Intoxication poster (Item # SIO-PS $9.95). Each stylish posters measures 11" x 17" and is laminated to reduce wear and tear. To order call 1-800-814-1132 or online at www.atlantic-pub.com.

- Post signs of intoxication and the rules about serving intoxicated customers where your staff will see the rules and be reminded of them. Periodically test your employees with quizzes on what to do in case an intoxicated customer continues to ask for drinks. If staff do deal with an intoxicated customer according to the regulations set out, be sure to praise the staff after hours and point out exactly what was done correctly. This will help enforce what needs to be done the next time.

Minors Can Mean Major Legal Problems

Serving alcohol or selling cigarettes to a minor is illegal. Unfortunately, many people who are underage routinely try to get served. Whatever reasons they have for drinking alcohol, minors can be quite a nuisance to bar managers. The frustrating thing for many managers is that while minors know that underage drinking is illegal, minors will often go to great lengths to conceal their age, often relying on borrowed, stolen, or fake IDs in order to buy alcohol. What is even more frustrating for the bar manager is that minors caught drinking will rarely find themselves in much legal trouble, but the bar that served the minors will generally face an entire array of legal problems and may be shut down. The problems will be worse if the minor is involved in another illegal activity or is hurt or injured after drinking. This means that every bar manager needs to take great care to make sure that no minors are served at his or her bar.

There are a number of ways that minors attempt to get served. The most

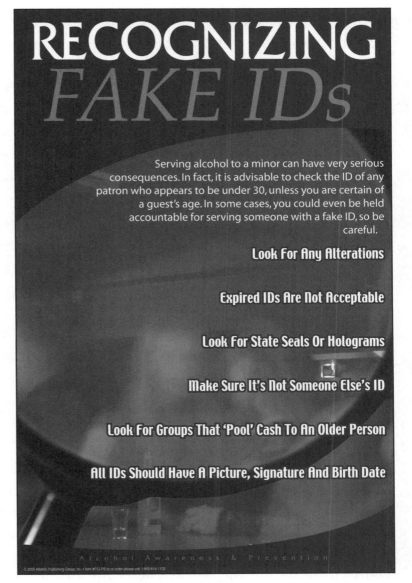

This poster will help employees recognizes fake IDs. To order, call 1-800-814-1132 or online at www.atlantic-pub.com (Item # FID-PS, $9.95).

popular method is by using fake IDs. Unfortunately, with scanners and high-quality printers available to almost every high school student, fake IDs are easier and easier to make—and harder to spot.

You need to make sure that all employees check the ID of anyone who seems underage. Train your staff to spot fake IDs. Staff should first look at the type of ID being given to them. Acceptable forms of ID include driver's licenses or state identification for non-drivers, passports, and United States Uniformed Service Identification. The ID must contain a picture, the person's name and date of birth, a physical description, and a signature. The ID must be valid to be accepted at the bar (many fake IDs are made from found expired IDs). Your bar staff should always look to see whether the picture of the person and the description match the person standing in front of them.

Fake IDs can be spotted a number of ways. Marks of cuts around a date of birth or different fonts within an ID are often giveaways that an ID is fake. Valid IDs have protective holograms. Look for these features. You can help your staff by getting an ID checker, which uses the magnetized strips on IDs to check whether they are fake.

If you are unsure whether an ID is valid or fake, it is acceptable to ask for another piece of ID. Many adults will have more than one piece of identification and will be happy to show it to you. Even other picture ID can show you whether the names and signatures on the various IDs match or not.

Using fake ID is not the only way minors attempt to be served. Some minors simply borrow valid ID from someone who looks like them but is older. This can be harder to spot since the ID is valid and cannot be easily discounted. Plus, if the person borrows ID from someone who is a sibling or friend, they may know enough (middle names or other identifying information) to pass as that person. If you suspect that a minor is trying to get into the bar this way, you can ask the minor for a signature sample to compare to the ID. Many minors will get nervous and leave before signing. Even if they do provide a signature, this can easily be compared against the signature on the ID.

Some minors will simply drop by a bar with older drinking-age friends and drink the beer served to the friends. This is still illegal, even if the minor promises not to drink any alcoholic beverage but then does so. Many bars counter this sticky problem by simply not allowing minors into the bar without parental supervision or by barring minors entirely. This also means that your staff has to check the ID of anyone who appears to be underage—even if that person is with an older group.

Some minors simply rely on looking older than they appear. With some makeup, older clothing, and the dim lighting of many bars, it is not difficult for a seventeen-year-old to appear several years older. One way to counter this problem is to simply ask all patrons under the age of thirty to show their IDs. Most older patrons will actually be flattered to be mistaken for someone younger, and few patrons will mind that you are taking such care to prevent underage drinking.

Some minors will even attempt to bribe your bartender or rely on friends that they have on staff to get served. The best way to prevent this problem is to make sure that your staff are reliable and trustworthy. Savvy bar managers always run background checks and will often send in an older teenager as a test to see how staff are able to detect and deal with the minor. Remember, even one minor served in your bar is too many, and no bar serves just one minor. In many cases, a minor will brag about being served, causing a whole stream of minors to try to get into your establishment.

Make sure that your staff know the laws concerning minors and alcohol sales, and make sure that they have the authority to turn away anyone they think is underage. Staff are often timid about turning away customers because they feel that it is bad for business. In some cases, they may fear making a mistake or offending someone or causing a scene. It is important to stress that you will never be angry about staff turning away someone who they thought might be underage. Tell your staff to trust their gut feelings and give them specific actions to take if they suspect that someone underage is trying to enter the bar or order a drink. In general, staff should fill out a denial-of-service form for turning away a minor, just as they would for turning away someone who is intoxicated. They should write down the time, date, a description of the person, and why they felt the person was a minor. In case of any problems, this paperwork will help your bar face any legal hassles.

Other Factors That May Lead to Lawsuits and Legal Problems

The most common cause of legal problems involving bar patrons has to do with intoxication. In many of cases, bars are held responsible (at least partly) for things a customer has done while intoxicated. However, there are other causes for legal problems that the bar manager needs to be aware of:

- **Illegal workers.** It is important to ensure that all staff members you hire are legal to work in your area. Immigration officers do check bars and restaurants, which tend to harbor disproportionate numbers of workers who are not legally allowed to work in the country.

- **Pickpockets and scam artists.** Bars are a heavy concentration of people, and many of those people are focused on their drinks or the company they are with. This makes pickpockets and other scam artists view these bars as a haven. They may distract the waitstaff or bartender with questions while stealing. By the time a customer realizes that a crime has taken place, the thief is usually long gone. The best defense here is often a sharp-eyed staff and a security camera that can catch the perpetrator on film. In many cases, women's purses, casually left on the back of a chair or empty seat make an ideal target. Offering a coat check or at least reminding customers to keep bags stowed can reduce the chances of robbery or theft.

- **Sexual crimes and harassment.** Where drink and groups of people are involved, it is always possible that some person will try to grab or sexually assault another. Many cases of date rape or sexual assault involve alcohol. The best way to defend female customers and staff is to refuse alcohol to anyone who is intoxicated. Sex crimes are escalating. In some cases, though not all, a man may begin with leering or saying obscene things. He should be promptly evicted from the bar at this point and security staff should not let him in again. A zero-tolerance policy is generally best in these cases. A few men who seem to be following or crowding around a woman should also be approached. The woman in question should be asked if she needs a taxi cab called on her behalf.

One common problem today is so-called date-rape drugs. These substances are often introduced into alcoholic (or nonalcoholic) drinks at bars and parties. The victim loses consciousness or becomes unable to fight off her attackers, who take advantage of this situation to assault her. Obviously, this is a very serious crime, and not the type of situation any manager wants in his or her bar. The best way to guard against this is to ensure that only the bartender or qualified staff have access to drinks and mixing equipment. Servers should be alert for signs of intoxication or illness in someone who has not had much to drink. If it is suspected that a drug has been given to the customer, police should be called and the victim should be given medical attention.

- **Robbery.** Because of the expensive inventory of bars and because of the money that passes through such establishments, bars are very popular targets for burglars. Customers' purses, tip jars, cash, alcoholic beverages, and even cigarettes are all popular targets of burglars. In some cases, ex-employees who know the bar schedule or policy surrounding money take advantage of their knowledge after they no longer work for the company. In general, you should keep as little cash as possible on your premises. After closing, it is the usual practice to remove all cash from the premises and leave the till open so that would-be thieves can see that it is empty. You may want to change your money storage system every few months so that robbers cannot find an easy target. If you are robbed during business hours, your only priority is to ensure that no staff or customers are hurt. In case of an armed robbery, hand over all money and cooperate as far as possible. Try to remember as many details about the robber as possible and contact authorities as soon as it is safe to do so.

- **Assault.** Bar fights are something of a stereotype, but they do happen. If your bar gets a "reputation" as a place where this sort of activity occurs, you are likely to attract a clientele you may not want. Customers and bystanders can also get hurt in a fight. Refusing to serve intoxicated customers is one way to ensure that things do not get out of hand. Having at least some staff members large enough to intervene in case of an argument is another. If a fight breaks out, it should be stopped as quickly as possible. If weapons are involved, staff should be trained to take care that they are not hurt. Police should be called in such an incident, and other patrons of the bar should be moved to a safer place until help arrives.

- **Accidents.** Whether it is someone falling on an icy step, cutting themselves on glass, or an employee hurting themselves on the industrial blender, accidents cause a lot of distress to everyone. You can help avoid accidents—and the legal and physical pain they cause—by keeping on top of spills and potential danger areas. All steps should be clearly indicated to prevent tripping. Staff should be properly trained to deal with bar equipment and with customers who may need help.

- **Zoning laws and licensing.** Some of the laws surrounding alcohol are straightforward, but there are many laws concerning who can sell alcohol where and at what time and how many miles alcohol has to be from the nearest school. Not knowing about a law is no excuse, so before you open your bar, review your local food and liquor laws with a fine-tooth comb. There are legal consultants who can help you sort out the laws. While such an expense may seem large when there are so many other things to pay for, paying a lawyer ahead of time to understand your local laws can help prevent a lot of legal hassles down the road.

- **Illness in the bar.** If someone becomes ill in your bar, either because of something they ate or drank or simply in a twist of fate, you need to take swift action. An ill patron is your responsibility, and you should train your staff to get help immediately for anyone who seems to be in distress.

- **Drugs.** Alcohol does not necessarily breed drugs, but drug peddlers do often try to sell their wares in bars, cafés, and dance clubs. Being on the front page as the location of a drug crack-down is certainly not the type of press you want for your establishment. Your staff should keep an eye out for suspicious activity and report it at once. Any person who has been selling drugs on or near your bar should be reported and refused future admission to your bar.

Reducing the Chances of Legal Trouble

The longer you own a bar, the greater the chance that you will run into legal trouble of some sort. We live in a litigious society, and one that seems, in some ways at least, to be getting more violent. No one wants to see another person hurt. Luckily, there are a few ways to make your bar a safer place:

- **A great staff is often your best defense against trouble.** An observant and experienced staff can often notice crooks and other trouble before it happens. Bartenders are often legendary for being able to size up a person at a glance. Hire well and you will save yourself plenty of problems.

- **Good training.** Be sure to train your staff to observe customers and to help them when necessary. Your entire staff—from servers to coat checks—should know what to do in an emergency. Your bar likely has a fire-escape plan. Determine exactly what staff should do in case of a problem, and review the procedures with them regularly.

- **Reduce temptation.** You can often reduce temptation for robbers and other would-be thieves by eliminating larger amounts of money in tip jars and by keeping as little money as possible on the premises. Some bars reduce temptation even more by proudly advertising that they offer free meals to police officers with police ID. Few criminals would be tempted into robbing a bar where a police officer may be dining.

- **Hire security staff.** Security staff can add a touch of class to your bar and can also ensure that there is always a pair of eyes devoted to keeping your bar safe. Plus, if trouble does break out, security personnel are specially trained to handle the situation.

- **Keep things visible.** Bright lights outside the bar and easy access to full lights in the bar can help ensure full visibility the minute something happens. Being able to see can help stop a crime.

- **Keep things clear.** Reduce clutter and obstacles that can help criminals get away. The fewer shadowy places there are to hide, the less activity will be going on that you are not aware of.

- **Consider security systems**—but don't rely on them. Items such as buzzers, security cameras, and other devices may help after a crime, but these expensive systems are rarely as effective as a sharp-eyed security staff that can stop an incident before it occurs. Criminals aware of your security system will generally find ways to thwart it.

- **Lock up well, and know who can get in.** Each night, be sure that the bar is well locked up. Change locks after employees are fired or quit, and control who has keys to what.

- **Know your customers.** Knowing who patronizes your bar, what their habits are, and what type of people they are may help you spot things out of the ordinary. If your clientele changes suddenly, you will be alert that something suspicious is going on.

- **Don't be afraid to refuse service**—and don't be bullied into serving someone you should not. It is illegal to refuse service without good reason. A drunken customer may try to talk their way into another drink and then threaten to sue if refused service. In some cases, there is very little except a strong hunch to tell a server that something is amiss and a patron should not be served. Servers may be tempted to serve a customer who insists that they will sue if not served, but there are plenty of good reasons not to serve a customer, and servers should know exactly when to stand their ground. Most threats to sue are empty anyway. Even if they are not, the bar manager who honestly refuses service for a legitimate reason will not likely find themselves in trouble. The chances of trouble if the wrong customers are served, on the other hand, are very high.

Make customers aware that you have the right to refuse service. To order, call 1-800-814-1132 or online at www.atlantic-pub.com (Item # RTR-PS, $9.95).

No matter how careful you are, legal problems can occur. For this reason, get the very best insurance you can. Legal problems and crime can cost a fortune. If you have borrowed money to establish or expand a bar, you simply may not have the money for legal or rebuilding costs, so one problem could put you out of business for good. Bars should have excellent liability insurance, which protects in case someone sues the bar for injury or harm that befell them as a result of the bar. You will also want to invest in the best injury, fire, theft, employee, and property insurance you can so that any theft or accident will not cost you your establishment. Talk to a qualified insurance agent in your area, who can let you know what insurance types are available for bars in your area. Also, talk to other bar owners to get a sense of the types of insurance they have had to draw on over the years. Whatever you do, though, do not scrimp on liability insurance, which is often what will protect your business financially in case of a lawsuit.

The Cost of Each Drink

As a bar manager, you will need to make sure that you understand the costs and profits of even the smallest aspect of your bar. Usually, the smallest profit and cost margin you will need to worry about is each drink. How much you spend and make on each drink will help determine how much your bar profits each month and year. For this reason, you will want to consider how much each drink costs well before you ever open your bar. Before you open, you will have to know what type of profit is to be made on each drink and how you should price each item of the bar. In order to do this, consider the following tips:

- **Calculate the Cost per Ounce.** There are 33.8 ounces in a liter and 25.35 ounces in a standard 750-mL bottle. Each time you look at a bottle, you need to divide the price by the number of ounces to get a sense of the typical price that a serving will cost you.

- **Calculate the Total Beverage Cost.** For each drink that your bar offers, make sure that you understand how much the drink costs in total to make. Add up how much each ounce of liquor in the drink costs, and add up garnish costs, serving costs, and glass costs (costs of possible breakage and cleaning costs add up to a fraction of a cent per drink but must be considered), as well as the costs of any additional materials such as juices or sodas that are added. The total will be your beverage cost for that drink. Your price needs to be higher to make a per-drink profit. However, if price is too high above the beverage cost, customers will generally feel they are getting a poor value and may head to a competitor for better prices.

- **Calculate the cost percentage for each drink you sell.** To do this, for each drink you will need to divide the ounce cost by the sale price you've established for the drink. Then multiply the number you get by 100. The final number is the percentage of the final drink price that you are spending in order to buy the contents of the drink. A lower number means that you are making a larger profit. You can play around with this formula in order to find the drink price that will net you the largest profits. To compute what must be charged for each drink, simply plug different prices into the formula listed below until you reach the desired liquor cost-of-sales percentage:

Total Drink Cost ÷ Price = 18%–25% Liquor Cost of Sales

- **Calculate the Gross Profit Margin.** Subtract the cost price from the sale price of each drink to get each drink's gross profit. Divide the resulting number by the sales price and multiply it by 100 to calculate the gross profit margin. In most bars, drinks will vary widely in terms of gross profit margin. The savvy bar manager will do what he or she can to encourage sales of the higher-profit margin drinks in order to ensure a larger overall profit. If you know what your highest-profit drinks are before you open, you can advertise these drinks as a specialty.

Develop a Price List

You need to know how much each of your drinks will cost. However, while understanding how much each drink is costing you is a good place to start pricing, it is not enough. There are several other factors you need to consider when making up your price list:

- **Market research.** If you have done your homework, your market research will help guide your pricing. Compare your prices to the competition. Do you need to offer lower prices to lure customers away from the competition or can you charge more and still make a profit? Who are you trying to sell to and how much is your potential customer base willing to spend per drink? Pricing too low can be as much of a problem as pricing too high, so price carefully.

- **Don't make your pricing list too complicated.** Similar prices help ensure that bar staff can quote the right price to a customer. Three-tier pricing for well items, middle shelf, and top-shelf items keeps things simple; for example, well items might cost $4, middle shelf $4.50, top shelf $5.00. Also, be sure to keep all prices of all items clearly listed on menus or on price lists at each table so that patrons know how much each drink costs.

- **Include tax in your prices.** This allows customers to know exactly how much they are going to be paying for a drink and also allows you to round off prices to make cash handling less complicated. For example, if a drink's taxes push the drink up to $3.95, you can charge $4.00 and make life much easier for your staff and your patrons. Just make sure that you are tabulating taxes correctly. Sales tax, and especially the taxes on liquor, can be very complicated. It varies widely from state to state and tends to change every so often. This means that before you establish drink prices, talk to your accountant and state Department of Revenue to make sure that you correctly charge taxes.

- **Tweak your prices before you open.** Once you are open, you will occasionally need to change your prices, as operating costs change or as profits differ from projections. However, it is best to do your research thoroughly so that you will not need to change prices too often or too quickly. Frequent price changes make things harder on your staff, who have to memorize the new prices. Frequent price changes are unappealing to customers, who like to know what to expect from a bar's price list.

Protect Your Profits Before Your Bar Opens

The rules and profit projections that you set down before your bar even opens can dramatically affect how profitable your bar is. Make sure that your bar implements these rules to keep profits at a maximum:

- **Control pours.** Regularly test to make sure that employees are not under-pouring or over-pouring. Pouring too little of each ingredient affects drink quality and customer satisfaction. However, if many of your staff are pouring just a little too much each time, then your bar is effectively giving away free (costly) drinks on a regular basis. The more drinks that are prepared this way, the more your bar is losing. Post recipes for popular drinks and the exact measurements of each ingredient, and then make sure that each staff member is preparing drinks according to instructions. Also, do not let staff free-pour. Always have staff use pourers or control pour spouts to ensure drink quality and no wasted ingredients.

- **Reduce spills and waste.** Spilled alcohol, even in small amounts, is money thrown away. Make sure that your staff does not do anything that will cause even small spills. This looks sloppy and displeases the customer as well as reducing profits. Make sure that your staff are not simply lining up glasses and pouring without lifting the bottle at each glass, for example.

- **Computer liquor-control systems** are the latest ways that bar managers are using to control liquor pouring amounts. In these systems, a device is attached to the neck of each bottle. It measures how much alcohol is poured and then allows the manager to relay this information to a computer. These systems can be expensive, but they let you control each drink down to the drop and helps ensure quality. Many customers also enjoy knowing that they are not being short-changed on drinks at bars that use such a system. This technology gives both managers and customers more control over drink quality, something that is sure to be appreciated by all. Controlled pouring and computer liquor-control systems are covered in depth in Chapter 9.

Your Budget—Your Key to Financial Planning

If you are going to be running a successful bar, then you will need a good budget. A good budget does several things:

- Sets up a long-term plan that lets you see how much money the bar will be earning and when. This lets you plan ahead financially.

- Tells you what your operating costs actually are and lets you control these costs.

- Lets you solve cost and financing problems before they occur by letting you spot potential problems on paper.

- Lets you notice any discrepancies or mistakes before your next audit—so that you have time to fix them.

- Allows you to control costs.

- Allows you to account for sales.

- Lets you see how effectively your bar is working and lets you pinpoint areas that need improvement.

- Lets you maximize profits by letting you see where you are making your profits and where your money is going.

- Can help you get financial support if you need a loan or if you need to expand. It will also make your business easier to sell if you decide to move on in a few years.

- Will protect you from the more unpleasant aspects of audits.

It is important that you develop a working budget now—before you open your business. That way, you will be able to keep accurate records from the start. Plus, you will be able to get comfortable with your budget plans so that by the time your business opens, you will be able to take care of the financial side of things in only a few hours a month.

It is best to use a monthly budget system because the very nature of the bar business ensures that your finances will change rapidly. A monthly budget may seem like a daunting idea, but once you develop a good working plan for keeping track of your finances, there will be no problem of keeping track of your expenses and profits. Think of a budget as a tool that will allow your bar be more successful.

One of the first things that you will have to determine for your budget is the operational costs. This part of the budget is sometimes called the Operational Budget. It not only lets you know what you are spending initially, but it lets you forecast what you will be spending in the near future so that you can budget accordingly. To follow are a number of items you will need to account for in this part of the budget:

- **Total Sales.** Trying to predict total sales is very important, but it can also be one of the trickiest parts of budgeting. Your bar will take in different amounts each day and each week, and at first it may be very hard to tell how much you will be making in any particular stretch. Within a few months, however, you will be amazed at how easy it is to predict how much money you can expect to earn in a month as patterns will develop as you establish a client base. In the first 4 or 12 weeks, it is normal to have very high overall costs and low profits. No matter how carefully you have done your homework and no matter how hard you try, it takes some time to get a business going and to start recouping the money that was used to start the bar. You should not panic and start making cutbacks. Just move forward and work on establishing a client base. Profit will follow.

    To estimate total sales, follow a few simple steps. If you have been open for a while, figure out how many customers you had last year or last month. If you do not have these figures available due to only being open a short time, make an estimated guess (remember, your initial budget will not be accurate; it will get more precise with time). Next, note how many days are in the calendar month that you are budgeting for and calculate the number of customers you expect on each day. Be sure to note any holidays or special events; adjust the customer expectations for these days. Next, multiply the number of days by the number of customers. To this number, add the number of holidays multiplied by the expected number of customers for those days. The idea is to get a total number for the month.

    Again, if you have been in business for a while, you are working with actual customer numbers and can use these numbers to note any changes or customer trends that you need to be aware of. If you are not yet opened, then you are trying to get the hang of budgeting and trying to make an educated guess how many customers your bar needs to plan for.

    If you can work with actual customer numbers, compare similar months (that is, months with the same number of holidays and weekends) to see whether you are gaining business or losing customers.

Next, calculate the food and beverage sales. To do this, divide the total sales by the food type of last month's sales. For example, if your bar has budgeted for $10,000 in sales, and your bar sells 70 percent liquor and wine, 20 percent beer, and 10 percent food, then you would have a breakdown of $7,000 for liquor and wine, $2,000 for beer, and $1,000 for food sales.

Finally, use the total expected customer and sales amounts to determine daily sales budget amounts. To do this, divide the total expected sales by the number of business days in the month. You will be able to use this to see which days you are under budget. You may want to indicate these days in red or use some other marker.

- **Material costs.** Material costs are those costs that you need to spend in order to make sales. In fact, sales and material costs are so closely linked together that they should not only be side by side in your budget, they should always be reviewed together. It is often best to see material costs as a percentage of costs, rather than just as a large number standing on its own. You can get this percentage by dividing the cost of a specific category (beer, wine, mixed drinks, liquor) by the total sales of the category.

- **Salaries.** The manager's salary is generally fixed while staff salaries are usually at least somewhat variable. To calculate the costs of the managing staff's category on any given day, total all the managerial salaries for a year and divide by the number of days in the year. Employee salaries are more tied to total sales. There is also a point at which employee salaries are covered by profits. This is a break-even point. When this point is reached, net profit will go up because the percentage of employee salaries will go down. In other words, the longer your bar runs with a profit, the less expensive employee salaries will be to you and the more carefully you need to choose your employees (as the more sales that employees manage to get, the more efficient and, thus, less expensive these salaries will be in the total budget). Even the cost of training will eventually pay for itself.

- **Overtime.** Overtime is costly and should be avoided where possible. A well-run bar should have little overtime. To avoid overtime, make sure that schedules for staff are well planned and that any employees wanting to switch shifts have managerial approval before actually switching work times.

Operating costs that are fixed include expenses such as rent. These costs must also be calculated in your budget:

- **Rent.** The rent or lease of the bar needs to be tabulated each month.

- **Taxes.** Taxes may be calculated in your lease or rent. If this is the case, you do not need to tally taxes separately. However, if your rent or lease agreement makes you responsible for taxes, simply divide property taxes by twelve to see how much you are paying in taxes per month. If you have not yet opened, you can find out how much the previous owners of the building paid in taxes the previous year and estimate based on this amount.

- **Insurance.** To budget monthly insurance, tally all the insurance premiums for all your insurance policies and divide by twelve. The result is the amount you pay for insurance each month.

- **Entertainment.** You must estimate how much you can or want to spend on bands, disc jockeys, and other performers each month.

- **Equipment rental.** Whether you plan to rent equipment for specific events or for long-term purchases, you need to add this expense to your budget.

- **Marketing and advertising.** Each bar manager needs to decide how much to spend on marketing and advertising each month. This amount includes newspaper ads, advertorials, and radio ads, as well as free giveaways and promotions.

In your budget, you will also need to account for costs that are considered "controllable." These costs give you a chance for savings because these costs can be altered a bit:

- **Supplies.** China and flatware, kitchen supplies, glassware, bar supplies, and dining room supplies should all be a specific amount and percentage of sales during each month. In general, you should seek to spend a small amount on these products without compromising on quality—buying on discount, researching suppliers, and comparing prices before you shop are your best bets for finding a good price on these items.

Because office supplies (pens, paper, computer supplies, etc.) are important but a comparatively small amount of money spent in a bar business, you will want to have a fixed amount each month to spend on these supplies.

- **Uniforms.** Some localities allow employers to charge their employees for their uniforms. If this is the case in your own state, uniforms will not figure in your budget. If you live in a state in which this is not allowed, though, you will need to factor in this expense as well.

- **Linens.** It is most cost effective to buy tablecloths, napkins, and other linens in bulk twice a year (or once a year, for a smaller business) for best savings. For this reason, linens are generally one fixed expense on your monthly budget.

In addition to fixed and variable costs, you will need to factor in the services that your bar will need to pay for in order to stay in operation:

- **Security.** Security should be the same fixed cost each month in your budget.

- **Laundry.** To tabulate laundry costs, multiply last month's budgeted sales by the percentage of cost for last month. Laundry is directly related to total sales and, as such, fluctuates. You will also need to factor in price increases, as laundry services tend to increase in cost over time.

- **Legal.** Legal fees vary and are not linked to any variable such as percentage of cost. Of course, you do not want to face a large legal bill (and the hassle it brings), but you need to budget for this possible event. In general, many bars find that once in a while they are faced with a large legal bill. Savvy bar managers will budget a small fixed amount each month to cover the occasional large legal bill.

- **Shipping/Freight.** Not all bars need to worry about freight or shipping expenses; your suppliers may simply calculate this along with your purchase and arrange for shipping. In general, you will only need to worry about this expense for specialized deliveries. If your bar is located in a remote place, though, this expense may amount for a large percentage of costs each month, as suppliers will not always deliver to out-of-the-way areas.

- **Accounting services.** Depending on the accounting services or personnel you use, accounting fees may or may not be fixed. With time, the operation of your bar should be running so smoothly that these expenses will remain quite fixed. You will still need to budget for larger costs twice a year for tax time, however.

- **Payroll.** Payroll will change depending on the hours you are open each month and depending on the number of staff.

- **Maintenance.** Maintenance of your machines and equipment is a must, but it can become very difficult to budget for if you use an on-call service, which charges high fees for each visit. Having one maintenance person on staff can make maintenance a fixed amount but will generally cause the bar to spend more on maintenance than necessary. Many bar managers have found that contracting a reputable maintenance service company helps keeps costs fixed each month and easier to budget for.

In addition, you will need to budget for the utilities that will keep your bar running:

- **Water.** Water will change slightly as an expense from month to month, but over time you should have a general range of what to expect from your water bill.

- **Gas.** Gas can be variable or semi-variable. If you are using gas to heat the bar, then you will spend more for this utility in the winter than the summer.

- **Telephone.** This should be relatively fixed. The one thing you will want to watch is personal phone calls made from the bar. In general, you will want everyone using the phone to jot down any long-distance calls, and then you will want to compare this record against the bill. Some bar managers have cut down on possible conflict by having only local lines at the bar and a pay phone at the bar for any private calls that patrons or employees need to make.

- **Heat.** In your budget, you will want to account for any heat not covered by the electric or gas bills. For example, if your bar uses firewood, oil heat, or some other source, list the budgeted amount under "Heat." Otherwise, heat will be part of your other utility bills.

- **Electricity.** Electricity is somewhat variable, and bar managers can expect larger bills in the summer, when fans or other cooling systems are in place. Electric bills will also depend on the types of equipment that relies on this power source.

Finally, you may want to add certain miscellaneous expenses to your bar budget, depending on the needs of your establishment. For example, costs such as postage, trade fees, contributions to charities, licenses, travel expenses, and credit card expenses can all be added to the budget (and should be, if you incur these costs in your operation).

Preparing to Open

To open your bar, you will need to arrange:

- A space for your bar—either rented or bought.

- Setting up the space for your bar. You will need a bar, a kitchen, a food storage area, a drink storage area, plumbing and lighting fixtures appropriate for a bar, and a seating area, as a bare minimum. If you can get or rent an establishment that was either a bar or restaurant previously, you will be able to save yourself the expense of having to set up the plumbing, lighting, and other bar aspects that can be quite expensive to set up from scratch.

- **Inventory.** In a way, this will depend on the space you are renting and the customers you are selling to. If you are starting a small establishment, you may want to start with a handful of beers, wines, martinis, and liquors, and slowly work your way up from there. Many bar managers assume that a larger drink selection is always better, but starting with a huge drink selection creates huge expense and stress. You will need to store and buy all the drinks and train your employees to understand which drinks are available. If you do your research in your area, you will know which drinks are most requested by bars in the surrounding area. If you have the budget and a cellar, on the other hand, stocking a larger selection may allow you to specialize and draw a specific clientele from the beginning. Similarly, if you are renting or buying a bar space that has lines, pumps, and a beer room, you are better off taking advantage of this by offering as many beers as you can. When deciding what inventory to buy, the trick is to consider your clientele, your competition, and your space. The right inventory will make the most of all three and will bring in a tidy profit. When buying inventory, you will want to focus on a few areas:

1. **Alcoholic drinks.** This is where most of your inventory budget will likely go, and you should take care to at least buy some whiskeys, rum, gin, vodka, sherry, port, tequila, cognac, brandy, bitters, vermouth, wine cocktails, cordials, liqueurs, champagne, wines, bottled beers, and draft beers. See Chapter 3 to get a better sense of the alcoholic drinks you should be buying before opening.

2. **Nonalcoholic drinks.** Not everyone at your bar will want an alcoholic beverage, and many patrons like to end the night with a nonalcoholic beverage. Nonalcoholic drinks also give you something to mix with alcoholic drinks to create beverages. In general, you should stock a nice selection of sodas (including colas, diet colas, seltzers, ginger ale, tonic water, etc.), juices (including grapefruit, tomato, orange, pineapple, cranberry, lime, lemon, etc.), bottled waters, nonalcoholic beers, coffees, and teas. The nice thing about these items is that they are relatively inexpensive, so it is easy to establish a good supply.

3. **Foods and food products.** You will want to buy foods that are easy to prepare and serve as a nice snack. You will also want to buy milk products, such as creams and milk, and fruits that can be made into salads or snacks or served as garnishes for drinks

(cherries, lemon, limes, oranges and grapefruits are often standard in good bar kitchens). You will also want to keep hot sauce, pepper, salt, olives, onions, sugar, and other food products that can help you create drinks on hand.

4. **Miscellaneous bar supplies.** A successful bar needs basic equipment such as:

    - Blenders
    - Knives
    - Corkscrews
    - Can openers
    - Bottle openers
    - Glasses
    - Cutlery
    - Coasters
    - Stirrers
    - Straws
    - Napkins
    - Matches
    - Cleaning supplies
    - Toothpicks
    - Towels
    - Ashtrays
    - Cigarettes
    - Pens
    - Paper
    - Telephones
    - Telephone directory
    - Bar mixing recipe books or manuals
    - Newspapers

- First-aid kit

- Tongs

- Pourers

- Ice scoops

- Gloves

- Aprons

- Map of the town

- Legal licenses/permits

- Emergency numbers for cabs and police

Some local laws even stipulate specific items that bars must carry. Sometimes these require little besides a first-aid kit and fire extinguisher. In other cases, the requirements are far more complex. Check your local laws and make sure you understand exactly what sort of miscellaneous supplies you need to take care of before opening.

- **A theme.** You will want to decorate your bar, generally according to some theme or style. This does not have to be complicated, but a pleasant atmosphere should be created using décor and lighting. The bar should be inviting and should have a pulled-together look. This is easy to accomplish if you keep the color scheme consistent—and it's less expensive to stick with a few basic colors—and a general style (old-fashioned or modern, tough or fancy).

- **Employees.** You will need to look for employees and go through the hiring (which involves interviews, careful security checks, follow-ups) and training process. You may wish to hire just a bartender, cook, and servers or a more complicated staff including maitre d´, security personnel, and others.

- **Legalities.** You should spend plenty of time working on this aspect of your business well before opening. Laws about bars can be very complicated, and you need to make certain that you have taken care of all the legal aspects of your business (including licensing) before opening. You don't want to go through the trouble of opening a bar only to be closed after a few nights due to a zoning problem. Hire a lawyer or seek legal advice; it may spare you a costly legal mistake.

- **Bar extras.** You may want to consider extras such as theme nights, a dance floor, lottery machines, pool tables, and other entertainments that can bring in clientele to the bar. Just be sure to investigate the legalities surrounding adding any extras to your bar. If at this point your budget is strained, you can safely wait to add these extras.

Obviously, taking care of all these aspects will take some time. You will want to start your new business right away, but it makes sense to take the time to research each of these aspects of your business well before opening. This will allow your bar to run smoothly right from the start.

The Opening

Once you have arranged all the pre-opening matters, you can focus on opening the bar. Some managers like to open with little fanfare, and if your beginning budget is modest, this is fine. Not every bar needs a "grand opening"; many people will stop into a new bar even when it is not widely advertised, simply to try something new. If your bar is in a visible location, it may not need much advertising anyway. However, there are a few low-cost ways to generate interest in your new bar on opening:

- Note the opening date in the window in advance. This costs nothing and lets curious passersby know when to come back.

- Offer a special deal or extended "happy hour" (be sure to check your state laws regarding happy hours) on the first few nights and display a sign outside the bar to advertise the special.

- Generate some free advertising by sending out a press release about your new bar. A new bar opening is news, especially in smaller towns. Some newspapers may want to run a story on your new establishment (especially if there is something unique about your bar), which will give you invaluable free advertising.

- Consider small ads in newspapers or local magazines. These can be inexpensive and quite handy in letting potential customers know that your establishment exists.

- Invite friends and family (and their guests) to the grand opening. People passing by your bar will see a new establishment and their curiosity will be aroused. Plus, word-of-mouth advertising will circulate about your bar immediately.

- Consider hiring a local band to perform at your bar on opening night. This will help bring in at least some people without requiring a huge advertising budget.

- Set up a large sign outside so that passersby will see that you are open for business.

Of course, as you keep reading, you will learn all the tips and tricks you need to keep your bar successful from opening night to many years down the road.

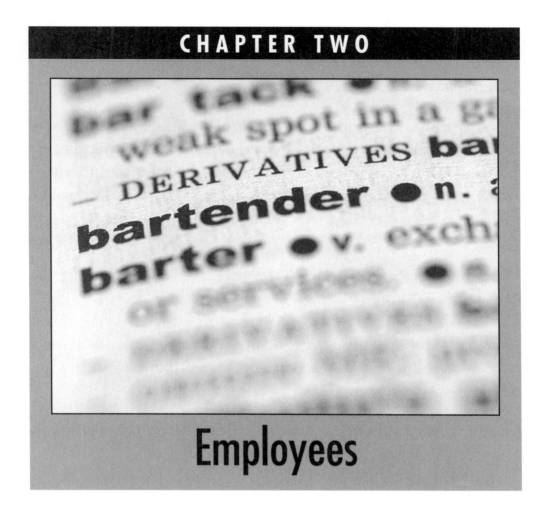

CHAPTER TWO

Employees

You can't run everything in your bar by yourself. You need a staff that can help you serve customers and can help you make your bar great. Bars are generally a team enterprise because they are all about serving others. A great bar staff can do several things:

- Ensure that each customer is served promptly and properly.

- Create atmosphere through a friendly and cheerful attitude.

- Help create the drinks and food that appeal to customers.

- Can help keep customers safe and resolve problems.

- Can help create a "buzz" about the bar by talking well of the establishment during off hours.

- Can offer useful suggestions and an unbiased viewpoint that can help you make changes to the bar.

- Act as liaison between the establishment and customers so that the bar management and bar patrons can agree or see "eye to eye" until everyone is satisfied.

Creating a good working relationship with your staff is essential if you want to have a successful bar. Trying to make a bar work with a poorly selected staff or with a staff that is not working with management is difficult; some successful bar managers would go so far as to say that it is impossible.

Qualities of a Good Employee

Whenever you interview someone for a position as a member of your staff, you will want to keep in mind the qualities of a good employee and the qualities of a bad employee. A good bar employee:

- **Responds well to direction and training.** He or she will follow your directions and guidelines for customer satisfaction.

- **Respectful.** It is important that all staff members treat all patrons— even those who have overindulged and have started to act in a less-than-dignified fashion—with due respect.

- **Is willing to speak up.** A good employee will ask if he or she is not sure why a policy is in place and will mention possible problems in a respectful manner.

- **Genuinely enjoys people.** A bar is a "people" place, and a good employee should be comfortable with others and not so shy as to be off-putting.

- **Is friendly** without being intrusive.

- **Projects genuine concern** for the customer.

- **Projects the right attitude**, self-confidence, and self-control, even in difficult situations.

- **Is willing to find out the answer to a question.** A good employee will never say "I don't know" when a customer asks something; they will respond "I'm not sure, but I can find out for you."

- **Is willing to learn about the beverages**, foods, and other aspects of the bar.

- **Is interested in working for the bar** for long enough to learn to do the job well.

- **Smiles.**

- **Is groomed.** A generally neat appearance—including tidy nails—assure the customer that the establishment the employee represents is similarly clean.

The less-than-ideal employee:

- **Is only interested in the paycheck.** Of course, not everyone wants to work in a bar as a career, but the employee who just wants a paycheck is likely to move on to the next job whenever a higher salary is offered.

- **Is judgmental or mean-spirited.** Customers who come to a bar to drink expect to be treated with respect and even a certain amount of discretion.

- **Communicates poorly.** All employees need to be able to speak effectively with customers and with the bar management, as well as with other staff. People who are not "people" persons are not the best candidates for a bar job.

- **Is sloppy.** Small details—not cleaning up glass, not following directions—can lead to huge problems at a bar. A good employee is careful to take care of the details of the job to ensure customer satisfaction.

- **Is not willing to take on extra work.** A bar often experiences "lag" time only to become incredibly busy in a short period of time. When things get very busy, the pressure is on to provide excellent customer service in spite of the rush. This means that bartenders may end up speeding up work and servers may end up preparing or pouring some drinks. An employee who refuses to go the extra mile during a busy time is a liability.

- **Is untidy.** Someone with dirty fingernails or someone who is not careful about the cleanliness of food hygiene or glassware cleanliness is bound to be a huge source of discomfort for customers and will ensure that some patrons do not return.

- **Is too friendly.** Someone who is too intrusive, tries to join customer conversations without asking, or comes by tables too often is more likely to be a nuisance to customers.

- **Is disinterested.** The bored employee who does not really care whether customers are happy is a common problem for many bars.

- **Shows favoritism.** While some customers will inevitably demand or require more attention than others, employees who visibly spend far more time with some customers than others leave a bad impression. If customers have to wait while a staff members finishes their private conversation with another patron, this mark of unprofessional behavior is likely to be resented—and quite rightfully too.

Of course, it's not always easy to tell which of these traits a potential employee has; all applicants and interviewees will try to put their best foot forward. As you keep reading, you will find the specific qualities you will need to find in staff members and ways you can determine which staff members are most likely to work out for your bar.

Employee Identity and Uniforms

Employees are the identity of your bar. An unfriendly bartender or server can cause you to lose business. In addition to their personalities, you need to consider how the employees will represent the identity of your business. For instance, will you be running a casual operation? Will you require your employees to wear uniforms? Will your employees wear T-shirts with funny sayings and your bar name printed across the back? Or will you have a nightclub atmosphere with glamorous and elegant cocktail servers? Obviously, the type of operation dictates the attire of the staff. Following are some sources for employee uniforms, covering everything from casual to classy:

- **Aprons, etc.** Offers a wide variety of products and a complete line of bar and server staff apparel. They can customize uniforms with your bar's logo or slogan. For more information or to find a distributor, visit **www.apronsetc.com**.

Uniform Vests with unisex styling. Available in 4-button front or no button in black, khaki, navy, royal, and red from Aprons, etc.

Black Polycotton Twill Tuxedo Apron Size 28" W x 32" H, center-divided patch pocket with adjustable neck strap from Aprons, etc.

Deluxe Waist Apron Size 23" W x 17½" H triple-pouch pocket 7" deep from Aprons, etc.

- Since its beginnings in 1922, Dickies has stood for quality and toughness. Their chef collection offers durable coats, pants, hats, aprons, and more. Items are available in a wide variety of colors and patterns. To find a distributor or view the collection, visit **www.dickieschef.com**.

- **Ann Carol** is an executive uniform and industrial clothing firm. They offer a complete line of uniforms for restaurants, bars, and hotels. For more information or to view the product line, visit **http://anncarol.com**.

Baseball cap, shirt, and pants from Dickie's Chef.

Types of Bar Employees

Before you start hiring, you will need to determine how many and what sorts of employees you need to open your bar. Whom you need to hire will depend on what size of bar you are planning to run, and what type of bar you want. In many places, several servers and a few bartenders are all that is needed. In larger establishments, you may need a whole team of bartenders to tend the

Professional apparel from Ann Carol

various bars, a sommelier, and a large staff of servers as well as DJs and bouncers. Before you begin hiring, consider some of the employees that make up a bar:

The Bartender

The bartender is the one who prepares drinks and pours. In some cases, he or she may also serve or give the drinks to the servers to give to customers. The most important trait of a professional bartender is that they are familiar with many types of alcoholic beverages and know how to prepare them well. In some cases, you may wish to hire bartenders who are proficient at flair bartending, meaning that they can prepare drinks in a way that exudes showmanship and visual excitement. Even if you choose not get a bartender who knows about flair bartending, you will certainly want a bartender who can prepare drinks gracefully and properly. In many cases, bartenders must be very adept at reading people and entering a role of listener or talker, as needed. The bartender needs to be chosen with great care, as bartenders have the largest impact of all your employees on your bottom line.

Some of the specific job responsibilities of the bartender include:

1. Adhere to the basic procedures of personal hygiene such as neat, clean, and pressed clothes, styled hair, and manicured hands.

2. Always greet customers with a smile and, if possible, by name. Recognizing new customers is critical; if you are busy, acknowledge her and indicate that you will be with her in a moment. Always place a cocktail napkin in front of the customer to show that she has been waited on.

3. When applicable, suggest the house specialty drinks and appetizers or offer the menu for perusing.

4. Be attentive to customers. Clean ashtrays, light cigarettes, and keep the bar and stools neat and clean. Raise outdoor patio umbrellas on hot days and generally respond to customer requests in an accommodating, friendly manner. Watch for empty glasses; politely ask if the customers would like another. Always ask before removing empty glasses.

5. Know how to operate the cash register correctly. Bartenders are responsible for accounting for every drink poured. Record all housed, manager, and complimentary cocktails accurately.

6. Make sure the cocktail waitresses'/waiters' tickets are accurate and complete. Do not fill any order until the prices are entered and totaled correctly.

7. Know all the bar prices.

8. Check questionable customers' IDs to ensure they are of legal drinking age. Check any suspicious bills to make sure they are not forged, but in a subtle way that does not offend the customer.

9. Communicate with coworkers throughout the shift.

WAYNE OVENSTONE IS CO-OWNER OF **TAPS PUB & GRILL** IN SOUTH AFRICA. TAPS PUB & GRILL HAS WON MANY AWARDS SUCH AS THE CHARLES GLASS AWARD, WHICH WAYNE BELIEVES IS THE EFFECT OF PERSONALIZATION OF CUSTOMERS AS WELL AS EMPLOYEES.

In our experience, the best bartenders (male or female) are trained in-house. Bartenders from a school tend to think that they are better than the home-grown bartenders. Why? Maybe because they are taught to throw bottles and things around? We just prefer people who get the job done, quickly and with the minimum of fuss and effort. We have written our own in-house training manual and run continual refresher courses for all staff. The one thing that we do that I have never seen anywhere else is that our managers are forced to work a single full day every month as a normal staff member (all management privileges are removed for each day in each area) in the kitchen, bar, and restaurant. They do not function as the head of these areas; they work as a normal staff member would with no privileges whatsoever.

We have a singles night on Tuesdays accompanied by a brilliant musician who plays the sax exceptionally well and really knows how to get the ladies going. Wednesday and Thursday nights we cater more for the sit-down diner who prefers a little peace and quiet while they eat. Friday nights are party nights—live music and anything goes. Saturday nights are dinner-dance nights, where we tone everything down a little and cater for the romantics. We also have big-screen TVs for sporting events during the day and some evenings.

10. Follow all the health and safety regulations as prescribed.

11. Follow all of the bar/restaurant regulations as prescribed.

12. Control and limit waste.

13. Communicate ideas and problems to management.

14. Attend all meetings.

15. Fill out all forms as prescribed.

16. Maintain all equipment and tools.

17. Follow all rotation procedures to ensure freshness of all products.

18. Follow management's instructions and suggestions.

Hostess/Host/Supervisor/Maitre D'

There is very often only one person in charge of the establishment during each shift. In some bars, this person is the bartender. In other bars, the bar manager or a specially hired host or hostess fills this role. In general, this person leads the bar and is the person who servers and other staff turn to for specific instructions and for problem management during the shift. The responsibilities of this employee are many:

1. Determine that proper lighting and cleanliness levels are adhered to before opening.

2. Ensure that employees and staff are doing their jobs and have the resources they need in order to do their jobs well.

3. Appear on the bar or dining room floor to seat customers and ensure customer satisfaction.

4. Resolve disputes or problems as they occur.

5. Ensure quality and speed of service as well as quality of food products and drinks.

6. Ensure that displays, including menus, are arranged properly.

7. Oversee any promotions or special events.

8. Oversee the end of shift, including table preparation for the next shift and cleaning procedures.

9. Ensure security of bar by overseeing proper closing procedures.

10. Follow all the health and safety regulations as prescribed.

11. Follow all of the bar/restaurant regulations as prescribed.

12. Control and limit waste.

13. Communicate ideas and problems to management.

14. Attend all meetings.

15. Fill out all forms as prescribed.

16. Maintain all equipment and tools.

17. Follow all rotation procedures to ensure freshness of all products.

18. Follow management's instructions and suggestions.

Servers

Although the main responsibility of servers is to serve drinks and food to customers, they also contribute other valuable services to the bar. The difference between good servers and bad ones is often the difference between a good bar and a bad one, in fact, because servers influence customer satisfaction the most of all your employees. Your servers will often determine how happy your customers are with your bar and how likely they are to return. The approach, attitude, and appearance of your servers will often affect your customers' experience at your bar more than just about anything else. Servers need to be professional, friendly, and have excellent social skills to put your patrons in the best possible mood. Servers have many responsibilities in your bar:

1. Maintain a neat, clean, and attractive appearance.

2. Ensure that all customers are relaxed and receptive prior to their

drinks or meals.

3. Ensure that all customers are served quickly. Always greet customers with a smile and, if possible, by name. Always acknowledge new customers; if you are busy, indicate that you will be with them in a few moments.

4. When applicable, suggest the house specialty drinks and appetizers or offer the menu for perusing.

5. Know all bar prices.

6. Write tickets neatly and accurately. Fill in all prices and totals before issuing to the bartender. Make a notation to the bartender when wine is served.

7. Be attentive to your customers. Clean ashtrays and keep the tables and chairs neat and clean. Watch for empty glasses and politely suggest another drink. Always ask before removing empty glasses.

8. Ensure that all bar tabs are forwarded to the correct dinner check.

9. Always add the cost of cocktails served in the dining room onto the dinner check. It will undoubtedly be an annoyance to the customer to stop eating in order to pay for drinks.

10. Always count out change by repeating the total ticket amount, then "count up": beginning with coins, name each denomination until you reach the amount received.

11. Assist the bartender in any way possible.

12. Check questionable customers' IDs to ensure that they are of legal drinking age.

13. Communicate to coworkers throughout your shift.

14. Follow all health and safety regulations as prescribed.

15. Follow all bar/restaurant regulations as prescribed.

16. Control and limit waste.

17. Communicate ideas and problems to management.

18. Attend all meetings.

19. Fill out all forms as prescribed.

20. Maintain all equipment and tools.

21. Follow all rotation procedures to ensure freshness of products.

22. Follow management's instructions and suggestions.

The Cook and Kitchen Staff

Kitchen staff prepare the food for your patrons, and although these staff members rarely meet your patrons, they have a huge impact on how much your patrons enjoy your bar. Kitchen staff can even affect your bar's legal status—a case of food poisoning or foreign objects in food can easily lead to a lawsuit. On the other hand, a reputation for great food will often keep your bar customers coming back again and again.

In some bars, a full kitchen staff is used to prepare complicated meals. In other bars, one or two people are employed in serving up prepared food for servers. You can also hire caterers as needed. Some bars do not hire any kitchen staff, and instead offer only small snacks from vending machines or from behind the bar. If your bar uses kitchen staff, your kitchen employees have several responsibilities:

1. Prepare the foods you have placed on the menu.

2. Prepare foods in an orderly and timely fashion.

3. Keep the kitchen area neat during work.

4. Note any problems with food supply and note which food items need to be reordered.

5. Communicate with servers regarding customer satisfaction of meals.

6. Communicate any problems or shortages in the kitchen to the staff so that the problem can be explained to customers.

7. Follow any special meal requests that customers make (such as dressing on the side or a vegetarian variation of a meal), where possible.

8. Attractively arrange meals or food on plates.

9. Control taste and size of food and meal served.

10. Follow all the health and safety regulations as prescribed.

11. Follow all of the bar/restaurant regulations as prescribed.

12. Control and limit waste.

13. Communicate ideas and problems to management.

14. Attend all meetings.

15. Fill out all forms as prescribed.

16. Maintain all equipment and tools.

17. Follow all rotation procedures to ensure freshness of all products.

18. Follow management's instructions and suggestions.

Cleaning Staff

Some bars hire occasional or regular cleaning staff while others use a professional cleaning service. Your bar's attractiveness will depend on how tidy your establishment looks, so choosing the right people to clean your establishment is crucial. A clean bar is also healthier and provides fewer opportunities for accidents or injuries. Since cleaning duties generally take place while the bar is closed, it is imperative that you research and hire a trustworthy staff or agency for this function. Your cleaning staff, then, has many important responsibilities:

1. Generally tidy the entire establishment.

2. Polish and shine all visible surfaces so that they are neat and free of dust or grime.

3. Clean under chairs, tables, and bars and all over floor to ensure a

clean and dust-free surface.

4. Clean and sanitize bathrooms.

5. Replace items such as paper towels, soap, and toilet paper in the bathroom.

6. Wash, scrub, and rinse dishes, cutlery, glassware, and plates (in some bars, a separate staff member is hired to do this).

7. Remove waste from the establishment and dispose of it.

8. Clean exterior surfaces such as windows and walkways.

9. Follow all the health and safety regulations as prescribed.

10. Follow all of the bar/restaurant regulations as prescribed.

11. Control and limit waste.

12. Communicate ideas and problems to management.

13. Fill out all forms as prescribed.

14. Maintain all equipment and tools.

15. Follow management's instructions and suggestions.

Security Staff

Security staff keep both your employees and patrons safe. They can help prevent minors from entering the bar, they can help remove unruly patrons, and they can act quickly if a problem arises. They can also help enforce a dress code or other standards you want in place. You will want to make sure that your security staff do not make customers feel uncomfortable. As society becomes more and more controlled, larger amounts of people resent being closely observed. A security staff that goes through every purse and stares down each customer may keep undesirables from your bar, but they may also make many desirable customers hesitate before returning to your bar.

Some bars hire their own security personnel while others use a security firm. Using a security firm reduces some of your control over who works at your venue. On the other hand, you may have fewer legal problems by hiring a security firm (the firm will be responsible, not you, in most cases, if someone sues after being ejected from your bar). Hiring a firm will also mean you will not have to worry about vacation times, compensation, and other matters related to employees. You will have to work harder, however, to hire a firm that will provide you with the type of security staff you want.

If you will be hiring your own staff, you will need to do a background check on each person being hired. You will also want to ask a lawyer to draw up an agreement between you and the employee to ensure that you are not held liable in case the security staff do something they are not permitted to do. Whether you hire a firm or your own security staff, ensure that you carefully lay down the rules for what the staff can and cannot do. You will have to hire your security staff carefully, as they have many responsibilities:

1. Check ID to ensure that all entering customers are legitimately allowed inside the establishment.

2. Control who enters and exits the premises.

3. Ensure that no customer or other person is bothering customers or staff.

4. Intervene in altercations.

5. Defend staff or customers who are being threatened, harassed, or upset.

6. Look for illegal or suspect activity occurring in the bar.

7. Telephone police or other authorities in case of a problem.

8. Ensure that barred patrons do not reenter.

9. Escort patrons who have been asked to leave.

10. Follow all the health and safety regulations as prescribed.

11. Follow all of the bar/restaurant regulations as prescribed.

12. Control and limit waste.

13. Communicate ideas and problems to management.

14. Attend all meetings.

15. Fill out all forms as prescribed.

16. Maintain all equipment and tools.

17. Follow management's instructions and suggestions.

You may also need to hire other staff, depending on your needs:

Temporary Staff

Temporary staff fills in during busy seasons or acts as assistance when a regular staff member takes time off. In general, temporary staff members should be made to feel part of the bar staff and should be given a quick abbreviated version of the training that the regular staff have gone through. Temporary staff have a number of responsibilities, including:

1. Perform all the duties of the staff member or members the employee is to replace or assist.

2. Follow all the health and safety regulations as prescribed.

3. Follow all of the bar/restaurant regulations as prescribed.

4. Control and limit waste.

5. Communicate problems and ideas to management.

6. Attend all meetings.

7. Fill out all forms as prescribed.

8. Maintain all equipment and tools.

9. Follow all rotation procedures to ensure freshness of all products.

10. Follow management's instructions and suggestions.

Publicist/Marketing Manager

If your bar grows enough, you may need to hire a full-time or part-time staff member to hire acts, arrange for publicity and interviews, and to market your bar. This person will often perform office duties as well as perform on-site marketing research. There are several responsibilities of the publicist and marketing manager:

1. Encourage and arrange the bar's appearance in media outlets.

2. Monitor the bar's appearance in media outlets.

3. Design and place advertisements.

4. Arrange and implement a marketing strategy.

5. Work with other companies in order to establish affiliate programs.

6. Work on the bar's Web site.

7. Act as liaison for media outlets and advertisers.

8. Suggest successful marketing and advertising ventures.

9. Arrange promotional materials and programs, including giveaways and entertainers.

10. Follow all the health and safety regulations as prescribed.

11. Follow all of the bar/restaurant regulations as prescribed.

12. Control and limit waste.

13. Communicate problems and ideas to management.

14. Attend all meetings.

15. Fill out all forms as prescribed.

16. Follow management's instructions and suggestions.

17. Conduct market research in order to determine and expand customer base.

DJ/Sound System Manager

The DJ is often a freelance worker, responsible for providing music and entertainment (including audio commentary and lights) for customers. In general, the DJ will come in nightly or a few times a week. Many bars either have one DJ they work with regularly or a number of DJs that come in to offer variety. Since most DJs only work in a bar for a short time, they require no training. In fact, a good DJ will be used to playing in just about any condition or establishment and will be able to quickly adjust to your bar. The responsibilities of a DJ include:

1. Select appropriate music and audio for the bar.

2. Work with manager and customers to select appropriate sound background for the bar.

3. Play selected music and provide some audio for customer entertainment.

4. Introduce live performers playing at the bar.

5. Encourage dancing or customer entertainment, if this is available.

6. Provide lighting that matches the music.

7. Take and play customer requests.

8. Ensure audience enjoyment of live and taped entertainment.

9. Bring own equipment or setup and maintain bar's sound and light equipment.

10. Follow all the health and safety regulations as prescribed.

11. Follow all of the bar/restaurant regulations as prescribed.

13. Communicate ideas and problems to management.

14. Fill out all forms as prescribed.

15. Maintain all equipment and tools.

16. Follow management's instructions and suggestions.

Live Entertainers

Live entertainers provide amusement for customers. Some patrons will travel a long way in order to see their favorite performers, so it is often a good idea to hire the best performers possible. Performers such as bands generally require a fee to play and traditionally get free beverages and food during the evening of the performance. When hiring entertainers, be sure to ask what equipment, space, practice time, and other variables are needed prior to and during a live performance.

While some bars have a regular performer, most establishments hire performers on the same basis as DJs: for nightly work. The best performers book quickly, so you will need to work hard and do plenty of shopping around in order to ensure a booking. Whether you book magicians, dancers, singers, comedians, mimes, actors, or other performers, the responsibilities are the same:

1. Entertain the audience.

2. Entertain and amuse bar staff without affecting their work.

3. Encourage audience participation.

4. Establish with bar manager when the performance will take place and what the duration of the performance will be.

5. Arrive promptly and perform as scheduled.

6. Arrange ahead of time any special requests or needs required for the performance.

7. Work with the available space to ensure the best possible entertainment effect.

8. React to audience response and work to ensure customer satisfaction and pleasure.

9. Be available for customer feedback, questions, and autographs. (Note: The entertainer always reserves the right to decide how to be available. Some performers only agree to a preset stage show; some take requests.)

10. Follow all the health and safety regulations as prescribed.

11. Follow all of the bar/restaurant regulations as prescribed.

12. Communicate ideas and problems to management.

13. Fill out all forms as prescribed.

14. Follow management's instructions and suggestions

Entertainment Booker

If you plan to have live performers regularly, you will need to arrange each performance individually. This can be a full-time job, especially if you plan to ask famous or requested entertainers to perform for your customers. An entertainment booker works on your behalf to make sure that performers are booked and ready to play at your venue. Responsibilities of the entertainment booker include:

1. Contact entertainers or their managers to request performances at your bar.

2. Follow up with performers or their agents or managers in order to arrange for bookings at your bar.

3. Book performances for your bar.

4. Select and book performances that are appropriate for your bar and that customers will enjoy.

5. Listen to bar management and customers in selecting entertainers that are appropriate for the venue.

6. Arrange with performers and their managers or agents any special needs or requests needed for the entertainment.

7. Arrange payment for the performers.

8. Determine and arrange additional cover charges and fees involved in entertainment.

9. Manage entertainment schedule for the bar.

10. Follow all the health and safety regulations as prescribed.

11. Follow all of the bar/restaurant regulations as prescribed.

12. Communicate ideas and problems to management.

13. Attend all meetings.

14. Fill out all forms as prescribed.

15. Follow management's instructions and suggestions.

Maintenance Crew

If you have lots of equipment (complicated registers, special ID-checking and bill-checking devices, sound, lighting, etc.), you may need to hire the services of a maintenance crew in order to keep this equipment in good repair. In many cases, bar managers simply call a maintenance service and pay per scheduled visit. In many larger bars, though, a staff is hired to ensure that someone is always available to fix equipment as needed. When the maintenance workers arrive at the bar, their responsibilities include:

1. Fix or repair any equipment that needs to be repaired.

2. Clean any equipment that needs to be cleaned or indicate what needs to be cleaned.

3. Check for the safety and operational status of bar equipment and machines.

4. Suggest resources for having bar equipment and machines fixed if the problem cannot be immediately resolved.

5. Bring proper tools and equipment to complete maintenance job.

6. Submit receipts for labor and part costs.

7. Order and install necessary parts for machines.

8. Find the most cost-effective ways to fix or replace existing machines or bar equipment.

9. Work to repair machines quickly with minimal customer disruption.

10. Follow all the health and safety regulations as prescribed.

11. Follow all of the bar/restaurant regulations as prescribed.

12. Communicate ideas and problems to management.

13. Attend all meetings.

14. Fill out all forms as prescribed.

15. Maintain all equipment and tools.

16. Follow management's instructions and suggestions.

The Hiring Process

Once you have determined who you might need to run a successful bar, you will have to start looking for appropriate staff to hire. For many bar managers, this can be a very daunting and time-consuming task. It can also be difficult to know where to find the best bar employees possible. Successful bar managers often use a number of techniques to help them find the right staff:

- **Advertise.** Putting an ad in the local paper, in the window of the bar, and in an online job bank will usually bring in many applicants, ranging from the novice job seeker to the experienced bar staff. The advantage of this method is that you will get many applicants. The disadvantage is that you will have to weed through many poor applications to find likely candidates. Most successful bar managers use this method occasionally to see who is out there, but few rely entirely on this method.

- **Targeted advertising.** Targeted advertising can help ensure that your ad is seen by the people you want to hire the most. For example, if market research shows that your targeted patrons will most likely be college students and you want to hire college students to work at your bar, try advertising in the student paper or the local college's student employment center rather than in the local paper. If you want to hire professional staff only, consider advertising in trade publications.

- **Recruiting.** The best experienced staff are generally already working for other bars. If you want to hire these employees for yourself, you will have to make them an offer yourself.

- **Ask around.** Your existing staff or other bar owners you know can make recommendations of people who have worked at a bar and are currently looking for work in your area.

- **Past applications.** People who have applied before to work at your bar and were a close fit can still be a great choice—and in the time between their last application and now, they could have gained valuable experience that can make them good employees now.

The Next Step in Hiring: Filtering

Once you have determined who you want to hire and once your advertising and searching have brought in some applicants, you will have to go through the difficult process of deciding who to hire. In general, if you have plenty of applications, you can start by filtering out those employees who do not seem to be a good fit for you. Read the applications and eliminate anyone who seems to switch jobs very often or who has no applicable skills that could help with working at your bar. There is no need to interview everyone who applies for a job with you.

Next, make a list of the qualities you want in each employee—these comprise the checklist you are measuring each applicant against. Also, note the type of traits that you want your bar to project. These are also traits to look for in employees. The more precise you are, the easier it will be for you to recognize the ideal employee when you see him or her.

Once you have narrowed down your list of applicants to a few candidates, ask them in for interviews. Before the interview, check all the person's references by calling each reference given and asking how long the employee worked for the reference, why they left the job, and whether the employer would rehire the worker. Before the applicant arrives, be sure to create a list of interview questions you want to ask them. There are several questions you will want to ask:

- **Questions about skills.** You may want to ask applicants about the skills they think they have that will help them work at your bar. This will give you a good sense of what the applicant thinks that the job involves and will give you a chance to see what skills the applicant has to work with. Stay alert not just for general statements but for proof. Any applicant can say, "I'm a real 'people' person." But the applicant who says; "I'm a real 'people' person; I have led camp three years in a row and have organized every social event for the debating team at my college," really is comfortable with others.

- **Integrity questions.** You can get a sense of how honest a potential bar employee is by asking questions such as, "Have you ever taken something that is not yours?" or "What do you think of taking something that does not belong to you?" Hesitation or a sudden jump in nervousness can indicate a potential problem.

- **Experience questions.** You can ask potential employees about what work they have done in the past and how that work applies to the work they will be doing at the bar.

- **"What if" and problem-solving questions.** "What if" and problem-solving questions can be a great way to gauge how well potential employees think on their feet (which is a key trait of bar staff). Questions such as, "What would you do if a patron asked for a 7-Up and you knew there was no 7-Up left at the bar?" can give you a great sense of how potential staff would respond to certain situations.

- **Life questions.** Asking about what the potential employee wants from life and what else they are doing currently gives you a better sense of the person as a whole. It can also tell you about potential problems—in general, those employees who have stable lives (students, family-oriented applicants) are more likely to work hard as they have the motivation to do so.

- **Goal questions.** Asking where the applicant sees themselves in a few years can be a useful way to gauge whether the employee will be happy in the job or whether the employee sees your bar as only a temporary way to make money while waiting for something "better."

- **Questions about concerns.** If you have any concerns, you may want to raise them. You should also give the applicant a chance to ask questions about the job. Sometimes these questions can be very revealing. Asking about vacation times and asking about how much creative control bartenders have in developing new drinks clearly reveals two very different qualities of employees.

During the interview, ask for a demonstration of skills, if appropriate. Ask a potential bartender to mix a drink or two and ask a server to balance three drinks on a tray. Also, be sure to jot down notes to yourself about the overall impression the employee makes. It's perfectly normal to be nervous during a job interview, but if the applicant is glum and does not meet your expectations at all, there is little hope that he or she will make a favorable impression on customers.

Remember, you cannot discriminate applicants based on their religion, race, or appearance. There are also some questions that you cannot ask under labor laws. Click on **www.dol.gov** for federal law regulations, and your state's Department of Labor Web site to find out what interview questions could land you in trouble.

After the interview, do a background check with a service such as **www .ussearch.com** to ensure that you are not hiring someone you shouldn't be. It is especially important to check out anyone who will be working with money and to check out your security staff. You may also want to run a credit check on any employee who will be handling larger amounts of money. These simple and low-cost checks can help save you lots of grief later.

If you would like more in-depth information on hiring employees, check out these books:

- *How to Hire, Train & Keep the Best Employees for Your Small Business: With Companion CD-ROM.* This book covers all the essential elements of employee management in an easy-to understand and practical manner. Topics include: recruitment strategies, hiring and interviewing, effective communication, training, motivation, leadership and team building. The companion CD-ROM contains dozens of employee training and human resource forms including unique employment applications, interview questions and analysis, reference checks, work schedules, rules to live by, reporting forms, confidentially agreement, and an extensive human resource audit form. Simply print out any form you need, when you need it. To order, call 1-800-814-1132 or visit

www.atlantic-pub.com (Item # HTK-02, $29.95).

- *501+ Great Interview Questions for Employers and the Best Answers for Prospective Employees*. This book contains a wide variety of carefully worded questions that will help make the employee search easier. These questions can help you determine a candidate's personality type, the type of work he or she is best suited for, and if the person will mesh with your existing employees and workplace. Once you learn the right questions to ask, you'll get the best employees. To order, call 1-800-814-1132 or visit at **www.atlantic-pub.com** (Item # 501-02, $24.95).

- *365 Answers About Human Resources for the Small Business Owner: What Every Manager Needs to Know About Workplace Law*. This book has 300 common questions employers have about employees and the law; it's like having an employment attorney on your staff. To order, call 1-800-814-1132 or visit at **www.atlantic-pub.com** (Item # HRM-02, $21.95).

Training

Once you have hired the best possible staff, you will still need to train them. Even if you are hiring staff who have worked extensively at other establishments, you will need to train your staff how things are done in your bar. Even if your employees have worked in a bar before, it is your responsibility to ensure that they have the knowledge and skills to do their jobs well and safely.

You need to train your employees:

- How to perform their jobs according to your specifications.

- The legal rules, directions, and conditions that they must follow.

- How you want specific problems to be resolved.

- How to control quality to your specifications.

- Safety rules and guidelines.

- What to do in case of an emergency (fire or crime).

Additionally, you will need to train your servers specifically:

- About the different types of alcohol.

- About the use of different glassware.

- The basic terminology of beverages and serving.

- Customer-service skills.

- Cash skills.

- Safety skills, such as when a customer should no longer be served.

- How to deal with difficult customers.

You will need to teach your bartender:

- What drinks you want served and exactly how you want the drinks prepared.

- How much interaction you want the bartender to have with customers not seated at the bar.

- When you want the bartender to stop serving alcohol.

- What roles and duties you want the bartender to perform.

- How much showmanship or creativity you want the bartender to display.

Key Training Points

Following are some important training points you will want to emphasize with your staff.

- **The big picture.** One problem of training employees is that sometimes staff members try so hard to follow bar policy that they ignore the major policy of encouraging bar customers. A classic example of this is the bouncer who tries so hard to provide security to the bar that he or she ends up making customers feel so unwelcome that they avoid entering the bar. When training, it is useful to start with the overall ambience you want to create at your bar, and be sure that you discuss how to handle customers who seem to be disrupting that goal.

- **Enthusiasm.** You likely had a vision for your bar before you opened. This vision of what you wanted to create was so powerful that it made you work to create the bar of your dreams. Share your dream with your employees, whether your vision is to provide a relaxed place for couples or a creative place for young professionals. If your staff understands the overall idea behind the bar—and likes it—they are more likely to understand how they fit into the staff overall. They are also more likely to look forward to work if they share your enthusiasm for the possibilities of the establishment.

- **Each staff member is responsible for ensuring quality.** If anyone notices a problem (chipped glass, hair in the food), they should return the product and explain the problem rather than serve it to the customer. Explain nice ways to point out a problem without offending coworkers. Role-playing is a good way to do this.

- **Each staff member should try to do their job promptly** as each person has an effect on how quickly a customer is served. How quickly someone gets their drink can set the tone and mood for the customer that evening. If the server does not arrive with the drink for ten minutes, the customer realizes his or her meal service will probably be equally slow. If the server is backed up, a host/hostess or manager should step in and see that the table receives its drinks quickly. As with food, women are generally served first.

- **Bartenders and servers should know which glasses are used** for which drinks. Make sure each staff member knows how to pick up glassware correctly. They should never touch the rim; glasses should be picked up by the handle or the base in the case of a wineglass.

- **Make sure each employee knows the difference between types of alcohol** and can describe this difference clearly and accurately to customers.

- **Make sure that staff know all the items offered on the menu.**

- **All staff should know which wines go with which food.** They should also be able to describe the nose, palate, and color of each wine the bar stocks. Some wine vendors offer training services or presentations to bar staff. Contact your vendor to see what services he or she offers. If your vendor offers wine classes, wine presentations, wine tastings, or other services, enroll your staff.

- **All staff members should know the basic laws and regulations of your area** regarding how food and alcohol are to be served.

- **All staff members should know the proper proportions of drinks.** Liquor is portioned not by weight but by volume. Volume is measured in shots or jiggers, which are liquid measurements ranging from ½ ounce to 2 ounces. Make sure your staff knows what types of volumes you want added to each drink.

- **Ensure that your staff knows where to turn for answers when they need them.** Inevitably, your staff will learn much while on the job. This requires some fast thinking. Your staff should know where to find maps, drink recipes, and other necessary items. You may also want to let your staff know where they should turn if a question comes up during their shift.

- **Your staff needs to know about the layout of the bar** and where to find everything they need to find in order to do their job well. Train your staff on finding their way around your bar and train your employees to return items back to their original places.

- **Make sure your staff knows what to do in a crisis or emergency.**

- **During training, stress questions as well as information.** Give your staff a chance to ask you questions about their jobs and about the procedures and policies of your establishment.

- **Make sure that your staff is trained to take responsibility for the legal aspect of their job.** You may want your staff to sign a Service-Refusal Agreement (a sample agreement is found in *Chapter 19: Forms & Charts*).

- **Make sure that your staff knows what paperwork they must fill out as part of their job** and how they are to fill out this paperwork. Some of the more common forms that may need to be filled out include a service-refusal form (to be filled out when an employee refuses to serve a customer—your staff should contact the supervisor first about the problem, then fill out the form). A sample Service Refusal Form can be found in *Chapter 19: Forms & Charts*.

- **Try to stress the fun side of training.** Organize group activities or step-by-step instruction. Rather than having your staff endure a grueling day-long session, aim to instruct staff over a period of days. Stress role-playing games in which some staff act as customers that other staff wait on. Offer prizes for fastest learning or as awards for training tests and quizzes.

- **Stress long-term learning.** The secret to successful training is repetition and practice. Your staff will no doubt get plenty of training on the job. However, you will want to encourage your staff to seek out training on their own (through reading or attending events). You may even want to purchase tickets for your staff to attend wine or hospitality seminars to learn more skills that would make them quality employees. At a minimum, you will want to hold mandatory "refresher courses" and meetings that will allow you to offer more training for your employees. This time will also give you a chance to listen to the suggestions and questions of your staff.

- **Start training immediately.** When a new employee walks through the door, don't keep him or her hanging around. However busy you are, nothing can be more important than making the new recruit feel welcomed and enthusiastic about joining the team.

- **Allocate the function of training** to an experienced and trusted member of staff. This works! The trainer feels honored and the trainee feels he or she has someone to turn to with queries, without "bothering" management all the time.

- **Choose quiet times to go through the specific routines and requirements of the job.** Also, make sure that you have the time to give each new employee an overview of the operation. Productivity improves if employees feel they are more than a cog in a wheel.

- **Orientation program.** All employees should be given a specific job description, plus information about the issues that affect their performance. Examples of the latter include information on periodic or annual performance reviews, emergency procedures, disciplinary and grievance procedures, personal conduct issues, work schedule expectations, and availability of additional training.

Do you find training overwhelming? Atlantic Publishing has a complete training reference specifically targeted toward restaurants with a special section for bar and beverage service. *The Encyclopedia of Restaurant Training: A Complete Ready-to-Use Training Program for All Positions in the Food Service Industry: With Companion CD-ROM.* From orientating the new employee to maintaining performance standards to detailed training outlines and checklists for all positions, this book will show you how to train your employees in all positions in the shortest amount of time. One of the best features of this book is that the companion CD-ROM contains the training outline for all positions in MS Word so you can easily customize the text. There are numerous training forms, checklists, and handouts. There are job descriptions for all positions. To order, call 1-800-814-1132 or visit **www .atlantic-pub.com** (Item # ERT-02, $79.95).

The Final Aspect of Training: Testing and Follow-Up

Once you have trained and hired your staff, you will have invested plenty of time in your employees. You may be tempted to sit back and congratulate yourself on your staff. Don't do it! Once you have trained your staff, you still need to test your employees periodically to make sure that they have the skills and have absorbed the knowledge they need in order to make customers happy. This is an essential part of training as it will let you catch any skills that need improving and will help ensure overall high quality of your employees' service.

You can do this a few ways. You can hold formal tests for your staff, in which you ask employees to submit written tests or prepare drinks in a test situation. You can also perform tests by having informal evaluations every few weeks. Evaluations mean simply that you review employee performance by watching the employee at work. You can include any customer feedback as part of the evaluation. In most establishments, this work review is what forms the basis for decisions about raises and promotions. There are several ways to tell whether your employees meet the expectations you have placed on them:

- Does the staff do everything possible to make customers happy, even when it is beyond their job description? The server who will not clean up a spill because it "is not in the job description" is not doing their job.

- Is the staff reading customer moods? When a customer first sits down, they should be treated with the warmth of an old friend. They should be engaged in light conversation, but the staff should retreat if the customer does not seem to want to talk.

- How is the staff doing in the presentation of food and drinks?

- How well is the staff doing in terms of providing speedy service?

- Are drinks correctly prepared and served in the right glassware?

- Are bar policies and procedures followed?

- Does the staff get along well with each other?

- Does the staff have a good grasp of bar terms and drinks?

- Does the staff seem happy with their jobs?

If an employee's evaluations are bad, you will need to consider why this may be so. Is the staff unhappy with the job? Is more training required? Are policies or expectations very complicated or confusing? In many cases, kindly sharing the problem and offering more training or asking the employee what sort of solution they might prefer works wonders. A few poor evaluations in a row generally indicate a more serious problem. If the problem is not resolved, you may have to seek another employee as a replacement.

Many managers only contact employees when there is a problem, and this is truly a mistake. As you hire employees, you should share your evaluation procedures and policies. If employees regularly meet or exceed expectations, they should be told this and praised for their performance. Failing to do so can make good employees feel taken for granted.

Employee reviews can serve as a platform for employees to bring forth questions and concerns. This can help increase employee dedication, creativity, and job satisfaction. You will have written records of your employees' performance, get more productivity, and clearly set compensation. Employee appraisals are critical to your organization but are time consuming to write. It is important to have a system in place for employee evaluations. You can easily standardize these with the manual *199 Pre-Written Employee Performance Appraisals: The Complete Guide to Successful Employee Evaluations and Documentation: With Companion CD-ROM*. These evaluations are professional, constructive, and direct. Simply find the review that pertains to your employee, open and edit the Word document on the CD-ROM, and you are done. To order call 1-800-814-1132 or visit **www.atlantic-pub.com** (Item # EPP-02, $24.95).

Keeping Your Staff Happy

Once you have hired and trained your staff, you will want to keep them happy and motivated so that they continue to work for you and continue to provide excellent work for you. There are a number of ways to provide incentives for your employees to work for you:

- **Accept staff as well as customer suggestions.** Many bars have customer suggestion boxes or at least take customer opinions very seriously. Few have similar ways to deal with staff suggestions, even though employees often have an excellent understanding of the drawbacks and advantages of an establishment. Offering a suggestion box for employees—where suggestions can be made anonymously—or encouraging employees to tell you how things are going at meetings or in between shifts can help ensure that you have the information you need to keep employees happy.

- **Provide adequate time off—and adequate hours.** Staff want to work enough to meet their financial goals, but not so hard that their health suffers. Always ask how much someone wants to work in the upcoming week or month, and schedule shifts accordingly.

- **Offer incentives.** Cash bonuses and incentives are best, but free food and drink, passes to parks, or entertainments are good too. Prizes for jobs well done will make employees feel appreciated and will ensure that all staff work hard.

- **Develop a team.** Your staff will work better if they get along. Occasionally organizing group outings, seminars, or workshops for the staff is one way to foster a sense of team spirit around the bar.

- **Get to know your staff.** It is inappropriate to ask your staff personal questions (some personal questions may even be illegal), but asking your staff general questions such as "What's new with you?" or "What has been going on lately?" allow you to get to know staff gradually. Showing genuine interest and noting new things in your own life encourages a good working relationship.

- **Make sure that you provide a good place of employment.** Staff should have breaks, manageable work loads, an employee area for rest, clean washrooms to use, and whatever else is necessary. If you are not sure if you are providing everything you need to provide for your staff, ask them whether there is anything at work that they need to make their jobs easier or more pleasant.

- **Pass on compliments.** If a customer notes a very good drink or positive experience with a server, be sure to pass the compliment on. Even general compliments about the bar should be passed on to employees—after all, it is the staff that help make the establishment what it is.

- **Be kind about problems.** While compliments should be shared, you want to be more subtle about problems you are having with an employee, especially if you are not sure what is at the root of the problem. You should never criticize an employee in front of customers or other staff, and you should never discuss problems you are having with an employee with other staff members. Instead, take the one employee aside and privately and calmly try to understand the problem. Try to keep your temper and attempt to work with the employee to find a mutual solution.

If you need additional ideas on how to motivate or reward your employees, check out *365 Ways to Motivate and Reward Your Employees Every Day— With Little or No Money*. This book is packed with hundreds of simple and inexpensive ways to motivate, challenge, and reward your employees. You will find real-life, proven examples from actual companies. Use this book daily to boost morale, productivity, and profits. This is your opportunity to build an organization that people love to work at with these quick, effective, humorous, innovative, and simply fun solutions to employee work challenges. Make your business a happy place to work and reap the benefits. To order, call 1-800-814-1132 or visit **www.atlantic-pub.com** (Item # 365-01, $24.95).

Staff Problems

No matter how much you try to choose your staff carefully and no matter how hard you try to keep your staff happy, employee problems may arise. Issues with work performance can often be worked out with more training and some frank discussion. A more awkward problem—and unfortunately one that is all too common—is the problem of the dishonest employee.

Some employees will routinely under-pour or over-pour, causing problems. Some will claim broken glasses when in fact the contents of the glass was offered for free to a friend or drunk on the job. Some bar employees will pocket money made from liquor they bring in on their own or will pocket the money from several short pours. In any case, these sorts of employees will cost your bar a lot of business and money.

There are many reasons why staff are dishonest. Some may see their actions as harmless. Some staff may need the money, be acting out of boredom, or may be seeking revenge on the bar for a perceived slight. Whatever the reasons, one of your best defenses against staff dishonesty is to let staff know the rules at your bar—and the results of breaking those rules. Note the importance of carefully accounting for each drink poured and dollar earned, and note the importance of honesty and quality in building the bar's reputation.

Your best bet in avoiding staff problems is to keep close control of the bar. Ask for full reports to be filled out at the end of each shift that detail any problems, any spilled drinks, any problems at all. Invest in good cash registers that cannot easily be skimmed, and make sure that all bar patrons have to fill out a claims form in order to get money back that they lost in the vending machines and pay phones. Check register receipts and inventory carefully, and occasionally show up unexpectedly to see how the bar is getting on when you are not supposed to be there. Make sure that amounts rung on the register can't be voided without the approval of a supervisor. If you suspect that theft is taking place, there are several security firms that will investigate for you at a small cost. The only real way to avoid this sort of dishonesty is to keep your eyes open and hire carefully.

CHAPTER THREE

Inventory

Inventory consists of those things that you will be buying in order to sell drinks at your bar. Well before you open, you will need to find sources for inventory and will need to arrange the financing to pay for your inventory.

Vendors

Vendors are basically sellers—they will be the people you deal with in order to buy wine, beverages, supplies, and even vending machines for your bar. Your relationship with your wine and beverage vendors will be very important, as it will help enable you to get the best-quality drinks to your customers. The marks of a good vendor include:

- **Services offered.** A good vendor will stand behind their products and will offer the services that ensure your complete satisfaction. A vendor, for example, should offer you free, no-hassle replacement of broken items and should offer you convenient delivery options to ensure that you get your liquor products (or food products) on time. If a vendor is offering you equipment (such as a vending machine), the company should offer you free or very low-cost maintenance on those repairs.

- **Range of products offered.** Wine vendors specialize in wines, while other vendors may specialize in beers or other products. The vendor that you select for each category, though, should provide you with enough choices and options so that you do not need an entire army of vendors to supply your bar.

- **Incentives and perks.** Many vendors offer small freebies (often passed down from food or beverage manufacturers) such as free wine tastings, free coasters, or other small freebies. While these freebies are not necessary, they can be quite useful and helpful for you. At the very least, these small bonuses are things that you can pass down to your customers.

- **Willingness to meet your needs.** Good vendors listen to the needs of your bar—and then strive to meet those needs. They know the tensions and difficulties of the bar business and work hard to make sure that things are as easy on you as possible. Good vendors, for example, make sure that delivery times and reordering is easy for you.

- **Affordable.** Good vendors will offer you products in your price range and will tell you about upcoming discounts and promotions so that you can budget for them.

- **Prompt and reliable.** Deliveries from your vendors should come when expected and should arrive complete and unharmed. Vendors that routinely fail to deliver quality products can cost your business a lot of money, so for the sake of your bar, discontinue your business with any vendors that cannot deliver on promises.

- **Convenient.** Good vendors will offer easy payment options, delivery estimates, delivery options, and easy ordering. It is generally not worth it to spend hours and plenty of frustration on a vendor that simply uses up too much of your time.

You can easily find vendors in trade publications and through trade groups designed for bar owners and managers (wine vendors and merchants as well as food and drink vendors will routinely advertise with such places). You can even look in your local Yellow Pages for a vendor. However, these are hit-and-miss methods. The best way to find a vendor that can supply your bar with wine, beer, and liquor is to look in one of two places:

1. **Other bars.** Your competition already have good relationships with vendors, and the reason why other bars choose a good vendor often has to do with good pricing and good value. Ask around to see which vendors other restaurants and bars in your area use. Chances are they use these vendors for a good reason.

2. **Trade shows.** By far the best place to find a vendor is through a trade show. There are food and wine shows held all the time exclusively for bar and restaurant owners and managers. These are excellent opportunities to actually meet the faces behind the vendors, get catalogues of vendors' products, test sample products, get new ideas for your bar, test new products, find out about special offers, and compare vendors—all in one place! Better yet, since vendors are all gathered together, they are competing for your business. You can often get terrific deals and incentives at these shows and easily make comparisons. Often this is also your first chance to find out about new companies and vendors opening for business. Savvy bar managers make it a point to take in many trade shows to make contacts, find new vendors and products, and to secure deals that will make their bar better.

Your state will determine who your vendor will be for liquor. In some states, the sale of liquor products is controlled so that only state-run vendors are allowed to sell liquor to bars. This means that you will have to purchase what the approved vendor allows, but you will generally be able to meet most of your needs through one vendor. If your state permits liquor to be sold by private vendors, you will be able to enjoy wider ranges of products, but you will likely need to order from several vendors in order to get all your drink inventory.

In most states, beer is bought from local suppliers. Luckily, these suppliers want to get their product into your bar, and they are often willing to install a draught system in your establishment at little or no cost. When deciding which draught supplier to choose, always select what beer most of your customers will request—this should be your draught beer. Ideally, your draught supplier will be able to provide you with many other types of beer rather than just the product you have on tap. Since you will be ordering many kegs from this supplier, you will often be able to get good discounts on any other products the supplier carries.

You will also need to order a number of food and nonalcoholic drinks in order to make snacks and mixed drinks. Some liquor distributors will be able to provide you with these items. If they cannot, your local food service suppliers will be able to give you what you need.

Always select your vendors carefully. You want to order as much of your products from as few vendors as possible. This will make life much easier on you, as you will need to make fewer orders, have less paperwork, and organize scheduling for fewer deliveries. If you order larger amounts from a few vendors, you will also likely be qualified for more discounts and incentives, so choose wisely.

Juices and mixers must be of the best quality you can afford. It makes little sense to pour quality liquor into a cocktail made with a low-quality juice or mix. Juices must be 100 percent real—no substitutes added. Mixers can be of any brand that has the quality level you are striving for. It is often advantageous to use brand-name items even if they cost a little more. Customers who sit at the bar should see that you are using high-quality, recognized liquors, juices, and mixers.

- **Look into ready-made bar mixers.** These can save a tremendous amount of time and preparation. Zing Zang manufacturers a complete lines of bar mixers. Visit **www .zingzang.com** for details or to view their product line.

There will be a high level of competition between the various suppliers for this part of your business. This is due in part to the fact that these products have a high profit margin. All suppliers stock at least some of these products. When comparing prices, remember to look at the whole picture. Consider how much this extra business will mean to each supplier. Due to the increase in volume, how will this affect the prices of the other items you purchase from the supplier? Are the services and delivery arrangements to your satisfaction? What are the credit terms? What is the finance charge? How much is the overall purchase actually costing?

Once you establish which liquor, beer, mixer, and garnishes you will be using, transfer them onto the order sheets. List them alphabetically and by category on the Liquor Order Form.

SOME COMMONLY USED BAR MIXERS, JUICES, AND GARNISHES

JUICES	MIXERS—MISC.
Orange juice	Sweet-and-sour bar mix (commercially prepared or own recipe)
Cranberry juice	Coconut cream concentrate
Pineapple juice	Grenadine
Grapefruit juice	Bitters
Tomato juice	Orgeat syrup
Lime juice	Worcestershire sauce
Lemon juice	Tabasco sauce
	Sugar-saturated water
FRESH FRUIT	**GARNISHES**
Oranges	Stuffed olives
Limes	Cocktail onions
Bananas	Kosher salt
Strawberries	Celery salt
Lemon peels	Super-fine bar sugar
Lemons	Celery salt
Pineapple	Super-fine bar sugar
Cherries	

SODA/WATER
Coke or Pepsi
Diet Coke or Diet Pepsi
Sprite or 7-Up
Ginger ale
Tonic water
Soda water
Sparkling or mineral water
Purified water

Storage

Storage may not seem like a very exciting concept to you, but it is a vital part of running a successful bar. There are several storage areas in a bar:

- **The bar itself.** Alcoholic beverages are often displayed behind the bar where patrons can see the items offered. Extra supplies are often kept under the bar while glasses are often kept above or behind the bar for a nice effect. In general, everything that is stored where customers will be able to see it should be made to look as attractive as possible. Labels should be facing the customer, and the bottles should be clean and dusted frequently. It is also important that the temperature where the alcoholic beverages are stored behind the bar is not too hot and is not exposed to strong sun (which can spoil the drinks).

- **The back rooms.** Most bars have storage rooms to store items such as glassware, flatware, alcoholic beverages that do not need to be cooled, and other items. It is important that the storage room be kept very clean and maintained at a constant temperature. A cool, dry place is needed to store most items. It is also important that food items be stored separately (away from cleaning products, for example). You may wish to create two separate rooms for food and non-food supplies.

- **The refrigerator and freezer.** Items such as dairy products and some food products (cut fruit, opened cans of olives and pickles) need to be stored in the refrigerator, and a walk-in refrigerator can be handy for keeping beverages such as beer cool. Ice and frozen food can be stored in the freezer.

- **Wine cellar.** Many bars do not have one, but if you have the space and the money, a wine cellar can be a great way to offer your customers a wider selection of quality wines. Wine cellars are specially designed to keep wine at the perfect temperature and in ideal condition. They also help keep your stock perfectly organized so that you can easily find the bottle that a customer has requested. If you do not have a wine cellar, it is important to keep your wine stored in a dark, cool, dry place. Wine should always be stored on its side or at an angle that allows the cork to stay wet; this helps keep wine from spoiling.

It is important to teach your staff to store things in proper places. This not only makes it easier for your staff to find what they need, but in some cases (such as food), proper storage can prevent spoiling. You need to make sure that if refrigerated food products including milk and cream are left out of the refrigerator for an entire night, they are thrown out rather than being placed in the refrigerator later. Thawed meat or meat that has been left standing at room temperature should be discarded rather than used. It is also important to keep expiration dates on all perishable products and discard any spoiled products or any products past their expiration date. Serving stale or spoiled products creates a terrible impression on customers and can lead to cases of food poisoning.

COMBINING HIS PASSION FOR IRISH PUBS AND LITERATURE, OWNER/PROPRIETOR DREW DVORKIN OPENED **THE DEAD POET** ON SEPTEMBER 1, 2000. DREW, A FORMER HIGH SCHOOL ENGLISH TEACHER, DESIGNED THE BAR TO CELEBRATE THE LIVES AND SPIRITS OF FAMOUS WRITERS AND POETS. DREW FEELS THAT MAKING THE CUSTOMER AT HOME IS A VERY IMPORTANT ASPECT OF HIS BAR.

"*We only sell a new product if the customer is asking for it. If they aren't asking for it, they are not going to buy it, so don't invest any time or money into it. One customer requested that we buy a frozen margarita machine and we did. The customer appreciated it but he was the only one! A good way to keep a customer coming back is to show them that you care about the business as well as them. Show them that every comment is appreciated and acknowledged and not just thrown in the garbage.*

The employees are the biggest factor. I personally show them how to do everything so that they know what to do. I make sure that my employees sign all memos so that they can never say 'I didn't know...' The staff is the #1 selling tool. The customers will buy whatever the you tell them to."

Food Rotation and Labeling

All food items need to be rotated to ensure that the oldest items in inventory are used first. The first in, first out (FIFO) method of rotation is used to ensure that all food products are properly rotated in storage. Label all boxes, cans, containers, bags, and shelves. It is a good idea to enforce these procedures with your employees by displaying posters. Atlantic Publishing offers a "First In, First Out" reminder poster for $8.95 (Item # FSP10-PS). Available at **www.atlantic-pub.com** or by calling 1-800-814-1132.

The FIFO method uses these principles:

1. New items go to the back and on the bottom.

2. Older items move to the front and to the left.

3. In any part of the bar/restaurant, the first item used should always be the oldest.

4. Date and mark everything.

Any food operator using the FIFO method of food rotation and operators who are following a Hazard Analysis of Critical Control Points (HACCP) program need to use labels. Labeling reduces spoilage and food costs when products are dated correctly and staff becomes accountable for managing food storage and preparation. Labeling also ensures product freshness and flavor. Properly documenting prep dates and use-by dates allows an operator to identify which foods need to be consumed by a specified date, thus eliminating the discard of food.

DayMark (**www.daymark.biz**) offers a variety of labels to be used in food rotation that comply with the FDA's storage requirements:

• Dissolve-A-Way (DissolveMark™)

• Removable (MoveMark™)

• Freezable (CoolMark™)

• Permanent (DuraMark™)

• Repositionable (ReMark™)

Storing Other Items

The storing, receiving, and rotating procedures of food items also pertains to liquor and all other items delivered to the bar. The manager and the person who placed the order should always be present when a delivery is received. Immediately after the order is checked for accuracy, it must be locked and secured in its separate room. The manager must be the only individual who has the key to the liquor storage room. Liquor may be stored at room temperature as long as the temperature remains relatively constant.

Train all staff members to look for the quality of a product. If they notice a poor quality product (strange smell, separated dairy products), they should return the product to the kitchen area rather than serve it. The bar manager should check all the expiration dates of perishables each day and discard those that are spoiled.

Supplies

There are a number of supplies that you will need in order to run a bar successfully. One of the most important of these—beverages—is discussed in Chapter 16. Besides the items that you will be selling to customers, however, there are a number of items that every well-stocked bar needs. Among these supplies is the basic bar hardware that helps in designing drinks, the basic supplies used in helping the customer, and the miscellaneous items that no bar should be without:

- **Ashtrays.** At the very least, you should have one ashtray for every two seats. If they are not entirely smoker friendly, many bars today at least have smoking areas. Buy the least expensive ashtrays that you can, especially if they are embossed with your bar's logo, as they tend to disappear.

- **Matches or matchbooks.** A must for smoking customers, these can also be nice freebies that feature the bar's name and phone number.

- **Bar spoons.** These long spoons are used for mixing a number of cocktails.

- **Napkins.** You need two kinds: those for dining patrons and those to be used as drink napkins (4-inch square paper napkins that are used as coasters and also serve for quick clean-ups).

- **Coasters.** Buy these only if you do not intend to use drink or beverage napkins.

- **Blender.** Get a powerful blender that can make quick work of ice. You will need an industrial-strength blender especially designed for use in bars (the type sold in stores simply may not stand up to nightly use over a long period of time). At the start, you may choose to get one very good blender and two smaller blenders. You should have at least two; one as a backup. Without a blender, many of the mixed drinks that customers favor are simply not possible, so never be without this item.

- **Papers, documentation, books.** You will need the documentation that shows that you are the owner of the bar, that you have all the proper licensing, etc. You will also need a phone book, a few recipe books, and a few books that detail the making of mixed drinks. A wine book or two is also a good idea. Customers will also often ask for an atlas, the current day's newspaper, magazines (or other reading material), maps, a Bible, TV program guide, a city guide, and even reference books (such as the *Guinness World Book of Records*). Keep all these on hand. Many customers will also want to write down something (a number, a recipe, directions). Always keep pens and notepaper under the main bar to offer. Small papers such as receipts, business cards, letters, advertisements, and many of the other papers that inevitably accumulate when a bar is in business will also be added to the mix. These papers and books do sometimes make the back of a bar look like a library. The successful manager keeps books and most papers tucked into an easy-to-find place where staff can easily access needed materials. Staying organized (especially with all those papers!) is a must.

- **Brushes.** Scrub brushes should be available to scrub glasses and dishes. A reserve of these is important as they tend to wear out fast. Brushes for cleaning the floor should always be kept on hand so that spills can be cleaned up as quickly as possible. Check out Tucel Industries, Inc. at **www.tucel.com** for cleaning tools designed for food and beverage operations.

- **Bottle and can openers.** You need a wide selection to open all sorts of bottles. A can opener, bottle openers, corkscrews, the flat portable openers that open bottles and pierce cans, and mounted bottle openers are all needed at a bar to help in opening various beverages. You can't go wrong with having more of these, especially as they are fairly inexpensive pieces of equipment.

- **Knives.** You need knives for cutting fruit for drinks, utility knives for opening shipments, knives for customers to use in eating, and sharp Swiss Army-type knives to use in opening bottle seals. If they need it, be sure to sharpen your knives regularly. Dull knives are dangerous and a nuisance to both customers and staff. They waste time and money.

- **Cutlery.** Find plain but attractive cutlery that customers can use when eating at your bar. Buy more than you think you will need, as it is embarrassing to be caught short. Avoid offering plastic cutlery unless you are on an extremely tight budget—it may give the impression of "cheapness" or cafeteria food.

- **First-aid kit.** In many cases, this is a legal requirement, but even if it is not, no bar should be caught without one. Consider purchasing a professional-quality first-aid kit, such as DayMark's patented first-aid cabinet. It is stocked with OSHA-compliant first-aid products for accidents

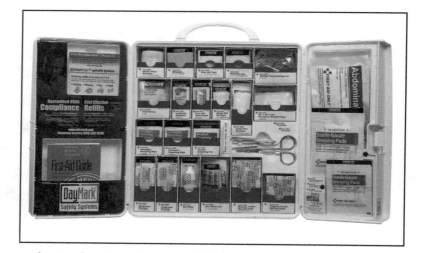

The Complete First Aid Kit is available from DayMark Safety Systems. To order, visit online at www.daymark.biz or call 1-800-847-0101.

that typically occur in the beverage and food service industry such as, burns, cuts, and sticks. This is only first-aid program with guaranteed OSHA compliance.

- **Cleaning equipment.** You will need a dustpan, mop, and broom up front to take care of any spills. You will also need all-purpose cleaner, glass cleaner, a vacuum cleaner, bathroom cleaner, toilet brush, scrub brushes, paper towels or rags, heavy gloves, dishwashing supplies, floor polish, feather duster (for tidying up display bottles). Even if you hire a cleaning service, all these things will allow you to tidy up any messes that develop during the night.

Combined with proper hygiene practices, DayMark's disposable aprons can help to reduce the possibility of cross-contamination and the potential for transference of viruses and bacteria by clothing.

- **Bathroom supplies.** You will need to provide clean bathrooms for patrons, and you will need to provide soap, sanitary napkin dispensers, toilet paper, paper towels, and other bathroom necessities as well. Be sure to buy in bulk so that you do not run out on a busy night.

- **Gloves and hairnets.** These are often a requirement by law. Even if they are not required in your area, they will help keep food perfect as it is being prepared. Heavy rubber gloves are also essential for keeping staff hands safe during cleanup. DayMark Safety Systems is a good source

DayMark's nylon hairnets promote proper hygiene.

for these types of safety products as well. For more information or to order any of the products pictured at right, visit **www .daymark.biz** or call 1-800-847-0101.

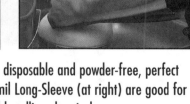

DayMark's Nirtile gloves (at left) are disposable and powder-free, perfect for food preparation. The heavier 22 mil Long-Sleeve (at right) are good for general cleaning and handling chemicals.

- **Cigarettes.** You will need a special license to sell cigarettes in most places, but it is well worth your while, as many people love to smoke and drink at the same time.

- **Clock.** An accurate and easy-to-see wall clock is essential in case your customers are meeting someone or have an engagement at a specific hour.

- **Glassware.** Glassware, of course, is a bar essential.

- **Mixing equipment.** You will need a strainer, spoons, mixing glasses, and shakers in order to prepare mixed drinks. You will also want to get pourers (small plastic spouts for bottles) to ensure that portion and shot sizes are the same for each drink.

SAF-T-ICE Totes

- **Ice and ice supplies.** No bar can ever have enough. You need ice buckets and ice scoops as well as plenty of fresh ice for drinks. You will also need an ice machine that is professionally installed and easily accessed by your bar staff. You will want a backup ice machine in case your main machine fails. Atlantic Publishing offers a number of supplies to keep ice sanitary, including:

SAF-T-ICE Funnel

  - *SAF-T-ICE Totes* helps you control ice transfer cross-contamination. They are made of tough, transparent, durable polycarbonate and will not nest, keeping dirt and bacteria from being transmitted by stacking. The 6-gallon size keeps the carrying weight at safe levels. It features a stainless steel bail handle for easy carrying/emptying.

SAF-T-ICE Scoop Caddie

  - *SAF-T-ICE Funnel* loads ice buckets faster and safer with less mess. Saf-T-Ice Funnel provides a fast, safe, efficient way to fill Saf-T-Ice Totes.

  - *SAF-T-ICE Scoop Caddie.* Keep the ice scoop safe from bacteria, dirt, and ice burial—designed to meet board of health guidelines everywhere. Features ribbed

Ice Scoops

bottom to keep scoop edge dry and a convenient hinged lid that covers scoop and allows for easy access. Easy-to-install bracket mounts with self-adhesive strips for screws.

– *Ice Scoops.* The easy-to-grip-and-hold sanitary plastic handle transfers less cold to hands. Made of a durable polycarbonate material. The 6-oz scoop is tapered to make pouring of ice into glasses easy and eliminate glass chipping; 32-oz Scoop and 64-oz Scoop also available.

For more information or to order, visit **www.atlantic-pub.com** or call 1-800-814-1132.

- **Pestle.** It may look old-fashioned, but this piece of bar equipment is key to crush sugar, ice, and fruit for drinks. The bar version is six inches and is known as a "muddler." A spoon can be used instead.

- **Stoppers.** These closures for bottles keep your open beverages fresh so that you don't waste a drop.

- **Standpipes.** These metal pipes fit into the drain hole of a sink and ensure clean water when the faucet is allowed to drip.

- **Stirrers.** These small plastic items can be plain or fancy, but order a great many of whatever type you decide on, as many drinks require them.

- **Tongs.** Tongs are the most versatile and practical of your bar supplies, so buy plenty. They are used when putting garnishes into drinks or when placing food on plates. In a pinch, they can be used to put ice cubes in a drink.

Browne-Halco is a prime supplier of small equipment in the United States. They offer in excess of 3,000 smallwares products, such as the stainless steel tongs above. For further details and to view the Browne-Halco product line, visit www.halco.com.

- **Straws.** So many drinks require them that you will have to buy lots. You may also want to buy some fancier ones for mixed drinks. Today some straws are so fancy that they act as garnishes.

- **Large frozen drink machine.** These are not essential pieces of equipment, but if you are not making do with blenders, then these machines can help prepare drinks fast. They are especially useful if you are having a special on a drink such as cosmopolitans. These machines hold plenty of mixed drinks, allowing bartenders to simply pour the drink rather than take the time to prepare it from scratch. As an added bonus, these large machines make the drinks look more interesting and can lead to increased sales.

This is a very general listing of the basic inventory needed. Refer to *Chapter 6: Types of Beverages* and *Chapter 17: Additional Equipment* for detailed information and equipment recommendations.

CHAPTER FOUR

Bar Layout (Nuts and Bolts)

The nuts and bolts of your bar are the basic structures that are in place. If you are leasing or have bought a facility that was already a bar before, you may not think about this aspect of your bar. Even if you have had to build up your own bar and eating areas, you may not give much thought to the way your bar is set up. After all, a bar is just a bar, right? Wrong! The way you have the mechanics of your bar set up can affect your success because it can affect customer experience. Consider the following:

Bar Hardware

The way your bar operates depends on many factors, one of the most important being the machinery of the bar. Sometimes, no matter how efficient your staff, the bar just isn't set up to allow maximum productivity. For this reason, think about productivity and your staff before you think of décor. The look of your bar is important, but service is more important still. If you set up your bar to allow for the best possible service, you will end up ahead of the competition. Below is a layout of a typical bar:

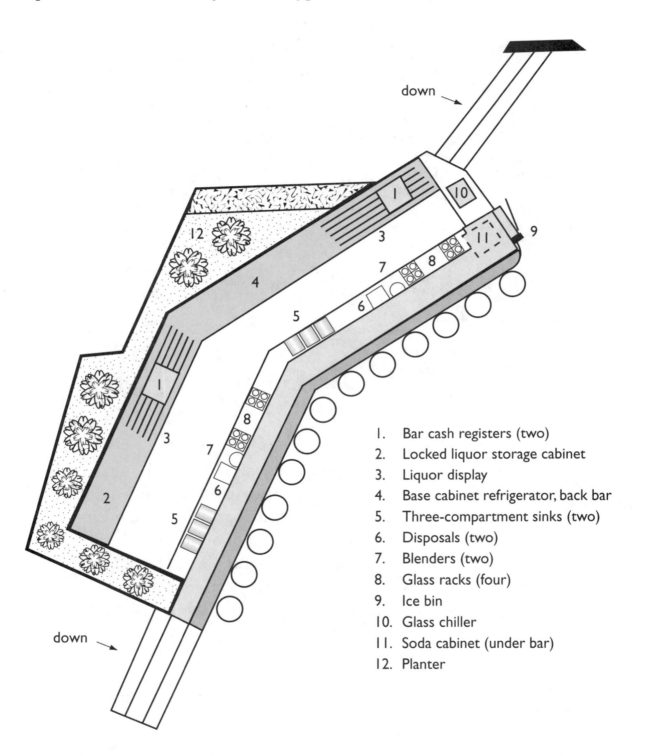

1. Bar cash registers (two)
2. Locked liquor storage cabinet
3. Liquor display
4. Base cabinet refrigerator, back bar
5. Three-compartment sinks (two)
6. Disposals (two)
7. Blenders (two)
8. Glass racks (four)
9. Ice bin
10. Glass chiller
11. Soda cabinet (under bar)
12. Planter

A good bar is one that allows staff to move around easily. A busy bar that only allows one bartender behind the bar at a time is sure to be a disaster, no matter how tastefully designed. A good bar also has plenty of room for supplies. If your staff has to keep running to the storage area for more drinks, they will get worn out and will serve fewer customers. Each drink will also take longer to make. Ideally, have enough space behind the bar for an extra refrigerator to store drinks.

Make sure that the bar design you decide on is simple and easy to clean. Lots of details look garish and can make cleaning difficult. Smooth surfaces not only look less cluttered, but they can easily be kept clean, which is more attractive to customers. A good bar should be truly impressive, upon first glance. An expansive selection of spirits and liqueurs can be an impressive sight. So, too, can a personable, neat, and tidy bartender in a well-pressed uniform, greeting the customers like an old friend—a definite draw. But the first time a customer finds anything less than clean about a bar, the impression they take home will be a bad one. Thankfully, a smart bar design can go a long way toward helping staff keep your establishment spotlessly clean.

- **Avoid "tight corners."** Some surfaces are a lot easier to keep clean than others. Nothing is surer to collect "bar gunk" than a tight corner. Your customers have a right to expect a comfortable level of cleanliness. Anything less is likely to draw their wrath, if not the attention of local health inspectors! Make sure your employees keep any tight corners as clean as they keep the flat surfaces. Do regular inspections to make sure.

* **Make it a habit to line all ice sinks with a plastic trash bag.** Whenever your staff needs to clean out the sink (either because of a broken glass or as part of regular bar cleaning) you can simply remove the bag, ice, water, and all. It is easy to replace, without inhibiting service. This will add a small cost to the maintenance of your bar, but the payoff is in terms of cleanliness and service.

* **Glass areas should be scrubbed several times a day.** These areas should always be out of the customers' field of vision. Your customers should never glimpse your bar's engine. Ensure that all boxes, empty glass racks, and dirty glasses are kept out of eyesight, either in "under-bar" sinks or out-of-view back-bar areas.

Seating

A good bar is attractive and comfortable. The seats at the bar should be padded and comfortable enough to allow for many hours of comfortable seating. Tables should be heavy duty and beverage-friendly. If your bar décor or lack of bar comfort is sending away customers, then your bar design is costing you money.

For a variety of high-quality products, check out Royal Industries, Inc. (**www.royalindustriesinc.com**). They manufacture a full line of food service products and furniture including:

- **Restaurant seating.** Commercial restaurant- and hospitality-quality seating, durably constructed, and offered in hardwood, bistro style, metal stackable, and youth chairs.

- **Bar stools.** They offer metal bar stools in both standard and bucket seat models.

Royal Industries, Inc. has a wide variety of styles and colors available to match your décor and provide comfortable seating. From left to right: bistro chair, classic chrome bar stool, and bucket seat bar stool.

- **Table tops and bases.** With heavy-duty reversible table tops, cast-iron table bases, and spiders, this table is a very durable product.

The Front Bar

The front bar is essential to pleasing customers and ensuring a loyal clientele. Make sure that your front bar is not too wide. Many bar managers assume that a wider bar is better as it allows for more room, but a wide bar can crowd out a bar staff and can make it quite hard for your staff and customers to chat and interact. If a customer has to yell over a wide bar to make their drink order heard, they are unlikely to return to your bar.

When designing your front bar, be sure that the space above the bar is not ignored. Although the tradition thing to place behind the bar and above the bar is mirrors, these are often a poor idea. They take a lot of time and money to clean and they can look foggy and dingy very quickly. Menu boards or artwork are better and less expensive options. Just make sure that the area behind the bar is attractive, and you are sure to draw more customers. A good bet is to keep a selection of inventory attractively displayed behind the front bar—this not only adds interest but can inspire customers to buy. Keeping menus or products before customers' eyes can not only tempt patrons and allow them to order easily, but such displays also cut down on the time your staff need to explain the bar's offerings.

When well designed, your front bar should give patrons a clear idea of what is offered without interfering with their line of vision or distracting the bar staff. To get a sense of whether your bar is well designed, order a drink yourself and see how easily the staff move to get your order prepared. Consider your own actions: Do you need to crane your neck to see a menu or to order? In a well-designed bar, both the customer and staff should be comfortable.

Streamlining Service

When designing your service area, you need to consider the necessary steps to prepare a drink and then make these steps as few as possible. The fewer steps your bartender needs to take to get a clean glass, to scoop ice from the ice bins, to get drinks from the spirit dispenser, and get the drinks from the soda guns, the easier each night's business will go. If your bartender has to walk to get each of these items, and then walk to yet another location to use the cash register, productivity will fall during the course of a night, even if each station is only a few steps away. If there is more than one bartender on duty, a bad setup can encourage spills and short tempers.

The service area should be large enough to handle more than one bartender comfortably. It should have everything needed to prepare drinks within easy reach. Since most people are right-handed, your bar should allow staff to pick up glasses with their left hand and bottles with their right. The floor of your bar should be uncluttered and contain no portable steps so that movement is not encumbered by anything.

Consider keeping buckets of ice under the bar with the most popular bottled beers in them. That way, staff can easily produce these bottles when things get busy at the bar. During slower times, these buckets can easily be refilled with ice and beer, dramatically cutting down on unnecessary trips to the refrigerator.

The Under-Bar

How well your under-bar is designed will determine how quickly your staff can prepare drinks and how much time your patrons spend stuck in bar traffic. Your goal in designing your under-bar is to make it as productive as possible. Ideally, the under-bar should have everything your staff needs to prepare most (about 80 percent) of their orders without walking away from the bar. This ensures fast service for the customer and even allows the bartender to strike up a quick conversation with the customer as the drink is being prepared.

Flooring

When designing your bar area, do not overlook flooring. The customer area of the bar should be designed to be attractive and safe. However, you will also want to add anti-slip and anti-fatigue floor mats behind the bar area. These mats will help keep your staff comfortable during shifts and will help prevent slips and glass breakage.

Grip Rock floor mats are suitable for any wet area.

- **Grip Rock and Super G floor mats by Matrix Engineering** are durable, long lasting, and lightweight. The Grip Rock safety mat was designed to be slip-resistant in wet, hazardous areas. This makes it especially useful behind the bar and in areas conducive to slips/falls. For more information, visit **www.griprock.com** or call 1-800-926-0528.

Climate Control

Body heat, cigarette smoke, sweat, outside temperature, and dance floor fog systems all affect how comfortable the bar feels. A too-cold or too-muggy and warm bar makes patrons feel like leaving. You can easily resolve this problem with a few handy devices and appliances:

- **A fresh-air exchange system.** This is in addition to your heating, ventilation, air-conditioning system. It works by constantly bringing in fresh air from the outside. Casinos use these systems to keep patrons from feeling sleepy. These systems can make any bar seem instantly well ventilated.

- **Fresh-air ducts.** These are especially useful over dance floors, so if your bar has one of these, consider a fresh-air duct. A fresh-air duct works by allowing you to bring in large bursts of fresh air from the outside whenever you decide that conditions are too clammy.

- **A smoke extraction system.** This type of system can help remove smoke and purify the air.

- **Heating.** Whether you choose electric heating, gas heating, or a fireplace, make sure that your heating system is doing its job on cold nights by keeping your customers comfortable. Remember that you will have to compensate for the door opening and closing as customers come in and exit your bar.

- **Air-conditioning.** Air-conditioning can help keep your bar nice and cool on hot days. It can also drive up your electricity bill. Many bars find that offering a patio and fans helps keep things cool as well.

Customer Comfort

The longer customers stay, the more likely they are to keep ordering drinks and giving your bar business. Make chairs comfortable and make sure that tables are not wobbly, lighting is comfortable, and music is at a good level (not blaring and not too quiet). If possible, install booths, which tend to make customers linger longer. Allow your customers to lean comfortably on the bar without getting cold elbows.

Don't overlook the bathrooms—they are customer areas as well. Keep nice-smelling soap in the bathrooms and easy-to-access paper towels or dryers. Extra touches in the bathrooms, such as sofas or small mint candies by the sinks, can make customers feel pampered and more likely to come again.

Color Schemes

Research has shown that certain colors promote specific feelings in consumers; for example, in restaurants decorated with reds and yellows, customers are more likely to experience hunger and may have a harder time settling down and relaxing—which may explain why so many fast-food places tend to use this color scheme. Researchers think that red and yellow may prompt a person who is already hungry to order more than they would if those colors were not present. Red and yellow are also likely to make a customer move on quickly once their money is spent, which is also ideal for the fast-food business.

Blues and greens, on the other hand, are likely to make customers settle down, according to researchers, thus are a better option for a bar that wants to encourage patrons to stay awhile. Some bars choose to add a little red and yellow to the food areas only (such as on the menu), which can encourage spending while overall décor can still work to keep customers at your bar for a while. Studies have also shown that plants can help your customers relax and want to stay awhile.

Bar Recipe and Procedure Manual

The purpose of the Bar Recipe and Procedure Manual is to ensure that the methods of preparing all cocktails are consistent among your bartenders. Most drinks can be prepared in many different ways. Therefore, it is imperative that all recipes and procedures are standardized to ensure that both the final product and cost is consistent. More importantly, all recipes and procedures for preparing drinks should be written down and given to all staff. Your bartenders should be tested to ensure that they know how each drink should be prepared. The Bar Recipe and Procedure Manual should be kept under the bar so that it can easily be referred to. It is an essential part of your bar's layout.

CHAPTER FIVE

Advertising and Marketing

Advertising is essential for the success of any business, and this is certainly true of the bar business, where new competition emerges constantly. However, you should not rely on only one form of advertising to bring in new customers. Savvy bar managers make use of a wide variety of strategies to turn potential customers into paying patrons. In this chapter, you will discover the secrets that successful bar managers use to create a buzz—even on a smaller advertising budget.

Advertising

Advertising means that you pay to have an ad placed in a newspaper or magazine or on a television or radio show in order to bring in customers. Advertising can simply be used to tell potential customers about your bar or it can be used to let customers know about special offers or promotions.

There are several places you can buy ads:

- On the sides of buses or taxi cabs

- In newspapers or magazines

- On television

- On the radio

- On the Internet (banner ads)

- On billboards

Prices for these advertisements vary widely. In general, the larger your ad and the more prominently it is being shown, the more you will pay for it. When placing an ad, you should make sure that you get what you pay for. That means that you should be certain to position your advertisement well.

Targeted Advertising

The way you advertise—and where you advertise—will affect how your bar is seen. You should have a clearly defined target market (see Market Research in Chapter 1) and advertise specifically to that market. Presenting a very young-looking ad in the local paper will draw a very different crowd than a quiet ad in the mall flyer. Advertise in the college newspaper if you want to attract a college crowd, and advertise in the local literary journal if you are looking for an artsy crowd. Talk to a professional who can help you get the effect—in words and pictures—that you want from your ad.

A market segment often overlooked is people relocating to new areas. Research studies shows new residents are five times more likely to become loyal "regulars." To reach this market, you may want to hire a company that specializes in tracking new residents in your geographic areas. Check out:

- **Moving Targets** solo mailings feature warm-hearted personal letters and attractive gift certificates. They have no contracts, no minimums, and no setup charges. Call 1-800-926-2451 for free samples, user references, and full details. Visit **www.MovingTargets.com** to see how many new movers are in your trade area each month.

Sample mailing from Moving Targets.

Target Repeat Customers

There is no better advertisement than a satisfied customer. Strive for repeat business and regulars. Here are few suggestions to establish a regular clientele:

- **VIP status.** Let your customers fill out forms to get on your VIP list, and offer these people extra incentives for coming back often such as coupons or a punch card where he or she gets a free drink after a set number of visits. Be sure to check local laws and regulations, as free drinks are regulated in some states.

- **Special mugs.** Offer regulars engraved, personalized glass beer mugs with his or her name on it. You can hang them in a special area and reuse them each time the customer visits.

Sample coupons from Loyal Rewards.

- **Offer incentives.** You can fax, mail, or e- mail repeat clients special offers or coupons. If you don't have time to develop an incentive program, you can hire someone to do it for you. For example, Loyal Rewards sends e-mail gift certificates with personalized offers to customers. It costs about For just 4.5¢ each and you do not need a computer. The service is 100 percent turnkey, and Loyal Rewards will even help build your database. Call 1-800-309-7228 or visit **www .LoyalRewards.com** for full details.

Marketing and Public Relations

Advertising is a simple way to tell people about your bar—you pay for ad space and provide an ad. Marketing is more involved—but generally gets better results. Marketing can be less expensive because it does not require selling ad space. With marketing, you are trying to create a "buzz" about your bar. You might print up business cards and leave them at offices if you are trying to attract the white-collar crowd, for example. You may contact your local television station or newspaper and offer to do an interview. Your interview will be an article that will let potential customers know about your bar—without you having to resort to the hard sell.

There are several ways to use marketing to your advantage without spending a lot of advertising dollars:

- **Open bar.** Offer local companies an open bar for an hour and/or a free buffet if they bring more than 25 people on a Friday night after work. Sure, initially you'll lose money on the deal, but if your venue is well run, fun, and offers good value for money, they'll stay on well past the free hour. Your venue could potentially become the company's new after-hours haunt.

- **TGIF promotion.** For example, anyone wearing a tie receives a discount on a Friday afternoon. Workplace get-togethers are a great source of large groups. If you can make your venue a regular weekly stop, those people will begin to bring friends and partners on other nights of the week too.

- **Live streaming video.** Offering live streaming video via a Web cam from your bar to your Web site or a popular local Web site can draw in customers.

- **Large industry groups.** Emergency workers, for example, often hold evenings for those in that industry to get together and let their hair down. Contact local unions, chambers of commerce, and any other representative body in your area. See if they'd be interested in hosting an event at your venue. If they need convincing, offer a discount on food and drink or suggest possibilities such as free DJ entertainment for the night. Every time you bring in one of these groups, you're showing your wares to hundreds of people who may otherwise never have set foot in your venue.

- **Get a really good Web site.** Design a high-quality Web site that makes your bar seem really enticing. Include items such as pictures of the bar, hours, contact information, and menu items. Add live streaming video to your site so that customers can really see what the bar is like before they step inside. Add your URL to business cards or in other places to beef up curiosity.

- **Contact a local radio station.** Suggest they run a live broadcast from your venue on a regular basis. This kind of publicity helps them and it certainly helps you to be seen as such a great venue that the local radio station wants to hang out there.

Word-of-Mouth Advertising

Word-of-mouth advertising is the most elusive yet the most powerful. It cannot be bought, but it can be generated. Word-of-mouth advertising is also the most effective form of advertising out there. Basically, if enough people are talking about a bar, then many patrons will go to that bar in order to see what the hype is about. You have likely experienced the powers of word-of-mouth advertising yourself. You may notice that suddenly everyone is buying a product or going to a new establishment, even though you have seen no advertisement for the product. There is simply a "buzz" around the hot trend.

While this "buzz" seems to arise almost naturally, don't be fooled. Savvy promoters have likely masterminded a whole campaign to get the product or service in question on everyone's lips.

If you want everyone talking about your bar, the easiest and most effective way to do this is to hire a public relations or advertising firm that specializes in branding and marketing. Such companies can develop an entire plan for getting people to talk about your bar. These companies will use ideas such as:

- **Hiring people to loudly talk about a bar** in a place where people can hear them (this sounds strange, but is actually one of the hottest trends of marketing right now—people overhearing parts of the conversation will often remember the name mentioned).

- **Placing the bar name on products** such as bottles of water, CDs, or other giveaway items to promote the establishment.

- **Arranging for product placement spots.** This means that someone on the radio, on television, or in film will mention the name of a product, seemingly naturally. This can be very expensive but is very effective.

These companies also have many more devices for making it seem that everyone is talking about your bar. If course, these services can be far more expensive than even an extensive advertising campaign, and for this reason many bars simply cannot afford this level of marketing. There are several ways that you can arrange to market your product yourself with time and effort but less money:

- **Get your friends involved.** If you know someone who works in radio, television, or some other media, consider getting them involved. Ask a DJ friend to casually mention your bar on a show—a very brief reference is fine, or ask a reporter friend to casually drop the name of your bar in an article. Ask a friend to perform live at your bar. They may say no, but you have nothing to lose until you ask.

- **Get published.** Write an online article or two and mention your bar, or contact local media outlets (weekly newspapers and small publications) that may need material. Offer to write an article if you can mention your bar in the byline.

- **Go online.** Keep it local, as that is where your potential customers are. However, there are likely several local forums—tourist guides, local chat groups—where you can mention that a new bar is opening. Keep it brief—mention the place and date and the bar's name, and you will reach some new customers.

- **Create a buzz.** Everyone loves a bit of mystery. Cover up your windows and put up an attractive "Coming Soon" sign. The sense that something new is going on will always draw the curious.

- **Contact the media.** Local radio, television, and newspapers often like to cover new businesses in the area, especially if there is something newsworthy about the new business. Is there something great about your concept, your new chef, or your décor? Decide what is newsworthy about your bar and contact the local news to see if a reporter wouldn't be interested in writing about your new establishment.

- **Get reviewed.** Offer to have your bar reviewed in a newspaper or guide and you will draw new customers.

- **Contribute.** If there is a local community event occurring, consider providing ice or nonalcoholic refreshments in exchange for a small banner that reads "Ice generously provided by [your bar's name here]." This is a great way to generate goodwill while still getting your name out.

Whatever method of marketing you choose, remember to keep at it—you do not want your bar's name to fade from collective memory.

Press Releases

Press releases are sent to the media and tell newspapers, radio, and other media the latest news about your bar or about your bar's promotions or upgrades. They are written in a concise style and contain everything that a reporter needs to write about your bar.

There are several things that a good press release does:

- It provides full contact information for you so that the media can contact you for a follow-up or interview.

- It has an effective title that will catch the attention of those looking for stories among press releases. Remember, your press release will be competing with many others, some of which are written by professionals.

- It gives a date for the press release and notes when the press release can be used by the media. This lets members of the media plan their publication schedule.

- It opens with the bare facts (what is noteworthy and newsworthy about the information in the press release).

- It provides quotes from you that can be used in news stories. Not all reporters and writers will contact you before writing your story.

- It provides all the major information about your bar, but it is not so long as to bore the reader.

- Is written in a professional style (this is no place for poetic flights of fancy).

Press releases have to be written in a specific style in order to be used. In general, you should be able to write a press release yourself quite easily. Before you begin writing your own, look at the example on the following page.

For more information contact:

J. Doe, Manager, Rick's Bar • 134 Boulevard Ave. • Anytown, Anystate USA

Phone: 555/ 555-5555 • Fax: 555/555-5556 • E-mail: j.doe@ricksbar.net

October 12, 2006

New Local Bar Is the First in State to Offer Customer Pampering

(Anytown, Anystate)—Rick's Bar, which has been in business since 1998, has recently renovated and reopened. It is now the first bar in the state to offer full spa services to customers all night long. Notes J. Doe, Rick's manager, "We have long been a dance bar, and on a trip to London I noticed how much more pampered the European bar crowd was. We decided to bring some of that pampering back home."

Rick's will now offer services on-site such as full manicures by a professional manicurist; foot, back, and hand rubs by the professional massage therapists; as well as hair and makeup touch-ups in an area adjacent to the bar. Says Doe, "Customers will be able to enter a special pampering area away from the bar, where in a controlled and quiet environment they will be able to request a number of spa services." It is expected that the bar will offer hot stone treatments and aromatherapy as well as other spa services. The cost of the services will be covered by the usual cover charge to get into the bar. Patrons will be able to bring their drinks with them into the spa area.

Doe notes that the idea will also help improve customer health, "The spa area will literally be an area where customers can relax and recharge after hitting the dance floor. Our professional spa staff will be able to smooth away any tensions and aches so that the customers will not be in pain due to a strained foot the night before." According to Doe, Rick's hopes to make the bar more attractive to its female clientele with these services, although he is quick to point out that the spa area is unisex.

The spa area will also serve bottled water and health drinks, which Doe claims are very trendy among European bar-goers. The bar's renovations will be competed by the end of September and a special grand reopening will take place on September 29. All are invited to attend; free door prizes will be given to some customers. A dress code is in effect.

For more information on marketing and advertising, check out these titles available from Atlantic Publishing:

- *Restaurant Marketing & Advertising: For Just a Few Dollars a Day* (Item # FS3-01, $19.95)

- *Restaurant Promotion & Publicity: For Just a Few Dollars a Day* (Item # FS4-01, $19.95)

To order, call 1-800-814-1132 or visit **www.atlantic-pub.com**.

CHAPTER SIX

Types of Beverages

Bar managers need to know some basics about various types of liquor. This is useful in determining what to stock and how much of each item to stock. Even though there are innumerable brands of liquor and many types of alcoholic beverages, all liquor can be divided into two groups:

Well Items

Well items are house brands. If a customer simply orders a "gin," the bar servers will serve the house brand. Some bar managers think that they can turn a profit by ordering the cheapest possible for their well items, but this is a mistake. Since your well items will be going into a number of drinks, you need to make sure that they are of high-enough quality to please customers. A medium-priced brand is usually the right combination of value and quality. You need to have a well item for each type of liquor that will be served, as customers will order a number of items (tequila, rum, water, and so on) without specifying brand.

Call Items

Call items are specific brands that a customer requests. When a customer asks for "Southern Comfort," for example, the patron is requesting a specific call item. Call items are usually more expensive and are often displayed at the back of the bar. It is unethical to serve well items and charge for call items if a patron has requested a specific brand. If you are out of the brand the customer requests, note which items you do have in stock.

There are a number of both call and well items that your bar will need:

Whiskeys

Whiskeys are made from fermented grains such as wheat, corn, rye, and barley. They are aged in oak barrels to give the liquor its taste, smell, and color. United States, Canada, Scotland, and Ireland all have their own special types of whiskeys, and the successful bar will want to have a selection of whiskeys from each of these countries.

STRAIGHT WHISKEY
Straight whiskey is unmixed with any other type of whiskey or liquor. It is often drunk alone or with ice ("on the rocks"). There are several types of straight whiskey:

Bourbon whiskey is made from 51 percent corn mash. Aged from two to six years in barrels of charred oak, it has a deep color and rather sweetish taste. Many fans of bourbon whiskey are very brand loyal and will generally order by brand name. Bourbon whiskey is sometimes called "just whiskey."

Tennessee whiskey is very similar to bourbon whiskey but has a more refined taste since it is filtered through maple charcoal. George Dickel and Jack Daniels brands fall into this category of whiskey.

Rye or American rye whiskey is now made from a blend of grains. The terms "rye whiskey," "American whiskey," and "blended whiskey" are often used interchangeably by patrons.

Bottled-in-bond whiskey is made under the supervision of the United States government to fit a number of standards:

- The whiskey is ages at least four years.

- It is bottled at 100 proof.

- It is produced in one distilling by a single distiller.

- It is produced and stored under government supervision.

BLENDED WHISKEY

There are several types of blended whiskey:

Canadian whisky is made under the supervision of the Canadian government. It is made from a blend of wheat, barley, malt, rye, and corn and is aged three years. Canadian whisky is considered mellow and light.

Scotch whisky is made only in Scotland. It is prized for its slightly smoky taste, which comes from the blend of the malt and grain whiskies that comprise it. This type of whisky is made by drying malted barley over open peat fires. Many fans of Scotch whisky have very specific brand loyalties, as different distilleries produce very different tastes by aging the whiskies for a longer or shorter amount of time or by adding special ingredients to their whiskies.

Light Scotch whiskies have become very popular in North America. They are basically Scotch whiskies that are light in color. The strength and, in many cases, the taste remain similar to other Scotch whiskies.

Single-malt Scotch whisky is whisky that is made at a single distillery. It has not been blended with any other whiskies. In many cases, this type of whisky has only local water and peat, making it quite strong tasting. The recipes for this type of whisky are a closely guarded secret, and in many cases, these whiskies are aged for many years. Both factors make the single-malt Scotch whisky more expensive than other types of whisky.

Irish whiskey is made only in Ireland. It is made like Scotch, only it is distilled three times and is not treated with peat smoke. The result is a very smooth, full, and heavy drink. The distilleries that make Irish whiskey are quite old, and one, Jamesons, claims to be the first whiskey producer in the world.

Other Liquors

Vodka was originally produced only in Russia, but it has become popular the world over and is now one of the hottest-selling liquor products around, mostly because it is used in so many popular mixed drinks. Vodka has often been prized for its clarity and for the fact that it leaves little odor, but it is not a "light" drink at all; in fact, vodka can come in proofs that ensure quite a strong drink. Bars need to stock plenty of this almost tasteless liquor, as demand for it is quite high.

Gin is distilled from a variety of grains and gains its unique flavor and aroma from juniper berries. It is bottled at 80 proof. In the past, it was the world's

⑧ Categories of Liquor

Rye Whiskey
Rye whiskey must be distilled from a fermented mash of grain containing at least 51 percent rye.

Popular Brands: Van Winkle Family Reserve Rye™, Jim Beam Rye™, Wild Turkey Rye™, and Old Potrero Straight Rye™.

Popular Drinks: Rye and Cola, Rye and Water, Rye Sling, Slider, Barnstormer, Black Manhattan and Whiskey Sour.

Tequila
Tequila is distilled from the fermented mash of the agave cacti. Tequila is usually clear, although some types may have a gold tint.

Popular Brands: Cuervo Tequila™, Hussong's, Lapis Anejo and Two Fingers Gold.

Popular Drinks: Margarita, Tequila Screwdriver, Bloody Maria, Mexican Coffee and Tequini.

Bourbon Whiskey
Bourbon whiskey was originally produced in Kentucky. Bourbon must be distilled from grain mash containing at least 51 percent corn.

Popular Brands: Maker's Mark™, Jim Beam™, Wild Turkey™, Evan Williams™, Jack Daniels™ and Pappy Van Winkle Family Reserve™.

Popular Drinks: Bourbon and Cola, Bourbon and Water, Old Fashioned, Mint Julep, Louisville Lady, Narragansett, and Stiletto.

Vodka
Vodka is made from a variety of grains, including wheat and corn. It is bottled at no less than 80 and no higher than 110 proof. It is colorless, odorless and virtually tasteless.

Popular Brands: Türi™, Absolut™, Belvedere™, Stolichnaya™ and Grey Goose™.

Popular Drinks: Screwdriver, Kamikaze, Long Island Iced Tea, Vodka Gimlet, Black Russian, Vodka Martini, Vodka and Tonic, Vodka Sour and Harvey Wallbanger.

Scotch
The unique smoky flavor of Scotch (produced only in Scottland) is derived from drying malted barley over open peat fires.

Popular Brands: Ambassador™, Ballantine's™, Glendronach™, Miltonduff-Glenlivet™, and Old Smuggler™

Popular Drinks: Rob Roy, Hot Scotch, Scotch Royale and Napoleon.

Rum
Rum is bottled at no less than 80 proof. Rums can be classified into two major types: light- and heavy-bodied.

Popular Brands: Bacardi™, Bundaberg Rum™, Captain Morgan Rum™, Cruzan Rum™, Flor De Caña Rums™, Malibu Rum™.

Popular Drinks: Rum and Cola, Cuba Libre, Rum Runner, Tom and Jerry, Piña Colada, Zombie, Mai-Tai, Rum Collins and Daiquiri.

Brandy
Brandy is traditionally distilled from a mash of fermented grapes or other fruits.

Popular Brands: Armagnac™, Christian Brothers™, E&J™ and Korbel™.

Popular Drinks: Brandy Alexander, Brandy Fizz, Apple Brandy Sour, Brandy Eggnog and Brandy Highball.

Gin
Gin is distilled from a variety of grains and is bottled at 80 proof. Every gin has its own distinctive flavor, aroma and is usually colorless.

Popular Brands: Beefeater™, Bombay™, Gordon's™, Plymouth™, Tanqueray™, Seagram's Extra Dry Gin™

Popular Drinks: Martini, Gin and Tonic, Tom Collins, Pink Lady, Gin Buck, Gimlet, Gin Manhattan, Gin Fizz, Gin Sour and Gibson.

© 2005 Atlantic Publishing Group, Inc.

This informative poster is an overview of the types of liquor. Appealing to customers and employees, it is available in full color and laminated to reduce wear and tear. It is 11" x 17" and available from Atlantic Publishing for $9.95 (Item # COL-PS). To order, call 1-800-814-1132 or visit www.atlantic-pub.com.

most popular drink because it was so inexpensive. Today it is mainly used in mixed drinks such as the "gin and tonic."

Beefeater is the only premium dry gin distilled in London. It is made by heating the prime grain spirit for a long time in a still with a mix of good ingredients or herbs. The result is a high-quality gin that many fans ask for by name. Some mixed drinks call specifically for this gin.

Holland or Geneva is a high-quality gin that has a very strong juniper berry flavor. For this reason, it is often drunk as a liqueur rather than in mixed drinks.

Cold compounded is a less expensive (and lesser quality) gin made by mixing the botanicals and prime grain spirits without heating at all. The liquid flavorings of herbs and fruits such as licorice, orange peel, lemon peel, coriander, almonds, angelica root, cassia bark, and orris root (botanicals) are simply stirred into vats of grain spirits before being bottled.

Rum is made from fermented sugar cane juice and molasses that has been aged for at least a year. Clear white rum, which is usually made in Puerto Rico, is the most popular in North America. Dark rums are white rums to which caramel has been added to change the taste and color. Some dark rums are made in Jamaica or Martinique, and these are known for their sweetness and strength. Bermuda also makes a strong dark rum, Goslings.

Aquavit is a Scandinavian version of gin in which caraway seeds add flavor. Often drunk chilled, it can also be added to mixed drinks as a substitute for gin.

Brandy is distilled fermented grapes, although the term is sometimes used to describe other fermented fruit spirits. By law, if brandy is made from another fruit (generally apricot, peach, pineapple, cherry, apple, plum, or blackberry), the labels needs to clearly reflect this, by stating "apple brandy," for example. Brandy is generally 80 proof and comes in many varieties:

Kirsch, also called Kirschwasser, is made in the Rhine Valley from whole black cherries.

Slivovitz brandy is made from plums and is distilled in Central Europe.

Pear William, also called Poire William, is a pear brandy made in France and Switzerland. Some distilleries actually bottle a whole pear in every bottle.

Cognac is produced only in the Cognac region of France and is considered the very height of brandy. The quality of grapes and the manufacturing process is carefully controlled to ensure maximum quality. As a result, cognac is very expensive. It is also a brandy that, in many cases, is aged for a long time. Cognac is labeled with letters rather than with dates, as so many distilled spirits of different years are used in the manufacturing process. On a cognac label, "V.S." signifies a "Very Superior" cognac that has been aged for at least one and a half years. "V.S.O.P.," or "Very Superior Old Pale," indicates an aging process of at least four and a half years. Some cognacs designated "V.S.O.P." have been aged for up to ten years. Cognac labeled as "X.O." means "Extremely Old" and has been aged for at least five and a half years.

Armagnac brandy is drier in taste than cognac and can only be made in the Armagnac region of France. Like cognac, it is strictly controlled. It is considered quite a high-quality brandy.

Spanish brandy, also called Spanish cognac, is made in Spain using the same distilling process as a brandy.

Marc is a French brandy made from the husks of grapes or the pulps of apples that are left over from cider or wine making. They are aged many years and made very strong.

Applejack, or apple brandy, is made from the cider of crushed apples. Calvados, a variation, is produced only in Normandy, France, where it is still a cottage industry. It can be made quite strong in this region, and some casks are aged up to 40 years. In the United States, Applejack is generally bottled-in-bond, meaning that its process is controlled by the government.

Metaxa is a sweetened Greek brandy with a wine-like flavor. Some versions are so sweet they can be considered liqueurs.

Grappa is an Italian brandy that is more of a grape spirit and is not truly a brandy, although it is often classified as one.

Tequila is usually produced in Mexico or the American southwest. It is distilled from the fermented mash of the aqua or century plants, which are cacti. Some types of Tequila are also made from apples, dandelion leaves, rice, dates, and other local products where the Tequila is made. Tequila is usually clear, although some types may have a gold tint. The smell and taste are distinctive. Tequila is used primarily in making margarita cocktails. Also in recent years there has been a wide increase in the variety of "premium" tequilas. Tequila can also be chilled and served straight as a "shooter" with a beer chaser.

Sherry is a fortified wine from Spain, meaning that it is a wine to which brandy has been introduced. Sherry gets its unique flavor from a special yeast that forms on top of white wine. This yeast, along with the actual manufacturing process, creates a range of sherry types. Some popular styles of sherry include sweet oloroso, amontillado, fino (which is very dry), and manzanilla (which is said to be salty, as it is aged by the sea). Sweet sherries tend to be dark due to the caramel color added, while dry sherries are generally the color of paler whiskey.

Port, a sweet fortified wine, is made in Portugal and comes in three types: Ruby, Vintage, and Tawny. Vintage port tends to be dry, deep, and full of flavor. Some describe it as a "nutty" flavored port. There is even a white port, made by using unpeeled grapes.

Marsala is a dark fortified wine that is often drunk after dinner. Patrons who enjoy something different or those who enjoy Italian food are often the biggest fans of this Sicilian wine.

Madeira and **muscat** are also fortified wines. They are imported from Portugal, France, Australia, and Spain. They are not strictly necessary for many bars, as they are rarely requested, but some bar owners who stress their wine list would do well to have at least a bottle or two on hand.

Cordials and Liqueurs

Cordials and **liqueurs** are created by the mixing or pre-distilling of neutral grain spirits with fruits, flowers, or plants to which sweeteners have been added. Cordials and liqueurs are colorful and very sweet in taste, which is why they are usually served as after-dinner drinks. There are a wide variety of cordials and liqueurs available. They are often served in tiny liqueur glasses and tend to be expensive items. A good selection of cordials and liqueurs would include 15 to 25 of these. There are approximately 10 to 12 different types that you must stock because of their popularity or because they are used in making certain cocktails:

Coffee liqueurs are de rigueur for any bar, as so many mixed drinks and specialty coffees call for these.

Bailey's Irish Cream, made from Irish Whiskey and cream, is essential in many mixed drinks and is even popular with ice, especially among female customers.

Orange liqueur is used in many martinis and is good to keep on hand. Margaritas and Sidecars call for this liqueur, and many mixed drinks that have lemon in them are even tastier with a slight hint of orange liqueur.

Benedictine, a neutral spirits liqueur, contains 27 herbs and spices and is dark amber in color.

Chambord is a raspberry liqueur that is used in many mixed drinks that call for champagne. It is also used in many mixed sweet drinks.

Chartreuse is brand-name liqueur that combines brandy, spirits, and herbs and spices. There is a yellow and green version popular, and both are good in mixed drinks.

Creme de cacao tastes like chocolate and is key to many mixed drinks. It is also a nice mix with Bailey's Irish Cream or many coffee liqueurs.

Creme de Cassis is a blackberry liqueur often mixed with white wine or nonalcoholic beverages to make mixes.

Creme de Menthe is a mint-tasting liqueur that comes in green and white and is key for many mixed drinks. It is also sometimes drunk with ice and water, especially in France.

Drambuie is a brand-name liqueur made of herbs and Scotch whisky. It is very sweet and essential for the very popular drink "Rusty Nail."

Creme de Noyau is an almond liqueur that is far less popular now but is still useful for cocktails.

Galliano is made from anise, vanilla, and licorice liqueur. This brand-name drink is rarely used in mixed drinks today but still comes in handy for occasional cocktails. This Italian drink is yellow in color and comes in a distinctive tall bottle.

Jagermeister is a sweet liqueur often served with ice or straight, often just before a beer. It is popular among younger bar patrons, so it is useful to keep this liqueur on hand, especially if you expect your clientele to include some younger customers.

Kummel is a caraway-flavored liqueur that is clear and made by several manufacturers. It is handy for a few different mixed drinks.

Midori is a brand-name liqueur based on melon. Made in Japan, this green liqueur is useful for the popular "Melon Ball" and a few other drinks as well.

Sambuca is an Italian liqueur that tastes like licorice. It is often drunk straight, with three coffee beans added to the snifter glass as a garnish.

Sloe gin is a liqueur based on the sloe plum and has a deep taste. It is mainly used in cocktails such as the "Sloe Gin Fizz," which although not as popular as they once were, are still ordered occasionally.

Southern Comfort is a brand-name bourbon that has a slight peach accent. There are still a number of people who request this drink regularly, so it is a good bottle to keep by the bar.

Pernod, **Ricard** and **Ouzo** are brand names that are all weaker versions of a strong wormwood-flavored liquor. These liqueurs turn colors when mixed with ice and water and generally taste of licorice and anise.

Kahlua is a brand-name coffee liqueur that is necessary for certain very popular cocktails such as "Black Russians" and "White Russians" and is essential for any bar.

Vermouth is not classified as liqueur or liquor at all but is actually a wine flavored with roots, berries, or various types of plants. In many cases, an herb called wormwood is used in vermouth. There are two basic types: Dry vermouth is usually produced in America or France. This variety has a clear to light golden color. It is used primarily in martini cocktails. One good well item is all that is required. Sweet vermouth is a darker reddish wine with a richer, sweeter flavor. It is most often produced in Italy. Sweet vermouth is primarily used in making Manhattan cocktails.

Beer

Beer requires its own category, as you will likely want to have a large selection. Restaurants can have one or two beers, but bars generally require more. In fact, some bars are successful by offering a huge range of draft beers on tap. This is because beer is one of the biggest-selling drinks at bars.

Beer is quite perishable and should be treated as a food product, meaning it should be kept in a refrigerator. This is because light and warmth can spoil the product. While the storage of beer can make it a rather expensive product to keep on hand, its popularity makes selling this beverage well worth the effort.

There are many types of beers made around the world. You will want to stock plenty of lagers in your bar, as these are the most popular types of beers on the market today. You will also want to keep on hand several ales, which are heavier beers made with more hops for a stronger flavor. You will also want to keep a selection of port, stout, and bock beers. These are generally made overseas and are heavy, rich, dark, and sweet when compared with other beers. You will want to have a good selection of domestic and a few foreign beers, such as Heineken, Guinness, Pilsner, Bass, and Whitbread, on hand. You will also want to have some light beers on hand for those who are watching their weight. There are even fruit beers which are quite sweet and have a high interest factor if not a huge following. If you have the room, a few of these beers are an excellent way to provide for those customers who crave something a little different.

You can buy beer in cans, bottles, or in kegs for serving on tap. In general, about twelve varieties will be demanded regularly by your customers. Some customers prefer their favorite brands to be on tap. A number of customers will prefer beer out of a bottle and will even disdain the glass. In general, you will not need to fuss with cans. Your most popular beers should be on tap and you should have as many bottled products as you can justify. If you have the means and space for it, having lots of beers on tap is a great profit-maker, as many beer fans will travel longer distances to try a variety of beers on tap. Microbreweries should also not be overlooked, as they are somewhat of a trend right now.

Once you have established a clientele, an excellent way to keep profits up is to provide draft beer. Draft beers produce excellent profit for a bar, as patrons develop huge brand loyalty and will gladly head to the pub or bar that offers their favorite draft beer. To find out which to stock, you only need to listen to what your patrons want and then supply it. The result is a steady stream of satisfied customers and a tidy profit for you. Draft beer is also nice in terms of bar profit because it requires so little expertise to serve. As long as it is served icy cold and in a perfectly clean glass, it will satisfy. Even your least experienced bartender or server can easily handle serving beer.

5 Categories of Beer

Lager

Lagers are the most popular types of beer. The name comes from the German word "lagern," which means "to store."

Brewing: Lager is brewed with bottom fermenting yeast at cooler temperatures. Many lagers will ferment over longer periods of time and at temperatures less than 55° F. Pale golden color, carbonated and lightly hopped, lager is a popular favorite.

Color: Golden.

Flavor: Smooth, crisp, refreshing and clean.

Food Accompaniment: Well-rounded flavor works well with many types of food including grilled foods, seafood, beef, poultry and, of course, pizza.

Popular Brands: Budweiser™, Bud Light™, Busch™, Corona™, Michelob™, Coors™, Miller Lite™, Miller Genuine Draft™, Leinenkugel's Original Premium™, Heineken™, Rolling Rock™, Samuel Adams™ and Stroh's™.

Ale

Ales share certain characteristics, typically fruitiness, acidity and a pleasantly bitter seasoning.

Brewing: Ales take less time to brew and age than lagers and have a more distinctive flavor or "personality." They tend to be less carbonated and fuller bodied. Ale yeast ferments at warmer temperatures and typically requires no refrigeration.

Color: Varies in color, can be a rich gold to deeper amber shades.

Flavor: Robust and complex, often fruity.

Food Accompaniment: Serve with hearty, strong-flavored food such as read meat, fish and sausage.

Popular Brands: Pacific Ridge Pale Ale™, Mac's Amber Ale™, Henry Weinhard's Pale Ale™, Redhook Extra Special Bitter (ESB) Ale™, Ballard Bitter Ale™, Wheathook Ale™ and Point Cascade Pale Ale™.

Bock

Bock is a type of lager beer and be can be pale, dark or double.

Color: Coppery to dark brown in color.

Flavor: Sweet, rich, slightly "malty."

Popular Brands: Michelob Amber Bock™, Point Spring Bock™, Leinenkugel's Big Butt Doppelbock™ and ZiegenBock™.

Stout

Stouts are considered a type of ale. They have a heavily roasted flavor and come in many different varieties.

Types of Stouts: Dry stout (dark, rich and bitter), flavored stouts (usually flavored stouts with dark fruits, coffee or chocolate), oatmeal stout (rich body, velvety texture and sweet flavor).

Popular Brands: Guinness™, Murphy's Irish Stout™ and Beamish, Young's Oatmeal Stout™ and Young's Double Chocolate Stout™.

Porter

Porter was originally a English beer that originated in London. It is actually a type of ale and is usually heavy, with a higher alcohol content (between 7–9%). It is sometimes described as bitter.

Color: Reddish to dark brown in color.

Flavor: Can vary from subtle dark malts to fully roasted, smoky flavors.

Popular Brands: Henry Weinhard's Porter™, Black Watch Porter™ and Black-hook Porter™.

© 2005 Atlantic Publishing Group, Inc.

This colorful and informative poster is an overview of beer. The facts are interesting for customers and a good reference for employees. It is available in full color and laminated to reduce wear and tear. The poster measures 11" x 17" and is available from Atlantic Publishing for $9.95 (Item # TOB-PS). To order, call 1-800-814-1132 or visit www.atlantic-pub.com.

clean glass, it will satisfy. Even your least experienced bartender or server can easily handle serving beer.

Nonalcoholic beer may seem to be a contradiction in terms, but it is actually growing in popularity. This drink offers the taste of beer without the alcohol—or at least with only trace levels of alcohol. It is often requested by people who are driving home or by people who want to taste a beer with their meal but are unable to drink alcohol. Carrying one of the more popular brands, such as Kaliber or Buckler, is a smart choice.

If you will be serving plenty of beer—and you will be if you are running a bar—then you will need to find a way to take care of the empty bottles. In a successful bar, these can quickly add up, and some larger bars actually have to hire extra personnel to take care of this. One simple way some successful bar owners have gotten rid of empty bottles is to offer them to someone. In areas where bottle returns yield five or ten cents a bottle, there are always people willing to take the bottles away in order to make a profit themselves.

Wines

Just a few years ago, many bars offered only two choices of wine: white or red. Today many bars now have extensive wine lists, with selections of wine from the common to the rare. Partly, this resurgence has to do with a renewed interest in wine. Wine tastings and wine classes are becoming more popular, and knowing something about wine is now considered quite desirable. As a result, bar patrons are becoming more knowledgeable and curious about wines. Recent studies suggesting that wine can be good for one's health when drunk in moderation are also adding to wine's popularity, and as wine's popularity continues to grow, on-premise consumption grows rapidly.

You will need to decide how much wine you want to keep in your bar. Some bars stock up wine cellars of hundreds of bottles while others serve only a few or even none at all. Wine always enhances meals and is still often ordered by the glass at bars. The best way to determine which wines to stock—and whether you should stock wines at all—is to look at your intended clientele and competition. If you decide to serve wine, you should develop a wine list to help you determine which of the many types of wine available you wish to keep in stock.

Wine is often served with food, and this makes wine a more complicated alcoholic beverage; one that is in a category by itself. Certain wines go with certain foods, and there tend to be more types of wine than types of other beverages. Both these facts suggest that the smart bar manager will learn at least the rudiments about wine and will ensure that his or her staff has a basic knowledge of wine as well. This will allow the bar staff to make suggestions to patrons, as customers often ask for recommendations about wine.

Wine is essentially a fermented grape juice that comes in three colors—white, red, and rosé. Three factors affect the quality of wine: the grape, the climate the grapes are raised in, and the human preparers of the wine. Some bar patrons will ask for a wine not by brand but by the type of grape used in making the wine (such as Chardonnay, Shiraz, Muscat, Cabernet Sauvignon, Cabernet, and others). Some patrons want wines from specific regions. This is because some regions of the world—due to climate and soil type—produce

Red Wine

Cabernet Sauvignon

A classic variety, sometimes called the "king of red wine." Associated with the Bordeaux region of France as a 100 percent varietal or in red blends. Typically aged in oak for over a year, and should age several more years in the bottle.

Flavor & Color: Medium- to full-bodied, intense and deep, dark fruits (black currant) flavor, usually with strong tannins. With age, it can develop bouquet nuances of cedar, violets or leather, and its tannic edge may soften and smooth.

Food Accompaniment: Excellent with lamb; it also pairs well with roasts, steaks and other red meats. Also a good accompaniment with ham, pasta and cheese.

Merlot

The Merlot grape produces wine with a chewy, almost opulent texture and produces a smooth and mellow red wine.

Flavor & Color: Merlot is less tannic, and is rich, full-bodied and deep in color. Flavors range from cherry, plum to chocolate. Fruity lingering aftertaste with a hint of vanilla.

Food Accompaniment: Recommended for medium-weight meats (duck, pork, veal) especially in slightly sweet dishes. Also good with poultry, pasta and cheese.

Syrah/Shiraz

A rich, full-bodied, complex, spicy wine that thrives in the Rhone region of France. Syrah can be successfully blended with many other wine grapes; it also can be made in a variety of styles ranging from soft and medium-bodied.

Flavor & Color: Usually dark red with high tannins. The aroma and flavors can vary from fruit flavors such as strawberry or raspberry to meaty or spicy flavors such as smoky or peppery.

Food Accompaniment: Serve with robust, flavorful foods such as grilled meat, game, spicy dishes or barbecue.

Pinor Noir

A difficult grape to grow, native to the cool Burgundy region of France, pinor noir is intense aromatic, with complex flavors and a silky texture.

Flavor & Color: Usually light to medium, ruby red with soft tannins, usually dry with a suggestion of sweetness. Frequently with an earthy quality and often fruity. Aroma and flavor varies from region to region. In California, the aroma may be berry-like or vanilla. In France, it is earthy with hints of prunes or plums.

Food Accompaniment: Works well with Asian foods and fish. Also good with pasta, meats, game and cheese.

Zinfandel

From California, a dry, full-bodied, intensely flavored red wine with substantial tannins. Often described as big, robust and incredibly concentrated.

Flavor & Color: Fruity, full of mixed blackberry and raspberry scents. Premium Zinfandels are rich, with a lush texture and ripe fruit flavors.

Food Accompaniment: Excellent with hearty, spicy or salty food. Grilled or barbecued meats are fine choices as well as pasta and cheese.

© 2005 Atlantic Publishing Group, Inc. • Item #RWP-PS to re-order please call 1-800-814-1132

This poster on red wine is part of a 5-part wine poster series from Atlantic Publishing. It is full color and laminated to reduce wear and tear. It is 11″ x 17″ and available for $9.95 (Item # RWP-PS). To order, call 1-800-814-1132 or visit www.atlantic-pub.com.

different taste sensations even with similar grapes. While warm and pleasant climates produce nice wines, it is often the worse-weathered regions that produce better wines. Experts think that wines from areas such as Burgundy offer better taste because grapes have to struggle through bad weather, gaining more flavor and maturing more slowly. Finally, the human factor, or the special recipes and decisions of the winemakers, plays a big part in wine quality. Some patrons will ask for wines from specific brands or vineyards because they find that those wines offer the taste that they desire.

Some patrons also want wines from specific years, as the climate or growing season of grapes may be more or less favorable from one year to the next. Of course, many patrons will have no idea what sort of wine they wish to try and will turn to you or your servers for suggestions. For this reason, developing a wine list of wines that you are familiar with and can control and describe is an excellent idea. Some suggestions:

White Wine

Chardonnay

Grown in nearly every wine-producing region of the world, this is the most purchased dry white wine. Bold, rich and complex, the best Chardonnays are aged in oak and medium-bodied, medium dry and high in acidity.

Flavor & Color: Often with buttery richness and toasty vanilla aromas. May also taste of ripe figs and peach, honey, hazelnuts and spice.

Food Accompaniment: Often served with rich fish and poultry dishes made with cream, butter or cheese.

Sauvignon Blanc

Also known as Fume Blanc, this grape is fresh and crisp, with a tart acidity. Typically light- to medium-bodied, it has a distinctive aromas of fresh-cut grass and herbs, green pepper and sometimes citrus.

Flavor & Color: Light to medium yellow in color, sometimes with a tinge of green. It has a grassy bouquet like the smell of a freshly cut lawn. May also display scents of lemons, asparagus and fig.

Food Accompaniment: Excellent with salads, fish and green vegetables.

Riesling

Riesling grapes produce both refreshing light-bodied wines and full-bodied table wines. With a very high natural acidity, Rieslings are both floral and fruity, and can be delicate, subtle, and low in alcohol.

Flavor & Color: Ranges from pale, dry and delicate to apricot-scented and sweet.

Food Accompaniment: A very food-friendly wine, good with fish, pork, foie gras, spicy Asian dishes, smoked foods, salty foods and rich dishes.

Pinot Gris

Typically quite dry, but can range from light and delicate to fairly full-bodied.

Flavor & Color: Yellow in color with a smoky or musky aroma. Dry, rich, full-bodied, with a pear-like flavor and creamy texture. Sometimes buttery with apricot or almond overtones.

Food Accompaniment: Excellent aperitif, or serve with salmon and other seafoods.

Chenin Blanc

This grape is grown widely in the Loire region of France as well as California and Washington State. It is typically turned into a light dry or semidry white with overtones of green apples and peaches and an acidity that can range from soft to zesty.

Flavor & Color: Pale to medium yellow. With moderate to high acidity, it may vary from dry to semi-sweet and sweet . It has a honey aroma with scents of hay as well.

Food Accompaniment: Excellent aperitif, partners well with chicken and fish dishes.

© 2005 Atlantic Publishing Group, Inc. • Item #WWP-PS to re-order please call 1-800-814-1132

This poster on white wine is part of a 5-part wine poster series from Atlantic Publishing. It is full color and laminated to reduce wear and tear. It is 11" x 17" and available for $9.95 (Item # WWP-PS). To order, call 1-800-814-1132 or visit www.atlantic-pub.com.

REDS

Light-bodied is often served with red meat, roasted poultry, and oily fish (suggested: 4).

Medium-bodied is often served with game, veal, pork, and other red meats (suggested: 4).

Full-bodied is served with all red meats, lamb, and duck (suggested: 4).

Semi-sweet are served with dessert or after dinner, alone, as they suppress appetite (suggested: 2–3).

WHITES

After beer, these are the wines most often ordered at bars, so keeping a good selection is well-advised:

Dry light-bodied is often served with shellfish and seafood (suggested: 2–4).

Semi-sweet often accompanies a seafood meal (suggested: 4).

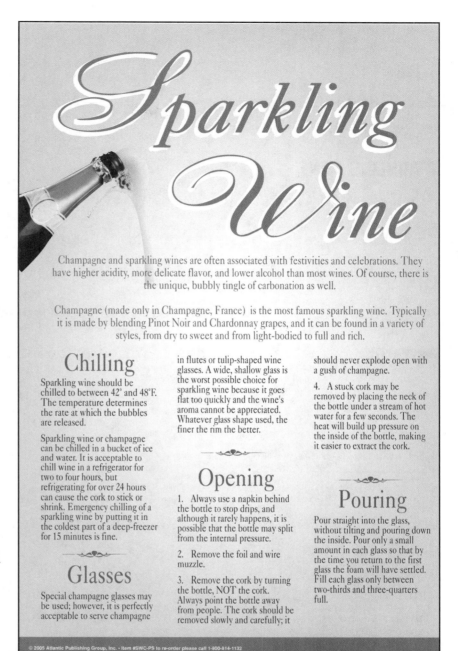

Sparkling Wine

Champagne and sparkling wines are often associated with festivities and celebrations. They have higher acidity, more delicate flavor, and lower alcohol than most wines. Of course, there is the unique, bubbly tingle of carbonation as well.

Champagne (made only in Champagne, France) is the most famous sparkling wine. Typically it is made by blending Pinot Noir and Chardonnay grapes, and it can be found in a variety of styles, from dry to sweet and from light-bodied to full and rich.

Chilling

Sparkling wine should be chilled to between 42° and 48°F. The temperature determines the rate at which the bubbles are released.

Sparkling wine or champagne can be chilled in a bucket of ice and water. It is acceptable to chill wine in a refrigerator for two to four hours, but refrigerating for over 24 hours can cause the cork to stick or shrink. Emergency chilling of a sparkling wine by putting it in the coldest part of a deep-freezer for 15 minutes is fine.

Glasses

Special champagne glasses may be used; however, it is perfectly acceptable to serve champagne in flutes or tulip-shaped wine glasses. A wide, shallow glass is the worst possible choice for sparkling wine because it goes flat too quickly and the wine's aroma cannot be appreciated. Whatever glass shape used, the finer the rim the better.

Opening

1. Always use a napkin behind the bottle to stop drips, and although it rarely happens, it is possible that the bottle may split from the internal pressure.

2. Remove the foil and wire muzzle.

3. Remove the cork by turning the bottle, NOT the cork. Always point the bottle away from people. The cork should be removed slowly and carefully; it should never explode open with a gush of champagne.

4. A stuck cork may be removed by placing the neck of the bottle under a stream of hot water for a few seconds. The heat will build up pressure on the inside of the bottle, making it easier to extract the cork.

Pouring

Pour straight into the glass, without tilting and pouring down the inside. Pour only a small amount in each glass so that by the time you return to the first glass the foam will have settled. Fill each glass only between two-thirds and three-quarters full.

© 2005 Atlantic Publishing Group, Inc. • Item #SWC-PS to re-order please call 1-800-814-1132

This poster on sparkling wine is part of a 5-part wine poster series from Atlantic Publishing. It is full color and laminated to reduce wear and tear. It is 11″ x 17″ and available for $9.95 (Item # SWC-PS). To order, call 1-800-814-1132 or visit www.atlantic-pub.com.

Full-bodied is often served with white meats and seafood (suggested: 4).

Medium-bodied is generally served with steak, roasted poultry, and fish such as salmon (suggested: 2–4).

ROSÉ

Dry light-bodied is generally served in place of either dry white or red wines (suggested: 1).

SPARKLING WINE

Dry is served in place of dry white wines (suggested: 1).

Semi-sweet tends to be served in place of semi-sweet whites (suggested: 1).

CHAMPAGNE

Dry is served alone or with any food item (suggested: 1).

Extra dry (Brut) is served alone or with any food item (suggested: 1).

The Language of Wine

Any bar manager who serves wine at their establishment quickly learns that wine comes with its own unique language. There are specific terms for describing wines. The successful bar manager will become at least somewhat familiar with this language. Being able to use the correct wine terms will make it easier to help customers who are confused about choices, and being able to use the language of wine will also allow the bar manager appear to be a more authoritative expert on the subject.

There are a few basic wine terms that are useful for every bar manager and employee to know:

Aroma: Refers to the scent of a wine. Words such as "fruity" or "sweet" are often used to describe a wine's aroma. The smell of a wine is also sometimes referred to as its "nose."

Light: Refers to the wine's body and/or alcoholic content. Light wines have a lower alcohol content.

Apertif: Usually a wine or fortified wine—served before meals.

Body: Refers to the fullness of the wine, its substantiality, which is described as light, medium, or full.

Color: Refers literally to the color of a wine. It is very useful to be able to tell a customer about subtle variations in color. Details such as whether a white wine is a deeper yellow or a more clear color can often help a customer make a better decision about what to order.

Corked wine: Refers to wine that has been ruined due to an insufficient or flawed cork.

Dry: Refers to the lack of sweetness in the wine.

Semi-sweet: Refers to the underlying sweetness of a wine.

House wine: Refers to wine that is served by the carafe or the glass. Serving it this way ensures that the sediment stays in the bottle. Also, patrons who order the house wine can be sure of getting a reasonably good wine even if they feel uncertain about ordering wine by brand name, region, or grape.

Jug wine: Refers to wine packaged and sold in large bottles or jugs. It is often less expensive than other types of wine.

Palate: Refers to the taste of a wine.

Words such as "dry" or "sweet" are often the basic words used to describe the taste of a wine, but customers may also want to know more. Being able to describe a wine as "fruity" or "peppery" or as tasting of a specific fruit or food is often helpful for customers.

You will want to be able to describe wine to customers in a way that is helpful and useful to them as they are making a choice. There are several accepted terms to use when doing this:

Bouquet: The complex fragrance that develops in a wine through fermentation and aging.

Buttery: Rich, creamy aroma and flavor. Some Chardonnays are usually described using this term.

Finish: The flavor a wine leaves in the mouth after the wine is swallowed. You may talk about the main taste of the wine and then mention the finish for a more complete description of a wine.

Legs: When wine is swirled in its glass, it may leave a type of residue or some drops of wine on the sides of the glass (much as syrup does). A wine with "good legs" leaves plenty of color on the sides of the glass as it is swirled.

Mature: Wine that is ready or aged enough to drink.

Bright: Fresh, fruity flavors.

Chewy: A wine that is heavy, tannic, and full-bodied.

Crisp: A wine that is noticeably acidic but pleasant. The acidity adds to the flavor.

Dense: A wine that is full-flavored or featuring a deep color.

Earthy: This word can suggest that a wine is clean and pleasant. In a negative sense, it can suggest a dirty wine that tastes funky. Because this word is vague, you may want to add other terms that clarify what you mean.

Fat: Full-bodied, high-alcohol.

Forward: Early maturing wine.

Fragrant: This word suggests that a wine has a floral aroma or bouquet.

Jammy: A sweet, concentrated fruit flavor.

Peppery: This word suggests a spicy, black pepper flavor.

Robust: Full-flavored, intense wine.

Round: Well-balanced, mellow, and full-bodied flavor.

Soft: Mellow and well balanced.

Aggressive: High tannins or acid taste. In many cases, this is a negative trait, but some customers prefer this taste.

Flat: This refers to an absence of flavor. Usually, flatness in wine is caused by lack of acidity.

Metallic: A wine with a tin-like flavor.

Off: A wine that is spoiled or faulty. It often clings to the teeth and may have an unpleasant vinegary or acidic taste.

Sharp: A wine with too much acid.

Just as you should teach yourself and your staff to talk about wine using these widely accepted terms, take care to ensure that every person on your staff can pronounce the different types of wines. Mispronunciation may seem to be a very small detail in a bar committed to serving great products, but mispronunciation can affect the way customers see your bar. If a server cannot properly pronounce the name of a wine, it may confuse the customer or make them view your bar as too uninformed about wines to provide proper service. When hiring new staff, make sure that all new employees can pronounce the following most common wine types:

Cabernet Sauvignon: Cah-bear-nay So-veen-yohn

Chardonnay: Shar-done-nay

Chenin Blanc: Chen-nahn Blohn

Fume Blanc: Foo-may Blohn

Johannisberg Riesling: Yo-han-iss-bairg Reez-ling

Merlot: Mare-low

Pinot Noir: Pea-no Nwar

Sauvignon Blanc: So-veen-yohn Blohn

The wine merchant or salesperson who sells you your wine will be able to point out which wines will fit into various classifications. It is not crucial that you can taste the difference between each, but it is very useful for the bar manager to understand the basics about wine. This will allow for better wine-buying decisions, better employee training, and better interactions with customers. It is also important that each group of wine is represented in your final list. As your bar expands and has been in business longer, you may want to offer an increasing selection of wines to appeal to customers who are more knowledgeable about wines and more likely to order wines by the glass.

Wine is an interesting and fun hobby to pursue. If you are interested in learning more about it, there are a number of excellent books covering all phases of the subject. There are also a number of classes that can be taken to help you understand the basics of wine. Even going on a wine-tasting tour will help improve your general understanding of wines. At the very least, you will want to invest in a guide to wines, which you can keep at your bar. You can refer to this guide to help you understand which wines to buy and distinguish which wines seem to be preferred by your customers.

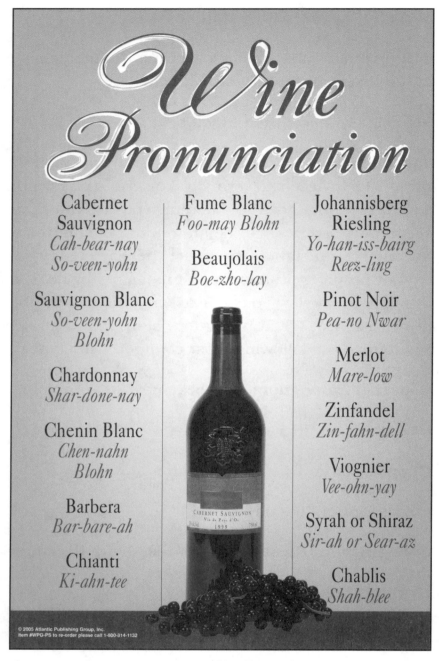

This poster on the proper pronunciation of wine is part of a 5-part wine poster series from Atlantic Publishing. It is full color and laminated to reduce wear and tear. It is 11″ x 17″ and available for $9.95 (Item # WPG-PS). To order, call 1-800-814-1132 or visit www.atlantic-pub.com.

A representative wine list must include wines of different prices and of different origins for each classification. There should be at least one moderately and one more expensively priced bottle for each classification. This allows customers who appreciate the better and more expensive bottles to do so, yet it allows the patron who may not know or care about the difference to enjoy some wine at a better price. A distinction should be made between moderately priced and cheap wines.

Although they have become increasingly popular, never use a wine that has a screw top. There is actually nothing wrong with the screw top itself, but it usually indicates a very cheap bottle of wine. The cork is traditionally used for wine bottles because the cork allows the wine to "breathe" somewhat and also imparts a specific flavor to the wine. Patrons who enjoy wine may be rather displeased to find a bar serving wine with a screw top. Also, the serving procedure for opening wine bottles is a very important part of the total wine experience that will be lost if a screw-top bottle is used.

At least one domestic and one imported wine should be listed for each classification. Imported wines are usually the more expensive bottles. In recent years, many of the notable California wines have rivaled or exceeded the quality (and price) of imported bottles. Wines from several different countries should be listed to give the customer the impression of a well-rounded and balanced list. Each of the wine-producing countries specializes in a particular wine variety. Your wine merchant or salesperson will be able to point them out to you.

People prefer to select what is familiar and of proven value to them. Thus, some wines should be of a recognized brand, such as Almaden, Inglenook, Paul Masson, Wolf Blass, Great Western, Taylor, etc. These wineries and labels are continually promoted and advertised and are very popular because of this exposure.

In addition to offering bottled wines, most bars/restaurants also sell a house or bulk wine, usually Chablis, Rosé, and/or Burgundy. Bulk wine may be purchased very inexpensively in gallon jugs or five-gallon casks. The wine is then portioned into and served from carafes. All the major California wineries produce a bulk wine. Because the wine is produced by a well-known winery and the price is often the lowest on the list, bulk wine tends to be a very popular item. House wine also seems like a good choice for many patrons who know little about wines but still wish to order wine from the menu.

Ordering Wine

The procedures for ordering wine are identical to those used in purchasing liquor. These orders may be prepared at the same time, since the liquor distributor will probably also carry most of the wines desired.

The computation of the beginning inventory of wine is also identical to that of liquor and food. The beginning inventory is the total dollar amount of the item prior to opening day. Based on this starting figure, you will then be able to project monthly wine costs.

When ordering wine, it is also useful to consider wine bottle size as well as types of wines possible. Most wine comes in standard 750-mL bottles. When customers order a bottle of wine, this is the size they are thinking of. It is also possible to order splits of wine, which come in bottles about half the size of a regular bottle. This is quite useful if you are offering a wine by the glass, as wine tends to lose its flavor and aroma once opened. A bottle that has been opened for days will simply not be enjoyed as much by customers in the know as a fresh bottle. Ordering some splits helps ensure that you can always offer customers a fresh and delicious glass of wine. Wines also come in larger bottles; it is economical to select these larger bottles when ordering your house wine.

Pricing Wine

The procedure for assessing the selling price of wines is similar to the one used in determining bar and menu prices. The first step is to compute a total portion cost for each item. Since wine is sold in the same unit as it is purchased, the total cost is the wholesale price at which each bottle was purchased. Although there are many other costs involved in serving wine—such as labor, wine books, glasses, corkscrews, carafes, decanters, utilities, and so forth—the only direct cost is the price of the bottle of wine. To compute the portion cost of bulk wine, simply multiply the cost per ounce by the portion size (glass or carafe).

A fair and customary markup for wine is approximately 1.5–2.5 times the bottle cost or, on average, 40 percent of cost of sales. Price out each bottle using the formula.

When pricing bottles that are commonly purchased at the local liquor store or supermarket, keep in mind that many of your customers will be fully aware of their retail price in these establishments. The markup described may cause customers to not only resist the wine purchase but also to examine your other prices with the same doubt. Unfortunately, 99 percent of your clientele are unaware of the operating costs of a bar and will not be able to see the justification for such a markup. *Why*, the hapless diner asks, *does the 1999 California Chardonnay from the liquor store cost $15; from your bar, $32; at ABC bar down the street, $38; and at a large chain, $24?* Many diners assume that the price of the wine they order in a bar or restaurant has been outrageously inflated, and they're sometimes correct. One of the issues in pricing wine is that the customer knows the retail price. If the perception is that your wine pricing is too high, customers may view all of your prices in that manner. In order to avoid this stigma of being over-priced, lower the prices on these bottles and make up the difference on some other varieties and bulk wine, which is an excellent low-cost item.

Careful examination of market trends and conditions will enable you to purchase wine at substantial discounts. You can then pass on these discounts to your customers, while still maintaining the desired profit margin.

Wine is a good profit item; it will average approximately the same cost of sales as food, but the labor and operating costs needed to present it are substantially less. This is why a good representative wine list, and a big effort on management's part to promote it, is advocated.

Later in this book, we will describe some simple and inexpensive ways to effectively increase wine sales.

CHAPTER SEVEN

Preparing and Serving Beverages

Serving beverages is a key function of bars, and one that you must be able to perfect in your own bar if you wish to be successful. After all, any potential customer can walk into a liquor store, purchase their own beverage, and prepare it at home. Many people go to bars not only to spend time with friends, but also to experience the service that bars offer. This means that you must be able to provide good service in order to get repeat customers.

When it comes to prepared beverages at bars, customers expect a few things:

- **Good service.** Customers not only want someone else to prepare a drink for them, but they want that drink prepared and served in a way that is friendly and kind.

- **Presentation.** Customers expect a drink that is presented nicely. This not only helps them feel pampered and well-attended to, but it also further stresses the fact that they are not drinking at home, but rather having professionals create their drinks for them.

- **Atmosphere.** Bar patrons want to enjoy the ambience of a place outside their home. Lighting, colors, décor, and other customers all work together to create a pleasant atmosphere.

- **New experiences.** Customers rely on the expertise of bars, bartenders, and servers to offer drinks that are new to them.

The bar manager who can consistently deliver on these four aspects of a successful bar can usually create a loyal following and manage a successful bar that other patrons want to visit.

Serving Wine

Wine is often the most complicated drink to serve and one of the easiest to prepare. To prepare, all one needs to do is ensure that the correct wine is poured from the wine bottle into a clean wineglass. Serving wine is more complicated than that, though. Since wine is delicate, it must be stored away from light, heat, and sudden movements before it is served. It should also be stored on its side or at an angle; this is to keep the cork moist. If the bottle is stored upright, the cork will soon dry out and allow air to seep into the bottle and spoil the taste of the wine.

The taste of wine varies with the temperature of the drink. Serve white and rosé wines at about 46°–50°F, serve red wines at about 62°–68°F, and serve champagnes and sparkling wines in an ice bucket at about 42°–48°F. When serving wine, remember that there is a fair amount of snobbishness about wine. Your goal (and your servers' goal) should be a happy balance between making the customer feel comfortable in his or her knowledge of wine and giving the customer a chance to decide how they want their wine served. For this reason, servers should ask when a guest wants wine served during the meal. If the customer seems unsure, it is acceptable for the server to make a gentle suggestion as to wine and the course to serve it with. The final decision rests with the customer, however.

Serving Wine Properly

There is a process in serving wine properly. Staff and servers should be taken through this process to ensure that the setting goes through without a hitch. Wine connoisseurs (and there are more and more of them today) may not return to your bar if wine is not served according to accepted rules:

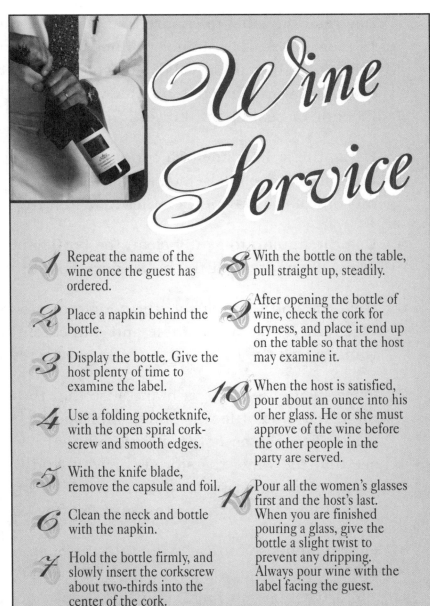

Wine Service

1. Repeat the name of the wine once the guest has ordered.

2. Place a napkin behind the bottle.

3. Display the bottle. Give the host plenty of time to examine the label.

4. Use a folding pocketknife, with the open spiral corkscrew and smooth edges.

5. With the knife blade, remove the capsule and foil.

6. Clean the neck and bottle with the napkin.

7. Hold the bottle firmly, and slowly insert the corkscrew about two-thirds into the center of the cork.

8. With the bottle on the table, pull straight up, steadily.

9. After opening the bottle of wine, check the cork for dryness, and place it end up on the table so that the host may examine it.

10. When the host is satisfied, pour about an ounce into his or her glass. He or she must approve of the wine before the other people in the party are served.

11. Pour all the women's glasses first and the host's last. When you are finished pouring a glass, give the bottle a slight twist to prevent any dripping. Always pour wine with the label facing the guest.

© 2005 Atlantic Publishing Group, Inc. • Item #PWS-PS to re-order please call 1-800-814-1132

Continually remind your servers on how to properly serve wine. This poster on wine service is part of a 5-part wine poster series from Atlantic Publishing. It is full color and laminated to reduce wear and tear. It is 11" x 17" and available for $9.95 (Item # PWS-PS). To order, call 1-800-814-1132 or visit www.atlantic-pub.com.

1. If serving red wine, uncork the bottle soon as it is at the table so that it can "breathe."

2. Place a napkin behind the bottle, with the label of the bottle facing the customer. Ensure that you have a good grip on the bottle (especially important if you are holding a cloth napkin that can easily cause the bottle to slip).

3. Approach the person who ordered the wine and present the bottle to him or her so that the label can be displayed. Wait until the person

has read the label to ensure that you have the bottle they requested. In most cases, a customer will nod slightly, make eye contact, or otherwise show approval of the wine. The cork should be slightly slanted toward the customer as well so that the customer can see any labeling or sealing on the cork.

4. Using the knife blade of a corkscrew, cut around the foil and remove the foil and capsule. Place these where the customer can reach them but out of the way of the other items on the table.

5. Use the napkin to gently clean the bottle and the bottle neck. A careful grip will ensure that the bottle does not slip.

6. Hold the bottle and insert the corkscrew about two-thirds into the cork. Place the bottle on the table and pull carefully on the cork. You do not want to jerk the bottle or push the corkscrew further into the bottle.

7. Once the bottle is open, make sure that the cork is not dry (which indicates the bottle was stored improperly). Place the cork on the table (wet side up so as not to stain the linen). This allows the customer to see that the wine was stored correctly and that the bottle was opened properly (no scarring on the underside means that the corkscrew was not punched in so far as to cause floating cork bits in the wine).

8. Pour a small amount of wine into the customer's glass. To prevent drips, use the napkin at the neck of the bottle and give the bottle a slight twist as you finish pouring. Drips not only look unsightly, they indicate a waste of the customer's money. The customer may reject the bottle of wine if there is something wrong with it; they cannot simply reject it because of the taste. If a bottle is rejected due to spoiling, it should be brought to management for investigation. For newer bottles, vendors will generally replace the item. Older vintages are usually not refunded.

9. Only once the customer has approved the wine should the others in the party be served. Serve women first and then the men, always ending with the customer who ordered the wine. Fill each glass only two-thirds full so that wine can be slightly swirled in the glass to release full aroma and flavor.

10. When a new bottle is ordered, new glasses should be brought and the process gone through again.

Although this process seems time consuming, servers need to be trained in this process until this method of serving wine is speedy, automatic, and even graceful. Proper wine service will favorably impress those who know about wine and will add a touch of class to the experience of those who enjoy wine but do not know much about it.

Serving Sparkling Wine and Champagne

Champagne and sparkling wine are served differently than wine. It is also important to stress proper serving of these drinks among your staff, as opening the corks on these bottles can be tricky and awkward. To follow are the steps for proper sparkling wine and champagne service:

1. Bring the bottle to the table in an ice bucket.

2. Place a napkin behind the bottle, as with wine. Show the bottle to the customer.

3. Using the knife implement, remove the foil from the bottle. Carefully remove the wire muzzle using your fingers.

4. Point the bottle away from the table, and turn the bottle carefully and slowly. The bottle should "steam," but no champagne should spill at all (especially important with very expensive champagne such as Dom Perignon). The cork should be placed on the table—it should not fly across the room.

5. Carefully pour champagne into champagne flutes, using the same care as with wine in order not to spill any. The process of tasting and approval is not necessary with champagne as the "fizz" of champagne shows the server that the champagne is not spoiled without a taste test being necessary.

Serving by the Glass or by the Bottle

Groups of bar customers will often order wine by the bottle or carafe. However, more and more bar customers are buying wine by the glass, even when they are meeting in groups, and this makes selling wine by the glass an important marketing tool. Many regular drinkers of wine today like wine-by-the-glass programs, and this clientele may make more of an effort to patronize your establishment if you offer such a program. The smart bar manager recognizes that a strong wine-by-the-glass program attracts customers who are willing to spend more for wine. A well-organized wine-by-the-glass program can, in fact, cause wine profits to more than double. With profit margins as high as 300 percent, premium wine served by the glass can be as profitable as specialty drinks!

Some successful pubs, bars, and restaurants offer a wine-by-the-glass suggestion for certain appetizers and for every entrée, which suggests to patrons which wines could enhance each dish. Even customers not considering a glass of wine with their meal may be tempted to buy a glass of wine when it is suggested to them. You should not rely on the waitstaff to recite the wine-by-the-glass list, though; the list is too long and the recitation may seem too intrusive or uninteresting to customers. A better idea is to use an attractive table tent or smaller menu design. Print the wine-by-the-glass list on a blackboard or sign that can be read from several areas of the dining room and bar. Even champagne sells better when sold by the glass. The fact is, many patrons who would not consider buying wine or champagne by the bottle might consider buying a single glass, especially if the suggestion is presented to them in an appealing manner.

Every successful bar managers needs to decide how many wines by the glass their bar should pour, and this is not always an easy decision. You might select to offer as few as 3 wines or as many as 15 or 20. The numbers will depend on your marketing program and your customers. In general, you want to be wary of offering more than 20 wines by the glass because of potential losses from wine spoilage. Yet the average number of by-the-glass offerings in bars and restaurants has grown steadily. Many restaurants now pour at least 30 percent more wine than they did five years ago, and their sales have benefited to a great extent. There are various wine-by-the-glass dispensing systems available today that can assist with your program. These systems will keep wine as fresh as the moment they were uncorked for up to six weeks, eliminating spoilage and waste. They are all temperature-controlled and use a nitrogen gas replacement system. The nitrogen gas instantly replaces the oxygen in a freshly opened bottle of wine with pure, odorless, tasteless nitrogen gas, thereby stopping the oxidation process that damages wine. There are a variety of manufacturers that now make these systems.

If you are offering wine-by-the glass programs—or are serving wine at all—you will need to consider wineglasses. The wineglass has a noticeable effect upon the taste of wine—the same wine will taste different in a fine crystal glass than in a cheap wineglass. Of course, crystal wineglasses are not very economical, especially since breakage can easily occur. Only the finest bars and restaurants can afford real crystal wineglasses. Nevertheless, you should try to purchase the best wineglasses that are affordable, and you should never try to buy wineglasses without testing what wine tastes like in them.

You do not need to use a separate glass for reds, whites, and champagnes. You can often save money by serving all wines in 10-ounce tulip-shaped glasses, which are quite suitable for any wine. Buying these glasses in bulk can also add up to substantial savings, especially when you are just starting out. You should invest in separate champagne glasses as soon as you can afford to do so, though, as many people prefer the look of them for their champagne.

When you are considering which glassware to buy, make sure that you buy glasses you can afford to break—in a bar, broken or missing glasses are quite common. Simple, clear glasses that are not cut, faceted, etched, or colored are less expensive and easier to replace as they break. Another advantage of simple glasses is that they actually allow you to see the wine more clearly. Always choose wineglasses with generous bowls, as this allows patrons to swirl the wine in the glass and release the wine's full flavor and aroma. A thin glass rim that tapers slightly inward will make the wine flow more evenly and easily from the glass and will also allow the wine's aroma to be maximized. Finally, be sure that the base—sometimes called the foot—allows the wineglass to stand firmly whether the glass is full or empty. Wobbly wineglasses spell disaster: lost wine, smaller profits, broken glasses, and irate customers.

Half Bottles and Decanters

For customers who want to purchase more than a glass of wine but less than a full bottle, half bottles and decanters often make an attractive choice, and for this reason, you will want to offer your patrons both options. Half bottles can save a bar money as they offer less spoilage than full bottles when used as part of a wine-by-the-glass program. Half bottles are also very much favored by single diners and couples. However, storing half bottles can be challenging as most storage racks are not designed to handle these bottles.

You can avoid this problem quite readily by using the case carton type as a storage bin—simply turn it on its side.

Decanters are usually used for older wines. Wines that are older than ten years often have sediment in them, and pouring the wine into a carafe or decanter allows the sediment to be removed before serving, which is important for customer satisfaction.

To decant wine:

1. Place a candle on the table alongside the bottle and decanter.

2. As you pour, watch through the lit bottle for sediment to appear in the neck; when it does, stop pouring.

3. The remainder of the wine may be discarded or strained through cheese cloth in the kitchen.

Wine Service Innovations

There are a number of innovative products that can help regulate wine service as well as store and preserve wine. You may be interested in:

*   **Winekeeper** produces a line of dispensing and preserving systems for wine. Their use makes enjoying fine wine an extended and pleasurable experience. Winekeeper units consist of handcrafted, custom-quality cabinetry and employ proven nitrogen

gas preservation technology. Single bottle units to larger commercial units are available. Custom applications, designs, and finishes are available. For more information, contact Winekeeper at 625 E. Haley Street, Santa Barbara, CA 93103, phone 805-963-3451, or visit **www.winekeeper.com**.

- **OZ Winebars** are another option for serving wine by the glass. The traditional way for wine refrigeration is opening a bottle and placing it in a refrigerator. It is not only slow and inefficient, it ends up speeding up the deterioration of the wine through oxidation, reducing your wine sales profitability. With un-refrigerated wine, this process is even faster. OZ Winebars is a wine refrigerator designed specifically to store and dispense both red and white wine. OZ Winebars has an advanced commercial system for managing, refrigerating, preserving, and serving opened wines. OZ Winebars extends the serving life of your wines and provides your staff a clean, efficient vehicle for your wine service program in an exciting, authoritative ambience for your customers. For more information, contact OZEM Corp, 832 Harvard Drive, Holland, MI 49423, phone 866-617-3345, or visit **www.ozwinebars.com**.

Wine Storage and Presentation

If wine is an important of your bar or nightclub, you may want to invest in a wine cellar, cabinet, or other wine accessories. There are a huge variety available for every type of service and décor. Following are just a few examples:

- **Vinotemp** offers a wide selection of wine cellars and wine cellar accessory equipment: storage systems, cooler systems, wine racks, wine storage cabinets, humidors, liquor cooler cabinets, wine cellar design, and wine storage. They have a wide design range of models, door styles, various woods, numerous finishes, and a variety of refrigerator and rack design options, as well as thousands of unique wine cellars and storage cabinets available, even custom-designed units. For more information, visit **www.vinotemp. com** or call 1-800-777-VINO (8466).

The 700 Monaco Modern by Vinotemp. Two decorative glass doors, special furniture trim design with fluorescent light, and individual redwood and aluminum racking. Dimensions: 59" W x 33" D x 92" H. Approximate bottle capacity: 550.

Beer Pouring

On the surface, pouring beer may seem very easy. After all, most people at home simply snap open a beer can to drink. However, pouring beer in a bar is more complicated than that, so it is important that your servers and bartenders know how to pour beer correctly. There are two ways to pour beer in a bar: 1) from a bottle or 2) from the keg. In both cases, it is essential that the poured beer be icy cold—about 40°F. This is especially important for draught beer, which is un-pasteurized and can make your patrons ill if served or stored warm. It is important that the beer be poured into thick, cold glasses that are spotlessly clean. Icy glasses will help keep the beer cold while cleanliness will help ensure that the beer does not fall flat. In general, servers should rinse beer glasses before serving beer and should take special care to provide a new glass with each beer order.

When pouring draught beer, one of the most important elements you should pay attention to is the head, or the foam that settles on the top of the beer before fizzing away. It is important that the head not be too large or too small.

Ideally, the head should rise just above the rim of the glass or pitcher. A head that is too large will make the bar patron feel cheated. To pour the perfect beer, follow these steps:

1. Start with a clean, cold glass. Ideally, it should be made of thick glass and have a handle so that the beer is not warmed by the drinker's body temperature. Hold the beer mug or glass at a 45-degree angle under the spout without letting the spout touch the glass. If the angle is too steep and the beer flows down the sides of the glass or mug, there will be no head. If the glass is held straight up so that the beer splashes into the glass directly, there will be too much head.

2. Open the tap quickly and start the pour, moving the glass into an upright position once the glass is half-filled. You should have an ideal head of ½ to 1-inch thickness.

3. Serve immediately before the head disappears.

Practice will make this technique quick and automatic for most servers and bartenders.

One other concern regarding draught beer is the cleanliness of the taps themselves. Unlike bottles, which are fresh with each new beer, taps and the lines that carry the beer get clogged and dirty with repeated pours. It is important to get a tap and line cleaner to carefully clean the lines through which the beer flows. You should have this done once a week. This will help ensure a tasty beer each time and will also ensure proper hygiene for all your customers.

Bottled beer is simpler in some ways: Bartenders only need to open the beer and either pour it into a mug or bring the mug and bottle to the table so the patron can pour it themselves. In the past, bar staff routinely poured beer into mugs or glasses for customers, but now more and more customers seem to prefer drinking straight from the bottle. This cuts down on glass washing, certainly, but it also does create confusion: How to create customer satisfaction if customers have different perceptions about bottled beer. An ideal solution is simply to ask any ordering patron whether they would like a glass or mug; this gives the customer a chance to tell your server which glass (if any) is expected. Foreign beer is almost always served in a glass or mug, and many bars simplify by serving all beer in mugs or glasses, unless a customer specifically asks otherwise.

Mixology

Mixology refers to the practice of mixing alcoholic beverages with each other and with nonalcoholic components to make cocktails or mixed drinks. Bartending schools tend to stress this part of bar management and bartending, even though the same types of mixed drinks get requested over and over. There are always "drinks of the moment," since drinks, like clothes, experience fashions. The cocktails of the 1920s are as unlikely to make a comeback as cloche hats. That's why it's important for the bar manager to make sure that his or her staff know how to make the popular drink of the moment (you can find out the hottest drink right now simply by watching drink trends or by doing some quick online market research) and by making sure that your staff can make the most commonly requested drinks.

In general, you should have the recipes for the most common and the currently most popular drinks behind the bar. This will allow servers to quickly and discreetly look up what belongs in a drink and prepare it for the customer. In the back, a few books of cocktail and drink recipes are a good idea in case a customer makes a request for something more exotic. Of course, you will also need to make sure that you have the ingredients and drinks on hand to make mixed beverages. You need to stock up on the items that go into the most popular cocktails and the "drinks of the moment," as these supplies will tend to run out quite fast.

You will also need to have a handy conversion chart for working with metric, non-metric and "odd" measurements (yes, the dash is really a measurement in bartending!). Post this handy chart in your bar where the bartender can easily refer to it as needed:

STANDARD BAR MEASUREMENTS

UNIT(S)	EQUALS
1 dash	1/16 teaspoon
1 teaspoon	1/8 ounce
1 tablespoon	0.5 ounce
1 pony	1 ounce
1 jigger/bar glass	1.5 ounces
1 wineglass	4 ounces
1 split	6 ounces
1 cup	8 ounces
METRIC CONVERSIONS	
1 fluid ounce	29.573 milliliters
1 quart	9.4635 deciliters
1 gallon	3.7854 liters
0.0338 fluid ounce	1 milliliter
1.0567 quarts	1 liter
10 milliliters	1 liter
10 centiliters	1 deciliter
10 deciliters	1 liter
OTHER MEASUREMENTS	
ENGLISH	METRIC
Fifth	4/5 quart
1/5 gallon	25.6 oz
750 ml	25.36 fl oz
Pint	0.5 Quart = 16 fl oz
500 ml	17 fl oz
Half-pint	0.5 pint = 8 fl oz
200 ml	6.8 fl oz
Half-gallon	64 fl oz
1750 ml	59.7 fl oz
1 quart	32 fl oz
1000 ml	33.814 fl oz

You can use these measurements when making the 25 of the most commonly ordered mixed drinks. These drinks are:

- Screwdriver

- Sombrero

- Mai-Tai

- Piña Colada

- Old-Fashioned

- Tequila Sunrise

- Gimlet

- Margarita

- Martini

- Cosmopolitan

- Manhattan

- Gibson

- Bloody Mary

- Stingers

- Coffee Drinks

- Collins Drinks

- Fizzes

- Daiquiris

- Sours

- White Russian

- Black Russian

- Alabama Slammer

- Gin and Tonic

- Long Island Iced Tea

- Juice/Punch Drinks

There are a few drinks that your bartender should be able to make without referring to the manual at all. Test your bartender to make sure that he or she can make the following quickly:

Screwdriver

1½ oz vodka
4 oz orange juice

Add vodka to a tall glass with ice; fill with orange juice.

Sombrero

1½ coffee liqueur/Kahlua
½ oz Half & Half

Combine ingredients in snifter with ice.

Piña Colada

1½ oz light or dark rum
2 oz pineapple juice
2 oz cream of coconut

Mix ingredients in a shaker and serve over ice.

Old-Fashioned

1½ oz American or Canadian whisk(e)y
½ tsp superfine sugar
2 dashes bitters

Splash of club soda
Cherry and orange slice

Muddle the cherry (without stem), orange slice, and club soda. Add remaining ingredients and stir.

Tequila Sunrise

1½ oz tequila
½ oz grenadine
Orange juice
Orange slice

Pour grenadine into tall glass. Add tequila and fill with orange juice. Garnish with orange slice.

Gin and Tonic

1½ oz gin
Tonic
Lime wedge

Add gin to a glass filled with ice; fill with tonic. Add lime wedge.

Margarita

1 oz tequila
1 oz triple sec
1 oz lime juice
Lime wheel

Blend ingredients with crushed ice. Serve in salt-rimmed glass. Garnish with lime wheel.

Martini

2 oz gin
Dash of extra dry vermouth
Olive

Shake or stir gin and vermouth over ice. Strain and serve in a cocktail glass. Garnish with an olive.

Daiquiri

1½ oz light rum
½ oz sweetened lemon juice

Shake or blend with ice.

Highball

1½ oz American whiskey
3 oz ginger ale

Combine and stir.

In addition to the above, customers may request any number of other drinks. Some patrons enjoy the sound of a drink and may not be able to describe how it is made. It is up to your staff to do research to determine whether the drink can be made. A few more obscure and some popular drinks that may be requested include the following (please note that some of the names of these drinks may be offensive).

57 Chevy

1 oz pineapple juice
1 oz vodka
1 oz Grand Marnier
1 oz Southern Comfort

Mix ingredients in a shaker with ice. Serve in a Highball glass.

747

½ oz Irish crème liqueur
½ oz amaretto
½ oz Kahlua

Pour and serve ingredients in a shot glass.

Affinity

1 oz Scotch

1 oz dry vermouth

1 oz sweet vermouth

2 dashes orange bitters

Cherry

Stir ingredients with ice; strain into chilled glass. Garnish with cherry.

Afterburner

1 part Rumple Minze

1 part Tia Maria

Pour and serve ingredients in a shot glass.

Alabama Slammer

1 oz Southern Comfort

1 oz amaretto

½ oz sloe gin

½ oz fresh lemon juice

Shake or stir first three ingredients with ice. Strain into chilled glass filled with ice; add lemon juice.

Algonquin

2 oz blended whiskey

1 oz dry vermouth

1 oz pineapple juice

Shake ingredients with ice; strain into chilled cocktail glass or serve over ice cubes in an Old-Fashioned glass.

Almond Lemonade

1½ oz vodka

½ oz amaretto

Lemonade

Shake with ice and strain into a shot glass.

Amaretto Sour

1½ oz amaretto
½ oz lemon juice
Orange slice

Mix ingredients in shaker with ice. Strain into chilled cocktail glass. Garnish with orange slice.

Angel's Delight

1 part grenadine
1 part triple sec
1 part sloe gin
1 part heavy cream

Layer this drink in the order listed.

Anti-Freeze

1½ oz vodka
½ oz Midori

Shake with ice, strain, and serve.

Apple Pie

½ oz apple schnapps
½ oz vodka
½ oz pineapple juice
Dash of powdered cinnamon

Shake with ice and strain into shot glass.

Apricot Cocktail

1½ oz apricot brandy
½ oz fresh lemon juice
½ oz fresh orange juice
1½ tsp gin or vodka

Shake ingredients with ice; strain into chilled glass.

B-52

1 part Grand Marnier

1 part Kahlua

1 part Baileys Irish Cream

Shake with ice. Strain or serve over ice.

Baileys & Coffee

1½ oz Baileys Irish Cream

5 oz coffee

Pour Baileys Irish Cream into a cup of steaming coffee.

Banshee

1 oz white crème de cacao

1 oz crème de banana

1 oz cream

Shake ingredients with ice; strain into chilled glass.

Bay Breeze

1½ oz Absolut Vodka

3 oz pineapple juice

1 oz cranberry juice

Stir ingredients. Serve over ice.

Beachcomber

1½ oz Puerto Rican white rum

½ oz lime juice

1 oz orange juice

1 oz grenadine

Shake ingredients. Serve straight up or with ice.

Bellini

1 peach half
4 oz champagne
Simple syrup

Muddle the peach in a champagne glass with a little simple syrup. Fill the glass with champagne.

Bermuda Rose

1 oz Bombay gin
½ oz apricot-flavored brandy
½ oz lime juice
Dash of grenadine

Shake with ice and strain.

Between the Sheets

1 part Remy Martin cognac
1 part Cointreau
1 part Bacardi light rum
Dash of lemon juice

Shake with ice. Strain into a sugar-rimmed glass.

Billy Taylor

2 oz gin
1 oz fresh lime juice
1 tsp powdered sugar
Cold club soda

Shake all ingredients except club soda with ice. Strain into chilled glass filled with ice cubes. Top with club soda; stir gently.

Black and Tan

1½ oz Irish whiskey
1 oz dark rum
½ oz lime juice
½ oz orange juice
½ tsp superfine sugar

6–8 ice cubes
4 oz chilled ginger ale

Combine Irish whiskey, rum, lime juice, orange juice, sugar, and 3–4 ice cubes in shaker; shake vigorously. Put the remaining ice in a glass. Strain the mixture into the glass and fill with ginger ale.

Black Devil

1½ oz Puerto Rican light rum
½ oz dry vermouth
1 pitted black olive

Stir well with ice and strain.

Black Russian

1½ oz vodka
½ oz coffee liqueur

Add vodka and then coffee liqueur to a glass filled with cubed ice. Stir briskly.

Black Velvet

6 oz cold Guinness
6 oz cold dry champagne or other dry sparkling wine

Pour ingredients at once into chilled glass; don't stir.

Blizzard

3 oz bourbon
1 oz cranberry juice
½ oz lemon juice
1 Tbsp sugar
½ cup crushed ice

Combine all ingredients in a blender. Cover and process at medium speed until smooth; about 20 seconds. Pour into chilled glass.

Blue Lagoon

1½ oz vodka
½ oz Blue Curacao

3 oz lemonade
Cherry

Combine ingredients over ice in a Highball glass. Garnish with a cherry.

Blue Margarita

1½ oz tequila
½ oz lime juice
½ oz Blue Curacao
Lime wedge

Moisten chilled glass rim with a little lime juice, then dip rim into salt. Shake first three ingredients with cracked ice; strain into glass. Garnish with lime wedge.

Blue Whale

1½ oz Blue Curacao
1 oz Puerto Rican rum
½ oz pineapple juice

Shake with ice and strain into a shot glass.

Boilermaker

1½ oz Irish whiskey
10 oz beer

Serve whiskey in a shot glass with a glass of beer on the side as a chaser.

Bolero

1½ oz light rum
½ oz apple brandy
½ tsp sweet vermouth

Stir ingredients with ice; strain into chilled glass.

Bonny Prince

1½ oz gin
½ oz Lillet blanc

½ tsp Drambuie
Orange twist

Shake liquid ingredients with ice. Strain into chilled glass; drop in orange twist.

Bootleg

1 part Jack Daniels
1 part Sambuca
1 part Southern Comfort

Combine ingredients in a Lowball glass.

Bootlegger Martini

2 oz Bombay gin
½ oz Southern Comfort
Lemon twist

Stir gently with ice; serve straight up or over ice. Garnish with lemon twist.

Boston Breeze

1 oz cream of coconut
1½ oz rum
3 oz cranberry juice
1 cup ice

Blend and serve in a Margarita glass.

Bourbon Street

1½ oz bourbon
½ oz amaretto

Shake with ice and strain into a shot glass.

Brandy Alexander

1½ oz brandy or cognac
½ oz dark crème de cacao
1 oz sweet cream or ice cream

Shake with ice and strain.

Bronx

1½ oz gin
½ oz dry vermouth
½ oz sweet vermouth
½ oz orange juice

Shake with ice and strain.

Brown Derby

1½ oz Puerto Rican dark rum
½ oz lime juice
⅙ oz maple syrup

Shake with ice. Serve straight up or over ice.

Bubble Gum

½ oz melon liqueur
½ oz vodka
½ oz crème de banana
½ oz orange juice
Dash grenadine

Serve in a shot glass.

Bullshot

1½ oz vodka
1 tsp lemon juice
Dash Worcestershire
Dash Tabasco
4 oz chilled beef bouillon
Dash salt and pepper
Lemon wedge

Shake and serve in a glass. Garnish with a lemon wedge.

Buttery Finger

½ oz Irish Cream
½ oz vodka
½ oz butterscotch schnapps
½ oz coffee-flavored liqueur

Combine in a shot glass.

Candy Apple

1 part apple schnapps
1 part cinnamon schnapps
1 part apple juice

Shake with ice and strain into a shot glass.

Captain Morgan Sour

1½ oz Captain Morgan Spiced Rum
1 oz lemon juice
1 tsp sugar

Shake and serve over ice or straight up.

Caribbean Grasshopper

1½ oz cream of coconut
1 oz crème de cacao
½ oz crème de menthe

Combine ingredients. Serve straight up over ice.

Cement Mixer

½ shot Irish Cream
½ shot lime juice

Pour ingredients directly into the glass. Let drink stand for 5 seconds and it will coagulate.

Chambord Iceberg

½ oz Chambord
½ oz vodka

Combine in a champagne glass packed to the top with ice.

Chi-Chi

1 oz cream of coconut
2 oz pineapple juice
1½ oz vodka
1 cup ice

Blend until smooth.

Chocolate Martini

1 oz Absolut vodka
½ oz chocolate liqueur
Lemon twist

Shake over ice; strain into a chilled cocktail glass. Garnish with a lemon twist.

Cocomotion

4 oz cream of coconut
2 oz lime juice
1½ oz dark rum
1½ cups ice

Blend and serve in a Margarita glass.

Coffee Cream Cooler

1½ oz light or dark rum
Cold coffee
Cream

Pour rum into a tall glass half filled with ice. Fill with cold coffee and cream to desired proportions.

Colorado Bulldog

1½ oz coffee liqueur
4 oz cream
Splash of cola

Pour first two ingredients over ice. Add a splash of cola. Stir briefly.

Cranberry Martini

1 part Godiva liqueur
1 part Absolut vodka
1 part cranberry juice
Lemon twist

Combine with ice and shake well. Garnish with a lemon twist.

Creamsicle

1½ oz Stoli Ohrang vodka
½ oz Irish Cream

Combine over ice.

Cuba Libre

1½ oz Bacardi rum
Cola
Juice of half a lime

Add rum to a glass filled with ice. Fill with cola. Add lime juice and stir.

Daiquiri

1½ oz light rum
½ oz lemon juice

Shake or blend with ice.

Dirty Harry

1 oz Grand Marnier
1 oz Tia Maria

Shake with ice and strain.

Double Gold

½ oz Jose Cuervo Gold tequila
½ oz Goldschlager

Shake with ice and strain into a shot glass.

Emerald Isle

½ shot Irish whiskey
½ shot green crème de menthe
2 scoops vanilla ice cream
Soda water

Blend the first three ingredients and then add soda water. Stir after adding soda water.

Emerald Martini

2 oz Bacardi Limon
Splash extra dry vermouth
Splash Midori

Stir with ice. Serve on ice or straight up.

Fireball

2 oz cinnamon schnapps
Dash Tabasco

Combine in a shot glass.

Foggy Day Martini

1½ oz dry gin
½ oz Pernod
Twist of lemon peel

Shake and pour over ice or serve straight up. Garnish with a lemon peel twist.

Fog Horn

2 oz gin
½ oz lime juice
Cold ginger ale
Lime slice

Put 4 to 5 ice cubes in chilled glass; add gin, lime juice, and ginger ale, stirring gently. Garnish with lime slice.

Fuzzy Navel

1½ oz peach schnapps
3 oz orange juice

Pour schnapps over ice in a glass. Fill with orange juice and stir well.

Gibson

2 oz dry gin
Dash extra dry vermouth
Cocktail onion

Stir with ice. Add the cocktail onion. Serve straight up or over ice.

Gimlet

1½ oz vodka
½ oz fresh lime juice

Mix vodka and lime juice in a glass with ice. Strain and serve in a cocktail glass. Garnish with a lime twist.

Gin and Tonic

1½ oz gin
Tonic
Lime wedge

In a glass filled with ice, add gin and fill with tonic. Add a lime wedge.

Gin Fizz

2 oz fin
1 tsp sugar
Juice of 1 lemon
Club soda

Shake first three ingredients with ice and strain. Fill with club soda.

Girl Scout Cookie

½ oz peppermint schnapps
½ oz coffee liqueur
3 oz Half & Half

Shake with ice and serve over ice.

Godfather

1½ oz Scotch
½ oz amaretto

Combine in a rocks glass over ice.

Godmother

1 oz vodka
½ oz amaretto

Combine in a rocks glass over ice.

Golden Cadillac

½ oz Liquore Galliano
1 oz white crème de cacao
1 oz cream

Mix in a blender with a little ice at a low speed for a short time. Strain into a champagne glass. A scoop of vanilla ice cream can be substituted for the cream.

Golden Martini

7 parts extra dry gin
1 part French vermouth
Lemon peel twist

Stir gently with ice. Serve straight up or over ice. Garnish with a lemon peel twist.

Grasshopper

½ oz green crème de menthe
½ oz white crème de cacao
½ cream

Combine in a blender with ice and blend until smooth. Strain into a Margarita glass.

Green Hornet

½ oz vodka
½ oz Midori
½ oz sweet & sour mix

Shake with ice; serve straight up or over ice.

Gremlin

1½ oz vodka
½ oz Blue Curacao
½ oz rum
½ oz orange juice

Shake with ice, strain, and serve straight up.

Greyhound

1½ oz vodka
Grapefruit juice

Pour vodka over crushed ice in a tall glass. Fill with grapefruit juice.

Half & Half

3 parts gin
3 parts vodka
1 part dry vermouth
Lemon twist

Shake with ice; serve straight up or on ice. Garnish with a lemon twist.

Hawaiian Highball

3 oz Irish whiskey
2 tsp pineapple juice
1 tsp lemon juice
Club soda

Combine the whiskey with the lemon juice. Add ice and fill with soda.
Stir gently.

Heat Wave

1 oz dark rum
½ oz peach schnapps
Splash grenadine
Pineapple juice

Add rum and schnapps to a Highball glass with ice. Fill with pineapple juice.
Add a splash of grenadine.

Highball

1½ oz American whiskey
3 oz ginger ale

Combine and stir.

Hot Toddy

1½ oz Seagram's V.O. whiskey
1 lump sugar
2 cloves
Hot water

Pour Seagram's into hot water. Add sugar and cloves. Stir.

Hurricane

1½ oz dark rum
4 oz pineapple juice
2 oz orange juice
Splash grenadine

Combine over ice.

Irish Coffee

1½ oz Irish whiskey
Hot coffee
Sugar
Cream

Pour whiskey in a warm glass or mug. Fill with coffee. Stir in cream and sugar to taste.

Italian Russian

½ oz Sambuca
1 oz vodka
Orange peel twist

Pour over ice cubes in small rocks glass. Stir well. Twist an orange peel over the glass and drop it in.

Jack & Coke

1½ oz Jack Daniel's whiskey
3 oz Coca-Cola

Combine over ice and serve.

Jamaican Coffee

1 oz Jamaican rum
1 oz Tia Maria or other coffee liqueur
6 oz hot coffee
Heavy whipping cream or whipped cream
Ground allspice

Combine first three ingredients in warm mug; stir to combine. Float cream on top by slowly pouring it over the backside of a spoon; don't mix. Or, top with a large dollop of whipped cream. Sprinkle lightly with allspice.

Jell-O Shots

1 (3 oz) package any flavor Jell-O gelatin
6 oz boiling water
6 oz vodka, rum, gin or other spirit

Pour gelatin in medium bowl. Add boiling water; stir until gelatin is dissolved. Stir in liquor; refrigerate until cool. Pour into glasses; refrigerate until set. Serve cold.

Jelly Bean

1 part anisette
1 part blackberry brandy

Combine in a rocks glass over ice.

Jolly Rancher

½ oz peach schnapps
½ oz apple schnapps
2½ oz cranberry juice

Combine in tall glass with ice.

Kamikaze

1 oz vodka
½ oz Cointreau
½ oz lime juice

Shake with ice and strain into a shot glass.

Kandy Kane

1 part Rumple Minze
1 part Hiram Walker Crème de Noya

Layer Crème de Noya over Rumple Minze.

Kangaroo

1½ oz vodka
½ oz dry vermouth
Lemon twist

Stir liquid ingredients with ice. Strain into chilled glass; drop in lemon twist.

La Jolla

1½ oz brandy
½ oz crème de banana
2 tsp lemon juice
1 tsp orange juice

Shake ingredients with ice; strain into chill glass.

Lazer Beam

1 part bourbon
1 part Rumple Minze
1 part Drambuie

Shake with ice and strain into a shot glass.

Leap Frog

1½ oz gin
Dash of lemon juice
Ginger ale

Combine gin with lemon juice and ginger ale in a Highball glass.

Leprechaun

1½ oz Irish whiskey
3 oz tonic water
3–4 ice cubes
Lemon peel

Put whiskey and tonic water in a rocks glass. Add ice cubes and stir gently. Drop in a slice of lemon peel.

Lifesaver

1 part Malibu rum
1 part Absolut vodka
1 part Midori
1 part 7-Up

Shake with ice and strain into a shot glass.

Long Island Ice Tea

½ oz vodka
½ oz rum
½ gin
½ oz Triple Sec
½ oz tequila
Cola

Shake the first five ingredients over ice and strain into a glass. Fill with cola.

Madras

1½ oz vodka
2 oz cranberry juice
2 oz orange juice

Pour vodka over ice in a tall glass. Fill halfway with orange juice; top off with cranberry juice.

Mai Tai

1 oz light rum
1 oz dark rum
1 oz Triple Sec
½ oz grenadine
½ oz orgeat syrup
½ lime juice
Pineapple spear
Cherry

Shake liquid ingredients with ice. Strain into chilled glass over ice cubes. Garnish with pineapple spear and cherry.

Mandeville

1½ oz light rum
1 oz dark rum
½ oz lemon juice
½ oz cola
1 tsp anise-flavored liqueur
½ tsp grenadine

Shake ingredients with ice; strain into chilled glass over ice cubes.

Manhattan

2 oz whiskey
Splash dry vermouth
Dash Angostura bitters
Cherry

Stir. Garnish with cherry.

Margarita

1 oz tequila
1 oz Triple Sec
1 oz lime juice

Blend with crushed ice. Serve in a salt-rimmed glass. Garnish with lime.

Martini

2 oz gin
Dash extra dry vermouth
Olive

Shake or stir gin and vermouth over ice. Strain and serve in a cocktail glass straight up or over ice. Garnish with olive.

Melon Ball

½ oz Midori
1 oz vodka
4 oz orange juice

Combine in a glass and stir.

Mint Julep

2 oz bourbon
½ oz sugar syrup
5 mint leaves

In a silver sup, mash 4 mint leaves with sugar syrup. Fill the cup with crushed ice. Add bourbon and garnish with mint leaf. Serve in silver cup.

Mud Slide

½ oz coffee liqueur
1 oz vodka
½ Irish Cream
Cola

Combine first three ingredients in a glass with ice and fill with cola.

Navy Grog

1 oz light rum
1 oz Jamaica rum
1 oz 86-proof Demerara rum
½ oz lime juice
½ oz passion fruit or guava nectar
½ pineapple juice
½ oz orange juice
½ oz orgeat syrup
½ cup crushed ice
Mint sprig
Lime slice

Combine first nine ingredients in a blender. Cover and process until smooth, about 15 seconds; pour into chilled glass. Garnish with mint and lime.

Nervous Breakdown

1½ oz vodka
½ oz Chambord
Splash cranberry juice
Soda

Combine first three ingredients in a tall glass. Fill with soda.

Old-Fashioned

1½ oz whiskey
½ tsp superfine sugar
2 dashes Angostura bitters
Splash club soda
Cherry and orange slice

Muddle the cherry (without stem), orange slice, sugar, and splash of club soda. Add remaining ingredients and stir.

Orange Crush

1½ oz vodka
½ oz Triple Sec
2 oz orange juice

Shake with ice. Strain or serve over ice.

Paradise Cocktail

1 oz apricot brandy
½ oz gin
½ oz orange juice

Shake ingredients with ice; strain into chilled glass.

Peppermint Patty

½ oz crème de cacao
½ oz peppermint schnapps

Pour crème de cacao into glass. Slowly add peppermint schnapps, pouring it over the backside of a spoon so that it floats on top; don't mix.

Piña Colada

1½ oz light or dark rum
2 oz pineapple juice
2 oz cream of coconut

Mix in a shaker and serve over ice, or blend with crushed ice.

Pink Lady

1½ oz gin
2 tsp grenadine
3 oz Half & Half

Shake with ice and strain into a cocktail glass or serve over ice.

Pink Squirrel

4 oz crème de almond
1 oz crème de cacao
4 oz cream

Shake all ingredients over cracked ice. Strain.

Purple Haze

1 part Chambord
1 part vodka
1 part cranberry juice

Combine in a shot glass.

Queen Elizabeth Martini

1½ oz gin
1 oz dry vermouth
1½ tsp Benedictine

Stir ingredients with ice; strain into chilled glass.

Razz-Ma-Tazz

1½ oz vodka
½ oz Chambord
1½ oz club soda

Serve over ice in a tall glass, chilled.

Red Devil

2 oz Irish whiskey
1½ oz clam juice
1½ oz tomato juice
1 tsp lime juice
Few drops Worcestershire Sauce
Pinch pepper

Combine with ice and shake gently. Strain straight up.

Red Hot Mama

1½ oz rum
4 oz cranberry juice
2 oz club soda

Combine over ice.

Rob Roy

2 oz Scotch
Dash sweet or dry vermouth

Stir over ice and strain.

Root Beer

1 part Kahlua
1 part Galliano
1 part cola
1 part beer

Combine in a shot glass.

Rusty Nail

1 oz Scotch
1 oz Drambuie

Combine in a rocks glass; add ice; stir.

Salty Dog

1½ oz gin or vodka

3 oz grapefruit juice

Mix with ice and pour into a salt-rimmed glass.

Scotch 'n Soda

1½ oz Scotch

3 oz club soda

Stir with ice.

Scotch 'n Water

1½ oz Scotch

3 oz water

Stir with ice.

Screwdriver

1½ oz vodka

4 oz orange juice

Add vodka to tall glass with ice; fill with orange juice.

Sex on the Beach

½ oz vodka

½ oz peach schnapps

½ oz orange juice

Shake ingredients with ice; strain into chilled glass.

Sidecar

½ oz Cointreau

½ tsp lemon juice

1 oz brandy

3–4 ice cubes

Combine all ingredients in a shaker vigorously. Strain into chilled cocktail glass.

Silver Bullet

2 oz gin or vodka
Splash Scotch

Float Scotch on top.

Singapore Sling

1½ oz gin
½ oz cherry-flavored brandy
3 dashes Benedictine
Dash grenadine
Dash lemon mix
Club soda

Shake first five ingredients and pour into a tall glass. Top with club soda.

Slippery Nipple

1 part Sambuca
1 part Baileys Irish Cream

Shake with ice and strain into a shot glass.

Sloe Gin Fizz

1½ oz sloe gin
3 oz lemon mix
Club soda

Shake gin and lemon mix; pour into a glass. Top with club soda.

Sloe Screw

1½ oz sloe gin
4 oz orange juice

Pour ingredients into chilled glass filled with ice cubes; stir well.

Snowball

1½ oz gin
½ oz anise-flavored liqueur
½ oz cream

Shake ingredients with ice; strain into chilled glass.

Sombrero

1½ oz coffee liqueur
½ oz Half & Half

Combine in a snifter with ice.

Stinger

1½ oz cognac/brandy
½ oz white crème de menthe

Shake well with ice.

Tango

2 parts gin
1 part sweet vermouth
1 part dry vermouth
2 dashes orange Curacao
Dash orange juice

Shake with ice and serve.

Tequila Sunrise

1½ oz tequila
½ oz grenadine
Orange juice
Orange slice

Pour grenadine into a tall glass first; add tequila and fill with ice and orange juice. Garnish with orange slice.

Tom Collins

1½ oz gin
Juice of 1 lemon
Club soda

Shake first two ingredients and pour over ice. Top with club soda.

Tootsie Roll

1 part Kahlua
1 part vodka
1 part orange juice

Combine in a shot glass.

Vodka and Tonic

1½ oz vodka
3 oz tonic
Lime wheel

Stir ingredients with ice in a glass. Garnish with lime wheel.

Vodka Martini

2 oz vodka
Dash dry vermouth
Olive

Stir ingredients with ice and strain. Garnish with olive.

Whiskey Sour

1½ oz whiskey
½ oz lemon juice
1 tsp superfine sugar

Shake with ice. Serve straight up or over ice.

White Russian

1½ oz vodka
½ oz Kahlua
½ oz cream

Shake and serve over ice.

Wild Irish Rose

1½ oz Irish whiskey
1½ tsp grenadine
½ oz lime juice
Club soda

Fill a Highball glass with ice. Add Irish whiskey, grenadine, and lime juice. Stir well. Fill with club soda.

Yellow Morning

1 part crème de banana
1 part Cherry Heering
1 part cognac

Layer this drink in the order listed.

Zombie

½ oz light rum
½ oz dark rum
½ tsp Bacardi 151 rum
1 oz pineapple juice
1 oz orange juice
1 oz lemon or lime juice
1 tsp powdered sugar

Mix the first two rums and all juices with ice in a shaker or blender and pour into a tall glass. Garnish with a pineapple spear and a red cherry. Float ½ tsp Bacardi 151 on top with 1 tsp powdered sugar.

At the very least, the successful bar manager will want to make sure that the cocktail recipe books at the bar have recipes for each of these drinks, as some customers delight in requesting the obscure drink. When faced with an unfamiliar drink request, servers should be instructed to tell the customer that they will check whether the drink is available. They should then look up the recipe, determine which ingredients are necessary, and determine whether those ingredients are on hand. If they are not, servers should explain what is missing and suggest a similar drink.

Determining which drinks can be made is much easier if the bar staff keeps a list of ingredients on hand. A sample list might look something like the following:

INGREDIENTS	QUANTITY	LOCATION
Orange juice	2 cartons	Refrigerator
Lemons	12	Basket beside refrigerator

Such a list can help staff build even the more obscure drinks. As long as the list is kept updated, the customer will be able to get their drink order quickly.

Drink Recipes

A good bartender can make a tasty and attractive drink with originality, panache, speed, and skill. However, all truly great drinks begin with a bar manager. Those bars that consistently serve good drinks almost always have a bar manager who arranges the bar and its operations so that great drinks are easily a matter of course. Developing your own recipes and ensuring that they are followed is essential to consistent profits and customer happiness. As a bar manager, you should determine the drink menu so that your servers will know what is served at your bar. A big part of establishing a drink menu also involves the rules of how you want drinks to be prepared: in what amounts, in which glassware, and with which types of garnishes. Of course, if a customer asks for a drink prepared in a special way, your staff should be able to accommodate the request as far as possible. However, most customers will ask for a drink by name, and then it is up to your staff to adhere to the rules you have set down to prepare the drink. Setting down the rules for drink recipes is quite simple if you follow a few basic tips:

- **Give recipe lists to staff and post the recipe lists behind the bar.** New staff need to be given detailed recipe lists to take home and look over before they start work. Your staff should know as much as possible about the right way to mix drinks in your bar before they start work. This will make them more effective workers, as they will be able to tell customers exactly what drinks are available and what goes into each drink. They will also be able to prepare drinks

Atlantic Publishing offer two posters with drink recipes for classic and popular cocktails. The posters are full color and laminated to reduce wear and tear. It is 11" x 17" and available for $9.95 (Item # PC-PS). To order, call 1-800-814-1132 or visit www.atlantic-pub.com.

quickly without having to look up recipes. Keeping the recipe list posted allows staff to consult the list rather than confuse an order. With a posted list, even new and temporary staff can prepare drinks according to your directions.

- **Menus.** Just as you provide your staff with detailed information about drinks, you should provide customers with the same information so that they can make informed choices. On a menu at each table, provide not only the name of the drink, but also alcohol content for each drink and a full ingredient listing. This lets your customers stay safe by avoiding drinks that contain ingredients they may be allergic to and also ensures that your patrons can keep tabs on how much alcohol they are consuming. If you use premium brands in your drinks, be sure to point this out on your menu by listing the brand names used. This

will help show that you provide better quality than other bars and will act as an advertisement for your drinks.

One of the most creative and exciting aspects of creating your own recipe list is the possibility of creating your own signature drinks. Creating your own drinks has several advantages:

• It allows you to offer a unique drink that your competition cannot offer.

- It ensures new customers—customers who want to try your drink will have to come to your bar.

- A new drink that becomes successful can help put your bar on the map and can ensure effective marketing for your bar—all without you not having to do a thing.

- Creating and naming a new drink can be creatively fun and satisfying in its own right.

Of course, not all successful bars have their own drinks. It is perfectly possible to run a very successful bar without developing your own unique mixed beverage. Just serving already established drinks in a way that makes customers pleased enough to return is generally the big secret to successful bars. However, if you do develop your own drink, be sure to make the most of it. Begin by ensuring that no one else has developed the same drink (you can do this by checking bar recipe books for similar drinks). If you really have developed a new type of drink, get it trademarked. This will help ensure that your competition cannot market the same drink. Be sure to advertise your new drink. A sign at your bar that indicates "Home of the _____ drink" will let customers know about your product.

Mixology Tips

Making a good mixed drink involves small details that can contribute to turning your creation into something just that is a little better than the norm. These tips can help ensure maximum profits and happy customers by keeping your mixed drinks fresher and easier to prepare than those of your competition. Consider the following:

- **Waste.** Mixed drinks require small combinations of alcohol. In some cases, opening a new bottle of some beverages—such as champagne or sparkling white wine—results in waste as the bottle of the product cannot be used again or can spoil quickly. This can quickly become wasteful and expensive. Invest in bottle closures and a champagne bottle re-sealer, and teach your staff how to use these products to keep all your beverages fresh and ready to use.

- **Improvise.** If you have a steady flow of champagne drinks in your bar, just drop the handle of a metal spoon into the top of the champagne bottle and put it back in the refrigerator. This will keep the sparkle in your champagne for up to 12 hours.

- **Make the most of citrus fruits.** Many bars go through large amounts of oranges, lemons, and limes, especially since these products are a key ingredient in many mixed drinks. You can make the most of oranges and lemons by soaking them in warm water for a while before juicing them. This will help you yield more juice—and more profits—from each citrus fruit.

- **Teach your staff to never shake mixed drinks that contain clear liquids or carbonated beverages.** Stirring such drinks will ensure that the drink does not go flat and that the taste is not ruined.

- **Tell your staff that mixed drinks that contain ingredients such as juices, sugar, eggs, cream, milk should be shaken** (never stirred) thoroughly. These ingredients are hard to mix, and not shaking the mix for long enough can result in a sludgy and unpleasant drink.

- **Any drink that contains eggs should have an ice cube added** to the shaker to help blend the egg. You should also always indicate to customers when a drink contains eggs—some people will not drink beverages that contain eggs due to the dangers of salmonella.

- **Keep drips to a minimum.** Customers who see that their ordered drink has dripped may feel that they are getting less value for their money. Dripping can also look messy and unprofessional. A clean piece of wax paper rubbed along the rim of a wine or champagne bottle will prevent any dripping when you pour.

- **Ensure that drinks are placed in clean glasses and presented properly.** Beer, for example, should be served ice cold. If it is poured into a mug or glass, it should have little foam on top.

Flair Bartending

When you are considering how you want your staff to mix drinks (see *Chapter 9: Bar Controls* for controlling pouring), you will need to consider flair bartending. Flair bartending is a hot trend right now, and thanks to its ever-growing popularity, it is expected to become a fixture at many successful bars. If you have seen movies such as "Coyote Ugly" or "Cocktail," then you know what flair bartending is—it is a way of serving drinks that adds a certain visual flair and sportsmanship to the process. Rather than simply mixing and stirring, bartenders treat bartending almost as a sport, flipping and catching bottles and moving their entire bodies as they mix drinks.

Flair bartending costs extra money: you will need to either train your current bartenders or hire bartenders who already know flair bartending (and they are not inexpensive employees). Flair bartending, on the other hand, will bring in money. Rather than getting live entertainment from singers they can see elsewhere, customers will be drawn to your bar because you offer a form of entertainment that is likely not available anywhere else in your city. Plus, flair bartending makes even simple drinks seem extra special, ensuring that customers keep ordering—at your bar. Flair bartending is also great for special occasions, such as celebrations or parties, when the visual flair is likely to attract more customers—and more orders for special events. Flair bartending simply brings in lots of money.

Flair bartending is also known as performance bartending, cocktail bartending, ultimate bartending, and even Olympic bartending. Whatever you wish to call it, there are two types of flair bartending: Working or simple flair bartending involves small tricks or moves that can be done during work. These small moves can generally be performed after a little practice and often do not interfere with work. They are less risky and are usually performed with low-cost items, reducing the risk of major breakage or waste. Any bartender who has flipped a lime into the air before cutting it up and throwing it into the drink has exhibited this kind of flair bartending. The major advantages of this type of bartending is that they are low risk, require little expensive training, and allow interaction with the customer. In fact, one aspect of this type of bartending is that the bartender will often joke with the customer while flipping the items or mixing the drink. Where possible, encourage bartenders to practice this type of working flair bartending, and offer incentives for them to do so.

Performance flair bartending is the more serious form of flair bartending. It often involves flipping entire bottles and performing choreographed moves. It is far more risky and can involve breakage. It usually includes long practice hours and training. Usually, this type of bartending is used for special shows and for competition. However, some bars are now incorporating nightly floor shows with this type of bartending. It certainly draws an audience, and if your bartender competes as well, the publicity from a competition win can easily improve your business. This type of bartending does slow down drink making, but many patrons dazzled by the show do not mind too much.

For more information about flair bartending, an excellent recourse is the Flair Bartenders' Association, Inc. (FBA), which can be reached at:

FBA
PO Box 190466
Boise, ID 83719-0466
www.barflair.org

FBA provides useful information about training and bartending that may inspire you and your employees.

You should never put flair above sheer bartending skill. A personable bartender who knows how to prepare a variety of drinks is more worthwhile than the bartender who can flip bottles but has no interaction or interest in bartending, per se. Ideally, you want someone who has both qualities, but if this proves unlikely, concentrate on the flair-less bartender who is amiable and good at his or her job.

Keeping the Quality of Mixed Drinks High

The difference between a good and great martini is very small, but it often makes the difference between a satisfied customer and a customer who will visit your bar again and bring a friend. You should take all the steps you can to ensure the highest possible quality for mixed drinks. This will make your bar the one customers patronize.

The way mixed beverages look is key to making customers happy. Bartenders can easily change the look of a drink by placing it in a different glass or by changing ingredients. Servers should ask customers about the presentation preferences for their drink. This will impress customers with your bar's service and will ensure that the customer gets the drink that will most suit him or her. A little showmanship in the preparation of a drink may slow the process down. However, a good performance can also thrill customers on a busy night and can give some extra excitement to drink preparation. Garnishes are another very inexpensive and quick way to add sparkle and interest to a drink. You will certainly want to add pizzaz to drinks using a few garnishes. Some bars are even offering novelty glassware included in the price of a drink. In many cases, where the glassware is attractive, customers rush to get the glass for only the cost of a drink.

Garnishes and Other Special Touches

One of the things that make mixed drinks so pleasing to customers are the garnishes and special touches often added to cocktails at bars and restaurants. Garnishes, straws, miniature umbrellas, and other extras enhance the entire drinking experience and should not be overlooked. At the same time, some garnishes can be more costly or time consuming than others. The smart bar manager will stress to their staff the importance of garnishes but will also set down

This poster from Atlantic Publishing is a great way to remind staff of the proper garnish for all types of drinks. The posters are full color and laminated to reduce wear and tear. It is 11″ x 17″ and available for $9.95 (Item # DG-PS). To order, call 1-800-814-1132 or visit www.atlantic-pub.com.

guidelines for garnishes on drinks. This will make drinks uniform and ensure consistent quality without wasting money or time. You do not want one drink to take so long to garnish that other customers are left unsatisfied any more than you want plain-looking drinks that leave patrons unsatisfied.

You should make sure that you and your bar staff are familiar with the types of garnishes that can add interest, taste, and style to drinks:

- **Real whipped cream.** While preparing it is a pain, using real, fresh whipped cream made with a small amount of sugar and real vanilla can improve the quality of a drink. Any additional cost is often passed on to the customer in the form of slightly higher prices. Most customers do not mind the cost, as the quality of real cream is so much better than canned whipped cream.

- **Freshly squeezed juices.** Freshly squeezed lemon, lime, and orange juices are more fragrant and flavorful. They also do not offer the chemical aftertaste of many fruit drinks or frozen juices. Your bartender can easily squeeze some fresh juice with a juicer. You will gain customers by advertising the fact that you only use freshly squeezed juices—and by delivering on better-quality drinks as a result.

- **Novelty garnishes.** Novelty items or unusual garnishes are excellent attention-getters. When customers see a pair of sunglasses, a doll's hat, or plastic animals hanging off a cocktail, they may be tempted to order the drink—even if they have no idea what is in the cocktail! Dry ice; a triple garnish of orange, lime, and lemon slices; a cluster of grapes for the glass of wine; a tiara or glow-in-the-dark necklace draped around a glass; a choice of olives, such as almond- or garlic-stuffed olives; a lemon twist wrapped around a coffee bean; a keychain snapped around the base of a stem glass; a skewer of oversized cherries; a deck of cards fanned around the base of a drink; or a pickled okra sprout—these are all unusual garnishes that can really make your bar gain a reputation for serving eye-popping drinks. Develop your own list of garnish ideas and really let yourself go wild with them! Just make sure that any garnishes touching the drink itself (rather than just the glass) are foods or food-safe. Plastic novelty items are safer just used to decorate the glass.

GARNISH GUIDELINES

- For alcoholic beverages, one straw should be used for every drink with ice.

- For kiddie cocktails, an orange flag or two cherries for every drink.

- For drinks with miniature swords, use one onion per sword and submerge the garnish in the drink.

- For drinks with miniature swords, two olives per sword can be used in lieu of onions. The garnish should be in the drink.

- Cherries should not be served in drinks with a miniature sword.

- For drinks calling for lemon peel, the lemon peel is used to flavor the rim of glass, then dropped in drink.

DRINK GARNISHES

DRINK	GARNISH(ES)
Manhattans	Cherry
Gibson	Cocktail onions
Martini	Olives or a twist (ask customer's preference)
Collins and Sours	Orange speared with a cherry
Tonic Drinks	Lime wedge
Rob Roy	Cherry
Old-Fashioned	Cherry and orange slice
Drinks with Bloody Mary mix	Lime wedge, celery stalk, or pickle
Coffee Drinks	Whipped cream, ground cinnamon
All Coolers	Lime wheel or wedge
Pineapple Juice Drinks	Pineapple wedge speared with a cherry
Orange Juice Drinks	Orange speared with a cherry
Margaritas/Daiquiris	Lime wheel or wedge

One simple way to ensure that mixed drinks are served in a quality-controlled way is to write down the recipe for all common drinks—including garnishes—and place it where the bartender can refer to it. This helps ensure that all patrons requesting the same drink get the same quality of drink. No customer will feel that a patron at the next table has received preferred treatment, and the profit from all drinks will be uniform. A simple table such as the following can be used for all drinks:

ITEM:
Glass:
Garnish:
Ingredients:
Procedure:

Keeping this list by the bar will also help new bartenders and servers have all the knowledge about the bar's drinks that they need.

Glasses and Glassware

Glasses and other containers are much more than just the receptacles that you serve drinks in, and they should never be ignored. What you serve your drinks in can be just as important as what you serve—not only are containers part of the overall impression that customers get of your drinks, they can also be an important part of the service of drinks. Beverage containers and glasses can also be among the more dangerous parts of serving alcohol, and, in fact, a number of lawsuits involving bars have revolved around improper use or storage of glasses or glassware, so bar manager beware. You and your staff should pay attention to glasses to prevent lost customers, lost profits, and other serious problems.

One of the biggest dangers of glasses has to do with broken glass. You should do all you can to ensure that no broken glass injures an employee or customer, and you should train your staff to take these same precautions. Staff should be taught to never use glasses as ice scoops. This can cause pieces of glass to fall into the ice and then be served to customers. Any time a glass breaks in or near an ice bin, the entire ice bin needs to be emptied and the contents thrown away so that no glass finds its way into the drinks. If any glasses are broken in or near food that is being prepared, the food should be disposed of and prepared again, for the same reason. Broken glass in the customer area or behind the bar should be cleaned up quickly to prevent injury.

Glass hygiene is also essential to creating a good customer impression and in ensuring safety. Staff should never touch the upper half of a glass when serving a drink. Glasses need to be washed in hot soapy water and rinsed well before each use. They should also be individually examined before they are used in a drink order. Any cracks or dirt will turn off a customer or could lead to injury. More delicate glasses, such as stem glasses used for wine or champagne, may need to be washed by hand and handled even more carefully in order to prevent breakage. Clean glasses will ensure not only customer satisfaction but will show off drinks to their best advantage. Any residue left on glasses can make some drinks, such as beer, look flat or taste unpalatable.

Special Glasses for Special Drinks

Glass appearance is also important in creating an effective presentation. Simple glass designs are not only often less expensive, but in many cases they also set off drinks to the best advantage. Replacing lost or broken plain glasses is often much easier than replacing complicated patterns. Buy simple but nicely proportioned glassware for your bar and buy accessories, such as napkins, coasters and trays, that set off the glasses and glassware to their full advantage.

- **Snifter glasses.** You can warm these before serving brandy. This gives a nicer aroma to the drink that is preferred by many customers. To heat, place in hot water and dry before serving. You can also heat a glass by filling with water and microwaving for 15 seconds (make sure the glassware is microwaveable). Pour out the water and serve the drink.

- **Mugs.** You should heat these as described above to keep coffee, hot chocolate, or tea warm in the mug.

- **Beer mugs.** Frosting beer mugs helps keep beer cool and also makes the mugs look great. Simply place the dry mugs in a refrigerator at 31°–33°F. When they are taken out, condensation will leave a thin layer of ice on the mugs.

- **Cocktail glasses.** For mixed drinks that call for no ice, chill the glasses well before serving. Place them in a refrigerator or freezer. Gently shake them off before using.

- **Flaming liquor glasses.** If you are serving any drinks that need to be set on fire before being served, you will need to warm the glass before igniting to ensure that the glass does not break and cause injuries—never light a cocktail on fire if the drink is in a chilled glass. Also be sure to follow all fire regulations to ensure that you do not have an emergency on your hands.

Nonalcoholic Drinks

All bars should offer nonalcoholic beverages such as water, colas, juices, teas, and coffees. These less expensive drinks are favored by those who do not or cannot drink, those who are designated drivers for the night, and those who wish to top off their night's drinking with another type of beverage. The nonalcoholic drink menu should be prominently displayed and made available to all. At least three or four nonalcoholic items should be offered, and these should be suggested to any patron who has been refused drinks because he or she is intoxicated. They can also be suggested to people who seem to be getting ready to leave—many patrons will like to linger over a cup of coffee or tea at the end of a long evening. In general, some tips for serving nonalcoholic beverages include:

- **Virgin drinks** (nonalcoholic versions of alcoholic drinks) should be served exactly as their alcoholic counterparts. For example, nonalcoholic beer should be served in frosted or chilled beer mugs at ice-cold temperatures. A smart bar will also offer a number of virgin cocktails, as many non-drinkers enjoy the garnishes and drinks of beverages and may wish to try the nonalcoholic versions for themselves.

- **Offer hot coffee in a mug.** Always ask the customer whether he or she takes sugar, milk, or cream, or present all these choices with the coffee. Ensure that the customer has a small teaspoon with which to serve the coffee.

- **Serve tea piping hot in a mug.** It can be served one of three ways: an empty mug can be served with a small tea kettle full of tea; a mug of hot water can be served alongside a tea bag; or the tea bag can be placed in a mug of hot water and served to the customer. Orange pekoe is the traditional tea served in most places, but offering many tea types will often appeal to a wider range of customers. Always serve sugar and a teaspoon with tea, and ask whether the customer takes milk or lemon with their tea. Offering honey as a sweetener is also a good choice.

- **Serve colas, sodas, juices, and waters in simple glasses with a straw and ice.** All are usually served ice cold. It is a good idea to ask customers whether they prefer ice in their drink. You can also offer to rim the glass with sugar, if that is the bar policy. Colas and drinks can be served with garnishes such as lemon slices and other garnishes, although this is not strictly necessary.

Servers: The Key to Serving Great Drinks

The servers who deliver drinks to customers are a key part of the service of drinks. Rather than just providing drinks, servers add to the presentation of drinks and to the drinking experience. Friendly and helpful servers who make a good impression on customers are worth their weight in gold. No matter how good your bar drinks and bar décor, no customer will want to return to your bar if your servers tend to make customers feel uncomfortable or ignored. On the other hand, an average bar can easily get a regular clientele simply by having servers and staff who make customers feel like a million dollars.

If you want your staff to make a lasting and great impression on customers, here are a few tips that can help:

- **Make sure that you treat your serving staff well.** Let them know that they are much more than just the people who serve drinks—they are the ones who can really help customers get the best service and experience possible. Encourage your serving staff to come to you with customer complaints and their own suggestions, and make it a point to listen to what your serving staff is telling you. Your servers are on the "front lines" of service in a bar, and they can often tell you about what is going on with the customer who is affecting your bar.

- **Be sure to add incentives to keep your servers and staff happy.** Bonuses, wage increases, and non-monetary gifts, such as passes to wine shows, amusement parks, or concerts, keeps staff happy and makes them more willing to work harder for you and your customers.

- **Make your bar a pleasant place to work as well as a pleasant place to drink.** Some bar managers work so hard to please customers that they all but ignore their staff, and this is terrible. Happy staff simply leads to happy customers, so make sure that you treat your staff well. Provide staff with the space and time they need, hire extra staff to make work loads manageable, and always stay open to staff suggestions about making the workplace better. Every customer prefers being served by a smiling and content staff!

- **Make your bar staff visible.** When a customer looks around for help or to place an order, they should easily be able to spot a server. Uniforms, aprons, or trays can all help indicate who staff members or servers are. Better yet, attractive aprons or uniforms or novelty trays add to the décor and ambience of the bar.

Your staff will be able to communicate far more effectively and take detailed orders more quickly if they learn some of the basic shorthand that is used by servers to indicate beverages and specific instructions. The following list of abbreviations should be given to all staff. Staff should learn these in order to reduce order mistakes and ensure speedy drink delivery.

BAR ABBREVIATIONS

POURING INSTRUCTIONS	
Back	Bk
Blended	Blnd
Double	Dbl
Dry	Dry
Extra dry	xDry
Mist	Mist
Neat	Nt
Perfect	Perf
Rocks	X
Shot	Sht
Splash	Spl
Tall	Tall
Virgin	Vgn
With	w/
WELL LIQUOR ABBREVIATIONS	
Bourbon	B
Brandy	Br
Gin	G
Rum	R
Scotch	S
Tequila	Teq
Vodka	V
MIXER ABBREVIATIONS	
Coffee	Cof
Coke	/C
Cranberry juice	/Crn
Diet Coke	/Diet or /DC

MIXER ABBREVIATIONS (continued)	
Ginger ale	/Gngr
Grapefruit juice	/Grp
Half & Half	/Cr
Orange juice	/OJ
Pineapple juice	/Pine
Soda water or seltzer	/s
7-Up	/7
Sweet & Sour	/SS
Tomato juice	/Tm
Water	W

DRINK NAME ABBREVIATIONS	
Black Russian	Bl Rs
Bloody Maria	B Maria
Bloody Mary	B Mary
Brandy Alexander	B Alex
Brandy Manhattan	Br-Man
Cosmopolitan	Cosmo
Daiquiri	Daq
Dry Manhattan	Dry-Man
Dry Martini	Dry-Mar
Fuzzy Navel	Fuzzy
Golden Cadillac	G Cad
Grasshopper	Grass
Greyhound	Grey or V-Grape
Harvey Wallbanger	Harv
Irish Coffee	Irish C
John Collins	John C
Kamikaze	Kami
Lemon Drop	Lem D
Long Island Iced Tea	Tea

DRINK NAME ABBREVIATIONS (continued)	
Manhattan	Man
Margarita	Marg
Martini	Marti
Old-Fashioned	OF
Piña Colada	Piña
Pink Lady	P Lady
Pink Squirrel	Sqrl
Presbyterian	Press
Rob Roy	R Rob
Rusty Nail	Nail
Screwdriver	V-OJ
Seabreeze	Breeze
Singapore Sling	Sling
Sombrero	Kah-Cr
Stinger	Sting
Tequila Sunrise	T Sun
Toasted Almond	TA
Tom Collins	Tom C
Vodka Gimlet	V-Gim
Vodka Martini	V-Marti
White Russian	W-Russ
NAME BRAND LIQUOR & LIQUEURS	
Absolut 80°	Absol
Absolut Citron	Ab Citron
Absolut Mandarin	Ab Mand
Absolut Peppar	Ab Peppar
Bacardi Light Rum	Bac
Bacardi Limon	Bac Limon
Bacardi Select	Bac Select
Bailey's Irish Cream	Baileys

NAME BRAND LIQUOR & LIQUEURS (continued)	
Beefeater	Beef
Belvedere Vodka	Belved
Benedictine & Brandy	B&B
Benedictine	Bene
Bombay Sapphire	Bom Sapph
Bombay	Bom
Booker Noe Bourbon	Booker
Bushmill's Irish	Bush
Canadian Club	CC
Chivas Regal	Chivas
Chivas Royal Salute	Salute
Chopin Vodka	Chopin
Cointreau	Coin
Courvoisier VS	Cour VS
Courvoisier VSOP	Cour VSOP
Crown Royal	Crown
Cuervo 1800	1800
Cuervo Esp. Tequila	Gold
Cutty Sark	Cutty
Dewar's White	Dewars
Di Saranno Amaretto	Amo
Drambuie	Dram
E & J Brandy	E&J
Frangelica	Fran
Galliano	Gall
Gentleman Jack	Gentleman
Glenfiddich	Fiddich
Glenlivet	Livet
Glenmorangie	Moran
Godiva Chocolate	Godiva

NAME BRAND LIQUOR & LIQUEURS (continued)	
Goldschlager	Schlager
Grand Marnier	Marnier
Herradura Tequila	Herradura
Irish Mist	Mist
J & B	JB
J. Walker Black Label	Black
J. Walker Blue Label	Blue
J. Walker Gold Label	Gold Label
J. Walker Red Label	Red
Jack Daniel's	Jack
Jägermeister	Jäger
Jameson Irish	Jameson
Jim Beam Bourbon	Beam
Kahlúa	Kahlua
Leyden Gin	Leyden
Maker's Mark	Makers
Midori	Midori
Myers's Jamaican	Myers
Ouzo	Ouzo
Patrón Tequila	Patron
Peppermint Schnapps	Pep Snp
Pinch 12-Year Scotch	Pinch
Rumple Minze	Rumple
Sauza Hornitos	Horn
Sauza Triada	Triada
Seagram's Seven	s7
Seagram's V.O.	VO
Smirnoff	Smirnoff
Smirnoff Black	Smir Black
Southern Comfort	Comfort

CHAPTER EIGHT

Food & Sanitation

Many of the patrons who will come into your bar for a drink will also want food. In some cases, alcohol stimulates appetite. A group of people out to have a nice time will want to combine good drinks with good food.

Of course, from the bar manager's perspective, food complicates things considerably. Not only will more perishables have to be bought and stored, but the hiring of a cook and more servers is often needed. Some establishments resolve this issue by having two different areas—a dining area and a bar—complete with different servers. Other bars keep things simple with a very small or modest menu that is easy to prepare and easy for servers to remember. If you are trying to weigh the costs of offering food against the costs of not offering a menu, consider the following:

- Patrons who are hungry or who are with someone who is hungry may leave to patronize another bar in order to get something to eat.

- Traditional "bar food"— wings, burgers, appetizers, snacks—is quite inexpensive to buy and simple to prepare.

- Bar patrons who might not otherwise come in for a drink might come into a pub for the food. By offering a bar menu, you are, in fact, expanding your possible clientele.

- A good chef or cook can prepare dishes that are as memorable as your specialty drinks; in other words, food that will create repeat customers.

- Food can be used as effectively as theme nights to draw in more customers. Offering free food is often less expensive than offering inexpensive drinks during happy hour, yet the profits can be greater. People coming in to eat food will be more likely to order drinks, which is likely the most high-profit item on your menu.

- Food makes customers linger, which increases the chances of repeat drink orders per customer.

Of course, the most important factor for including food in your bar menu is:

- **Food makes customers happy.** Many customers associate eating with fun social times, which is likely what you are trying to create for your customers. Offering even a small menu will help you provide something that improves customer experience and ensures that customers will leave with a smile on their faces.

You will want to keep your offerings simple, especially at first. A basic bar menu might consist of the following:

- **Appetizers or snacks (3–7 items on the menu).** This can include hors d'oeuvres, nachos, mozzarella sticks, a sampler platter of small items, wings, perogies, French fries, and other items. These are inexpensive items that go well with food and are ordered by patrons who are a bit hungry but not in the mood for a big meal.

- **Meal items (3–7 items on the menu).** These can include items such as pizza, hamburgers, fish and chips, seafood platters, larger orders of nachos or wings, steaks, or pastas. You can serve foods as a buffet or in a restaurant setting. In general, for evening hours when you are most likely to be busy, restaurant-style serving will ensure the best order. Many bars find that offering a buffet for lunch encourages people to drop into the bar during office hours for a quick break.

- **Desserts (3–7 items).** Developing a reputation as the bar to go to for a nice dessert and a good, relaxing drink is great way to build a reputation. Offering a selection of items such as ice cream, brownies, bread pudding, cheesecake, cakes, and other items is a good business idea. Desserts can look spectacular in a display case and draw customers. Some people also crave alcohol with sweets, and some types of beverages such as champagne, some wines, and some sweet drinks are marvelously complemented by sweets. Offering desserts may also make your bar into a popular destination place for couples, which, again, will help ensure steady business and a regular clientele.

- **Vegetarian or healthful items (3–5 items).** Just as many more bar customers are now turning to light beers for their lower calorie content, many people are trying to eat better. Healthier fare, such as clear soups, salads, grilled vegetables, sandwiches or vegetable wraps, or pastas, will help ensure that your menu appeals to most customers. Some of your healthful items can overlap with the main meal and appetizer options; just make sure that you have at least a few items that the health-conscious can enjoy.

- **Breakfast items (2–3 items).** Not all bars offer breakfasts, but if you plan to stay open late or open early, having a breakfast option can be quite attractive to some customers. All-day breakfast choices are quite popular at many pubs and bars.

The exact items you choose to offer on your menu, of course, will depend on the type of bar you want to create. A bar with a Tex-Mex theme will offer nachos, of course, and a sports bar will do well to offer wings, burgers, and other items that go well with beer and the game on TV. Peanut bars may offer only hamburgers and platefuls of nuts. Bars hoping to appeal to a fancier clientele may offer entire gourmet dinners. You can make bar food as plain or as simple as you wish, but you need to make sure that the food you choose matches the clientele and the bar. A sports bar may not do as well by serving escargot. If you listen, your customers will be more than glad to tell you which items would please them and which would not.

If you plan to offer food at your bar (and from this chapter, it should be clear that you should at least seriously consider having a menu), you will need to consider the legal and health aspects of food. Some cities or locations require specific licensing in order to allow food and liquor to be sold together. All cities have specific laws governing the safety and sanitation of food. You will need to check local regulations to make sure that you are selling food according to law. You will also need to take extreme care to ensure all food—especially meats—are properly prepared and cooked. An inexperienced chef or a case of food poisoning could close your bar. More importantly, such a situation could make potential customers shy away from your establishment long after the problem is resolved. If you serve food, you need to make absolutely sure that all of it is perfectly cooked and the area where it is prepared is spotless.

You will need to make sure that food is offered in an appealing and comfortable way. Relying on servers is often the worst way, as it ensures that servers are delayed at a table each time a customer wants to hear the menu. Your best bet is to either have a menu printed (if you plan to have a menu that is more or less permanent) or having the menu prominently displayed on a chalkboard (if you plan to change the bar menu each day or every few days). Always name your dishes in an appealing way and provide a description of the food. If you use fresh ingredients or have a very talented chef, be sure to highlight the fact on your menu.

When the food is presented to your customers, it should look as good as it tastes. Providing nice but simple cutlery and linen napkins adds plenty of style at a low cost. Plain white square dishes and plain bowls look great for most meals, while paper-lined baskets for snacks and wings are both inexpensive and attractive. Get your kitchen staff to arrange food nicely on the plate and ensure that food is colorful and appealing; adding red peppers to a green salad, for example, adds visual appeal as well as taste. These small touches often make the difference between an enjoyed meal and a meal that is recommended to friends.

You will also need to ensure food quality. Many successful bar managers find that they can save money and provide high-quality ingredients by arranging for a food buyer that can provide local, fresh products in season. This helps ensure variety in the menu and also helps ensure the highest food quality at the lowest prices, which is exactly what customers want. In ensuring quality, you will have to work with your kitchen staff closely. You will want to establish the following guidelines with your kitchen staff:

- Consistent portion sizes.

- Ingredients and techniques to be used in preparing food.

- The food that is to be offered and what is to be done when a customer asks for substitutions.

- Proper cleanup procedures.

Establishing these guidelines and sharing them with your staff is key, as it will ensure that consistent food quality is maintained. It is not excessive to have these guidelines (which are different at every bar and restaurant) printed and posted in the kitchen area.

Good Food, Happy Customers

The food you serve can sometimes be as, or even more, profitable than the drinks you sell. No matter what size your venue is, a decent menu of bar snacks doesn't need a humongous kitchen to exist.

- **Basics.** The number-one bar food staple is still the humble hamburger. With a small grill and some basic ingredients, you can offer your customers well over a dozen different burger varieties. With the addition of a few other easy-to-prepare staples, such as nachos, sandwiches, chicken wings, fries, mozzarella sticks, deep-fried mushrooms, and the trusty salad, you can provide a wide array of bar food with only a grill, toaster oven, and deep fryer.

- **Why stop at the predictable beef hamburger?** Turkey burgers, veggie burgers, chicken burgers, even teriyaki, tandoori, and buffalo burgers offer a great source of variety to the burger connoisseur. Ingredients like mozzarella, Gorgonzola, Cajun spices, pepperoni, salsa, and guacamole can add the kind of panache that will see people come from far and wide to tuck on in.

- **Cook your own.** Some venues have gone a step further with their bar food and provide a "cook-your-own" facility, where customers can choose their ingredients, slap them on a large grill, and cook their meat, cheese, vegetables, bun, etc., to their heart's content. While a setup such as this requires a certain level of investment and a high level of staff supervision, the returns can be outstanding.

- **To charcoal or not to charcoal?** Many operations feature a flame grill as a selling point for their bar food, but many savvy chefs say that when cooking burgers, it's best to use a flat grill so that the juices don't run and the burger doesn't dry out. Along these lines, it's best to not put any weight on the burger as it is on the grill, as this, too, tends to dry out the meat.

- **Add a touch of originality to bar food.** Consider a touch of international flavor. A pasta bar, containing a variety of pasta and sauce types that customers can mix and match, is a very inexpensive alternative to standard bar snacks. Likewise, tempura, Chinese, curry, and pizza can not only feed hungry mouths but also attract a new stream of clientele looking for something that's a step up from burgers.

If you find that ordering ingredients, controlling food portions for each customer, and arranging a menu are too complicated, you can often find a local caterer who can provide simple foods for your bar at a reasonable cost. Look to see where other bars get their food and you will likely find a number of caterers who consistently provide good bar food to a number of establishments in your area. At the beginning, especially, getting food catered can be an elegant and attractive idea for the bar manager. A kitchen staff (or kitchen) can often be added later, especially if the bar being opened is quite small.

When serving food, ensure a few basic guidelines are followed:

- As soon as they are seated, pour water for customers who are at your bar to eat. Offer to take a drink order as they wait.

- Take food orders as quickly as possible. List any specials before taking orders.

- Remove extra place settings from tables before taking food orders.

- When taking food instructions, note any special orders (how a steak is to be prepared, special instructions, possible sides, etc.).

- Always bring drinks and food on a tray and serve customers from their left. Serve all liquids from the right (except soups).

- Use the left hand to place and remove dishes when working at the left side of the guest, and the right hand when working at the right side of a guest.

- Never place your finger in a cup or glass, even if it is empty and you are clearing the table. Always handle cutlery by the handles.

- Appetizers are served first, cold appetizers before hot ones. Remove appetizers before serving main courses.

- When guests order dinner, make a few suggestions about possible wines that may complement the dinner.

- Take care that food served is the right temperature, especially when serving soups, meats, and seafood.

- When serving the main course, ask whether anything is needed (condiments, more drinks). Promptly deliver anything needed.

- Return five minutes after serving the meal to ask whether everything is all right. Quickly deliver anything that is needed or resolve any complaints with the meal.

- Keep an eye on each dining party, but do not hover. Most customers will look around and make eye contact or wave a server over if they need further help.

- Once everyone at a table has finished their meal, clear all plates and ask whether anyone wants dessert or another beverage. If someone has left food on their plate, ask whether they want it wrapped up.

- Wipe any crumbs onto a plate (not the floor) before returning with drinks and dessert.

HACCP & Sanitation

If you do decide to add food service to your bar, you need to practice proper sanitation procedures. Every bar/restaurant employee is responsible for preparing and serving quality and safe food products. Each employee must be thoroughly familiar with basic food safety and sanitation practices. This section will describe the fundamental methods and procedures that must be practiced in order to control food contamination, the spread of infectious diseases, and personal safety practices.

Management must provide employees with the training, knowledge, and tools that will enable them to establish and practice proper food handling and sanitation procedures. Through the use of this section, and under the guidance of your local health department, you and your staff can obtain training and knowledge. First, however, the bar must be equipped with the proper tools and training and working conditions. Employees will never establish good sanitation procedures if they do not first have the proper environment in which to practice them.

Aside from what is required by law, management should provide training materials; proper training sessions or clinics; hand sinks at every station; hand and nail brushes; labels for dating and rotation procedures; disposable towels; gloves; first-aid kits; germicidal hand soaps; employee bathrooms and lockers; scrub brushes; uniforms; hairnets; thermometers; test kits; and quality, color-coded utensils.

Food service establishments may harbor all types of bacteria, bugs, and pests. Restaurants can attract these health hazards with the three basic ingredients necessary to sustain life: food, water, and warmth. Any environment that provides these three elements for an extended period of time will become host to these intruders. In order to eliminate contamination, all that is necessary is to make the living conditions unfavorable for these unwanted intruders.

What Is HACCP?

Hazard Analysis of Critical Control Points (HACCP) is a system for monitoring the food service process to reduce the risk of food-borne illness. HACCP focuses on how food flows through the process—from purchasing to serving. At each step in the food preparation process there are a variety of potential hazards. HACCP provides managers with a framework for implementing control procedures for each hazard. It does this through identifying critical control points (CCPs). These are points in the process where bacteria or other harmful organisms may grow or food may become contaminated.

Why Use HACCP In Your Facility?

You are responsible for protecting your customers by serving safe and wholesome food. To accomplish this, you have to educate your employees and motivate them to put into practice at every step what they've learned about food safety. To do this, you need a systematic process for identifying potential hazards, for putting safety procedures in place, and for monitoring the success of your safety system on an ongoing basis. HACCP helps you do all of these things.

Using HACCP, you can identify potentially hazardous foods and places in the food preparation process where bacterial contamination, survival, and growth can occur. Then you can take action to minimize the danger.

Using HACCP

HACCP is based on this principle: If the raw ingredients are safe, and the process is safe, then the finished product is safe.

Implementing HACCP involves seven key steps. As you proceed through these steps, you will:

1. Assess the hazards.

2. Identify critical control points.

3. Establish critical limits.

4. Monitor the critical control points.

5. Take corrective action as needed.

6. Develop a recordkeeping system.

7. Verify your system's effectiveness.

HACCP Step 1: Assess the Hazards

To assess the hazards present at each stage of the preparation process, track each HACCP food from purchasing and receiving through serving and reheating.

To begin, review your menus. Identify all potentially hazardous foods, as well as those foods that may become contaminated during the process.

At this point, you may even want to reduce risks by removing highly hazardous food items from your menu. For example, you may want to avoid egg salad sandwiches if sandwiches must be transported and held before being served.

Once you have surveyed the foods on your menu, evaluate general preparation and cooking procedures to isolate any points where contamination might occur. Next, rank these hazards in terms of severity (how serious are the consequences) and probability (how likely are they to occur).

HACCP Step 2: Identify Critical Control Points

Identify the points in the process where hazards can be controlled or prevented. Develop a flowchart or list the steps involved in preparing each potentially hazardous food. Then, identify procedures to prevent, reduce, and eliminate recontamination hazards at each step you have listed.

In general, food service workers can reduce the risk of food-borne illness by:

1. Practicing good personal hygiene.

2. Avoiding cross-contamination.

3. Using proper cooking and cooling procedures.

4. Reducing the number of steps involved in preparing and serving.

HACCP Step 3: Establish Critical Limits

In order to be sure a food passes safely through a critical control point, you need to establish critical limits that must be met. These critical limits should be standards that are observable and measurable. They should include precise time, temperature, and sensory requirements.

Specify exactly what should be done to meet each particular standard. For example, instead of saying that a "food must be thoroughly cooked," the standard might say, "Heat rapidly to an internal temperature of 165°F within two hours." In addition, make sure employees have calibrated, metal-stemmed, or digital thermometers and that they use them routinely.

Make sure recipes state: 1) end-cooking, reheating, and hot-holding temperatures, and 2) specific times for thawing, cooking, and cooling foods. Schedule sufficient staff in peak hours to prepare and serve foods safely.

HACCP Step 4: Monitor the Critical Control Points

Using your flowcharts or lists, follow potentially hazardous foods through every step in the process. Compare your operation's performance with the requirements you have set. Identify any areas of deficiency.

HACCP Step 5: Take Corrective Action

Take corrective action as needed. For example, if products' temperatures are unacceptable when received, reject the shipment. Similarly, if:

1. Food is contaminated by hands or equipment, rewash or discard it.

2. Food temperature is not high enough after cooking, continue cooking to the required temperature.

3. Food temperature exceeds 55°F during cold prep or serving, discard it.

HACCP Step 6: Develop a Recordkeeping System

Develop a recordkeeping system to document the HACCP process and monitor your results. This may be any simple, quick system, such as a log, in which employees can record their compliance with standards at critical control points. These records are crucial and may provide proof that a food-borne illness did not originate at your establishment.

HACCP Step 7: Verify Your System's Effectiveness

Verify that the HACCP process in your facility works. You can do this in a number of ways.

For starters, be alert to how often you need to take corrective actions. If you need to take corrective actions frequently, this may indicate a need to change, or at least fine-tune, your system. In addition, think of tests you can do, like measuring the strength of your sanitizing solution. Also, examine your records and make sure employees are entering actual, valid data. An inspection by the health department can provide a good assessment of whether or not your process is working.

On the following pages, you'll find a sample HACCP checklist. Use this checklist to determine areas in your operation that require action. Once a month, make observations during production and take corrective action if needed.

In order, we'll look at:

1. Purchasing

2. Receiving

3. Storing

4. Preparing

5. Cooking

6. Serving and holding

7. Cooling

8. Reheating

There are multiple hazards at, and specific preventative measures for, each step.

Step 1: PURCHASING

The goal of purchasing is to obtain wholesome, safe foods to meet your menu requirements. Safety at this step is primarily the responsibility of your vendors. It's your job to choose your vendors wisely. Suppliers must meet federal and state health standards. They should use the HACCP system in their operations and train their employees in sanitation. Delivery trucks should have adequate refrigeration and freezer units, and foods should be packaged in protective, leakproof, durable packaging. Let vendors know up front what you expect from them. Put food-safety standards in your purchase specification agreements. Ask to see their most recent health department sanitation reports, and tell them you will be inspecting trucks on a quarterly basis.

Good vendors will cooperate with your inspections and should adjust their delivery schedules to avoid your busy periods so that incoming foods can be received and inspected properly.

Step 2: RECEIVING

The goals of receiving are: 1) to make sure foods are fresh and safe when they enter your facility, and 2) to transfer them to proper storage as quickly as possible.

Let's look more closely at two important parts of receiving:

1. Getting ready to receive food.

2. Inspecting the food when the delivery truck arrives.

There are several important guidelines to keep in mind and tasks to complete as you get ready to receive food:

- Make sure your receiving area is equipped with sanitary carts for transporting goods.

- Plan ahead for deliveries to ensure sufficient refrigerator and freezer space.

- Mark all items for storage with the date of arrival or the use-by date.

- Keep the receiving area well lit and clean to discourage pests.

- Remove empty containers and packing materials immediately to a separate trash area.

- Keep all flooring clean of food particles and debris.

When the delivery truck arrives, make sure it looks and smells clean and is equipped with the proper food storage equipment. Then inspect foods immediately:

- Check expiration dates of milk, eggs, and other perishable goods.

- Make sure shelf-life dates have not expired.

- Make sure frozen foods are in airtight, moisture-proof wrappings.

- Reject foods that have been thawed and refrozen. Look for signs of thawing and refreezing such as large crystals, solid areas of ice, or excessive ice in containers.

- Reject cans that have any of the following: swollen sides or ends, flawed seals or seams, dents, or rust. Also reject any cans with foamy or bad-smelling contents.

- Check temperature of refrigerated and frozen foods, especially eggs and dairy products, fresh meat, and fish and poultry products.

- Look for content damage and insect infestations.

- Reject dairy, bakery, and other foods delivered in dirty flats or crates.

Step 3: STORING

In general, there are four possible ways to store food:

1. In dry storage, for longer holding of less perishable items.

2. In refrigeration, for short-term storage of perishable items.

3. In specially designed deep-chilling units for short periods.

4. In a freezer, for longer-term storage of perishable foods.

Each type of storage has its own sanitation and safety requirements.

DRY STORAGE

There are many items that can be safely held in a sanitary storeroom. These include, for example, canned goods, baking supplies (such as salt and sugar), grain products (such as rice and cereals), and other dry items. In addition, some fruits (such as bananas, avocados, and pears) ripen best at room temperature. Some vegetables, such as onions, potatoes, and tomatoes, also store best in dry storage. A dry-storage room should be clean and orderly, with good ventilation to control temperature and humidity and retard the growth of bacteria and mold. Keep in mind the following:

- For maximum shelf life, dry foods should be held at 50°F, but 60°–70°F is adequate for most products.

- Use a wall thermometer to regularly check the temperature of your dry-storage facilit.

- To ensure freshness, store opened items in tightly covered containers. Use the "first in, first out" (FIFO) rotation method, dating packages and placing incoming supplies in the back so that older supplies will be used first.

- To avoid pest infestation and cross-contamination, clean up all spills immediately, and do not store trash or garbage cans in food storage areas.

- Do not place any items—including paper products—on the floor. Make sure the bottom shelf of the dry-storage room is at least 6 inches above the ground.

To avoid chemical contamination: Never use or store cleaning materials or other chemicals where they might contaminate foods! Store them, labeled, in their own section in the storeroom away from all food supplies.

REFRIGERATED STORAGE

Keep fresh meat, poultry, seafood, dairy products, most fresh fruit and vegetables, and hot leftovers in the refrigerator at internal temperatures of below 40°F. Although no food can last forever, refrigeration increases the shelf life of most products. Most importantly, because refrigeration slows bacterial growth, the colder a food is, the safer it is.

Your refrigeration unit should contain open, slotted shelving to allow cold air to circulate around food. Do not line shelves with foil or paper. Also do not overload the refrigerator, and be sure to leave space between items to further improve air circulation.

- All refrigerated foods should be dated and properly sealed.

- Use clean, nonabsorbent, covered containers that are approved for food storage.

- Store dairy products separately from foods with strong odors like onions, cabbage, and seafood.

- To avoid cross-contamination, store raw or uncooked food away from and below prepared or ready-to-eat food.

- Never allow fluids from raw poultry, fish, or meat to come into contact with other foods.

- Keeping perishable items at the proper temperature is a key factor in preventing food-borne illness. Check the temperature of your refrigeration unit regularly to make sure it stays below 40°F. Keep in mind that opening and closing the refrigerator door too often can affect temperature.

Many commercial refrigerators are equipped with externally mounted or built-in thermometers. These are convenient when they work, but it is important to have a backup. It's a good idea to have several thermometers in different parts of the refrigerator to ensure consistent temperature and accuracy of instruments. Record the temperature of each refrigerator on a chart preferably once a day.

DEEP CHILLING

Deep or super chilling—that is, storing foods at temperatures between 26°F and 32°F—has been found to decrease bacterial growth. This method can be used to increase the shelf life of fresh foods, such as poultry, meat, seafood, and other protein items, without compromising their quality by freezing. You can deep-chill foods in specially designed units or in a refrigerator set to deep-chilling temperature.

FROZEN STORAGE

Frozen meats, poultry, seafood, fruits and vegetables, and some dairy products, such as ice cream, should be stored in a freezer at 0°F to keep them fresh and safe for an extended period of time.

As a rule, you should use your freezer primarily to store foods that are frozen when you receive them. Freezing refrigerated foods can damage the quality of perishable items. It's important to store frozen foods immediately. It's also important to remember that storing foods in the freezer for too long increases the likelihood of contamination and spoilage. Like your refrigeration unit, the freezer should allow cold air to circulate around foods easily. Be sure to:

- Store frozen foods in moisture-proof material or containers to minimize loss of flavor as well as discoloration, dehydration, and odor absorption.

- Monitor temperature regularly, using several thermometers to ensure accuracy and consistent temperatures. Record the temperature of each freezer on a chart.

Remember that frequently opening and closing the freezer's door can raise the temperature, as can placing warm foods in the freezer. To minimize heat gain, open freezer doors only when necessary and remove as many items at one time as possible. You can also use a freezer "cold curtain" to help guard against heat gain.

Step 4: PREPARING

THAWING AND MARINATING

Freezing food keeps most bacteria from multiplying, but it does not kill them. Bacteria that are present when food is removed from the freezer may multiply rapidly if thawed at room temperature. Thus, it is critical to thaw foods out of the temperature danger zone. Never thaw foods on a counter or in any other non-refrigerated area!

Some foods, such as frozen vegetables and pre-formed hamburger patties and chicken nuggets, can be cooked from the frozen state. It is important to note, however, that this method depends on the size of the item. For example, cooking from frozen is not recommended for large foods like a 20-pound turkey.

The two best methods for thawing foods are:

1. In refrigeration at a temperature below 40°F, placed in a pan on the lowest shelf so juices cannot drip on to other foods.

2. Under clean, drinkable running water at a temperature of 70°F or less for no more than two hours, or just until the product is thawed.

Always marinate meat, fish, and poultry in the refrigerator—never at room temperature. Never save and reuse marinade. With all methods, be careful not to cross-contaminate!

CAUTIONS FOR COLD FOODS

When you are preparing cold foods, you are at one of the most hazardous points in the food preparation process. There are two key reasons for this: First, cold food preparation usually takes place at room temperature. Second, cold food is one of the most common points of contamination and cross-contamination.

Chicken salad, tuna salad, potato salad with eggs, and other protein-rich salads are common sources of food-borne illness. Sandwiches prepared in advance and held un-refrigerated are also dangerous. Because cold foods such as these receive no further cooking, it is essential that all ingredients used in them are properly cleaned, prepared, and, where applicable, cooked. It is a good idea to chill meats and other ingredients and combine them while chilled.

Here are several other important precautions to keep in mind:

- Prepare foods no further in advance than necessary.

- Prepare foods in small batches and place in cold storage immediately. This will prevent holding food too long in the temperature danger zone.

- Always hold prepared cold foods below 40°F.

- Wash fresh fruits and vegetables with plain water to remove surface pesticide residues and other impurities, such as soil particles.

- Use a brush to scrub thick-skinned produce, if desired.

- Beware of cross-contamination! It's crucial to:

    – Keep raw products separate from ready-to-serve foods.

    – Sanitize cutting boards, knives, and other food contact surfaces after each contact with a potentially hazardous food.

    – Discard any leftover batter, breading, or marinade after it has been used with potentially hazardous foods.

Step 5: COOKING

Even when potentially hazardous foods are properly thawed, bacteria and other contaminants may still be present. Cooking foods to the proper internal temperature will kill any existing bacteria and make food safe.

It's important to remember, however, that conventional cooking procedures cannot destroy bacterial spores nor deactivate their toxins.

Keep in mind the following safe cooking tips:

- Frequently stir foods cooked in deep pots to ensure thorough cooking.

- When deep-frying potentially hazardous foods, make sure fryers are not overloaded, and make sure the oil temperature returns to the required level before adding the next batch. Use a hot-oil thermometer designed for this special application.

- Regulate size and thickness of each portion to make cooking time predictable and uniform.

- Allow cooking equipment to heat up between batches.

- Never interrupt the cooking process. Partially cooking poultry or meat, for example, may produce conditions that encourage bacterial growth.

Monitor the accuracy of heating equipment with each use by using thermometers. In addition, always use a thermometer to ensure food reaches the proper temperature during cooking. Use a sanitized metal-stemmed, numerically scaled thermometer (accurate to plus or minus 2°F) or a digital thermometer. Check food temperature in several places, especially in the thickest parts, to make sure the food is thoroughly cooked. To avoid getting a false reading, be careful not to touch the pan or bone with the thermometer. Always cook food to an internal temperature of 165°F.

Step 6: SERVING AND HOLDING

Food that has been cooked isn't necessarily safe. In fact, many outbreaks occur because improper procedures were used following cooking. Although it may be tempting to hold food at temperatures just hot enough to serve, it is essential to keep prepared foods out of the temperature danger zone. This means, specifically:

- Always keep hot foods in hot-holding equipment above 140°F.

- Always keep cold foods in a refrigeration unit or surrounded by ice below 40°F.

For safer serving and holding:

- Use hot-holding equipment, such as steam tables and hot-food carts, during service but never for reheating.

- Stir foods at reasonable intervals to ensure even heating.

- Check temperatures with a food thermometer every 30 minutes.

- Sanitize the thermometer before each use, or use a digital infrared thermometer that never touches the food.

- Cover hot-holding equipment to retain heat and to guard against contamination.

- Monitor the temperature of hot-holding equipment with each use.

- discard any food held in the temperature danger zone for more than four hours!

To avoid contamination: Never add fresh food to a serving pan containing foods that have already been out for serving!

SOME KEY POINTS

1. Always wash hands with soap and warm water for at least 20 seconds before serving food.

2. Use cleaned and sanitized long-handled ladles and spoons so bare hands do not touch food.

3. Never touch the parts of glasses, cups, plates, or tableware that will come into contact with food.

4. Never touch the parts of dishes that will come into contact with the customer's mouth.

5. Wear gloves if serving food by hand.

6. Cover cuts or infections with bandages, and if on hands, wear gloves.

7. Discard gloves whenever they touch an unsanitary surface.

8. Use tongs or wear gloves to dispense rolls and bread.

9. Clean and sanitize equipment and utensils thoroughly after each use.

10. Use lids and sneeze guards to protect prepared food from contamination.

To avoid contamination: Always wash hands, utensils, and other food-contact surfaces after contact with raw meat or poultry and before contact with cooked meat or poultry. For example, do not reuse a serving pan used to hold raw chicken to serve the same chicken after it's cooked, unless the pan has been thoroughly cleaned and sanitized.

SANITARY SELF-SERVICE

Like workers, customers can also act as a source of contamination. Unlike workers, customers—especially children—are, generally, not educated about food sanitation and may do the following unsanitary things:

1. Use the same plate twice.

2. Touch food with their hands.

3. Touch the edges of serving dishes.

4. Sneeze or cough into food.

5. Pick up foods, such as rolls or carrot sticks, with their fingers.

6. Eat in the food line.

7. Dip their fingers into foods to taste them.

8. Return food items to avoid waste.

9. Put their heads under sneeze guards to reach items in the back.

Be sure to observe customer behavior and remove any foods that may have been contaminated. Also, as a precautionary measure, serve sealed packages of crackers, breadsticks, and condiments, and pre-wrap, date, and label sandwiches if possible.

Step 7: COOLING

Here, as at other critical points, every move you make can mean the difference between the safe and the unsafe.

It is often necessary to prepare foods in advance or use leftover foods. Unfortunately, this can easily lead to problems, unless proper precautions are taken. In fact, problems at this stage are the number-one cause of food-borne illness. The two key precautions for preventing food-borne illness at this point in the process are rapid cooling and protection from contamination.

CHILLING IT QUICKLY

All potentially hazardous, cooked leftovers should be chilled to an internal temperature of below 40°F. Quick-chill any leftovers larger than half a gallon or 2 pounds.

Quick-chilling involves five simple steps:

1. **Reduce food mass.** Smaller amounts of food will chill more quickly than larger amounts, so cut large items into pieces or divide food among several containers or shallow pans. Use shallow, pre-chilled pans (no more than 4 inches deep). Use stainless-steel containers when possible; stainless steel transfers heat better and cools faster than plastic.

2. **Chill.** Ideally, place food in an ice-water bath or quick-chill unit (26°–32°F) rather than a refrigerator. These options are best for two

reasons:

- First, water is a much better heat conductor than air. As a result, foods can cool much more quickly in an ice bath than they can in a refrigerator.

- Second, refrigeration units are designed to keep cold foods cold rather than to chill hot foods. They can take too long to cool foods to safe temperatures.

Another option is to pre-chill foods in a freezer for about 30 minutes before refrigerating.

Separate food items so air can flow freely around them. Do not stack shallow pans. Never cool at room temperature.

3. **Stir frequently.** Stirring accelerates cooling and helps to ensure that cold air reaches all parts of the food.

4. **Measure temperature periodically.** Food should reach a temperature of 70°F within two hours and 40°F within four hours. It's important to note that this time must be reduced if food has already spent time in the temperature danger zone at any other point in the preparation and serving process.

5. **Tightly cover and label cooled foods.** On labels, include preparation dates and times.

To avoid contamination: Be aware that although uncovered foods cool faster, they are at increased risk for cross-contamination. Be sure to store uncovered cooked and cooled foods on the upper shelves of the cooler, and cover them when they reach 45°F. Never store them beneath raw foods.

Step 8: REHEATING

While assuming leftovers are safe might seem reasonable, it's not. In reheating and serving leftovers—just as in all phases of the food preparation process—you must be careful to avoid contamination.

To safely reheat and serve leftovers, be sure to:

- Boil sauces, soups, and gravies, and heat other foods to a minimum of

165°F within two hours of taking the food out of the refrigerator.

- Never reheat food in hot-holding equipment.

- Never mix a leftover batch of food with a fresh batch of food.

- Never reheat food more than once.

Heat or chemicals can be used to reduce the number of bacteria to acceptable levels. They can also be used for certain other harmful microorganisms.

Heat sanitizing involves exposing equipment to high heat for an adequate length of time. This may be done manually by immersing equipment in water maintained at a temperature of 170°–195°F for at least 30 seconds or in a dishwashing machine that washes at 150°F and rinses at 180°F. For either method, it is important to check water temperature frequently. Thermometers and heat-sensitive tapes and labels are available for determining whether adequate sanitation temperatures have been achieved.

Chemical sanitizing can be accomplished by immersing an object in, or wiping it down with, bleach or sanitizing solution. For bleaching, use ½ ounce or 1 tablespoon of 5 percent bleach per gallon of water. For using commercial products, follow the manufacturers' instructions.

Chemical sanitizers are regulated by the EPA, and manufacturers must follow strict labeling requirements regarding what concentrations to use, data on minimum effectiveness, and warnings of possible health hazards. Chemical test strips are available for testing the strength of the sanitizing solution. Because sanitizing agents become less effective as they kill bacteria and are exposed to air, it is important to test the sanitizing solution frequently.

SANITIZING PORTABLE EQUIPMENT

To properly clean and sanitize portable equipment, you must have a sink with three separate compartments: for cleaning, rinsing, and sanitizing. There should be a separate area for scraping and rinsing food and debris into a garbage container or disposal before washing, and separate drain boards for clean and soiled items.

To sanitize a piece of equipment, use the following procedure:

1. Clean and sanitize sinks and work surfaces.

2. Scrape and rinse food into garbage or disposal. Presoak items, such as silverware, as necessary.

3. In the first sink, immerse the equipment in a clean detergent solution at about 120°F. Use a brush or a cloth to loosen and remove any remaining visible soil.

4. Rinse in the second sink using clear, clean water between 120°F and 140°F to remove all traces of food, debris, and detergent.

5. Sanitize in the third sink by immersing items in hot water at 170°F for 30 seconds or in a chemical sanitizing solution for one minute. Be sure to cover all surfaces of the equipment with hot water or the sanitizing solution and keep them in contact with it for the appropriate amount of time.

6. If soapsuds disappear in the first compartment or remain in the second, if the water temperature cools, or if water in any compartment becomes dirty and cloudy, empty the compartment and refill it.

7. Air-dry. Wiping can re-contaminate equipment and can remove the sanitizing solution from the surfaces before it has finished working.

8. Make certain all equipment is dry before putting it into storage; moisture can foster bacterial growth.

SANITIZING IN-PLACE EQUIPMENT

Larger and immobile equipment should also be washed, rinsed, and sanitized. Use the following procedure:

1. Unplug electrically powered equipment, such as meat slicers.

2. Remove fallen food particles and scraps.

3. Wash, rinse, and sanitize any removable parts using the manual immersion method described in steps 3 through 5 above.

4. Wash the remaining food contact surfaces and rinse with clean water. Wipe down with a chemical sanitizing solution mixed according to the manufacturer's directions.

5. Wipe down all non-food contact surfaces with a sanitized cloth, and allow all parts to air-dry before reassembling. Sanitize cloth before and during sanitizing by rinsing it in sanitizing solution.

6. Re-sanitize the external food contact surfaces of the parts that were handled during reassembling.

7. Scrub wooden surfaces, such as cutting boards, with a detergent solution and a stiff-bristled nylon brush; then rinse in clear, clean water; and wipe down with a sanitizing solution after every use.

A First-Rate Facility

Safe and sanitary food service begins with a facility that is clean and in good repair. The entire facility—work areas as well as equipment—should be designed for easy cleaning and maintenance.

It's important to eliminate hard-to-clean work areas as well as faulty or overloaded refrigerators or other equipment. Also get rid of dirty surroundings and any conditions that will attract pests. Remember, the easier the workplace is to clean, the more likely it will stay clean.

FLOORS, WALLS, AND CEILINGS

Floors, walls, and ceilings should be free of dirt, litter, and moisture. Clean walls regularly by swabbing with a cleaning solution or by spraying with a pressure nozzle. Sweep floors, then clean them using a spray method or by mopping. Swab ceilings, instead of spraying them, to avoid soaking lights and ceiling fans. And don't forget corners and hard-to-reach places!

VENTILATION

Good ventilation is a critical factor in maintaining a clean food service environment. Ventilation removes steam, smoke, grease, and heat from food-preparation areas and equipment. This helps maintain indoor air quality and reduces the possibility of fires from accumulated grease. In addition, good ventilation eliminates condensation and other airborne contaminants. It also:

- Reduces the accumulation of dirt in the food preparation area.

- Reduces odors, gases, and fumes.

- Reduces mold growth by reducing humidity.

To ensure good ventilation, be sure to:

- Use exhaust fans to remove odors and smoke.

- Use hoods over cooking areas and dishwashing equipment.

- Check exhaust fans and hoods regularly to make sure they are clean and operating properly.

- Clean hood filters routinely according to the instructions provided by the hood manufacturer.

STOREROOMS

Like all areas of the facility, storerooms must be kept clean and litter-free. To accomplish this, be sure to sweep and scrub walls, ceilings, floors, shelves, light fixtures, and racks on a routine basis. Check all storage areas frequently—this includes your refrigerator and freezer as well as your dry-storage room. When checking storage areas:

1. Look for damaged or spoiled foods, broken or torn packages, and bulging or leaking cans.

2. Remove any potentially spoiled foods immediately, and clean the area thoroughly.

3. Make sure foods and other supplies are stored at least 6 inches from the walls and above the floor.

To avoid chemical contamination: Store cleaning supplies and chemicals in a separate area away from food supply areas and other chemicals so they do not pose a hazard to food or people.

RESTROOMS

Restrooms should be convenient, sanitary, and adequately stocked with the following:

- Toilet paper

- Liquid soap

- Disposable paper towels and/or air blowers

- Covered trash receptacles (the trash receptacle lid should open with a foot pedal)

Scrub restrooms daily and keep the doors closed. You may also want to provide brushes to wash fingernails and sanitizing solution for soaking the brushes.

Bacteria are everywhere: in the air, in all areas of the restaurant and all over one's body. Most bacteria are microscopic and of no harm to people. Many forms of bacteria are actually beneficial, aiding in the production of such things as cheese, bread, butter, alcoholic beverages, etc. Only a small percentage of bacteria will cause food to spoil and can generate a form of food poisoning when consumed.

Bacteria need food, water, and warmth in order to survive. Their growth rate depends upon how favorable these conditions are. Bacteria prefer to ingest moisture-saturated foods, such as meats, dairy products, and produce. They will not grow as readily on dry foods such as cereals, sugar, or flour.

Bacteria will grow most rapidly when the temperature is between 85°F and 100°F. In most cases, the growth rate will slow down drastically if the temperature is hotter or colder than this. Thus, it is vitally important that perishable food items are refrigerated before bacteria have a chance to establish themselves and multiply. Certain bacteria can survive in extreme hot- and cold-temperature ranges. By placing these bacteria in severe temperatures, you will be slowing down their growth rate, but not necessarily killing them.

The greatest problem in controlling bacteria is their rapid reproduction cycle. Approximately every 15 minutes, the bacteria count will double under optimal conditions. The more bacteria present, the greater the chance of bacterial infection. This is why food products that must be subjected to conditions favorable to bacteria are done so for the shortest period possible.

An important consideration when handling food products is that bacteria need several hours to adjust to a new environment before they are able to begin rapidly multiplying. Thus, if you removed a food product from the walk-in refrigerator and had inadvertently introduced bacteria to it, advanced growth would not begin for several hours. If you had immediately placed the item back into the walk-in, the temperature would have killed the bacteria before it became established.

Bacterial forms do not have a means of transportation; they must be introduced to an area by some other vehicle. People are primarily responsible for transporting bacteria to new areas. The body temperature of 98.6°F is perfect for bacterial existence and proliferation. A person coughing, sneezing, or wiping their hands on a counter can introduce bacteria to an area. Bacteria may be transmitted also by insects, air, water, and articles onto which they have attached themselves, such as boxes, blades, knives, and cutting boards.

Dangerous Forms of Bacteria

The following section describes a number of harmful bacteria that may be found in a restaurant. The technical names and jargon are given for your own information. The important points to retain are the causes and preventive actions for each.

CLOSTRIDIUM PERFRINGENS

Clostridium perfringens is one of a group of bacterial infectious diseases that will cause a poisoning effect. These bacteria are extremely dangerous because they are tasteless, odorless, and colorless, and therefore nearly impossible to detect.

Clostridium perfringens bacteria are usually found in meat or seafood that was previously cooked and then held at room temperature for a period of time. These perfringens are anaerobic. They do not need air in order to survive. They can thrive in masses of food or in canned foods in the form of botulism. In order to survive, the bacterium will form a spore and surround itself. The spore will protect the bacterium from exposure to the air and give it a much wider temperature range for survival than normal bacteria: 65°–120°F. These bacterial forms may survive through long periods of extreme temperature and then multiply when the conditions are more favorable.

Keeping cooked food consistently above 148°F or below 40°F eliminates clostridium perfringens bacteria.

CLOSTRIDIUM BOTULISM

This is another of the poisoning forms of bacteria. Botulism is a rare infectious disease but it is far more lethal than the other types. Botulism bacteria exist only in an air-free environment like that of canned goods.

These bacteria are most often found in home-canned goods; however, several national food packers have reported outbreaks in their operations.

Symptoms such as vomiting, double vision, abdominal pain, and shock may occur anytime from three to four hours after ingestion to eight days later. Examine all canned goods closely before using. Look for dented, leaking cans and swollen cans or jar tops.

STAPHYLOCOCCI POISONING

Staphylococci bacteria (Staph) are perhaps the most common cause of food poisoning. Staph bacteria can be found everywhere, particularly in the human nose. The bacteria by themselves are harmless. The problem arises when they are left uncontrolled to grow in food items. Food that has been left out, un-refrigerated, for just a few hours can produce the poisonous toxins of Staph bacteria.

Symptoms will appear two to six hours after consumption. Common symptoms are vomiting, muscle weakness, cramps, and diarrhea. The sickness ranges from very severe cases—sometimes lethal—to a relatively mild illness. To prevent Staph poisoning, follow refrigeration procedures precisely. Only remove the refrigerated food items that you will be using right away.

SALMONELLA INFECTION

Salmonella infection is caused directly by the bacteria themselves, after consumption by a human. In certain cases, death has resulted; however, usually Salmonella cause severe—but temporary—illness. Symptoms include vomiting, fever, abdominal pain, and cramps. Symptoms usually show up 12 to 24 hours after consumption and may last for several days.

Salmonella are found in the intestinal tract of some animals. They have been discovered in some packaged foods, eggs, poultry, seafood, and meat. Thorough cooking and following refrigeration procedures can keep Salmonella growth to a minimal amount.

Hepatitis, dysentery, and diphtheria are some of the other infectious diseases that are bacterially derived.

Controlling Bacteria

The first step in controlling bacteria is to limit their access to the restaurant. Make certain that all products entering the restaurant are clean. Follow the prescribed bug-exterminating procedures to stop bacteria from being transported into the restaurant. Keep all food products stored and refrigerated as prescribed. Clean up any spills as you go along, making the environment unsuitable for bacteria to live. Keep all food refrigerated until needed, and cook it as soon as possible.

The quality known as "pH" indicates how acidic or alkaline ("basic") a food or other substance is. The pH scale ranges from 0.0 to 14.0—7.0 being exactly neutral. Distilled water, for example, has a neutral pH of 7.0. Bacteria grow best in foods that are neutral or slightly acidic, in the pH range of 4.6 to 7.0. Highly acidic foods, such as vinegar and most fresh fruits, inhibit bacterial growth. Meats and many other foods have an optimal pH for bacterial growth. On the other hand, some foods normally considered hazardous, such as mayonnaise and custard filling, can be safely stored at room temperature if their pH is below 4.6.

Lowering the pH of foods by adding acidic ingredients, such as making sauerkraut from cabbage or pickles from cucumbers, may render them non–potentially hazardous. This is not a foolproof prevention method, however. For example, although commercially prepared mayonnaise has a pH below 4.6, adding mayonnaise to a meat salad will not inhibit bacteria. The moisture in the meat and the meat's pH are likely to raise the pH of the salad to a point where bacteria can multiply.

ACIDITY VS. ALKALINITY — pH Levels of Some Common Foods			
Vinegar	2.2	Carrots	5.0
Lemons	2.2	White bread	5.1
Cola drinks	2.3	Tuna	6.0
Commercial mayonnaise	3.0	Green peas	6.0
Grapefruit	3.1	Potatoes	6.1
Dill pickles	3.2	Chicken	6.2
Orange juice	3.7	Corn	6.3
Pears	3.9	Steamed rice	6.4
Tomatoes	4.2	Fresh meat	6.4
Buttermilk	4.5	Milk	6.6

Avoid Bacterial Cross-Contamination

One of the most common causes of food-borne illness is cross-contamination: the transfer of bacteria from food to food, hand to food, or equipment to food.

Food to food. Raw, contaminated ingredients may be added to foods, or fluids from raw foods may drip onto foods that receive no further cooking. A common mistake is to leave thawing meat on a top shelf in the refrigerator where it can drip down onto prepared foods stored below.

Hand to food. Bacteria are found throughout the body: in the hair; on the skin; in clothing; in the mouth, nose, and throat; in the intestinal tract; and on scabs or scars from skin wounds. These bacteria often end up on the hands where they can easily spread to food. People can also pick up bacteria by touching raw food, and then transfer it to cooked or ready-to-eat food.

Equipment to food. Bacteria may pass from equipment to food when equipment that has touched contaminated food is then used to prepare other food without proper cleaning and sanitizing. For example, cross-contamination can occur when surfaces used for cutting raw poultry are then used to cut foods that will be eaten raw, such as fresh vegetables.

Coverings, such as plastic wrap and holding and serving containers, can also harbor bacteria that can spread to food. A can opener, a plastic-wrap box, or a food slicer can also become a source of cross-contamination if not properly sanitized between uses.

Personal hygiene is the best way to stop bacteria from contaminating and spreading into new areas. Hands are the greatest source of contamination. Hands must be washed constantly throughout the day. Every time an individual scratches her head or sneezes, she is exposing her hands to bacteria and will spread it to anything she touches, such as food, equipment, and clothes. Hand and nail brushes, antibacterial soaps, and disposable gloves should be a part of every bar/restaurant, even if not required by law. Proper training and management follow-up is also critical.

Every employee must practice good basic hygiene:

- Short hair, and/or hair contained in a net.

- Facial hair contained in a net or clean shaven.

- Clean clothes/uniforms.

- Clean hands and short nails.

- No unnecessary jewelry.

- A daily shower or bath.

- No smoking in or near the kitchen.

- Hand washing prior to starting work, periodically, and after handling any foreign object: head, face, ears, money, food, boxes, or trash.

An employee who has the symptoms of the common cold or any open cuts or infections should not go to work. By simply breathing, he or she may be inadvertently exposing the environment to bacteria. Although it is rarely practiced in the food industry, all employees should be required to have a complete medical examination as a condition of employment. This should include blood and urine tests. A seemingly healthy individual may unknowingly be the carrier of a latent communicable disease.

"ARE YOUR HANDS REALLY CLEAN?"

Hand washing is perhaps the most critical aspect of good personal hygiene in food service. Workers should wash their hands with soap and warm water for 20 seconds. When working with food, they should wash gloved hands as often as bare hands. Hand washing is such a simple yet effective method for eliminating cross-contamination. Try the following exercise:

You'll need a fluorescent substance and a black light. (One possible source for these is Atlantic Publishing's Glo Germ Training Kit. See **www.atlantic-pub. com** or call 800-814-1132.) Using these materials, you can show trainees the "invisible dirt" that may be hiding on their hands:

1. Have employees dip their hands in the fluorescent substance.

2. Tell employees to wash their hands.

3. Have employees hold their hands under the black light to see how much "dirt" is still there.

4. Explain proper hand-washing technique.

5. Have employees wash their hands again, this time using the proper hand-washing technique.

6. Have employees once again hold their hands under the black light.

AIDS

AIDS is not an airborne, waterborne, or food-borne disease. It cannot be transmitted through air, water, or food. The only medically documented manner in which HIV, the virus which is believed to cause AIDS, can be contracted is by sexual contact, by shared needles (usually associated with drug addiction), by infusion of contaminated blood, or through the placenta from mother to fetus.

- You cannot contract AIDS through casual, social contact.

- You cannot contract AIDS by touching people.

- You cannot contract AIDS through shared bathroom facilities.

- You cannot contract AIDS by breathing air in which people have sneezed or coughed.

- You cannot contract AIDS by sharing food, beverages, or eating utensils.

This means that, with regard to AIDS, food service operations are safe places to work and dine.

Bugs, Insects, and Animal Pests

Bug and insect infestation is the result of poor sanitation practices. Aside from being a nuisance, they are a threat to food safety. Flies, cockroaches, and other insects all carry bacteria, and many, because of where they get their food, carry disease. Bugs, insects, and animals require the same three basic necessities of life as bacteria do: food, water, and warmth. When healthful, thriving bugs and insects are visible, this is an indicator that proper sanitation procedures have not been carried out. Eliminate the environment that these pests need to live, and you will be eliminating their existence. Combining proper sanitation practices with periodic extermination spraying will stop any problems before they start.

To prevent the spread of flies in your establishment, keep all doors, windows, and screens closed at all times. Ensure that garbage is sealed in airtight containers and is picked up regularly. All trash must be cleaned off the ground: flies can deposit their eggs on the thinnest scrap of food. Dumpsters must be periodically steam cleaned and deodorized. They should never contain any decaying food scraps.

All doorjambs and building cracks, even the thinnest ones, must be sealed. Be cautious when receiving deliveries; bugs may be in the boxes or crates. The greatest protection against cockroaches is your exterminator. Of course, the exterminator will be of little value if you do not already have good sanitary practices in place. Select an exterminator who is currently servicing other bars and restaurants. Chemicals sprayed in a bar or restaurant must be of the non-residual type. These are safe and approved for use in food service establishments. Rodents are prolific breeders, producing as many as fifty offspring in a life span of one year. They tend to hide during the day, but they can be discovered by their telltale signs, including the following:

- Droppings

- Holes

- Nesting materials

- Gnawing

- Tracks on dusty surfaces

Animal pests, such as rats and mice, may be very serious problems for the bar/restaurant operator. These rodents can eat through a cement wall to gain access to your building. They are filthy animals that will eat any sort of garbage or decaying food available. Rats are infested with bacteria and, often, disease. They have been known to bite people, as have their fleas, which also spread their bacteria and disease. Rats and mice have evolved into creatures highly developed for survival. Once they have become settled in an area, they are very difficult to get rid of. They are prolific breeders and spread rapidly.

Rats and mice, like flies, are attracted to exposed garbage. They are extremely strong and can easily gain access to a building through a crack or hole no larger than a quarter. Ensure that your building's foundation is airtight. Keep all food products at least 6 inches off the floor; this enables the exterminator to get under the shelving to spray. Rat bait, a poisoning capsule resembling food, is particularly effective when spread around the building and dumpsters. As with any poison or chemical you use, make certain that it is labeled clearly and stored away from food storage areas.

Kitchen Safety

By its nature, the food service environment is full of potential hazards to employees' safety. Knives, slicers, grinders, glass, hot surfaces, and wet or greasy floors are only a few of the hazards food service workers face every day. Fortunately, most accidents also involve human error and, therefore, can be prevented.

Heat and Burns

There are many ways employees can get burned in a food service environment unless they're very careful. Burns can result from contact with hot surfaces such as grills, ovens, burners, fryers, and other heating equipment. Burns can also be caused by escaping steam or by hot food or drinks that are splattered, splashed, or spilled.

To prevent burns:
- Use thick, dry potholders or mitts, and stir food with long-handled spoons or paddles.

- Turn on hot-water faucets cautiously. Wear insulated rubber gloves for rinse water that is 170°F. Follow instructions for the use of cooking equipment—particularly steam equipment. Be sure all steam is expelled from steamers before opening the doors.

- Lift cooking lids and similar equipment away from yourself to avoid burns from steam.

- To avoid splattering and splashing, don't fill kettles too full. Also, don't allow food to boil over.

- Remember that oil and water don't mix, so be sure food is dry before you place it in a fryer.

- Point pan handles away from foot traffic, but also within reach, to avoid knocking over other pans.

- Do not crowd cooking surfaces with hot pans. Remove cooked foods from cooking surfaces immediately.

- Allow oil to cool, and use extreme caution when cleaning fryers.

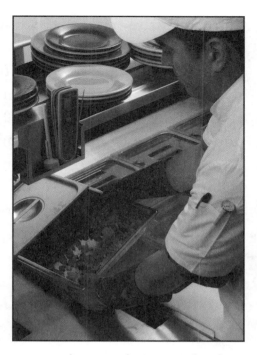

DayMark's SteamGlove™ provide safe and sanitary protection to employees who are working in wet and messy applications. This watertight protection withstands oven range temperatures and hot oil without melting.

- Use caution when removing hot pans from the oven. Wear insulated gloves or mitts, and be certain no one is in the removal path.

- Do not wear clothing that may drape onto a hot spot and catch on fire.

To follow are some resources for kitchen safety products:

- **DayMark Safety Systems** carries a wide assortment of gloves from food protection and sanitation gloves to the toughest cut and work gloves available.With a complete line of BurnGuard® with VaporGuard™ gloves, mitts, hot pads, and aprons, DayMark will help keep your staff free of burns, with products that will keep you safe up to 900°F. For more information, contact **www.daymark.biz** or call 1- 800-847-0101.

Duncan Industries also produces a full line of hand safety products including oven mitts and hot pads. They are designed to increase safety, hygiene, and sanitation in your kitchen and catering operation. They repel water, steam, and liquids and provide maximum protection from painful steam burns caused by wet protection equipment. Textured crosscut fabric provides a safer grip and increased control in busy operations. They are dishwasher safe and stain resistant. They are also sub-zero safe, so you can handle freezer foods, even dry ice. For more information, visit **www.kitchengrips.com** or call 800-785-4449.

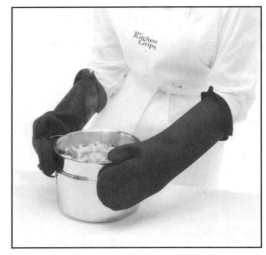

Cuts

Just as they need to take precautions to prevent being burned, food service workers also need to be careful not to get cut. And it's not just knives that can cause trouble.

Workers can hurt themselves—or their coworkers—with the sharp edges of equipment and supplies or with broken glass. Nails and staples used in food packaging can also be dangerous.

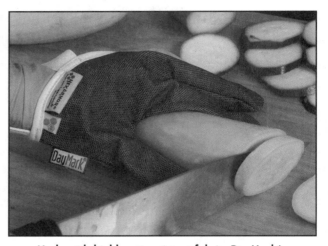

Made with highly cut-resistant fabric, DayMark's FingerArmor™ Cut Gloves protect workers from accidental cuts and pokes by shielding the most vulnerable parts of the hand—the middle finger, index finger, and thumb. Dual sided for superior protection, FingerArmor™ Cut Gloves can be worn under latex, vinyl, nitrile, or poly gloves, making them ideal for food preparation. With their flexible fit, FingerArmor™ Cut Gloves give operators full range of motion, significantly reducing slippage. The gloves are machine washable and can be easily sanitized.

To prevent cuts, take the following precautions:

- Use appropriate tools (not bare hands) to pick up and dispose of broken glass. Immediately place broken glass into a separate, clearly marked garbage container.

- Take care when cutting rolls of kitchen wrap with the cutter.

- Be careful with can openers and the edges of open cans. Never use a knife to open cans or to pry items loose.

- Use a pusher to feed food into a grinder.

- Turn off and unplug slicers and grinders when removing food and cleaning.

- Use guards on grinders and slicers.

- Replace equipment blades as soon as they are cleaned.

- Be aware that left-handed people need to take extra care when working with slicers and similar equipment. This is because the safety features on this equipment are usually designed for right-handed people.

In addition:

- Keep knives sharp. Dull blades are harder to work with and cause more cuts than sharp ones.

- Never leave knives or equipment blades in the bottom of a sink.

- Carry knives by the handle with the tip pointed away from you.

- Never try to catch a falling knife.

- Cut away from yourself on a cutting board.

- Slice, do not hack.

Also, when you're storing or cleaning equipment, be sure to:

- Store knives and other sharp tools in special places when not in use.

- Wash dishes and glasses separately to help prevent them from being crushed by heavier objects and breaking in the dishwasher or sink.

- Do not stack glasses or cups inside one another.

- Watch out for nails, staples, and protruding sharp edges while unpacking boxes and crates.

Electrical Shock

Because of the variety of electrical equipment used in food service, electrical shock is a common concern.

To prevent electrical shock:

- Properly ground all electrical equipment.

- Ensure that employees can reach switches without touching or leaning against metal tables or counters.

- Replace all worn or frayed electrical cords.

- Use electrical equipment only when hands are dry.

- Unplug equipment before cleaning.

- Locate electrical switches and breakers to permit rapid shutdown in the event of an emergency.

Strains

Carrying equipment or food items that are too heavy can result in strains to the arms, legs, or back.

To prevent strains:

- Store heavy items on lower shelves.

- Use dollies or carts to move objects that are too heavy to carry.

- To move objects from one area to another, use carts with firm shelves and properly operating wheels or casters.

- Don't carry too many objects at one time; instead, use a cart.

- Don't try to lift large or heavy objects by yourself.

- Use proper lifting techniques. Remember to bend from your knees, not your back.

Slipping and Falling

Anyone who slips and falls onto the floor can be badly hurt. Be sure your facility does not have hazards that put workers at risk.

To prevent slips and falls:

- Clean up wet spots and spills immediately.

- Let people know when floors are wet. Use signs that signal caution, and prominently display them.

- Wear shoes that have no-slip soles.

- Do not stack boxes or other objects too high. They can fall and cause people to trip.

- Keep items such as boxes, ladders, step stools, and carts out of the paths of foot traffic.

Fires

More fires occur in food service than in any other type of operation. Fire extinguishers should be available in all areas where fires are likely, especially in the kitchen near grills and deep fryers. But be careful: Don't keep extinguishers so close to the equipment that they will be inaccessible in the event of a fire.

All employees should be trained in avoiding fires as well as in the use of fire extinguishers and in evacuation procedures. Remember: Always call the fire department before using a fire extinguisher!

Choking

As kids, probably we all heard our parents say: "Don't eat so fast! Chew your food properly!" They may have added, "Don't talk while you're eating," and "Drink your milk carefully!"

It's good advice for children—and for adults. Anyone can choke on food if he or she is not careful. That's why an important part of food service safety is being alert to your customers.

Here's what to look for and what to do:

- If a person has both hands to the throat and cannot speak or cough, it is likely he or she is choking.

- If this person can talk, cough, or breathe, do not pat him or her on the back or interfere in any way.

- If this person cannot talk, cough, or breathe, you will need to take action. Use the Heimlich maneuver, and call for help immediately.

All food service employees should be trained in the use of the Heimlich maneuver, and posters with instructions on how to perform it should be posted near the employee dining area.

Exposure to Hazardous Chemicals

Improper exposure to cleaning agents, chemical pesticides, and chemical sanitizers may cause injury to the skin or poisoning. To protect workers from exposure to hazardous materials, special precautions need to be taken, including certain steps that are required by law.

For example, the U.S. Department of Labor's Occupational Safety and Health Administration (OSHA) requires food service establishments to keep a current inventory of all hazardous materials.

Manufacturers are required to make sure hazardous chemicals are properly labeled and must supply a Material Safety Data Sheet (MSDS) to be kept on file at the food service facility. The MSDS provides the chemical name of the product and physical hazards, health hazards, and emergency procedures in case of exposure.

Information about each chemical—including its common name, when it is used, who is authorized to use it, and information from the MSDS—must also be provided to workers.

To prevent improper exposure to hazardous materials, make sure:

- Only properly trained workers handle hazardous chemicals.

- Employees have safety equipment to use when working with hazardous chemicals.

- Employees wear nonporous gloves and eye goggles when working with sanitizing agents and other cleaners.

Improper handling of food products or neglecting sanitation and safety procedures will certainly lead to health problems and/or personal injury. A successful bar/restaurant must develop a reputation for serving quality food in a safe environment. Should there ever be a question in your customers' minds as to the wholesomeness or quality of a product, the bar/restaurant will quickly lose its hard-earned reputation. The sanitation and safety procedures described in this section are very simple to initiate, but management must follow up and enforce them.

Continue to communicate important safety information to your employees by posting these colorful, four-color, informative safety and human resource posters throughout your workplace. Each poster is 11" x 17" and is laminated for long-term protection. Posters are available in English or Spanish.

Topics include First Aid for Burns, First Aid for Cuts & Wounds, First Aid for Choking, Proper Lifting, Emergency Phone Numbers, Drug-Free Workplace, Fire Extinguisher Use, CPR Guidelines, Falling, and Sexual Harassment. To order, call Atlantic Publishing at 1-800-814-1132 or visit www. atlantic-pub.com.

English (All 10 Posters) • Item # WPP-PS • $79.95

Spanish (All 10 Posters) • Item # WPPSP-PS • $79.95

These eye-catching posters help you ensure compliance with FDA/USDA regulations and best food-safety practices. Make sure your employees are aware of critical requirements and practices with these quality, affordable posters. Display in key work areas so important food-safety messages will be continually reinforced. Posters include a message in both English and Spanish. Each 11" W x 17" H, easy-to-read poster is built to last. Heavy, 3-mil lamination with sealed edges protect against damage (set of 16). Item # FSP-PS $99.95 Topics covered are: Wash Your Hands; Step-By-Step Handwashing; Wash Your Hands After...; Clean Up Spills; Don't Contaminate; Personal Hygiene; Keep It Clean; Manual Dishwashing; 7 Principles of HACCP; Wear Food-Safety Equipment; Separate, Don't Contaminate; Cooking Temperatures; Keep Doors and Windows Closed; Food Rotation (First In, First Out); Proper Food Storage; and Thermometer Calibration. To order, call Atlantic Publishing at 1-800-814-1132 or visit www.atlantic-pub.com.

CHAPTER NINE

Bar Controls

Controlling liquor and its cost is a continual battle for the bar manager. Liquor is one of the most commonly pilfered items in bars and restaurants. Every employee has access to it at some time. It's valuable, desirable, and difficult to account for. Unlike food items, liquor is not generally in exact portions, so it is difficult to determine if a small amount is missing, except when using the computerized bar. Only one person—the bartender—controls the portion size; no one generally checks on his or her pouring until it is too late. The greatest control you can establish in the bar is to employ honest, mature, and concerned employees.

Described in this section is a system where every bottle is accounted for so you will be able to determine if one is missing. However, when the bartender is pouring, he or she is controlling the cost. Every month a liquor cost of sales will be projected, but should there be a cost problem, you will not realize it until the end of the month. Management must take an active daily involvement in the bar in order for it to be a financial success. The systems outlined in this section are based upon this crucial point.

First Step: Security

The first step in developing control over liquor cost is to ensure that it is received and stored properly. The manager must be present and take an active part in receiving the liquor delivery. Once verified, the delivery must be placed immediately into the locking storage room. With the exception of wine, nothing but liquor should be stored in the liquor storage room. Again, the manager must be the only person (apart from you, the owner) with a key to the storage room; the control system described in this section is based upon this certainty. The door to the storage area must have non-removable hinges and a sliding bolt lock.

Juices, mixers, and other bar items of this nature may be stored at the bar or in the food storage area. They cannot be kept in the liquor storage room, as the bartender will not have access to this room. The manager should not get into the habit of lending out his or her keys; if an article is needed from a locked storage room, the manager should retrieve it or accompany the employee retrieving it.

The bar itself needs to be as secure as the storage room. Every bottle must be locked up at the end of each shift. Many bars have sliding doors or removable panels that can be locked to cover the shelves of liquor. These are excellent devices, but make certain the hinges are non-removable and on the inside. Locks and latches should be commercial grade and of tempered steel. Refrigerators and coolers usually have locks on the handles, but most of these are weak and can be jimmied with a knife blade; replace them with latches and locks.

The walk-in where the beer and kegs are stored must be separated from the food area. If you do not have the room or capital to build a separate walk-in, section off an area for the exclusive use of the bar. Screened partitions with lockable doors can be purchased from your food service supplier or made locally by a welder. If the beer system does not already have one, install a cut-off valve in the walk-in. This will enable the system to be shut off after each shift.

The number of bottles of liquor stored at the bar is an integral part of the control system. Each type of liquor and each brand must have only two bottles at the bar at any time: one opened bottle and one unopened bottle for backup. Unless you have an extremely busy lounge, this amount will suffice. Should the bar run out of a particular bottle, the manager will have to go to the storage room to retrieve one.

Bartender's Procedures

Once an open bottle is exhausted, remove the pouring spout and place the spout on the unopened backup bottle. Do not throw the empty bottle out. Store it in a box along with the other empties under the bar.

At the end of the shift, complete a Liquor Used and Restocked Form. List the exhausted bottles and the number of each under the appropriate columns. The "Restocked" column of this form will be completed by the manager. Double-check to be sure that the empty bottles correspond to the ones listed on the form. Give this form to the manager when checking out.

Liquor Restocking

On a daily basis the manager must restock, from the storage room, all the liquor used the night before at the bar. First, compare the Liquor Used and Restocked Form completed by the bartender with the empty bottles at the bar. Each entry on the list must correspond to an empty bottle in the case. This will ensure that the bottle was actually used at the bar. After verification, the empty bottles may be thrown away or stored for the recycle center. Using the list completed by the bartender, restock the bottles needed from the storage room. Under the "Restocked" column of the form, fill in the number of bottles restocked. When the restocking is completed, there should be two bottles for each type of liquor at the bar. Should there be less than two, either the bartender made an error or a theft has occurred.

This system of restocking replaces every emptied bottle with a new one. Since the manager is doing the actual restocking, no bottle will ever become lost or stolen from storage. This system enables you to pinpoint areas that are cost problems. If the liquor cost-of-sales percentage is high at the end of the month, you can be certain that the bartender is responsible. He or she is either over-pouring or not following some other procedure, which resulted in a cost increase. You can base this assumption on the fact that every bottle delivered to the bar was accounted for; only under the bartender's control did the cost problem arise.

Inventory Controls

At the bar itself or in storage, an accurate liquor inventory is vital in controlling costs and maintaining profitability. There are a number of computerized systems available that can help with this process. To follow are some examples:

- **AccuBar** is an excellent example of a computerized inventory system. Customers report a 50 to 80 percent time savings when using the AccuBar system. It's easy to learn: most users are up and running within 30 minutes. The patented technology eliminates the need to estimate levels; simply tap the fluid level on the bottle outline. Once you tap the bottle outline, data entry is complete. There is no further human intervention. Since no data entry or third party is involved, reports are generated immediately. It also provides a running perpetual inventory. Transfers between locations and returns of defective items are also covered. AccuBar also helps gauge which items aren't selling, allowing you to consider stocking something else that might bring a better return. AccuBar also recommends what needs to be ordered from each supplier based on current perpetual, par, and reorder points. The order is totally customizable. When a shipment arrives, simply scan the items; any discrepancy from what was ordered is caught immediately. AccuBar can also track food, glassware, china, and other essentials.

- **The Accardis Liquor Inventory System** is another option to save time and money and eliminate over-pouring and theft. Since 1987, Accardis Systems has been controlling liquor inventory costs. Accardis was

Cyclops Falcon Inventory System Overview: First, identify the product by scanning the bar codes or using the find key. Next, weigh open bottles. Quantities are automatically sent to CYCLOPS with precise electronic accuracy. Third, enter quantity. Use the keypad to enter full unit quantities or to estimate open bottles if scale not used. Finally, generate reports and download data to a PC via the Falcon Docking Cradle.

the originator of scanning and weighing bottles to control inventory. The alcohol inventory system has proven to be fast and accurate. It will lower your costs while increasing your profits. Most clients recover the cost of the liquor inventory system in only a few months. The Cyclops Falcon scans and weighs liquor bottles electronically and then downloads the data to the PACER 4.0 for Windows software. Pacer prints out all the management reports on a station-by-station basis. The liquor inventory system also tracks all purchases and requisitions and can be used for liquor, beer, wine, supplies, hats, T-shirts, etc. Cyclops Falcon gives the user complete control of beverages at a fraction of the cost of most other systems. For more information, contact Accardis Systems, Inc., 20061 Doolittle Street, Montgomery Village, MD 20886. Call 1-800-852-1992 or visit **www.accardis.com**.

Controlling Mixed Drinks

Drinks need to be closely controlled in order to keep profits and customer satisfaction high. Customers who feel they are getting less for their money are unlikely to return. On the other hand, if your bartender consistently over-pours, even by a small amount, then you are effectively giving away free drinks for no reason. Controlling pours, then, is a major concern for bar managers everywhere, and a number of solutions have been put forth to help bars deal with this common problem.

In deciding how much liquor should be poured into each drink, try out several drinks and decide based on drink quality. In most bars, shots range from $\frac{9}{8}$ of an ounce to 1½ ounces. Any more or less affects quality. In many bars, the standard is one ounce. In general, you should make pours consistent. If you make some of your mixed drinks with ⅞-ounce shots, some with 1-ounce shots, some with 1½-ounce shots, and so on, you will create extra work for your bartender, as he or she will need to refer to your recipes for each drink, slowing down service and creating frustration all around.

Controlling Pouring

You want to give your bartender the tools needed to create drinks according to your specifications. By eliminating over-pour and spillage, bar owners and managers save money on every bottle served. If your bartender over-pours just ⅛ ounce per drink, your loss could be up to four drinks per bottle.

Liquor-control systems (LCS). Use of technologically advanced portion-control systems is becoming increasingly commonplace in today's drinks industry. LCSs are particularly effective at controlling liquor costs. They can also virtually eliminate employee theft. LCSs are marketed on the basis of a typical return on investment within 12 months. The following suppliers offer LCSs:

Berg Company
www.berg-controls.com
608-221-4281

AzBar
www.azbaramerica.com
214-361-2422

Bristol BM
www.bristolnf.com/liquor.htm
709-722-6669

Easybar Beverage Management Systems
www.easybar.com
503-624-6744

Precision Pours
www.precisionpours.com
1-800-549-4491

- **Easybar Beverage Management Systems** (**www.easybar.com**) has multiple solutions for beverage portion control. The Easybar CLCSII is a fully computerized beverage-dispensing system that controls beverage pour sizes, improves bartender speed, and ensures perfectly portioned drinks and cocktails. This 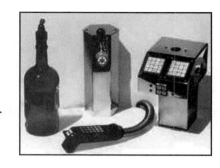 system also prevents product loss by eliminating over-pouring, spillage, breakage, and theft. It accounts for all beverages dispensed through the system and boosts receipts by lowering costs and increasing account-ability. Also available is the Easypour Controlled Spout System. This offers control for drinks that are dispensed directly from a bottle. The controlled pour spouts allow only preset portions to be dispensed and will not allow drinks to be dispensed without being recorded. Easybar's Cocktail Station creates cocktails at the touch of a button. The cocktail tower can dispense up to 48 liquors plus any combination of 10 juices or sodas. It mixes cocktails of up to five ingredients, and ingredients dispense simultaneously to cut pour time. All ingredients dispense in accurate portions every time.

- **Precision Pours** (**www.precisionpours.com**) manufacturers measured liquor pours, gravity-feed portion control systems, and bar accessories. By eliminating over-pour and spillage with the Precision Pour™ 3 Ball Liquor Pour, users save money on every bottle served. The Precision Pour™ 3 Ball Liquor Pour allows bartenders to pour liquor with one hand while mixing with the other, speeding up drink production. Also, since there is no need to use a messy shot glass, additional time is saved on cleanup. It also strictly 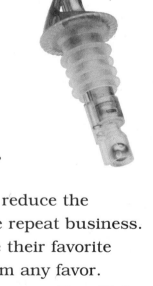 regulates alcohol. A drink that is too strong will likely reduce the number of drinks customers will order and discourage repeat business. Your customers want their favorite drinks to taste like their favorite drinks. Pour them a stiff one and you're not doing them any favor. Under-pour and you're likely to rile them. With the Precision Pour™ 3 Ball Liquor Pour, you'll get the same great taste every time, no matter who's pouring. The Precision Pour™ 3-Ball Liquor Pour features:

  – A new third ball bearing to guarantee accuracy.

– A primer ring surrounding the ball bearing to ensure no sticking, even with cordials.

– A bottom made from a solid piece of surgical plastic guarantees that the ball bearings cannot fall out into your bottles.

– A new cork that will fit all your liter bottles including Absolute, Crown Royal, and Jack Daniels.

Free Pouring

Another alternative for controlling the amount of liquor is to use the free pour. In the free pour, the bartender uses liquor pour spouts or shot glasses to measure liquor amounts. The liquor is measured and then mixed into the drink. Bar management does lose control of the amount poured in this system since the bartender is the one controlling the pours, but this is not a problem if you trust your bartender to pour the amounts you have designated for each drink. The advantages

BarVision gives the illusion of free pouring with wireless liquor pour spout that allows you to track liquor inventory usage automatically in real time.

of free pouring include more showmanship and personality to each drink, which many customers prefer, and less expensive setup of materials needed. The free-pour system does rely more on a dependable and skilled bartender, however.

Modern technology has influenced free pouring as well. BarVision combines free pouring with wireless liquor inventory control. It allows you to track liquor inventory usage automatically in real-time. Every pour is transmitted to BarVision by a wireless liquor pour spout. Every empty liquor bottle is reconciled automatically—eliminating the need for manual inventory procedures. BarVision reports provide extensive flexibility, whether you need a usage summary for a quick grasp on your open liquor inventory or a journal detail for reconciling your POS/register receipts. It does not require extensive wiring or hardware installation.

Here's how it works:

1. Bartenders free-pour drinks.

2. The pour spouts transmit data about the pours to the receiver.

3. BarVision "talks" to the receiver and keeps a journal.

4. Managers print reports from BarVision's journal.

For more information, visit **www.barvision.com** or call 480-222-6000.

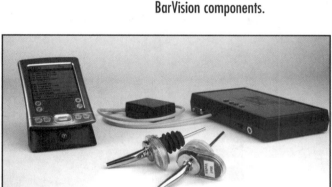

BarVision components.

Automation

In the future, you may even be able to do away with bar staff completely. Check out this automated option:

- **Motoman's RoboBar.** This is a complete, self-contained robotic bar that serves mixed drinks, draft beer, wine, sodas, and juices, highlighting potential applications in the growing service sector. RoboBar features a UPJ dual-arm robot with a compact NXC100 controller housed in the base of the robot. The two manipulator arms on this unique robot each have five axes of motion, and the base also rotates to provide an eleventh axis of motion. The end-of-arm tooling consists of simple parallel grippers. A safety enclosure is included. Programming is easy, and the user interface is intuitive and graphics-based. The system is designed to use a magnetic card scanner to authorize drink service. After a valid card swipe, the customer uses a touch screen to choose a beverage. The Motoman UPJ dual-arm robot selects a cup, and then fills it with the appropriate beverage(s) and ice, if desired. The robot then passes the drink to the customer via an automatic turntable located at the side of the cell. "Robots are fascinating to watch, and the entertainment factor alone makes RoboBar a customer magnet," says Ron Potter, Motoman's Senior Director of Emerging Robot Markets. "But RoboBar not only out-draws the competition, it also out-pours and out-performs, while improving profits and pleasing customers—giving establishments a big advantage in the 'bar wars,' " he continues. "RoboBar doesn't take tips, so customers can spend more money on drinks. RoboBar is never late for work and doesn't get tired. Interaction with customers is always friendly. Plus, it doesn't drink on the job or dip into the till—and smoke doesn't bother the robot," he explains. For more information on Motoman products and services, visit the corporate Web site at **www .motoman.com**, call 937-847-6200, or write to Motoman Inc. at 805 Liberty Lane, West Carrollton, Ohio 45449.

Point-of-Sale Systems

The most widely used technology to help control costs in the food service and beverage industry is the touch-screen, or point-of-sale (POS), system. The POS system is basically an offshoot of the electronic cash register. Touch screen POS systems were introduced to the food and beverage industry in the mid-1980s and have penetrated 90 percent of establishments nationwide. The touch screen is effortless. In fact, a child could be trained to use it in a few minutes. Such systems will pay for themselves. According to information published by the National Restaurant Association, an operation averaging $1,000,000 in food-and-beverage sales can expect to see an estimated savings of $30,000 per year. Understanding the numbers collected by a POS system will give the operator more control over inventory, bar revenues, labor scheduling, overtime, customer traffic, and service. Understanding POS ultimately clarifies the bottom line, knocking guesswork out of the equation.

A POS system is comprised of two parts: the hardware, or equipment, and the software, the computer program that runs the system. This system allows waitstaff to key in their orders as soon as the customers give them. Additional keys are available for particular options and specifications.

The order is sent through a cable to printers located throughout the establishment: at the bar and in the kitchen and office. All orders must be printed before they are prepared, thus ensuring good control. When a server has completed the ordering, a guest check can be printed and later presented. Most POS systems allow certain discounts and require manager control over others. Charge cards, cash, and checks can be processed separately, and then reports can be generated by payment type.

Some benefits of using a POS system:

- Increases sales and accounting information.

- Custom tracking.

- Reports waitstaff's sales and performance.

- Reports menu-item performance.

- Reports inventory usage.

- Track credit card purchases.

- Accurate addition on guest checks.

- Prevents incorrect items from being ordered.

- Prevents confusion in the kitchen.

- Reports possible theft of money and inventory.

- Records employee timekeeping.

- Reports menu-sales breakdown for preparation and menu forecasting.

- Reduces time spent walking to kitchen and bar.

As the labor market continues to diminish, touch-screens POS systems will become necessary. Many POS systems have been greatly enhanced to include guest books, online reservations, and fully integrated systems with real-time inventory, integrated caller ID, accounting, labor scheduling, payroll, menu analysis, purchasing and receiving, cash management, and reports. Up-and-coming enhancements and add-ons include improved functionality across the Internet, centralized functionality enabling "alerts" to be issued to managers and voice-recognition POS technology.

The following are some sources for POS systems:

- **Exadigm.** ExaDigm has taken a fresh new approach to POS connectivity with the launch of the Mate Plus point-of-sale terminal and in turn created a whole new way of doing business. With its unique modular format and interchangeable modems supporting IP  (Ethernet), WiFi, cellular, and dial-up connections, the Mate Plus offers speed, portability, mobility, changeability, and universal connectivity.

Featuring a fully modular design and PC-based Linux operating system, merchants now only need to purchase a single terminal that offers multiple connectivity options, easy software upgrades, and simple configuration to adapt to new technologies. The Mate Plus terminal delivers a solution that is easier, faster, and ultimately cheaper—and that means a drastically streamlined product for both the merchant and those that support it. For more information, visit **www.exadigm.com**.

InTouchPOS

- **InTouchPOS®-Advanced Restaurant POS System**. InTouchPOS® is an advanced and user-friendly touch-screen point-of-sale system capable of handling every type of food service or beverage operation. Visit **www.intouchpos.com** or call 800-777-8202 for more information.

- **Vital Link POS** is another comprehensive and cost-effective point-of-sale system. With a robust set of integrated order, delivery, and management reporting features, Vital Link POS delivers efficient operations, increased profitability, and greater control. Spend less time worrying about business operations and more time spent improving the bottom line. Vital Link POS is specifically designed for easy order entry of complex menu choices. Vital Link POS offers your bar a comprehensive point-of-sale solution. For more information, visit **www.vitallinkpos.com** or call 877-448-5300.

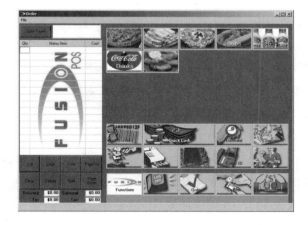

Vital Link POS Screen

Accounting for Bar Sales

There are many different ways to control or account for liquor sales. This section will outline some basic operating procedures that may be instituted in any bar using a manual ticket system.

Liquor sales are derived from three sources: 1) customers at the bar, which the bartender governs, 2) orders from the lounge, which are usually handled by the cocktail waitress/waiter, and 3) customers in the dining room. The control system for accounting for each liquor sale will be similar to the one used in the dining room for food items. Substitute the cocktail waiter for the waitress and the cashier, the bartender for the cook and dishwasher, and it is exactly the same setup as food sales.

Only one person—the bartender—is responsible for operating and accounting for the cash register. The manager will issue the cash drawer, bar tickets, and bar keys to the bartender at the same time the cashier drawer and server tickets are issued to the cashier. The bartender report is similar to the cashier report. It lists all the information necessary to account for all sales received at the register and to break them down into accounting terms for the bookkeeper. The cash drawer is prepared by the bookkeeper, and cash figures must be verified by the manager at the beginning and end of each shift. At the bottom of this form, spaces for verifying and issuing the bar tickets are listed.

Liquor, wine, and food sales must be kept separate when entered into the register; use a separate key for each.

Bar tickets may be the same as those used in the dining room. They should consist of two parts: the first being the heavy paper copy on which the order and other pertinent information is written; the bottom section is the tear-away customer receipt. The second is a carbon copy of the first; this is the slip from which the bartender prepares the order. Before starting any order, the bartender must make certain that the prices entered on the ticket are accurate and the bill is totaled.

Drink orders received at the bar by the bartender must be written like regular orders. The stiff paper copy of the ticket should be placed in front of the customer. Additional drinks may be written below the first one; this will ensure that all drinks are recorded on a ticket. A common ploy used by dishonest bartenders is to not write the order on a ticket at all—when the tab is paid, the bartender pockets the money. Prevent this problem by making it a mandatory procedure to record every drink served on a ticket and to place the ticket in front of the customer. A periodic stop by the bar to make sure all customers have bar-tab tickets is all that is needed to enforce this policy.

The easiest system to account for sales in the lounge is to keep a running tab of each customer at the bar. When the customer is finished, the cocktail waiter will pick up the money and the tab and give them to the bartender, who will ring the sale into the register. This system is impressively accurate; there is no way a sale could become lost. The disadvantage to this arrangement is that it tends to slow down the bartender, as he or she will spend more time at the register.

Most employees steal from their employers as a way to get even for some perceived injustice. Either they are unhappy with their pay scale or feel they are being otherwise treated unfairly. They compensate themselves by stealing. The easiest way to avoid this atmosphere of deceit and mistrust is to make certain that all employees are treated equally and fairly. Grievances should be aired before bad feelings can develop.

Get employees on your side by involving them in monthly inventories. Let them see what your costs are and that you are very concerned with what is taking place in the bar. Monthly bonuses or other incentives for maintaining consistent cost-of-sales percentages will compel the bartenders to become involved and concerned with controlling costs.

Controlling Wine

The manager must be present when a wine delivery is received to ensure it is accurate and accounted for. Wine must be put away immediately after delivery and locked securely. The manager must be the only person with the key to the storage area.

Wine should be issued by the bartender and restocked by the manager. Chilled wines may be stored in a cooler set at the proper temperature. Reds may be stored in a locked cabinet under the bar. Each serving area should be stocked with three of each type of white chilled wine and two types of each red. This will be more than sufficient for most bars.

When an order for wine is taken, the waiter goes to the bar and requests the bottle from the bartender. The bartender retrieves the bottle while the waiter fills out the ticket. The ticket should contain the following information: date, wine's name, table number, and the waiter's name. The bartender must check to make sure the information and price are correct before issuing the wine. The hard paper part of the ticket remains with the bartender and will be used to verify the issuance. The carbon copy is attached to the customer's bill; this is to ensure that the wine will be charged for. If for some reason the waiter does not enter the amount on the customer's check, there will be a record of the bottle ordered from the bar.

The cashier will total the bill, ensuring that the price entered is correct. At the end of his or her shift, the bartender will deposit the ticket receipts, with the liquor breakage form, in a place designated by the manager.

The following morning, the bookkeeper will prepare and present to the manager an itemized list of the bottles sold and verified by the cashier. This list must match the receipts left by the bartender.

As the liquor is being restocked, the manager should also restock the wine used. After restocking is completed, there should be three chilled whites and two reds for every variety. Should this count not reconcile, recheck the itemization and the bartender's receipts. If everything reconciles, consider the possibility of theft.

Bulk wine may be issued by the gallon and portioned into carafes. The bartender will list the number of carafes prepared at the beginning of the shift and the number left at the end. This information may be recorded on the Liquor Used and Restocked Form. The carafes may then be treated as though they were full bottles.

Controlling Communications

Controlling communication is another import (and often overlooked) bar control. With multiple shifts and numerous employees, a communication system is essential. We recommend implementing a communication manual. You can set up your own to keep track of scheduling, employees, and bar information or invest in a pre-formatted system.

- **COMMLOG** is a unique, fully customizable manager communication log. Created by hospitality professionals, COMMLOG's unique structure guides users through all parts of leaving a great note, improving communication and follow-up. COMMLOG utilizes a plastic coil binding so your log lays flat when open. It is available in either letter (8.5" x 11") or legal size (8.5" x 14"). COMMLOG covers all the important aspects of your business, with plenty of room for all your notes. COMMLOG is available in several formats, or you can customize it to fit your needs at no charge! There are many variations available, including a manager log and bar log. For more information, visit **www.commlog.com** or call 800-962-6564.

Controlling Cleanliness

Whether you hire a full-time cleaning staff or not, staff at every shift will need to ensure proper cleanliness before starting and after ending each shift. This ensures maximum cleanliness and hygiene for your bar. During each shift, you will want to adhere to the following cleaning practices:

Before each shift or day's work:

- Ensure that forms and paperwork are correctly filled out, filed, or sent to the proper persons. For example, restocking forms should be promptly delivered to suppliers to ensure that no important ingredient runs out.

- Ensure that tabletops are properly clean and set up with candles, ashtrays, and cutlery, as needed according to proper bar procedures.

- Ensure that side stands are clean.

- Look over the bar's general appearance—it should present a positive impression.

- Set lights to desired levels. Light candles, if used.

- Ensure that temperature is set to comfortable levels and there is adequate ventilation for pleasant dining.

- Ensure that walls are clean.

- Ensure that windows are clean and drapes or window treatments are either opened to let in light or closed to prevent glare (as is deemed best for customer comfort).

- Ensure that floors are clean and look nicely waxed.

- Ensure that furniture is properly arranged and looks polished. Tables and chairs should be checked to make sure that they don't totter.

- Look over glassware and cutlery to ensure that it is clean and ready to be used.

- Clean exterior of the bar, sweeping steps or shoveling the sidewalk if snow has fallen.

During each shift or day's work:

- Fill out and file forms as needed during work hours.

- Ensure that tabletops are properly clean and set up with candles, ashtrays, and cutlery, as needed according to proper bar procedures.

- Ensure that side stands are clean.

- Ensure that the bar's general appearance continues to present a positive impression.

- Set lights to desired levels. Relight candles, if used, as they burn out.

- Adjust temperature as needed to ensure that it stays at comfortable levels so that customers remain as comfortable as possible.

- Ensure that walls are clean.

- Ensure that windows remain clean and drapes or window treatments are either opened to let in light or closed to prevent glare (as is deemed best for customer comfort).

- Clean floors of any spills or breakages that occur during the work shift.

- Ensure that furniture continues to be comfortable. Rearrange furniture in order to accommodate preferred customer seating or larger parties.

- Keep an eye on glassware and cutlery to ensure that it is clean and free of chips and breaks. Clean glassware and cutlery regularly to ensure that fresh items are available for customers.

- Greet and serve customers, following as many customer suggestions as possible to ensure patron satisfaction.

After the day's work/shift:

- Ensure that forms and paperwork are correctly filled out, filed, or sent to the proper persons.

- Wipe down and clean tabletops and set up as needed according to proper bar procedures.

- Clean side stands.

- Clean exterior of the bar—sweep steps or shovel snow.

- Look over the bar's general appearance—it should present a positive impression.

- Turn of lights after all employees have left.

- Tally the day's earnings and expenses and remove all money from the premises.

- Turn down temperature to minimal night levels.

- Ensure that walls are clean.

- Ensure that windows are clean and drapes or window treatments are clean. Close windows securely and draw drapes or blinds as well.

- Clean and wax floors.

- Clean work areas.

- Clean bar.

- Clean kitchen and bathroom thoroughly.

- Polish furniture and arrange properly. Most bars will place chairs on tables to allow for easier cleaning of the floors.

- Lock up safes, liquor cabinets, and other secure areas well.

- Clean all glassware and cutlery to ensure that it is ready to go for the next shift.

- Leave till open.

- Put up "closed" sign and lock up all windows and doors. Double-check that all is secure.

CHAPTER TEN

Money

While every bar manager likes to see a hefty profit, money matters tend to be the least favorite part of running a business. In this chapter, you will learn the money facts that you need to understand, and you will learn valuable tips for coping with the money side of bar management.

Maximize Profits

Once your bar is open, it will start making profits on each drink sold. However, in today's competitive marketplace, a profit is not always enough to keep a bar in business. In many cases, you need to focus on getting more per drink in order to make your bar a success. There are several ways that the bar can help ensure a larger profit:

- **Offer your bar staff incentives** to make sure that you are getting the business you need. Your staff can help customers find a venue (your bar) for functions or can promote a drink that is a known profit maker if they know that they will get more money for it. If a staff member books an event that brings in $500, a $50 incentive for the staff member is well-spent money indeed.

- **Know which drinks make the most profit and advertise them.** Knowing which drinks can help bring in the money is key. Once you have figured out which items bring in the most money, make sure that you advertise them. Have staff mention these drinks by name, and make these drinks more visible and more visually appealing. In many cases, suppliers will help by providing you with coasters, posters, or other items that advertise certain brands.

- **Make sure your customers get value.** Too many business owners (and bar managers) cut corners, thinking that spending less means more profit. Studies have shown that the opposite is true—if the customer thinks they are getting more than they can expect, they will often respond in kind by patronizing the bar and bringing their friends.

- **Make it easy to linger.** Have interesting television on in the background. Have your staff ask "How about a round of coffee?" rather than "Would you like the bill?" The longer people linger at your pub or bar, the more they will buy. Also, if your bar has some people in it, it will be more appealing and lively to other customers. Customers are valuable—never rush them out.

- **Stay flexible.** Keep eyeing the crowd, and if you notice shifts in the crowd, be flexible enough to change to suit the crowd. Did a bachelor party just come in? Adjust by running a one-off special on beer or by turning on dance lights. Is there a more sedate crowd tonight? Bring things down a notch with softer music and lights. Your customers will appreciate the extra touch and will be more likely to stay if your place is just what they're are looking for.

- **Make sure that there is always someone on staff who can make executive decisions.** If there is a profit to be made and a customer to be satisfied by veering from the ordinary (by preparing special drinks or booking special functions), be sure that someone on staff can make the right decision for the bar, fast.

- **Cut down on how often you say no.** There is no way to satisfy each customer, but do try to keep a variety of things on hand so that you can make the drinks and snacks customers demand. Don't spend lots of time or money trying to buy every item, but do stock up on items that can be used in the near future (sodas, non-perishables). Make sure your staff know what is on hand and have them suggest an alternative when the customer asks for something that is not available. Whenever someone at your bar says no, they are giving a patron an excuse not to return.

- **Consider merchandise.** A great logo on T-shirts, pens, golf shirts, baseball caps, key chains, lighters, and glasses takes up little room but can bring in as much money (or even more) than your beverage items.

- **Consider vending machines.** Vending machines are easy places for customers to get anything from antacids, breath mints, phone cards, bottled water, condoms, feminine products, snacks, to cigarettes. Vending machines allow you to make a profit without taking much effort. Your local Yellow Pages can easily put you in touch with vending suppliers near you. You can even place your snack vending machines outside the bar proper so that you keep earning money while the bar is closed.

The Closeout and Audit

At the end of each month, it is important to close out all expenses and sales and balance all accounts. This process ensures that finances are being monitored and helps prevent financial problems down the line. It also lets you, the bar manager, see whether the bar is making a profit or not and what changes (if any) need to be made to operations.

Closeout actually depends on what goes on financially in your bar all month. It is essential that all expenses are recorded each day. Not having a reliable list of expenses incurred is sure to result in inaccurate bookkeeping and many problems at audit time. You need to record all expenses—including those that are prepaid or those for which you get a bill.

Monthly Audit Procedures

On the last day of the month:

1. Gather the completed inventory forms for food, liquor, wine, and operational supplies.

2. Using current invoices and past inventories, cost out the Inventory Form. The unit cost (or price) entered on the Inventory Form must correspond to the item and unit in the actual inventory. Correct prices are ensured by continual evaluation of invoices and/or contact with the suppliers.

3. Ensure that the employees organize and clean the storage areas and walk-ins so that the ending inventory may easily be taken the following morning. Combine all containers and bottles. Organize and label all shelves.

4. Schedule the bookkeeper and the employees involved in taking the physical inventory—the assistant manager, kitchen director, bar manager, and general manager—to arrive early in the morning prior to the start of business on the first of the month.

5. Schedule the preparation cooks to arrive an hour after the inventory crew so that you may inventory the food areas without disturbing them.

On the following morning, the first of the month:

6. The bookkeeper should arrive as early as possible in order to complete all of his or her work prior to management's completion of the inventory:

   A. Reconcile and record all the transactions from the previous day, as usual.

   B. Enter the information on the Daily Sales Report Form. Total, double-check, and verify all the columns.

C. From the employee time cards complete, total, double-check, and verify the Labor Analysis Form.

D. Ensure that all purchases are recorded in the Purchase Ledger. Complete, total, double-check, and verify the Purchase Ledger for each company. Total the purchases in each expenditure category: food, liquor, wine, and each individual operational category.

Ensure that all paid-outs entered on the Cashier's and Bartender's Reports have been posted into the appropriate Purchase Ledger categories. Total the cash paid-outs. Add this figure into the purchase total for each expense category.

COMPUTATION OF KEY PERCENTAGES	
Bar Supplies ÷ Bar Sales =	Bar Supplies Cost Percentage
Beer Cost ÷ Beer Sales =	Beer Cost Percentage
Food Cost ÷ Food Sales =	Food Cost Percentage
Labor ÷ Total Sales =	Labor Cost Percentage
Liquor Cost ÷ Liquor Sales =	Liquor Cost Percentage
Paper Cost ÷ Food Sales =	Paper Cost Percentage
Other ÷ Total Sales =	Other Cost Percentage
Wine Cost ÷ Wine Sales =	Wine Cost Percentage

Making Money Matters Easier on You

New bar managers, especially those who have never owned a business before, often find the process of caring for money matters quite daunting. There are a number of ways to make the process easier:

- **Keep excellent records.** Staying organized and holding on to all receipts is crucial. Invest in a filing cabinet and make sure to file all your receipts in a simple method that makes sense to you. Ideally, you want to be able to find any financial paper within minutes.

- **Set aside a time and place for money matters.** Each day, you should spend time considering the financial side of business. You should look at and file receipts, make payments, tally profits and debts, etc. This will make staying organized a habit. It will also prevent a buildup of financial matters that seems insurmountable.

- **Consider an accountant.** An accountant can help you by showing up once a week or once a month to help you complete your financial statements. Hiring an accounting service will mean an additional bill to pay, however. You will also want to go over the accountant's work on your own, to see how the financial side of things works. In general, it is a mistake to leave the entire financial management of your operation to another person. If you hire an accountant, stay involved in the financial work of your bar. An accountant, however, can be handy in the beginning, when you are just starting to learn the ropes.

- **Get tax help.** One place you will want help is in taxes. Tax laws are so complex that you will likely miss write-offs and other items if you do them yourself (unless, of course, you are a pro at doing taxes for business).

- **Consider financial software.** There are many titles out there that are made especially for small businesses, and they make managing money very easy. You can use the software to print checks, keep track of profits and debts, and you can even scan receipts right into virtual file folders—all without bulky filing cabinets. If you know your way around a computer, financial software can help make taking care of profits a snap.

- **Have a backup plan in case you suddenly can't use your cash registers.** Power failures and sudden mechanical problems can cost you a lot of money and always seem to occur at the worst time. Keep paper receipts and a calculator or small manual register under the bar so that staff can continue to serve customers, no matter what.

Making the Most from Sales

The savvy bar manager knows how to maximize profits and get the most sales possible without sacrificing ethics or drink quality. You can do the same if you follow a few simple tips. One simple way to maximize profits is by offering promotions or discounts. The small cost factor involved in initiating these promotions make them a good promotional vehicle.

"Happy hour," for example, a period of time when drink prices are generally reduced, can be an effective means of increasing bar sales. However, to be substantiated, it must draw a large volume of customers. "Happy hour" is most often run prior to opening the dining room, usually between 4 and 6 p.m. Drinks are sold at half-price or at a substantial discount. Hors d'oeuvres and salty snacks are often served, which will induce the customer's thirst.

In order to offset the enormous increase in the cost of sales due to the lower drink prices, total liquor sales must be increased substantially. A restaurant that lowers all drink prices by 50 percent during "happy hour" will be simultaneously doubling its cost of sales. When analyzing the feasibility of a "happy hour," you must also consider the additional cost of labor during a non-operating period; the food cost of hors d'oeuvres and other snacks; and any variable costs, such as the use of additional utilities.

The gross profit margin during any "happy hour" is small, though it can be substantiated with sufficient sales. An increase in revenue, small as it may be, will be created where none had previously existed.

There are other possible benefits from initiating a "happy hour." Lounge customers will be exposed to the restaurant and may wish to return at a later date to try the dining room. Customers may stay past the "happy hour" period and purchase cocktails at the full price or remain for dinner.

Employees will also benefit from a "happy hour" by an increase in income through increased hours and tips. This point is an important consideration, as employees may become discouraged during periods of slow or seasonal business. A "happy hour" that may not provide the restaurant with the desired profit may be deemed worthwhile for increasing employee morale and decreasing job turnover, eliminating the costly expenditure of rehiring and retraining new personnel.

Bar Tabs

Another way to maximize spending, and your bar's profits, is with bar tabs. Bar tabs make it easier for customers to spend without hassle, encouraging multiple orders of drinks. To allow bar tabs or not is a policy that can be debated from both sides with sound reasoning. Many bars and restaurants have been victimized by customers who walk out and do not pay their tabs. A policy of no bar tabs will alleviate the initial problem, but it will certainly be inconvenient—and possibly insulting—to some customers.

A bar tab should always be run if a customer so desires. The lounge is a place where the customer may relax and enjoy a cocktail before dinner. He should not be inconvenienced by paying for each drink order as he goes along. Drinks should also be automatically added to the dinner bill unless the customer wishes otherwise.

Money Losers

Money losers in a bar come in many forms, and you will want to check your financial records carefully to make sure that you are not being affected by one of these:

- **Imbalance in items.** Many managers think that by selling very low-priced drinks or by selling lots of high-priced items, profits will be optimized. Words like "most profitable" and "high price" often have a magic effect on bar managers who want to ensure a good profit. In fact, too much of any good thing is a problem because what customers really want is a decent variety of different prices and different items. If your menu is unbalanced your profits will veer up and down, with a general downward trend in many cases. Offer a decent variety, based on market research that suggests what customers want, and your profits will stay securely up.

- **Lack of local products.** Many bar managers will justify their lack of local beer by stating that their bar's style or type does not call for local beer. In fact, local beer and local food products are often the best-selling items in any bar. Many customers like or support the local beer, and visitors from other areas are often eager to try the local fare. Always offer local products, even if your bar has a uniquely international or exotic theme. As an added bonus, local products are often easier and less expensive to ship and buy, ensuring higher profit on your initial investment.

- **No plan.** Many bar owners have no clear plan of where their bar is headed and what they need to purchase and do to get there. Many say "I only want to run a bar." However, running a bar, like anything else, is a goal, and goals always require a plan. You should know where you will be expanding and how. You should know what products you need to order and when. Keeping everything on paper in the form of a business plan and purchase orders can help make it clear to you.

- **Theft.** Whether it is employees or customers that steal, every time something is taken from your bar, it is money out of your pocket. Many managers do not notice theft until after it has been going on for a long time. The best prevention of theft is careful checks and balances. Knowing how much inventory you have and checking registers and daily receipts is a good way to quickly spot discrepancies.

- **Spoiled food and drinks.** Spoiled product is lost profit. In some cases, such as a major power disruption, this can be hard to avoid. In most cases, though, spoilage is caused by ordering too much. This is avoidable. Keep track of your inventory and past purchasing patterns and buy those products that you need in the quantities they were needed in the past. Frequent checks on inventory tell you when you are running low and when you need to stock up on certain products.

- **No daily check.** Each day you need to be checking quality, prices, and invoices as well as the cash register tapes. Not doing so means that your bar is not being managed, and you are relying purely on fate to make a profit. Daily checks are the only way to keep quality high and spot problems (such as theft, discrepancies, bookkeeping problems, etc.) before they spiral out of control.

- **No control of storage area.** The liquor storage area should be locked and only the bar manager should have the key. However, all storage areas need to be controlled. This does not have to be complicated; simply have everyone taking something from the storage area write down when they removed something, what they took, and their initials. This information should be noted on a clipboard by the storage area. This will make it easier for you to control what is in inventory and where products have gone. Reordering and keeping track of use will be much easier.

- **No physical inventory.** If you do not regularly count the physical products on your shelf and compare them to what you think you have, you are sure to be in for a nasty surprise. Even though counting inventory is boring and very time consuming in a larger bar, it is necessary. Without this process, you have no real way of knowing what is on your shelves. You could be the victim of theft and not realize it.

- **Cutting corners on quality.** Many bar managers use a variety of ways to reduce quality. In many cases, they do this not to consciously deprive customers, but out of the mistaken belief that low quality costs less. They think that offering less for more will result in larger profits, when, in reality, cutting corners usually keeps customers from coming back. Quality products—be it fresh fruit in drinks, generous portions of drinks, or pleasant bathrooms—will bring the types of repeat customers who will ensure that you make money.

- **Staffing problems.** There are many staffing problems that can cost you money. Hiring or keeping unqualified or unproductive staff (because they are friends or family members, for example) is terrible for your bottom line. Selecting the wrong staff is a problem that can cost you a lot of money.

- **No rotation or improper rotation.** If you do not rotate your stock and inventory, those products will spoil, costing you money. Making sure that no perishable inventory is overlooked and allowed to spoil can save you money.

- **Inventory problems.** If you do not keep inventory adequately stocked, you will not be able to give customers the drinks and products they are requesting. If you cannot deliver the items that are on your menu because of poor reordering and inventory control, your bar will appear unreliable, and you will lose money by losing repeat business. Your bar should always be able to make the items on the menu.

- **Waste.** Whether bartenders spill a small amount of liquor with every pour or whether food is ordered in larger-than-needed amounts and then discarded, waste in any form takes away from your bottom line.

Pour controls and careful management of what needs to be ordered in what amounts is your best defense against waste and the money it costs your bar.

- **No set recipes and portion sizes.** While every experienced bartender may have his or her own idea about what goes into a drink, and while every cook may have their own idea about what constitutes a meal, these portions and recipes may not be what is best for your bottom line. Additionally, if every bartender and cook has different ideas about recipes and portion sizes, customers are going to be getting very different quality products from your bar. You need to control portion sizes and recipes of both drinks and food at your bar. Instruct your bar staff how you want drinks prepared and what sizes are appropriate. Make sure that all staff are following directions.

- **Poor storage, wrapping, and handling of liquor and foods.** Beer that is left out to get warm, meat that is thawed and allowed to spoil, and food and drinks that are incorrectly handled can mean waste or even food poisoning for your customers. You do not want the health department investigating your bar for poor management of food and drink. Make sure that you control how food and drinks are stored and handled. Food and drink preparation areas should be clean, and staff should keep all products that need to remain cold in the refrigerator or freezer. Food and drinks should be stored and served at their appropriate temperatures to ensure that your customers stay safe.

- **Employee dishonesty.** Employee theft and other forms of worker dishonesty cost employers in North America enormous sums of money each year. Bars, like any other places of employment, can provide the opportunity for embezzlement. Bar managers must keep close control over money and inventory to ensure that nothing suspicious is going on. Any suspicious or unexplained financial problems should be investigated as soon as they are discovered. Bars can also protect themselves from employee dishonesty by carefully checking references and, if appropriate, running background checks before hiring staff. Even temporary staff should be checked carefully before being hired to ensure that money loss will not come from poor staffing choices.

- **Poor attitude or atmosphere.** Customers want a place where they can relax and get great service. If your bar is unpleasant, you will lose money by losing customers. You need to make sure that your bar is an inviting place not only to drink and eat, but also to linger.

- **No customer concern or no customer market research.** Bar managers are busy people, and while they may not overlook customers on purpose, far too many lose sight of bar patrons as they worry about the many other elements of running a bar. Not catering to customers, however, can ensure that a bar will lose a lot of money. Not only will unsatisfied customers not return, but they will often share their experiences with other people—potential patrons. In order to avoid losing money, it is important for bar managers to not only please customers, but to impress them enough to make them wish to return. Regular market research will reveal not only who your bar's customers are, but also what they want.

Sample Forms for Your Business

To follow are a number of useful forms for your bar business. You can find additional forms in Chapter 19.

SAMPLE MONTH LIQUOR PURCHASES BY BOTTLE

BRAND	COST	NUMBER PURCHASED	TOTAL COST	$ PER DRINK	# OF DRINKS EA.	SALES BOTTLE VALUE/ SALES TOTAL VALUE
FRANGELICA	17.50	3	52.50	3.00	22.5	67.50 / 202.50
GALLIANO	12.55	1	12.55	2.50	22.5	56.25 / 56.25
BLUE CURACO	6.20	1	6.20	3.25	22.5	73.13 / 73.13
C BROS BRANDY	8.05	7	56.35	2.25	22.5	50.63 / 354.38
BL BER BRANDY	7.10	2	14.20	2.25	22.5	50.63 / 101.25
CHERRY BRANDY	7.10	1	7.10	2.25	22.5	50.63 / 50.63
CR DE CACAO DK	7.05	3	21.15	2.50	22.5	56.25 / 168.75
CR DE CACAO LT	7.05	1	7.05	2.50	22.5	56.25 / 56.25

BRAND	COST	NUMBER PURCHASED	TOTAL COST	$ PER DRINK	# OF DRINKS EA.	SALES BOTTLE VALUE/ SALES TOTAL VALUE
TANQUERAY	13.80	10	138.00	3.00	22.5	67.50 / 675.00
BOMBAY SAPPHIRE	14.80	2	29.60	3.00	22.5	67.50 / 135.00
BEEFEATER	13.85	11	152.35	3.00	22.5	67.50 / 742.50
ABSOLUT	13.15	3	39.45	3.00	22.5	67.50 / 202.50
STOLICHNAYA	12.70	10	127.00	3.00	22.5	67.50 / 675.00
SO COMFORT	7.90	3	23.70	2.50	22.5	56.25 / 168.75
AMARETTO	8.65	5	43.25	2.75	22.5	61.88 / 309.38
VERMOUTH	6.20	1	6.20	2.25	22.5	50.63 / 50.63
BUSHMILLS	14.90	10	149.00	3.00	22.5	67.50 / 675.00
KAHLUA	14.75	22	324.50	2.75	22.5	61.88 / 1361.25
BAILEYS	17.85	13	232.05	3.25	22.5	73.13 / 950.63
PEACH SCHNPS	6.35	8	50.80	2.25	22.5	50.63 / 405.00
RASPBERRY	5.70	1	5.70	2.25	22.5	50.63 / 50.63
CROWN ROYAL	5.75	6	94.50	3.00	22.5	67.50 / 405.00
MALIBU	8.65	20	173.00	2.75	22.5	61.88 / 1237.50
QUERVO GOLD	10.70	13	139.10	2.75	22.5	61.88 / 804.38
CUTTY SARK	5.70	7	109.90	3.00	22.5	67.50 / 472.50
DEWARS WHITE	15.50	7	108.50	3.00	22.5	67.50 / 472.50
RED LABEL	5.05	1	5.05	3.00	22.5	67.50 / 67.50
BACARDI LT	8.00	6	48.00	2.75	22.5	61.88 / 371.25
BARCARDI DK	8.00	3	24.00	2.75	22.5	61.88 / 185.63
MYERS DK	10.95	5	54.75	2.75	22.5	61.88 / 309.38
YUKON JACK	10.30	4	41.20	2.75	22.5	61.88 / 247.50
RUMPLE MINZE	12.90	5	64.50	3.00	22.5	67.50 / 337.50
WILD TURKEY	13.50	1	13.50	3.00	22.5	67.50 / 67.50
JIM BEAM	7.35	1	7.35	2.50	22.5	56.25 / 56.25
EARLY TINES	7.05	1	7.05	2.50	22.5	56.25 / 56.25

BRAND	COST	NUMBER PURCHASED	TOTAL COST	$ PER DRINK	# OF DRINKS EA.	SALES BOTTLE VALUE / SALES TOTAL VALUE
JACK DANIELS	10.95	27	295.65	2.75	22.5	61.88 / 1670.63
CANADIAN CLUB	10.25	2	20.50	2.75	22.5	61.88 / 123.75
SEAGRAMS 7	7.75	3	23.25	2.75	22.5	61.88 / 185.63
SEAGRAMS VO	10.25	18	184.50	2.75	22.5	61.88 / 1113.75
CANADIAN MIST	7.25	9	65.25	2.75	22.5	61.88 / 556.88
MACNAUGHTON	6.75	11	74.25	2.75	22.5	61.88 / 680.63
BLACK VELVET	7.10	23	163.30	2.75	22.5	61.88 / 1423.13
RICH & RARE	7.05	3	21.15	3.75	22.5	84.38 / 253.13
GILBYS	6.25	51	318.75	2.25	22.5	50.63 / 2581.88
MONTEGO BAY	5.75	56	322.00	3.25	22.5	73.13 / 4095.00
KANCHATKA	5.10	143	729.30	2.50	22.5	56.25 / 8043.75
TRIPLE SEC	5.65	14	79.10	3.25	22.5	73.13 / 1023.75
ARANDAS	6.65	20	133.00	3.25	22.5	73.13 / 1462.50
USHERS	9.70	30	291.00	3.75	22.5	84.38 / 2531.25
CANAD'N HUNTER	6.70	40	268.06	3.75	22.5	84.38 / 3375.00
ARANDAS GAL	14.65	4	58.60	3.25	52.6	170.95 / 683.80
PEPPERMINT	6.10	6	36.60	2.25	22.5	50.63 / 303.75
GLENLVT SCOTCH	23.75	2	47.50	3.00	22.5	67.50 / 135.00
APR TRIPLE SEC	6.10	8	48.80	3.25	22.5	73.13 / 585.00
FLSMN ROYAL	5.10	13	66.30	2.50	22.5	56.25 / 731.25
ARR TRPE SF	3.70	4	14.80	3.25	22.5	73.13 / 292.50
CAN LTD	6.25	2	12.50	3.00	22.5	67.50 / 135.00
TOTALS						5,673.20 / 44,541.93

MARKUP FOR SAMPLE MONTH

SALES PRICE: $44,541.93

COST MARKUP: $5,673.20

DRINK SALES SCOREBOARD

	MONTH:	YEAR:
Server		
Number of Carafes		
Number of Bottles		
Number of Glasses		
Server		
Number of Carafes		
Number of Bottles		
Number of Glasses		
Server		
Number of Carafes		
Number of Bottles		
Number of Glasses		
Server		
Number of Carafes		
Number of Bottles		
Number of Glasses		

BUDGET SAMPLE

	LAST MONTH'S PROJECTED	LAST MONTH'S ACTUAL	THIS MONTH'S PROJECTED
SALES			
Food			
Liquor			
Wine			
TOTAL SALES			
MATERIALS			
Food Costs			
Liquor Costs			
Wine Costs			
TOTAL COSTS			
GROSS PROFIT			
LABOR			
Manager Salary			
Employee			
Overtime			
TOTAL LABOR COSTS			
CONTROLLER OPERATING COSTS			
China & Utensils			
Glassware			
Kitchen Supplies			
Bar Supplies			

	LAST MONTH'S PROJECTED	LAST MONTH'S ACTUAL	THIS MONTH'S PROJECTED
CONTROLLER OPERATING COSTS (Continued)			
Dining Room Supplies			
Uniforms			
Laundry/Linen			
Services			
Trash Pickup			
Laundry Cleaning			
Protection			
Freight			
Accounting			
Maintenance			
Payroll			
Utilities			
Phone			
Water			
Gas			
Electricity			
Heat			
FIXED OPERATING COSTS			
Rent			
Insurance			
Property Taxes			

	LAST MONTH'S PROJECTED	LAST MONTH'S ACTUAL	THIS MONTH'S PROJECTED
FIXED OPERATING COSTS (Continued)			
Depreciation			
GENERAL OPERATING COSTS			
Labor Taxes			
Other Taxes			
Repairs—Equipment			
Repairs—Building			
Entertainment			
Advertising			
Promotion			
Equipment Rental			
Postage			
Contributions			
Trade Dues, etc.			
Licenses			
Credit Card Expense			
Travel			

CHAPTER ELEVEN

Customers

Few people venture into bar management with the idea of striking it rich. Many bar managers operate an establishment because the job seems interesting and fulfilling. In some cases, bar managers have a great idea for a bar; in other cases, they may hope to be able to showcase great acts. Whatever the dream, many bar managers have a vision that is heavily populated by people. If you ask many bar managers what they like to see in a bar, they usually respond that they like to see smiling customers. The most successful bar managers generally have a great interest in people.

This is what makes bar managers successful: good people skills translate into happy customers, which translates into a successful bar. The bar manager who does not care about his or her customers and who makes no effort to accommodate them is unlikely to run a successful bar.

The majority of bar drinkers—up to 40 percent by some estimates—are middle-aged men. However, that means that 60 percent are customers of every other description. Younger sets patronize specific establishments known for catering to singles. Customers also range from quiet drinkers to loud partiers to people who come in to meet a group of friends or even conduct business. No matter who your customers are and what their age or background, they demand specific things:

- **Prompt, courteous service.** Customers expect to be pampered a bit and to have some attention lavished on them. Good service at a bar usually involves a waiter or server who is prompt and friendly.

- **Paging systems.** If you need to keep customers waiting, consider implementing a paging system. Microframe's popular Guest Visual-Pager® System is the alternative to the vibrating coaster systems. A seating card is handed to the guest instead of a coaster, and when their table is available, the seating card number is entered in the keypad at the host stand and then displayed  on the Visual-Pagers. There is no limit to the Visual-Pagers that can be displayed in the main waiting area, the bar, or even outdoors. This system is very successful for a number of reasons: Guests can anticipate their number on the Visual-Pagers and this increases table turns; establishments are saving thousands of dollars annually because they are no longer losing expensive coasters, and the Visual-Pager System is maintenance-free. A complete Guest Visual-Pager System can be purchased for a fraction of the cost of a coaster system and is available in both wired and wireless versions. Visit **www.restaurantpager.com** or call 800-635-3811 for more information.

- **Privacy.** Customers like to have attention, but they also come to a bar to be alone in the midst of a crowd. Couples, especially, often like to be able to chat in a quiet corner without having a server hovering over them.

- **Safety.** As in any public place, customers rightly expect to be free from harassment and problems concerning their safety. They require food and drink to be safe.

- **A clean and pleasant atmosphere.** Customers of bars expect to enjoy not only their drink but also to enjoy the place where they are drinking. Wobbly tables, unsavory music, unpleasant smells, insects, and gritty tabletops and floors are all markers that indicate a bar that is not trying to please the customer.

- **Ambience.** A group of blue-collar workers may want a sports bar while a younger set may want a funkier, artsy look, but every customer wants a bar that reflects their personality—or what they imagine themselves as.

- **Quality food and drinks.** Bar-goers know what to expect for their money. Similarly, they have expectations about what type of service they should get. Bars that are unable to meet basic expectations will not do well.

- **Comfort.** Customers need good seating, a good view of any entertainment that is going on, bathroom facilities, and adequate lighting.

- **Customers want to feel special.** For the price of a drink, they want attention that makes them feel important. For this reason, bars that can afford to offer a little extra touch—VIP treatment—often have customers lining up.

Meeting customer demand is not as hard as you may think. Customer satisfaction starts with your bar. Your bar setup should be comfortable, pleasing, and attractive for the clientele you are aiming to attract. The bar should make it easy to relax and enjoy a few drinks alone or with friends.

Secondly, customer satisfaction can be ensured with a positive staff attitude. Train your staff to treat customers well, above all else. All staff should work hard to ensure smiling customers. Your employees already have an incentive to treat customers well: tips. Remind your staff that tips are not automatic. The word "tip" comes from the phrase "to insure promptness." Good service will generally result in better tips and in a better bar.

You may also want to institute a customer incentive program. These loyal, repeat customers occasionally deserve something to make them feel appreciated. Whether it is something as simple as a VIP pass, a free appetizer, or a free dessert, offering loyal customers an extra something makes them feel special and helps ensure continued business.

Expand Your Customer Base

One of the most important ways to keep customers coming back to your bar is to expand your customer base so that new patrons are always dropping by.

If you've been in business for a while, you've managed to bring together a core of regular patrons, but how do you go beyond the constrictions of that slice of the market and bring in a wider variety of customers without driving away your existing business? Consider the following:

- **Take it slow.** Transform your customer base slowly. Lure new customers over the long-term while making sure that your existing clientele are never made uncomfortable. If you change things too quickly, your core regulars may begin to feel that their favorite haunt is no longer "theirs."

- **Stand-up comedy.** Give the young crowd a reason to bring their friends along. Introduce a stand-up comedy night. It may bring in a group of people who might otherwise never have set foot in your bar.

- **Choose entertainers carefully.** The kind of crowd that would come to see a live punk band might be a rude shock to your over-45-year-old regulars. Your regulars are far less likely to take issue with a country and western band, a 70s cover band, or a solo act.

- **Attract female clientele.** A beer-guzzling sports bar crowd is never going to get into a wine-tasting night, but they may appreciate it when the ladies begin to arrive and the gender ratio starts to even out!

If you are trying to attract new customers and keep your current customers happy, you need to ask them directly what they are looking for. Savvy bar managers continue market research after they have been open for a while, because they know that customer needs change.

The term "market research" sends many bar operators into glazed-over-eyes mode, but knowing what your customers think about your establishment is vital. Ignore popular opinion at your own peril.

- Do more than ask the regulars what they think of your establishment. Talk to non-customers. Find out what it would take to bring them into your establishment. Lower prices? Live entertainment? Dancing? Can they see what you have to offer as they walk by? Do they know how good your food is?

- Try talking to your competition's customers. Find out where the other bars have you beat. Talk to them often, so when the landscape changes, you know about it.

- Keep asking questions about the neighborhood. For example, a geographic area can change markedly with a labor shift at a large company, or the redirection of a roadway, or even an alteration to a bus route.

- The competition is constantly shifting. A competitor can suddenly become a major player with one successful promotion, price adjustment, or addition to their list of products and services. Keep your finger on the pulse. Don't miss a golden opportunity.

- Is your market shifting? Take a look at the ratio of sales between your different types of alcohol (draft beer, bottled beer, spirits, liqueurs, wine). Has there been a recent increase in draft beer and spirits sales? Has there been an increased demand for bar snacks?

- Act on what your market research tells you. If something needs changing, change it. If something needs a small tweak, tweak it.

Here are some questions to ask your customers that can help streamline your business. For results, try the following:

- Do you sometimes visit a competitor's establishment? If so, why?

- Which nights are the other places you visit slow? Which nights are they busy?

- What would you like to see changed about our establishment?

- Which staff members are your favorite? Why?

- Do you like our food? Do you have any suggestions for new items?

- How did you first find us and what brings you back?

- Do you bring friends to our bar? If not, why not?

- Do our hours of operation suit your needs?

When possible, try to see the bar from your customers' perspective. Ask a friend to join you at the bar and ask for honest commentary about the bar. What are the things that may make a patron leave your bar? What things will draw him or her in and make them stay a while.

Do an Audit—From the Eyes of a Customer

If you really want to please customers (and get more of them), perform a satisfaction audit—from the customer's point of view. This works best if you can convince someone who does not work at the bar to conduct an audit (preferably someone who is not known to your staff), but in a pinch, the bar manager can do the audit. The idea is to drive or walk to the bar and then try to see the bar from the customers' eyes by ordering, spending some time in the bar, and leaving again. Done regularly, this can be a great way to tell what areas of your bar still need improving. Some elements of your bar audit should include:

- **Entrance.** Try walking to the bar. Is it easy to access on foot? Is it visible and easy to find? Is the walkway leading to the bar well lit and easy to negotiate? Try driving up to the bar. Is the bar easy to access by car? Is it visible from the road? What is the parking like? Do you feel comfortable in the neighborhood (if no, you may need to consider offering valet parking)?

- **Inside.** Who greets you? What first draws your eye? What is the first gut reaction you have to the bar? What are the other patrons like at a glance? Where is the attention on the room focused? What are the sounds, smells, and sights that greet you as you walk in? What could make you turn away and walk out again? What would make you stay?

- **Sitting down.** Sit down at the bar and then switch seats. How comfortable are you? What seating choices do you have? You should be able to choose a quiet place and a more social, visible place, depending on your wishes.

- **Ordering.** How soon is your order taken? How easy is it to order?

- **Service.** How pleasant is the staff? How easily accommodated are special requests? How fast does your order arrive? How is the drink or food presented? How does it taste? Do you feel like you are treated well at the bar? Is service prompt and courteous? Does your server smile at you and make conversation? How knowledgeable is the server about the price list and products offered? Can he or she make recommendations?

- **Bar.** How clean is the bar? How well-designed is it? Do you need to crane your head to see what you need to see (menus, etc.)? Look under the bar and under your seat. Are they clean? Look at the corners in the room and at the bar. Are they clean? Are the glasses clean? Do you see evidence of dirt?

- **Entertainment.** Is upcoming entertainment advertised? Is the stage in a place visible to all? Do any of the patrons need to crane their heads to see? Is the right equipment and space available for a wide variety of acts? Take in a show at the bar. What is your overall impression?

- **Bathroom.** Are the bathrooms easy to find and clearly marked? Are they well lit and easily accessible, even if you are feeling unwell? Are they very clean? Do they offer vending machines for essentials (sanitary products for women, for example)? Do they give a sense of calm or are they scattered and untidy?

- **Comparison.** Visit a few other bars the same night. How do the establishments compare? Where did you spend the most time and the most money (the results may surprise you)? Why was that the case?

Luciano Santini worked for "**The Standard**" in California that received very high awards. Luciano recalls communication being the most important aspect of being the general manager of the restaurant bar.

The biggest obstacle with staff is getting them to work as a team to reach the same goal. You have to get them to get over their personality clashes and be able to work closely together. Small five-minute talks before shifts, posting the night's specials with ingredients, making the staff comfortable, and making myself available were just some of the things I did to ensure communication between the staff and I.

"Communication between me and the guests was another important factor. I spent most of my time walking around the restaurant talking to guests making sure all was well with their service as well as food and drinks. You only get one opportunity to make a great first impression. I would often buy repeat customers a drink, appetizer, and sometimes their entire meal."

CHAPTER TWELVE

Tips to Making Your Bar a Success

There are many bars that go out of business each year. This is because the market for new bars is a challenging one. If you are in an area that has new bars opening all the time and a clientele who is always seeking the latest thrill, you need to work extra hard to ensure that your establishment stays exciting enough. There are many small details that can mean the difference between a bar that is merely surviving and one that is prospering beautifully. In this chapter, you will learn the small details that can push your success higher than ever. Not all of these tips are expensive. Many take only ingenuity and some effort, but the results can be spectacular!

Fill a Local Need

One of the first steps to ensuring that your bar is a success for a long time to come is to look around and make sure that you are offering value in the local area. Most of your business will be from people who can easily drive, walk, take a cab, or ride a bus to your bar. These same patrons will have the choice of many other bars in the area. There are a few ways to make sure that they select your bar:

- **Research the competition.** Take the time to sit in every competing bar. After you order your drink, take notes: Who frequents these bars? Older patrons? Younger patrons? Yuppies? Tradespeople? What sort of bar is it? How much do they charge? What does the bar look like? What are the drinks and food offered? What are the promotions? What kind of entertainment is offered? How busy are they and on which night are they busiest? What are they doing wrong? What are they doing right?

- **Consider lower prices.** If your competitors' prices are high, consider lowering yours. It will often get people to try your establishment for the first time. Your service and the quality of your bar will decide whether they return.

- **Service.** If your bar is known as the friendliest bar in town while your competitors tend to slack on service, you will make a profit. If your competition is already offering great service, you have to make your service stellar in order to compete.

- **Focus on what the competition is doing wrong.** If you notice something that the competition is doing wrong, make sure that your bar is doing that same thing right. It will encourage patrons to see your bar as the local establishment that offers more.

- **Set your hours to take advantage** of times when your competition is not available. If the competition stops food service early, think about extending your food service hours. Being able to provide something that the competition cannot or is not willing to provide is a great way to make sure that you lure in new regulars.

- **Do you know what the local patrons want?** If you do not ask them and conduct regular market research, you have little hope of knowing the very things that will draw patrons to your bar.

- **Look at the bars that are succeeding elsewhere.** What works in other cities and towns may work in yours. Pay special attention to the types of bars that are doing well in areas similar to your own (in towns or cities with the same demographics). These bars may have hit on an idea that may work well in your area as well.

- **Special promotions.** Avoid using your best ideas and resources trying to compete on someone else's strongest night. Offer special promotions and discounts on nights when other bars are not offering anything. It will help lure in customers looking for something great on a slower night.

Remember, if you can offer something special, you are more likely to get more customers. It pays to make the extra effort to find out what is needed in your area—and then supply that need. Customers will flock to you.

Make Each Customer Count

Your market and competitor research will likely reveal that most bars that are successful pay a lot of attention to customers. In fact, great service is one of the surest ways of drawing repeat customers. To draw more patrons to your bar on a regular basis, you do not have to spend a lot of money. However, you do have to think like a customer; you will likely notice a few things that need to change at your establishment:

- **Waiting lines.** If there's a line outside the door, all it takes is a little creativity to either bring the line inside or disguise it on the outside. Remember, those people waiting outside are probably thirsty and they'd be more than happy to do their waiting in a courtyard area, at a temporary bar, or in a cordoned-off outside area where drinking is permitted. Of those who are prepared to brave the line, most will do so gladly if they know they can be inside within 30 minutes. Also, it's simple to change waiting-time perceptions by making that wait a little more comfortable or entertaining.

- **Parking** can be a big hassle in many venues. If there tends to be a traffic jam outside your venue, consider installing a valet service on busy nights or posting a staff member outside to direct patrons to parking around the back or down the road. Signs pointing to parking areas also help.

- **Offer creative extras.** Whether it is free hand massages, glow sticks, or a live band outside, making the outside dazzling will make people all the more eager to see the inside of the bar.

- Think about your **TV screens and sound system** in relation to your waiting area. Can waiting people catch a glimpse of the big game? Can they hear the music inside? These things will keep a waiting person keen on staying around, whereas a blank brick wall and a disinterested bouncer isn't inviting to anyone.

- **Keep clientele informed.** If there's a wait for a table, set up an electronic sign indicating how long their expected wait will be. Add to this anything you can think of that will make their wait more entertaining—sports scores, trivia questions, coming events. It might be a little more work, but if you can keep just five people from leaving, it'll be worth it. Contact Daktronics (**www.daktronics.com**) by phoning 605-697-4000.

- **Freebies and incentives.** Offer your waiting patrons a little something extra and they won't just "not mind" waiting, they'll do so gladly. Coupons to be used on a later date are a good option.

- **Create a waiting area** if you know that there tends to be a wait to get into the bar. This can include comfy chairs or an outside patio where customers can wait and sit. This is a great way to make sure that customers do not get tired and leave.

- **It doesn't have to be expensive.** Giving your waiting customers something to do doesn't have to be expensive, high-tech, or take up your employees' valuable time. Consider offering free reading material in your waiting area or even Internet access.

- **Act first.** A long wait doesn't seem quite so long when a staff member keeps you informed on how long your table will take. Don't wait for the customer to ask you; go out and tell the customer.

- **Make your bar irresistible.** Why will some bar patrons wait forty-five minutes to get into a bar instead of giving up and going elsewhere? They have a sense of urgency to get inside. Whether you are offering a hot live act, celebrities, or some other enticement, make sure it is worth the wait.

- **Offer free appetizers to waiting patrons.** A tray with a nice selection of different foods from your menu can actually be a great advertisement and may even generate increased food sales.

- **Supply your customers with pagers.** Offering waiting customers a pager to notify them when their table is ready is a great alternative to the usual "public address" announcement or a yell over the crowd. When a table becomes available, your host simply dials the waiting customer's number, and wherever they are in the building (or outside), they know that their table is ready. Contact Bristol Business Machines **www.bristolnf.com** at 709-722-6669 for more information on customer paging systems, or check out **www.restaurantpager.com**.

- **Build suspense.** If it appears as though there is something really exciting going on in your bar, people will be willing to wait to get inside.

- **Make sure waits are fair.** Patrons who have been waiting for a while will get rightfully angry if it appears as though the staff are letting in people who are paying extra or who are simply "flirtier." Make sure that your security staff respect the queue and try to get everyone inside in an orderly and fair manner.

- **Keep your customers informed.** Be honest. If there'll be a half-hour wait, don't tell them it will be a fifteen-minute wait and hope they don't walk out. Similarly, ensure your staff keeps them updated on the wait so they know they haven't been forgotten. Small things like this make a big difference in the eyes of a waiting customer.

Customers are your mainstay in the bar business. If you treat them better than other bars would, you are ensured repeat business. Customers love to feel like VIPs, and the more patrons you make feel like this, the more business you will have. Share these tips with your staff to ensure they treat every customer as through he or she were a star.

Appearance

Most customers will be people who have passed you by in the past and decided to try your venue. In order for this to happen, you need to pay far more attention to the exterior of your venue than most bar operators do. Here are some easy ways to spice up your outside areas:

- **A graphic projection lighting system.** Also known as a "bat light," this type of system can provide a highly effective way to advertise your bar to passersby. It also looks great when used on the inside of your establishment. Bat lights use a light and optic setup to project your logo or other related graphics onto any surface, including walls, ceilings, the outside sidewalk, and more. They can be purchased or rented for far less than you might think. Talk to High End Systems about their Technobeam system (**www.highend.com**) to see if your budget can handle a little high-tech marketing.

- From how far away can your bar be seen? If you can't be seen at least a block away, consider **increasing your outside signage**. While this is not a small expense, there's no point in hiding the fact that your bar is nearby. If you talk to your distributors, you might find that one of them is prepared to subsidize the cost of your signage, in return for mention of their product.

- **Neon works!** Why do you think every bar has neon beer signs in the window? The answer is simple: because people notice them. An impressive neon sign is a local landmark. Think of those huge neon signs in Times Square and how many tourists know of them and send photos of them home to their family. You don't have to go to quite that scale, but a small investment in neon will bring people in to take a closer look.

- Don't discount the appeal of **a nice paint job**. Is your exterior freshly painted? A new paint job isn't just about aesthetics. The outside of your venue is usually assumed to reflect the inside. Consider asking your staff to come in after-hours and paint the walls for you, in return for a bonus. Most bar staff could use a few extra bucks now and then. It'll be a lot cheaper than hiring a professional.

- **Landscaping isn't a luxury.** Just as your exterior walls say a lot about your interior, so, too, do your grounds. If all you have outside your venue is a gravel-covered parking lot and a few beat-up pickup trucks, you're not going to attract a broad demographic, no matter what you offer inside. Plant some hardy greenery outside that will survive any weather extremes (choose varieties that will not need constant trimming and watering). This will soften the outside of your bar exterior. A few trees around the outside of the parking lot won't hurt, and some up-lights underneath them can offer a particularly breathtaking look, for not a lot of money.

- **Keep things neat.** Remove snow in the winter, have an awning to protect patrons from the elements, and make your entrance attractive to ensure that more people will peek into your bar.

- **Who is greeting your customers?** Is someone making them feel welcome right away or are they being greeted only by a suspicious security person? Do not give customers an excuse to walk away after they have made it all the way to your bar's door. Make them feel welcomed.

Some Enhancing Touches of Quality

Sometimes the only element that separates successful bars from those that fail is in the small professional touches of excellence. This extra effort implies that tremendous thought has been made all around to attain the highest level of quality possible. Professional bartenders and courteous cocktail waiters/waitresses can be found in any well-managed restaurant. However, it is the small, un-demanded touches and extra procedures that separate good lounges from superb ones. Described in this section are some simple, inexpensive suggestions that will give your bar the extra touches—the finesse—that will separate yours from the rest.

Simple signs of quality that make a big difference include:

- Real napkins and table linens.

- Fresh ingredients, real fruit juices, and high-quality garnishes.

- Elegant presentation of drinks—garnishes, fancy napkins, and pretty glassware can turn even ordinary drinks into extraordinary ones.

- Elegant cutlery and dinnerware.

- Fresh flowers and candles.

- Quality tables, chairs, and seating. Comfort is always appreciated.

- Entertainment. Giving patrons something to do or something to look at while drinking is appreciated, especially by those customers who arrive alone.

- Beautiful bathrooms. Many customers judge a bar by the bathrooms. If yours are beautiful, clean, and offer extras such as a sofa and breath mints, your bar will seem all the more impressive and wonderful to your customers.

- Elegant décor or a unique ambience. Even sipping a beer in a visually exciting place seems more interesting and fun than staying at home. Lights, colors, and artwork can easily create ambience on a small budget.

Signature Drinks

Many bars see the value in creating a special drink that becomes their signature creations. Such a lure can be a huge draw to your patrons, especially if it gives the customer great value, unique taste, and an original bar experience. Successful specialty drinks invariably have an intriguing, captivating flavor not easily replicated without being privy to the recipe. If customers want to taste it again, they have to come back. These tips might provide you with just what you need:

- **Reputation.** A truly great signature drink can further the reputation of your bar. The drink, however, doesn't need to be particularly highbrow to become famous. For every establishment that creates an exotic fruit-rum-champagne concoction with a ten-dollar glass, there are five small neighborhood venues that can prepare one simple drink, to perfection, for less money or in a unique way. A simple martini can be a signature creation if it's original looking and tasty enough to get people talking.

- **Your signature drink should not be overpowering.** Unless, of course, you want that to be its main draw! The idea should be for people to buy a lot of your signature drinks, not for them to buy one and stumble out the door into traffic.

- **Be sure to patent your drink or register it so that others cannot use the same name and recipe** as you. Guard your recipe as a secret. This will not only increase the mystery around the drink, but it will discourage imitators.

- **Do not get overly worried about how to create a signature drink.** A few changes to basic recipes, some off-the-wall experiments, and some unusual garnishes are all that is required. Set your bartender to work on a quiet afternoon and see what comes up.

- **Don't overdo it.** One very popular drink is all you need. You want your bartender serving the drinks that bring in customers, not working like a chemist to create new concoctions all the time.

- **Make your signature drink colorful or at least noticeably different.** A tiny squirt of grenadine, crème de menthe, or Blue Curacao can radically change the look of your signature drink without significantly altering the taste and cost of it.

- **Garnishes don't have to be boring.** A slice of lemon or a wedge of lime might be traditional, but it's not something that your customers will get excited about. Try something out of left field: a stick of beef jerky, a wedge of kiwifruit, or a chocolate Kit Kat. These might cost you a little more, but the novelty will leave a mark on your patrons.

- **Don't under-market your creation.** Promote it like you would any other selling point of your bar, even to the extent of including it in your marketing material; for example: "Welcome to Frankie's Bar: Home of the Flaming Death-Bringer."

- **Make it special.** Your signature drink should be special on every level—including the glass it is served in. A highball is not going to give an impression of excellence, so spend a little extra and put your drink in something that will add to the "ooh-aah" element.

- **Your signature drink should be fairly (or even heavily) discounted** to add to the drawing power of the beverage. Talk to your liquor distributor about whether they can cut you a deal to include one of their product lines in your creation so you can discount the sale price, but also what it costs you to make.

- **Value.** Customers want to feel like they're getting great value for their money. With a little thinking, you can have your clientele believing they're getting something with more alcohol than it actually has. For example, when pouring a Tequila Sunrise, pour the orange juice first, then drop in the tequila. The tequila will float to the bottom of the drink, ensuring that the customer's first sip from a straw will hit them like a brick. The drink will have no more alcohol than usual, and you shouldn't claim otherwise (that would be fraudulent), but it doesn't hurt for your patron to say to their friends, "Wow, they don't scrimp on the tequila in these things!"

- **Liquor on the glass rim.** Rubbing the inside rim of a glass with a liquor-soaked rim sponge will ensure that the first sip a customer takes will be the most memorable.

- **Hot cocoa, coffee, and tea make a great base for signature drinks.** All have an attention-grabbing aroma and familiar flavor, they combine nicely with lots of spirits and liqueurs, and they're very inexpensive!

- **Apple cider.** Consider hot apple cider as a signature drink base if your location is susceptible to cold weather. Cider marries well with many liqueurs to give a strong apple flavor to your patrons' favorite drinks.

Embrace Change

How much money people have to spend, what is considered trendy, even favorite ways to spend spare time; these things all change frequently. Bar managers notice these changes and wonder whether they should change their bars in response. If the area where the bar is located suddenly becomes upscale, would a trendier look make more sense? If reality shows are suddenly hot, would a reality-show theme make sense for a renovation? Once bars have been in operation for a while, the pressure is on to change, renovate, upgrade. Before you do, though, you need to consider a few things.

First, you need to know whether major changes would really bring in more profit. This means more market research and projections. For large renovations and moves, you may need to develop a new business plan and financial projections in order to determine whether a new idea will work. Before you make large changes, make sure that those changes will work.

Secondly, you must consider the cost of those changes. Some renovations may require contractors, equipment, new supplies, and new employees. Some larger renovations may require you to get new licensing or be affected by zoning laws. To prevent costly mistakes, figure out the total costs and legalities, including the costs of being closed during renovations, before you make a final decision. Of course, the total costs of your renovations must be covered by the profits you expect to make. You will want to make sure that your renovations will bring in enough increased profits to pay for the renovations.

A few words of caution: You can easily drive away regulars through major renovations. Patrons may find new places to get drinks while your bar is in disorder during a transition. More seriously, patrons may simply dislike your new concept. If you were a sports bar catering to older men and have installed a dance floor that brings in younger crowds, you may lose some regulars. If you have done your marketing and research well, the costs will cover this loss of business, but it can still be disconcerting and even frightening to notice that some familiar faces are conspicuously missing from your bar.

You also need to be very careful about debt. Many bars need business loans in order to make major renovations. However, these loans need to be paid back, and if your new profit-making ideas are not making the profit you thought they would, then your new debt may quickly become a burden. Many businesses have closed because they took out large loans for a renovation that proved to be unprofitable. Make sure that you do not make this same mistake.

Because of the risks and costs of expansion, many business owners try out new ideas for a night or two or they make small changes a part of regular promotions. Rather than renovating extensively to draw a younger crowd, for example, they change the bar slightly once a week. This costs less and comes with less risk, but it can still yield great business. A theme-for-a-night special or promotion is the ideal way to achieve this. Some ideas for themes-for-a-night that have worked for some successful bars include the following:

- **Margarita night.** Whether you try giveaways, décor, or great deals on tequila, margarita night tends to be quite successful.

- **Sports-minded.** You can easily buy some sports memorabilia and a pool table and turn a big-screen TV or the bar TV to a sports station. You can host a special party or offer drink specials during sports playoffs to really pack the bar.

- **TV.** If there is a popular show that is ending its season, you can host a party for the show. Have staff dress as characters from the show, serve special drinks based on the show, and turn the TV on to the season or series finale.

- **Tropical theme.** A tropical luau or barbeque is a great way to kick off summer, end it, or just celebrate it. All you need are some inexpensive leis, tropical music, and some summery drinks on sale to make this a money-making hit.

- **Holidays.** Whether it's Halloween or a civic holiday, offering special décor and drink specials can be great ways to lure in customers who want celebrate with a large group of people.

- **Festivals and launches.** There are likely many events going on in your town. Whether it's an independent film festival, book launch, jazz festival, or other event, by agreeing to be the venue, you can easily get great advertising and great business for a night.

- **Quiet room.** A quiet room in the back could be easily outfitted to be a "study bar." If there are college students in your area, all you need to provide is comfortable seating, larger tables, outlets for laptops, and good lighting. Students will be glad to meet at your bar for study sessions and drinks.

- **Irish pub.** Popular around St. Patrick's Day, your local vendor of Irish brews will likely be able to help turn your bar into an Irish oasis any time of the year. Brewing companies like Guinness have a vested interest in promoting the "Irish pub" theme.

- **Wine-tasting night** might bring in a new type of clientele. A regularly scheduled wine-tasting night might totally transform your establishment. Any wine distributor will gladly assist.

- **Cigar night.** In conjunction with a local tobacconist, consider setting up a cigar lounge. The event is likely to bring in a bigger-spending crowd than you're used to.

- **Live music.** Put an ad in the local alternative and college newspapers offering the stage area as a free rehearsal space for local bands (with volume restrictions, of course), during the daytime hours. You may well begin to draw a live music crowd in the process. Best of all, this is during your slowest bar hours.

- **Movie night.** Contact a local video store that can supply you with pre-release movies in return for cross-promotion. Not only will it bring in new business, it will also keep your customers seated for hours longer than they might normally have stayed.

- **Karaoke.** Often worth the outlay of a few hundred dollars to run a karaoke night, these nights are usually very successful at bringing in new and repeat business.

Expansion

There may come a time when you decide that the risks of expansion are well worth it. If you have done your research and tried out your idea through theme nights, you may be ready to expand.

The most popular way for a bar to expand today is via a nightclub. The nightclub industry is unlike any other, and when you have a popular bar and restaurant operation, many people will approach you with grand plans to expand into the club business, while portraying themselves as skilled experts in the nightclub field. While some do know what they're talking about, nightclubs have an incredibly high rate of failure; in fact, approximately 10 percent of the nightclubs make 80 percent of nightclub revenue. Don't just take anyone's word on opening a nightclub—know what you're doing before going in. While Chapter 16 covers nightclubs in depth, the following are some important details:

- **Research the nightclub business** before you spend a cent. There are plenty of resources, both offline and online, that can give you in-depth information on the dos and don'ts of opening a nightclub.

- **Check out the competition.** Spend a night in as many local clubs as you can—both successful ones and unsuccessful ones. Take notes on who is doing what, what seems to hit a chord with the locals, and what might work with your own establishment for a relatively small investment.

- **Make sure that your bar will work as a nightclub.** In general, nightclubs need far more open room than bars do. You will need all the supplies and equipment you have now, plus you will need room for sound equipment, live acts, and plenty of room for a dance floor. In fact, many of the most successful nightclubs today have multiple levels to cater to several crowds.

- **Develop your own niche.** You'll rarely take the industry by storm. If you find a decent-size sector of the market that is under-served and manage to fill that need well, you'll go a long way toward turning in a healthy and consistent profit.

- **Make sure you know what age group you are targeting.** Many nightclubs draw a younger crowd, but if market research suggests that this sort of crowd is not your forte, consider that many nightclubs that cater to the 35-plus crowd do well too.

Starting a nightclub can be daunting, but many bar managers like the fact that nightclubs encourage audiences to stay longer. It is unusual for people who want to dance to just show up for one song. Plus, since dancing is tiring, the possibility of buying drinks at the bar will be even more enticing for your customers.

If you are going to have a nightclub at your bar, or even if you are going to offer nightclub entertainments such as dancing, you will need music. Music is often what makes or breaks a club, so choose carefully. Unless you live in an area with many great local bands, you will need to hire either DJs or use computers to generate sound. There are advantages and disadvantages to each system:

- **MP3 mixer.** A computer system with a wide selection of MP3s and an auto-mixing program like MP3000f can keep the tunes rolling all night with the sort of seamless, non-stop sound that you'd normally get from a DJ. Though an MP3 mixer isn't capable of following the crowd's mood, it's a cost-effective means of putting together a DJ sound without spending a fortune. MP3000f can be downloaded at **www. disconova.com**.

- **Find a good DJ.** Though an auto-mixing system is a great cost-effective option, if you really want to keep a crowd at maximum pleasure level, a good DJ is a must. Finding a reliable DJ who puts the crowd above their own ego is often difficult. Run a competition for local hopefuls and offer the winner a regular gig.

- **Own equipment.** Many DJs have their own sound equipment, lighting, and music, but they also charge a higher price as a result. Purchase your own sound equipment and lighting. Pay a DJ by the hour; it's more cost effective. It also allows you to hire DJs without their own equipment, thus expanding your hiring possibilities.

- **Please the crowd.** Many DJs play music for their own pleasure, rather than the crowd's. As a result, the dance floor can become a little quiet sometimes. To ensure your DJ not only works the crowd well, but also brings people back every week, offer him or her a small percentage of the register take for the night. This consideration will not only have your DJ trying harder to keep the patrons there all night, but will also ensure they don't move on to a new job at the drop of a hat.

- **VideoCD and DVD.** Gone are the days when a quality establishment could get away with relying on a CD player behind the bar or a jukebox to keep the customers entertained. VideoCD and DVD are now taking over. If you create enough variety in these DVDs, your bar staff can conceivably throw on a disc and forget it for hours, while your customers dance to, sing along with, or watch their favorite music. Please note that establishments that play live or recorded music must be licensed with BMI and ASCAP. You can find them online at **www .bmi.com** and **www.ascap.com**.

- **Auto-changers.** If you elect to use a VideoCD system, auto-changers can be used to enable DJs or bar staff to mix up the programming without any manual tweaking over the course of the night. Tracks can be pre-programmed by the user or randomly selected by the player. VideoCD not only covers all of the popular music mediums, but it can also be customized and mixed—an option that DVD doesn't yet match.

Just about any bar establishment can benefit from an area set aside for dancing, even if only for a few nights of the week. If you are starting a nightclub, though, a great dance floor is a must. This is not as hard to create as you might think:

- **Square footage.** Most bar operators find that setting aside anywhere between 10 to 15 percent of the venue's total square footage for a dance floor is a winning formula. A dance floor should be large enough to hold a good number of people, but if it is too large, it can often feel empty and exposed. Many people who dance like the privacy a crowd offers them, so making your dance floor too large can detract from their enjoyment.

- **Lighting.** You will want your dance floor to have plenty of lighting options. While you do not want a floor that is brightly lit, you will want lots of lighting effects (strobe, soft lights, etc.) for different songs.

- **Rest areas.** If possible, comfy chairs or other seating needs to be provided near the dance floor so that dancers can sit and relax but still be part of the action.

- **A dance floor** doesn't have to be dedicated to one use. At times of the week when dancing isn't taking place, it can be turned into a stage area for live entertainment, or even removed altogether if you invest in a portable dance floor. Portable dance floor systems may be found at **www.tuffdeck.com** or **www.dance-2000.com**.

- **Slippery surfaces.** While a well-polished dance floor can be great for dancers, it can be a hazard for your customers—especially if they've had a little to drink. Place adequate warning signs on a dance floor when it is not being used for that purpose, to avoid costly injury claims. Make sure that your dance floor (and the area around it) is flat; stairs can be very dangerous on a busy floor.

- **Acoustics.** Your dance floor should have great sound all the time so that dancers can hear every part of songs.

- **Visuals.** Special effects, such as fog or bubbles, add to the dance floor experience and make dancing more fun for your customers. Some dance floors also have screens above the dance floor so that dancers can see videos or other parts of the dance floor.

- **Spaces and moods.** Many successful dance floors have several spaces and moods. Today's most successful nightclubs actually have several different floors, each playing different types of music so patrons can get a change of pace without leaving the bar. Even if you do not have the room for this, you should try to create different dance areas or platforms to give dancers different perspectives of the dance floor.

Sound Systems

Whether or not you're featuring live entertainment or a fully functioning dance floor, a strong and flexible sound system is an integral part of your bar operation. If you are going to begin a nightclub to complement your bar, you will need to invest in a sound system that can reliably deliver the sounds that will keep your customers coming back. Consider the following:

- When it comes to constructing a quality sound system, it's far better to overdo your capacity and cut back as you need to than to strain amps and fatigue speakers prematurely. Make sure that there are speakers and amps that deliver sound to every area of the bar. Cut out amps as needed. You can always use the equipment you bought on special nights. You do not need to use all your equipment each night for it to be a good purchase.

- Consider buying a used system. Bar managers are often horrified by the price tag of today's sound systems, especially when they consider all the other purchases they need to create a nightclub. Rather than buying a cheaper new system, consider a quality used system if your budget is small.

- Always listen to a sound system before buying, and take a sound file along as you shop. Many of your customers will be music fans. They will resent a sound system that makes their favorite recording artists sound weak. Test all systems at full volume and ask someone who knows about music to make sure that you get as little distortion as possible. Muddy sound is terrible on a dance floor.

- Arrange backup and maintenance. If your nightclub's sound system fails and you have no backup, you will have to close for the night, disappointing customers and losing business. You will be giving customers a chance to find a new favorite dance spot, so be sure to plan for emergencies before your system is installed.

- Loud music can be great, but it also interferes with the very interaction that your patrons have come to enjoy. If you can't set aside a quieter area for your customers to use when talking, consider lowering the volume of your music. This won't just make your customers more relaxed, it will also make the process of ordering a drink easier.

- Consider the acoustics of your venue when setting up your sound system. If the bar or seating area faces a dance floor or live entertainment stage, having your speaker system aimed toward the bar will only make service and interaction difficult during loud music periods. Consider positioning your speakers between the dance floor/ stage and bar areas. Point them away from the areas of your venue that will benefit from being quieter.

- Video walls. Pair these popular enhancements with a quality sound system. A video wall can produce an awesome effect that, while not adding to the sound, can certainly improve how the patrons perceive it. A 16-cube video wall isn't only a dance-floor supplement, it can also be great for daytime coverage of sporting events and is useful for presentations during corporate functions. Contact Multivision Video and Film at **www.vidwall.com**.

Promotions

Whether you decide to expand or not, promotions and sales will be a big way for you to draw in more customers. In many cases, customers will make a special effort to go to bars that they know are offering special promotions and drink sales.

Wine is a very profitable item that requires little preparation, little handling, and little additional cost to present it. Thus, the sale of wine should be energetically promoted. Described in this section are some simple and inexpensive yet very effective ways to increase wine sales—and the bar's bottom line.

A wine list is a great advertisement. It should be professionally prepared, laid out, and printed. There are special wine books that may be purchased to house the wine list. They are impressive to look at and practical. The bindings are of loose-leaf style so that they may be updated as needed. A good wine book lists the price and, if possible, exhibits the label. Labels are available from your distributor or directly from the winery. Wine lists may be a part of the table setting, which will almost guarantee that they will be looked at. Unfortunately, they are also collector items that many customers admire. You can alleviate this problem by giving each member of the waitstaff one list that can be brought around to each table at the appropriate time. This will also tend to remind the waitperson to suggest a bottle of wine to his or her customers.

Wineglasses should be set on every table, as they are an inducement to order a bottle of wine. Sometimes just suggesting a bottle will get the customer interested. The glasses should be removed if no wine is ordered. Whenever touching a wineglass, remember to hold it by the stem, otherwise you will leave fingerprints and smudges.

Some savvy bar managers suggestively set their tables with a bottle of wine and a small tent card to explain the wine and list the price.

Waitstaff must be thoroughly trained and knowledgeable about the wine list. They should know which wines may be served with which foods and the correct procedures for presenting and opening the bottle. Invest in some cheap bottles so that each waitperson may practice opening one. Your wine merchant will often be glad to set up a meeting with your staff. These people are very knowledgeable about wine and can be a great aid in training employees. Remember, it is in their best interest that you sell more wine. Once your waitstaff learns how to correctly pronounce each wine and serve it, they will know more than 75 percent of customers do.

Get your employees interested in wine. The best way to accomplish this is to have a wine tasting where they can all try the different varieties. The cost of this event will be easily substantiated by the increase in wine sales and employee morale. Often your wine merchant will be interested in subsidizing one of these events.

Show your waitstaff that it is in their best interest to sell more wine. The larger the checks, the larger the tips they will receive. Set up a wine contest: the waitperson who sells the most wine in a month might receive some sort of bonus; perhaps a bottle of very expensive wine. If two or more guests are considering wine by the glass, that's a server's cue to suggest sharing a bottle. Upgrading the order saves time.

Of course, you will not want to focus only on wine promotions. Mixed drinks and beer are also hot sellers at many bars, and the savvy bar manager will find out when many patrons are coming in for these items in order to offer a special sale on them. Do many blue-collar workers come in on Fridays? Offer a TGIF special that offers cheap pitchers. Where possible, try to offer discounts on larger amounts (pitchers of beer rather than pints, for example) as this will encourage customers to bring groups of friends and stay longer.

Do not forget to advertise your promotions and special theme nights. Post signs around town and in front of your bar. In most cases, in order for promotions to work, you will need to draw larger crowds. Resist the

temptation to go too low with prices; not only will customers be suspicious of quality if prices are too low, but you may not be attracting the demographic you want by lowering prices
too much.

Entertainment

Many bar operators like to keep their patrons entertained with a variety of eclectic means and don't mind spending a few dollars to do so. In fact, major sporting venues have been employing these kinds of halftime entertainments for years and finding great results. If your bar can offer unique and appealing entertainment, chances are very good that you will have plenty of clientele. Better yet, if your bar develops a reputation for providing great entertainment, customers will always be dropping by your bar to look at your latest entertainment options. Consider the following:

- **Trivia nights.** A handful of questions, a few slips of paper for answers, a running score, and $50 worth of vouchers for food and drink to give away—it all makes for a big night of entertainment. More venues are seeing the value of trivia competitions—luring customers in with the offer of freebies. These contests vary from huge nights run by live presenters to computerized interactive trivia games, where patrons compete against bars around the country via satellite. Either option does one important thing: brings people back.

- **Food tasting.** People love food, and if you offer free appetizers or snacks with your beverages, you will draw a crowd.

- **Theater.** Traditional theater (or mystery theater) gives customers a chance to look at something and encourages people to stay for an entire performance.

- **Karaoke.** The Japanese tradition of karaoke has come on in leaps and bounds in North America in the last ten years, but there's still a big difference between quality karaoke and most karaoke. It's far more than simply putting up a bunch of old songs with some fuzzy video. Your karaoke enthusiasts need variety in the music selection. Hire a good karaoke host who can keep things moving and draw a big crowd of listeners.

- **Board games.** A Scrabble or Monopoly night might be a simple idea, but it also works! Quieter nights of the week are an excellent time to try out a board game tournament. It instills a sense of community amongst your patrons.

- **Stand-up comedy.** It's more than possible for you to find four or five stand-up comedians who will keep your audience laughing without costing you more than a hundred bucks total. Live comedy is a great draw, and it tends to keep an audience planted until the finish. Try an open-mike night and see what you find!

Coins Machines

Coin-operated entertainment machines are a great source of extra revenue for a bar. The eclectic nature of most bars means that coin-ops of all styles, sizes, and functions can fit perfectly within your surrounds while adding to the fun and flavor of your establishment. The profits that coin-ops generate can be huge; they can also run a lot deeper than just the money inserted into the machines.

Coin-ops increase traffic, generate great repeat business, and keep people in your venue far longer. Coin-ops also give people who arrive alone a chance to do something as they sip their drinks. From high-tech games to virtual reality to pool tables, anything that gives your customers added entertainment is a good option, especially if it will bring you higher profits. These machines are cheaper than renovations but can contribute nicely to your profits.

- **Profit-based coin-ops.** Some coin-ops don't have to cost you a cent, but they can bring in a good source of revenue. Simply open the phone book and look under "Coin-operated" and you'll find a slew of companies that will bring you games and entertainment for your customers for no charge—other than a share of the profits. This kind of a deal can only be good for your business. No maintenance worries and you get a new machine whenever an old one stops earning money—all free of charge.

- **Deal directly with the machine manufacturers.** In a scenario like this, your venue will handle most of the daily maintenance required of the machines and the manufacturer's repairperson comes out only as needed. While this limits your selection of game alternatives, when you want to switch games, it's only a matter of changing a couple of computer chips. The actual game casing stays the same, but a completely different game appears, keeping your customers from getting bored with their options.

- **Don't forget change machines.** If you are going to offer coin-ops, make it easy for your customers to use the machines without taxing your staff too heavily for change. One change machines is all that is needed.

- **Responsibility.** If the machine is on your premises, take responsibility for it and either return the customer's money or see to it that your supplier can fix the malfunctioning machine A.S.A.P. There's nothing worse than wanting to play a machine and finding it switched off—again.

- **One of the biggest crazes at the moment is photo-machines.** Customers put up to five dollars into the machine and step in to have their photo taken. In a few minutes, they can have their image on stickers or postcards; they can even pick a background. These machines are huge moneymakers and can even incorporate an ad for your bar within the picture. Your local phone directory will list plenty of suppliers.

- **Lottery machines are very popular right now.** If your state allows them, they can be a great source of revenue. The latest machines work much like slot machines in Las Vegas, allowing customers the chance to win big.

- **Retro arcade machines and video game machines** are very popular and go well with bars. Many people love these games and gladly spend extra time at a bar in order to play them.

- **Dancing machines.** Patrons throw a dollar into the machine and step onto a stage that features a series of lights. They then try to step on whichever lights flash to keep in time with an on-screen dancer. These machines can be very addictive and often draw a large crowd—which can't hurt your bar's takings. Again, any amusement machine vendor in your local phone directory should be able to supply this machine.

- **Virtual reality** (VR) sports are becoming a reality. More and more bars are installing VR golf ranges, VR batting cages, VR racing games, VR bowling alleys, VR hockey games, and VR boxing machines. These machines are the same as any other coin-operated gaming machine, except they cost the customer more and deliver a superior product. While they take up more room, they give you far greater profitability and extensive replay value.

Coin-operated games come in many varieties. Just about any game you can think of has a coin-op version available. Football, air hockey, video games, shooting games, skee-ball, basketball games, even video poker and blackjack machines that fit into your bar-top—it's all available and it's all going to bring in a newer, younger customer for a minimum investment or no investment at all.

Pinball Machines

The trusty pinball machine has been around since the late 1800s yet still uses the same formula as the pinball machines of old. Lights, sound effects, the bounce of the ball, the sound of the flipper, and the lure of a high score. With a little smart thinking, your pinball machines can earn you a lot of money.

- **Install a pinball machine in your waiting area.** If you keep the noise levels down so nearby customers don't get annoyed, they can be a great moneymaker. Vendors can bring you the latest pinball machines for free and will split all profits with you at the end of the month. At 50 cents a game, a machine only needs to be played ten times a day to bring you $75 a month in profit sharing. Not a bad return on zero investment!

- **Vintage machines.** Invest in a vintage pinball machine rather than getting a coin-op company to bring in a high-tech modern machine on which you'll have to split your profits. Older machines cost far less to buy and a lot less to maintain, and the appeal of an old machine will bring back memories for your older patrons. Machines such as these can be purchased through online auctions such as eBay (**www.ebay. com**).

- **Outright purchase.** If you choose to purchase your own pinball machines, look in the classified ads in the newspaper or at local auctions for the best deal. Of course, purchasing your own machine will mean you're responsible for its maintenance, so look for a machine that either comes with an array of spare parts or that has been fully serviced recently. The older the machine, the tougher it becomes to track down spare parts when the time comes to repair them.

Darts

Long a bar game institution, the old dartboard has become high-tech.

- **New technology.** Look at what's available on the market today. The dartboard has received a technological boost. Coin-operated dart systems not only keep score for your patrons, but they also bring in a new source of revenue. Turnkey systems can be purchased or brought in under a profit-sharing deal.

- **Dedicated area.** Even if you can't be bothered with a coin-op version of darts, it still pays to set aside an area for a dartboard. Tournaments and leagues can bring in a steady flow of new customers.

Pool Tables

Who doesn't enjoy going out for an evening of pool? Many bars base their entire business on the lure of this age-old game. What's more, the money that can be brought in from the tables is perhaps the most lucrative of any coin-op game.

- **Investment.** If you're looking for a sound investment in coin-op machinery that won't cost you a lot to maintain, pool tables are the way to go. When they do need servicing, repairs are relatively simple. Unlike computerized coin-ops, they don't need to be updated frequently. Having a pool table supplier bring in tables for free is a valid option if you want to simplify things, but you'll be giving up half of your profits for that convenience. Spend a little, make a lot.

- **Space.** One of the worst things that a pool player can experience is a lack of space. Make sure you give each table ample room in which to play.

- **Maintain your pool equipment.** Bent cues, missing balls, no chalk on the end of the table; these are all small things that will drive a dedicated pool player elsewhere. Remember, a dedicated pool player will stay and drink and pump dollars into a table all night long.

- **Run a weekly pool tournament.** Offering a prize to the winner of a weekly pool tournament is bound to bring you many times that amount in beer sales from the contestants, their friends, and those who just like to watch. Increase your prize and increase your tournament's appeal.

- **Make your tables free for maximum customer draw.** Pool tables are a great source of income, but have you considered setting them to play for free for at least part of the week? It's an irrefutable fact that pool tables draw drinkers into your establishment, so if your venue is empty on a Monday, why not make that free pool night and fill the bar? You might as well fill the joint and make some money!

Jukeboxes

For years, hospitality venues have seen the appeal and profitability of the jukebox. Modern times haven't changed the jukebox's universal appeal. In fact, some venues not only make a fortune from their jukebox, they also serve as the venue's number-one draw.

- **Never bring a generic jukebox into your establishment.** The suppliers will fill your machine with music your customers have never heard before and are unlikely to pay to hear again, whereas purchasing your own jukebox and filling it with CDs that you know have local appeal is a far better option. It'll cost a little more initially, but if you get rid of the discs that don't pay and leave in the ones that do, you'll soon be earning a whole lot more—and not splitting profits.

- **Volume level.** Your bar staff should never let the jukebox get ridiculously loud, nor should they let it be so low that it can't be heard.

Beer Isn't the Only Beverage That Comes Brewed

Coffee-based beverages have long been a bar staple, but times have changed, and nowadays people aren't content to have their coffee from just any drip-coffee machine.

- **Espresso.** Today's coffee drinkers want to know that the coffee they're buying is quality. They want espresso or nothing. Over the last decade, coffee making has become more of an art form than ever. If you're keeping up with consumer trends, you better have an espresso machine on the premises.

- **Baristas.** Though a true barista is a whiz with the espresso machine and can command a far higher salary, for the most part you won't need an expert at the helm of your espresso machine—just someone competent who can train others to a similar level of competence. Make the coffee machine part of your orientation for new staff.

- **Investment.** While the initial investment in coffee-making hardware can be recouped in a matter of months, from that point on you're looking at a profit margin equal to, or even higher than, that of traditional alcohol sales. Make that investment now!

- **Promotions.** Promote your new coffee service, if need be, with giveaways or specials.

- **Ambiance.** An integral part of today's coffee-drinking experience is where you drink it. Create an atmosphere that is welcoming to today's coffee-drinkers.

There are a variety of manufacturers that offer high-quality coffee and espresso equipment. Check out the following:

- **ASTORIA espresso and cappuccino coffee machines by General Espresso Equipment** are available in a variety of commercial lines. The Astoria JADA Super Automatic is the most productive espresso and cappuccino machine in the world. Two independent brewing groups can dispense four espresso servings simultaneously. The JADA is controlled by an advanced user-friendly micro-processor system with easy-to-read, easy-to-operate touch pads and an illuminated electronic functions display. The Astoria Sibilla is available in one, two, or three brewing heads (groups) with six programmable/volumetric portion selections and an override semiautomatic button. It can produce up to 240 espresso servings per hour. For more information, visit **www.espressobrewer.com** or call 336-393-0224.

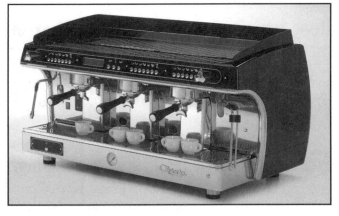

Bars Need Cigars

We all know that smoking is on the downward slide, but few realize that cigar smoking is actually on the rise. Affluent bar patrons and those merely seeking something different are turning to the humidor for a relaxing smoke. What this means to you is an opportunity to profit from supplying what your customers want. While cigars sales are well and good as a profit alternative, also consider the many other aspects of this trend that can bring you a fine profit. Cigar smoking is far more than a habit, it's a ritual, and if you're selling cigars, you need to supply the tools and atmosphere that go with the experience.

- **Start with a mood.** The cigar is all about relaxation, so replacing your standard bar-style tables and chairs with wooden coffee tables, leather chairs, and/or sofas is a great start. Keeping the music low, making sure there's a good ventilation system, and ensuring seclusion from the rest of your bar operation is the finishing touch. If you can outfit a room, or a section of your venue in this fashion, you'll find cigar smokers—and others who just enjoy a quieter experience—making a beeline for your door!

- **Accessorize.** Giving your customers something to take home with your logo on it is a great way to remind them to come back. Anything from matchbooks to lighters to cigar cutters is a great (and inexpensive) option for your venue.

- Don't open the door without a **humidor**. Cigars are susceptible to outside conditions, which mean savvy cigar bars provide a temperature-controlled humidor for their cigar products. These can be freestanding structures or built into the existing facilities. While a good humidor protects your cigars, it also serves as a great POS display for them.

- If you can't cut a cigar, you can't smoke it. There are multitudes of **cigar cutters** available for resale. The price of a good cutter depends on the style, blade, quality, and materials, but most range in price from as little as $2.50 to a thousand times that amount. Variety is key, and if you offer a good range of cutters for sale, some with your logo on them, you can bring in a great profit for a small investment.

- **Serving equipment.** This is another important part of the professional cigar bar. Presentation boxes that hold a number of cigars and can be brought to the table by a server are a very elegant touch. Individual cigar cases can be an excellent add-on product for when you make a cigar sale.

- **Cigar matches.** Very different from standard tissue matches, they offer yet another source of revenue for your cigar bar. Cigar smokers traditionally don't like the flavor that a common sulfur-based match gives their smoke, but cedar matches, which are slightly longer and emit fewer odors, are right up their alley. Cover any matchbooks you sell with your logo (every marketing opportunity is valuable) and sell them for a nominal fee or give them away free with every cigar purchase.

- **Cigar lighters** are also far different from the everyday cigarette lighter as they use butane. The reason for this variation is the same as the reasoning behind cedar matches—butane burns cleaner and imparts very little taste on the cigar itself, though it is more expensive. Stock up and sell to your heart's content!

- **Ashtrays.** While just about any standard ashtray can do the job, elongated ashtrays with deep cigar resting channels allow your smokers to put their cigars down without spilling them about. Cigar ashtrays come in many materials, from glass to ceramic, marble to metal. They top off the appeal of your cigar bar nicely.

Live Entertainment and Celebrities

Eventually all bars consider live entertainment. Few things draw in crowds like a live band. However, knowing which bands to book is not always easy—or affordable. If you have a small bar, consider open-mike night and opening your doors to local bands that need a venue to practice. This will bring some entertainment to your bar at no cost—and entertainers often bring their friends along.

For more ambitious booking, you may need to contact managers and publicists of more established entertainers. Prepare yourself by having the stats of your bar—how many customers you can draw, and what the crowd is like—ready. You should give the manager or publicist the reasons why your bar is a great place for the entertainer to perform.

Even celebrities will sometimes appear at smaller venues if there is a good reason for them to do so. If a celebrity will be in your area, contact the their publicist and give them the most compelling reasons you can for appearing at your establishment—be it a charitable cause or some other motivation. Celebrities tend to draw a crowd, and if your bar gets a reputation for celebrity sightings, you can expect a good crowd on any given night. Be sure to give them the ultra VIP treatment, and ask for an autograph that can be prominently but discreetly hung behind the bar.

CHAPTER THIRTEEN

Your Bar's Personality

"What's the bar like?" is the first question that someone will ask a friend who has visited a new bar or restaurant. They want to know who you cater to, what you offer, and what style you embody. Various elements make up a bar's personality—or what a bar is "like":

- Décor and ambience

- Advertising and marketing

- Themes

- Patrons

- Bar name

- Drinks and food offered

- Waitstaff

- Building structure

- Entertainments and incidentals

Décor and Ambience

The way you decorate your bar will leave a strong impression on customers that visit your establishment. Elements such as table linens, furniture selection, artwork on walls, the color scheme, window treatments, and lighting should all work together to give one impression. Combining two very different styles—such as a cowboy theme and pastel colors—is not a great idea. Keeping things simple—especially at first—is advised.

Themes

Not every bar has a theme, but many successful bars have either theme night or themes. If your bar has an overall theme, it is often easier to choose a color theme and décor, as you are working with an overall idea. There are millions of themes from which to choose. The only limit is your imagination. Some themes that bars have used successfully in the past include the following:

- **Movies and music.** Bars featuring movie posters, Oscar statue replicas, and director chairs as customer seating are quite popular. Plenty of people love movies, and this type of theme has the possibility of special "movie nights."

- **Old-fashioned.** Bars placed in old buildings can often play up that theme by acquiring antique furniture and appearing old-fashioned and quaint.

- **Local.** Local bars may have photos of the city or town as it looked over the years. They may also have local celebrity autographs and local fare to offer. These are often a big draw in tourist towns.

- **Marine.** Having portholes as windows, adopting nautical rope to place around the bar, and hanging up pictures of ships are a few of the ways that you can turn your bar into a marine-themed bar. It is very inexpensive to do and may draw customers because marine themes tend to lend a bar a "homey" look.

- **Futuristic.** Spare glass and metal furnishings can create a sci-fi feeling that can go quite well with techno artists or dancing. This sort of bar tends to be a hit with the younger, hip crowd.

- **Military.** If you are near a military base, camouflage gear, a menu titled "rations," and some military posters on the wall are all that are needed to create a place for service personnel to spend off-duty hours quite happily.

- **Biker.** If you love motorcycles, you can draw a like-minded crowd by decorating with bike decals and offering merchandise.

- **Smoking.** Many bars offer cigars and cigarettes, but some offer a huge array of cigarillos, fancy cigars, and chewing tobacco. Since plenty of bar patrons also smoke, offering a wide choice of smoking options ensures that cigar aficionados will visit such a bar in droves.

- **Comedy.** A number of comedy clubs are really bars with comedy entertainment. Plenty of people like to laugh, and drinks combined with laughter ensure a good time. Of course, you would have to find a steady stream of good acts in order to have such a themed bar, but the success of comedy clubs suggests that a good market exists for this sort of thing.

- **Cafeteria or market style.** Surprisingly, restaurants and bars that are arranged as traditional markets have done quite well recently. The wide array of fresh food and the outdoorsy atmosphere brings in customers.

- **Peanut bars.** At peanut bars, the attitude is often quite casual. In general, each table gets baskets of peanuts that can be peeled and eaten. The shells go onto the sawdust-covered floor. The advantage of this is that peanuts are cheap and often are a nice complement to beer. This would combine well with a sports theme.

- **Beer.** Beer bars sell other types of beverages but often emphasize a wide range of beers on tap. Some bars offer many dozens of beers on tap from all over the world, which ensures a steady clientele of serious beer drinkers.

- **Tropical.**
Whether it is in imitation of a Hawaiian island or a general tropical locale, a tropical theme lends itself well to exotic mixed drinks such as piña coladas as well as traditional island music. Bright, cheerful colors and a warm atmosphere  create a pleasant and relaxed mood. Many customers enjoy the feeling they get when they visit such bars.

- **Aquatic.** A few fish tanks and the color blue are all it takes to create a calming water theme. Candles in each table can rest in aquariums of water. This is a very inexpensive theme to adopt.

- **"Green."** An "eco" theme will often draw a younger, alternative crowd. Healthful meal choices, neutral colors, and soft candle lighting (from beeswax candles) are required for this sort of theme.

- **Literary.** Inkstand candle holders, books on the tables, coffee on the menu, and posters of authors on the wall complement this theme nicely. You can easily hold poetry readings at such a bar. If you like, you can also act as a used bookstore. If you have an upstairs room, you can let literary and writing clubs meet up there, ensuring a steady clientele.

- **Tacky.** The very strange—fuzzy dice, leopard print, bright colors—

appeals to a younger crowd. The décor is very easy to arrange and the theme is broad enough to include plenty of inexpensive items.

- **Adult.** Many bars feature exotic dancers to bring in extra clientele. While these bars will generally appeal mostly to men, couples do visit. Check licensing and zoning laws carefully, as these sorts of bars will generally be more controlled than other bars.

- **Dance.** Many bars are dance bars, offering live acts or DJs to encourage dancing. Although many appeal to the younger crowd, plenty of dance bars attract an older customer base as well, by advertising VIP lounges or  "front-of-the-line" preferential treatment for those customers over a specific age. One of the nice things about having this sort of bar is that customers will typically stay at the bar for a while to dance. Dancing will also encourage plenty of drink buying. In many cases, a dance bar can have an additional theme as well. To encompass this theme successfully, you will need a larger space to set aside for dancing.

- **Retro.** Retro bars are still very popular. Some are fashioned after malt shops of the past, and many feature 1950s, '60s or '70s posters and décor. Servers can easily adopt uniforms from retro years, and older cars can be parked in the bar as decoration.

- **Internet.** Internet cafés have been very popular for some time, but now many have become bars, offering alcoholic drinks and food as well as traditional coffees. Since many bar customers do business at the bar, offering Internet service is a logical step, especially if many of your customers are businesspeople. You will need to make sure that no drinks are spilled on the computers, though.

- **Girly.** While in the past bars were seen as places for men to meet, a number of bars have sprung up that appeal mainly to women. These bars may offer special treatment for female customers or male dancers. In many cases, martinis and  drinks such as the Cosmopolitan are quite popular in these bars.

- **Artistic.** Prints on the wall and paint splotches everywhere, some artist-style bars even encourage customers to draw on the walls and tables. These are bound to appeal to the younger bar customers as well as to the "alternative crowd."

- **Spa.** A few bars now have adopted spa services, offering customers massages and hair touchups (styling only, no cuts) as well as relaxing hot stone treatments. This makes customers feel comfortable and relaxed. It is also a nice idea for bars where women are the primary customers.

- **Jazz and blues.** These bars have been around for a long time, but continue to do well as so many people are ardent jazz fans. Live jazz and blues acts, a New Orleans-style décor, and southern cooking complement this style of bar nicely. This sort of bar will draw quite a variety of customers.

- **International.** Many bars have themes that focus on a specific location

(French, Italian, Irish, English). These bars tend to draw a wide range of customers as well. Many customers coming to these bars will expect a decent menu made up of specific cuisine. If you have a French bar, be prepared to serve French food as well as offer French music and décor.

- **Sports.** General sports bars have plenty of sports memorabilia on the walls and several television sets for watching games. People come to these bars to watch sports events with others. During big games, these bars tend to be crowded. The main clientele here is men, although some women enjoy stopping by sports bars as well. Some sports bars focus on a specific sport, but most are general sports bars.

- **Western themes** are quite popular because of the fans of country music out there. Genuine western décor may be a bit expensive to buy, depending on where you live, but if there is a country music station in your area, chances are that there is a customer base for this type of bar.

- **Warehouse or industrial.** Very popular among the younger crowd, this theme is also very inexpensive and simple to set up. All that is needed are some unpainted walls, dark lighting, some inexpensive exposed metal beams, and the theme is well established. Many bars that are established in older factories or buildings have this theme. As an added bonus, there is no need to worry about covering up exposed pipes or water damage with this theme—all the flaws of an older building complement the theme in this case!

You can get more ideas about bar themes by browsing through the travel section of your local newspaper—bars that work in other areas will generally at least have a chance where you live, as bar customers tend to want similar things across the country. Be sure to look at themes that the competition offers, and ask your friends and family about themed bars they have been to or heard of. You can always try a theme night to test out a theme you might want to take on a larger scale later on.

Patrons

The customers who visit your bar affect how your bar is perceived. A customer base of motorcycle enthusiasts will give a bar a much different style than a group of socialites. You can control who visits your bar to some extent by the policies and themes you set up for your establishment. A fashion-themed bar with a strict dress code is not likely to draw the sports-lover from the factory down the road.

Bar Name

The name you give your bar will reflect how it is seen. A French or Italian name may make the bar seem more exclusive. A single letter, such as "V," was popular for a while for very upscale and trendy bars. Your name—Fred's, for example—suggests a more casual atmosphere. You should think about your bar's name before you make your final decision. The name should be easy to pronounce but unique. A catchy name is more likely to be remembered by customers. A good name also drums up interest in a new bar.

Drinks and Food Offered

The drinks and food that are served will often affect how a bar is received. If a customer tells a friend that your bar serves "truffles in champagne sauce," it creates a very different impression than "fish and chips." The names of your menu items and what you offer can make your bar seem more exclusive or more approachable, more exotic or pretentious. In any case, if someone can call your food and drinks "tasty," you are well on your way to acquiring new customers.

Waitstaff

Service is so important that it is quite common for potential customers to ask their friends about the service they received at a particular venue. Almost everyone has had a terrible experience with bad service—slow service or a very surly server. Those who have had a bad experience will often want assurance that the bar they are considering will treat them well. If your customers can say that your service is "excellent," you are more likely to earn a great reputation, and your bar's personality is more likely to be seen in a positive light.

Building Structure

Whether the bar is large or small, in a new building, or in a historic mansion, structural details will affect how your bar is seen. Building structure can make a bar seem "cozy" or "spacious," "quaint" or "hip." There may not be much you can do about the building you have bought, but you can ensure that you use the space you have to your bar's best advantage.

GREGG IS THE OWNER OF AN INFORMAL PIANO BAR/CABARET ON THE UPPER EAST SIDE OF NEW YORK CITY. SINGING WAITRESSES AND BARTENDERS POUR THE DRINKS WHILE PROVIDING BACKUP TO THE PIANO PLAYER'S SHOW TUNES AND ROCK 'N' ROLL OLDIES. "INCREDIBLE FRIENDSHIPS BEGIN AT BRANDY'S" IS THE SLOGAN THAT HANGS ABOVE THE PIANO THROUGHOUT THE NIGHT.

---

*O*ur staff is the most important aspect of our business. We do not advertise a special drink or a special recipe, so when a guest comes in, our bartender recommends a drink. I spend most of my time behind the bar talking with the customers. We receive a lot of "regulars" during happy hour.

Our walls are decorated with posters of Broadway shows that our staff has performed in. We are the only bar in our area that provides guests with live music. Our biggest mistake on spending money on equipment was when we purchased a sound system that was supposed to be state-of-the-art and ended up being a faulty sound system.

CHAPTER FOURTEEN

Dealing with Problems

Bad Employees

Bad employees can mean everything from employees who steal to employees who do not provide the customer service that is required of them. If you are having problems with your staff, you will first want to examine what could be wrong. Is the staff member having some sort of personal problem? Is there a problem at work? Does the employee have the necessary training?

Define the problem and approach the employee in private. Explain the problem as kindly as possible and offer to help resolve the issue, if appropriate. Sometimes all that is needed is extra training or time off to cope with a personal problem. Once you have a solution, tell your employee when you will re-evaluate performance and discuss what specific changes (friendly service to customers, faster drink service) you want to see in place.

If we are looking for the top 20 percent of potentials, it helps if we have at least 50 applicants to screen from. One of the most productive ways we have found to gather a large response is to Web-vertise. It seems that today's workforce increasingly relies on the Web to scout opportunities. It gives the business the opportunity to screen by e-mail and see how the candidate responds in writing before having an interview.

Hiring a bartender who has gone through some sort of bartending training does allow customer service-oriented candidates to gain a base of knowledge before hiring. I would rather train a bartending graduate than take on potential bad habits of an experienced one.

Employees who do not improve or who are involved in illegal or dishonest activity at the bar should be let go. If you can, offer to act as a reference on the employee's next job hunt. Whatever the circumstances, wish your employee all the best and try to part on at least professional or somewhat polite terms.

Unhappy Neighbors

Some people are not at all happy about a new bar in the neighborhood, especially if your establishment has opened up in an area where there were previously no bars. If located near a residential area, people may complain about noise. If your bar is in a business area, other businesses may complain about the mess or damage your bar customers make on the way home from your establishment. If you work hard to ensure that your customers do not leave the bar intoxicated, it can be frustrating to be depicted as someone who lets an unruly bunch loose into the night.

Try to work with your neighbors. Sponsor neighborhood activities, show up for neighborhood meetings, and listen to neighbor complaints. Ask about suggestions for how you might improve neighbor relations. If you feel that your bar is being depicted unfairly, offer neighbors a free VIP pass to your bar so that they can see for themselves how the bar is operated. With time and a little patience (as well as a lot of communication), most neighbors will get used to the idea of a new bar in the area. You can help speed this process along by listening and being friendly and approachable.

Unhappy Customers

A complaining customer can be a serious problem, especially if he or she is complaining loudly enough for others to hear. Train your staff to deal with an irate customer. First, staff should aim to calm down the customer by directly addressing the problem. The staff should apologize for the problem and offer to fix it, if possible. If the food or drink is unpalatable, new food and drink should be brought at once. If service is slow, the customer should be seen to at once. If there is a problem with the order, the problem should be explained. If the staff is not able to appease the customer, staff should enlist management's help.

If you are called to resolve a dispute, it is important that you stay calm, even if the customer personally attacks you or the bar. Ask about the problem and what it would take to improve the situation. In some cases, free drinks and food vouchers for another meal will make things acceptable. In other cases, no effort will satisfy a customer. If possible, try to agree to disagree. Even the most irate customer is likely to see your attempts to resolve the problem in a positive light.

Disturbances Outside or Inside the Bar

Sudden yelling or shouting, inside the bar or outside of it, can be distracting to customers and can disrupt their evening. If the disturbance occurs inside, ask the offender to stop and lower his or her voice. Most people will gladly lower their voice to avoid irritating others. If this does not work, take the person outside or into your office to see if you can resolve the problem. If it is evident that the customer will not calm down, ask staff to remove the offender and offer to call for a taxi.

There is little you can do about outside disturbances. Construction work or other such noises outside may simply be drowned out with music. Close bar windows and doors to keep out dust and muffle noise. If the disturbance is caused by yelling or some other noise, a staff member should investigate to make sure that no one outside is in need of assistance. For a very upsetting noise, apologize for the ruckus in addition to offering an explanation. Offer to move any affected customers to quieter areas of the bar.

Bad Reviews

A bad review in a magazine, newspaper, Internet site, or guidebook can be upsetting, especially if you have been working hard to establish a good reputation. Realize that not every potential customer reads every review. A local newspaper review may do some damage, but plenty of potential customers will stop by out of curiosity. Studies show that most people pay more attention to reviews and recommendations of friends and acquaintances. If you continue to provide excellent value and service, your current customers will recommend you, and the review will have less impact.

Crime

If a crime occurs in your establishment, the legal ramifications may be expensive for you. If someone has been hurt in a crime, you also need to worry about the customer or staff affected. In any case, the unwanted publicity surrounding a crime at your establishment can be embarrassing and upsetting. The best way to get over a crime is to work on helping anyone who was hurt in the incident. You may want to review your security and safety policies and share them with the police so that you will be able to avoid incidents in the future.

No Customers

Try to figure out why you have fewer customers than you had anticipated. If you are not easy to spot from the road, you may need to advertise more. If you advertise, you may need to offer more incentives, such as entertainment or giveaways. You will also want to evaluate the impression you have made on any customers you have had. If customers are unhappy with the drinks, food, or service, you may need to change policies to ensure better customer care and put more effort into advertising to lure back patrons.

Too Many Customers

This may not seem like much of a problem. In fact, many bar managers may want to have as many customers as possible. However, too many patrons at one time can cause overcrowding and a less pleasant atmosphere for all your patrons. Too many customers at one time may also tax your staff and your supplies. In fact, too many customers can even close your establishment—most towns have fire regulations concerning how many people can safely be in one place at a time.

If you are expecting more customers than normal for a specific event or promotion, hire more staff and stock up on supplies in anticipation. Move furniture around to allow for maximum movement. Post bouncers at the doors to keep track of how many people enter to comply with fire regulations.

If you are regularly getting more customers than you can handle, you will want to hire more permanent staff members and make the most of the space you have. You may be able to open previously closed spaces to customers as well. You can also control how many customers visit your bar at any one time by controlling your promotions. For example, if you have a lot of business types and blue-collar workers patronizing your bar, you can offer a special business buffet for the businessperson and a special sports night, broadcasting the latest game. Directing marketing toward each group can help ensure a steady but manageable stream of customers. If your business continues to expand, you may have to simply expand your premises or move to a larger building.

Customer Accidents

If a spill occurs, the staff member should immediately apologize and offer a napkin to help the customer clean up the mess. The staff member should apologize at once and clean up any broken glass or dropped cutlery. The incident should be reported to the manager. If the customer is injured by the spill, because the spilled food or drink was hot enough to scald or burn, for example, the staff member should not touch the customer but should report the incident to management and get medical help for the customer immediately.

Food Poisoning

Greater awareness about food poisoning lets most people know that food poisoning can be fatal. People are far more cautious about dining at a place where someone has experienced food poisoning. Many people will also sue the establishment that made them ill.

If your business is affected by such a claim, take steps at once. If you are legally charged, seek a lawyer's help and follow all advice to the letter. If a charge is reported, ask for a health inspection of your bar to be conducted, and post the positive results in an obvious place. Find out what the possible problem was (meat, drink, another food item) and conduct your own investigation into the matter. Take any steps—such as finding a new supplier or implementing new storage policies—to help ensure that no food poisoning will occur in the future. (For in-depth sanitation and food safety-program information, read *HACCP & Sanitation in Restaurants and Food Service Operations: A Practical Guide Based on the FDA Food Code,* published by Atlantic Publishing; **www.atlantic-pub.com**, 800-814-1132.)

Small Profits

Be sure to evaluate your money situation closely. Are you keeping poor records, causing you to lose track of money? Hire an accountant or start looking over your books more closely. Are you spending more than you can? Cut back on unnecessary costs. Are you the victim of theft? Look over your paperwork carefully to see if you can spot the offender.

Intoxicated Customers

Working within the law is critical. But where does your staff draw the line? These pointers may help:

- **Doubles—to serve or not?** A double served with a mixer is more than twice as potent as a single shot diluted with a mixer. Take this into account before offering too many incentives for your clientele to move up to doubles.

- **Cut-off point.** Many experienced bartenders will talk to a customer before they get to the cut-off point and let them know that they're getting close to the line before they get too drunk and belligerent. This is an especially important tip for dealing with younger people. They're generally less able to read their own level of tolerance.

- **Make sure your staff is firm and direct when refusing service to a customer.** If a bartender shows the slightest bit of leniency, a problem drinker will zero-in on that person and take advantage. If your staff give in a little now, they may give in a little more tomorrow. Be firm!

- **Keep an eye on the people sitting with the customer who has been cut off.** Quite often, they will volunteer to get drinks for the person who is supposed to be cut off. If they do, your establishment is still liable for any injury.

- **Excuses.** Sometimes a customer will attempt to get another drink, telling you that they live locally and are walking home. Regardless of the truth of this claim, it's still illegal to serve a visibly intoxicated customer, no matter what their situation. Simply explain the law to the customer, and let them know that the bar could lose its license if they are caught over-serving customers.

- **Avoid embarrassment.** If you want to avoid embarrassing a good customer in front of others, simply ask to speak with them outside or away from listening ears. Explain the situation. A little consideration in this manner will mean a lot.

- **Nonalcoholic service.** When a customer is cut off from more alcohol, that doesn't mean they have to be cut off from service. Food, soda, coffee, iced tea; these are all great options to allow your intoxicated customer a way to continue enjoying their evening, without being sent home.

- **Other considerations.** Whenever you cut off a customer, make a small consideration to them in return. Offer to call them a cab, or even provide a free cup of coffee or bar snack. A small gratitude like this can only help you out of a tricky situation.

CHAPTER FIFTEEN

Myths About Managing a Bar That Could Hurt Your Business

Myth: Bartending School Is Vital for a Bartender

Many of the best bartenders learn most of their useful trade while at work. This is because bartending schools vary widely in quality. Some emphasize the preparation of rarely requested drinks without stressing useful skills such as bar management, customer satisfaction, and customer safety. If you are hiring a bartender, you should consider the school he or she has attended, but testing practical skills will give the best clue of how many useful skills the person has for waiting on your bar. If you are considering attending a bartending school, investigate the school to make sure that you will be taught skills such as organization and techniques of serving. A good bartending school or course will emphasize dealing with customers. Be wary of a bartending school that is more of a "drink mix" school, stressing mixing many types of drinks without teaching anything besides drink preparation. There are many of these sorts of schools out there, which claim that a bartender's greatest asset is knowing how to mix an endless variety of drinks. Learning to mix the latest drink is relatively simple once one looks up the recipe, and most patrons will order the most popular drink of the moment rather than some obscure mix. A bartender with a good grasp of people and basic bartending techniques is usually more useful than the bartender who only knows how to mix hundreds of drinks from memory but has few skills besides. In some cases, an employee with a hospitality degree is better able to handle the bar job than someone who has attended a bartender school.

Myth: If You Hire Experienced Employees, There Is No Need to Train Them

You still need to train your employees to ensure that they understand what you want them to do. In cases where an employee has worked at another establishment for a while, you may actually need to provide additional training to allow the employee to get used to the way you want things done versus how they did things at their previous job.

Myth: Hiring Younger Serving Staff Is Best

Many bar managers mistakenly believe that hiring young female servers will help ensure a high customer loyalty. This is based on the belief that middle-aged men are the main patrons of bars, which is no longer the case. When hiring servers or other staff, you should consider experience and skill over age or physical appearance. In most states, hiring based on age or appearance is discriminatory and can lead to lawsuits.

Myth: The Customer Is Always Right

Bar managers want the customer to be happy enough to return and satisfied enough to recommend the establishment to others. It is never wise to argue with a customer, and if the difference of opinion is something quite small, it is better to humor the customer in order to avoid making him or her feel embarrassed. On the other hand, if the customer insists that he or she is not intoxicated and can drink more, for example, then they should be refused further drinks.

Myth: Security Staff Is Vital in Today's Bar

Security does add a certain peace of mind, but at many establishments, it is still the bartender who acts primarily as the security force of the bar. Where your security comes from depends on your location and bar. If you decide you do not need a separate security staff, however, make sure that the bartender or some other personnel are willing to help customers in case of an incident.

Myth: To Run a Successful Bar, Just Serve Great Drinks

While quality drinks are a key to bar success, many people go to bars to spend time with others. If you serve good drinks but offer exceptional atmosphere and service, you are likely to do well. In today's competitive world, great drinks alone are not enough. Bar managers need to have good financial planning and careful advertising and marketing and offer great customer service in order to be a success.

Myth: To Increase Profits, Reduce Costs

Reducing costs or cutting corners (reducing the size of drinks or firing staff) is unlikely to help. Customers expect more from bars than ever before. Offering them less is unlikely to bring you the results you want. If you are just starting out, it may take months to see a profit. If you have been in business for a while, increasing customers and getting more from each customer by encouraging spending and lingering are far better strategies than downsizing in order to make a profit.

Myth: You Must Keep Expanding in Order to Make a Profit

Many bar managers think that in order to make a large profit, they need to dabble in everything. For this reason, many bars spend large amounts of money setting up dance floors, live acts, larger establishments, and restaurants. When you are just starting out, though, it is often best to keep things simple. Do not expand randomly, assuming that spending more money will bring in more money. Only expand after careful research and weighing the potential risks and benefits. You do not want to get into debt for a venture that is unlikely to work for your bar.

CHAPTER SIXTEEN

Nightclubs

Nightclubs are the glamorous big sister of the bar industry. If a bar is small, a nightclub is bigger. If a bar has a jukebox, then the nightclub has a DJ or even a band. If a bar has a bartender and a server for service, then a nightclub has more bartenders and servers working plus a series of doormen, valets, and security personnel. If a bar is dimly lit, then a nightclub has light shows. If a bar has an open mike, a nightclub will have karaoke nights and booked amateur comedians. Running a nightclub has all of the issues of managing a bar, only bigger and with more entertainment for their customers.

Nightclubs are entertainment destinations for customers. A nightclub is a place customers plan to go, and then stay for the evening. For nightclubs, their competition is not only other nightclubs, but also sporting arenas, movie theaters, plays, concerts, and shows. As nightclubs are the entertainment side of this industry, attracting and keeping customers is the most important consideration in this type of bar management.

Because of the focus on entertaining, managing a nightclub is slightly different from a bar. Nightclub owners and managers will work with agents to secure comedians, DJs, bands, and adult entertainers. The clientele are coming to see these people; the nightclub is merely the venue in which they perform. Nightclubs must stay on the cutting edge of their clienteles' entertainment wishes and book accordingly.

Types of Nightclubs

Within the broad category of nightclubs, there are several different types. Each type has its own unique challenges as well as clientele for their operations.

Dance Clubs

A dance club features "danceable" music spun by a DJ or band. Fast and slow songs are alternated for the patrons to dance to. Dance clubs can focus on one type of music, such as country-western, disco, reggae, salsa, hip-hop or rap, or may have several floors within the building featuring a different type of music on each floor. Some dance clubs will feature different types of music for each day of the week. Dance clubs attract dating couples and singles looking to meet other people. The usual age of dance club patrons is "just legal" to mid-thirties, although older clientele looking for some fun may be in the club as well. Dance club clientele go where they enjoy the music; each group will have different demographic profiles such as race, income level, and national origin.

Dance clubs need separate entertainment licenses, plus extensive sound and lighting systems. Soundproofing will be needed if more than one musical act is in the building at one time. Finally, mixing several different music selections may mean crossover guests, and the possibility that the different groups will not interact well with each other. Security may be needed to keep the groups separate, or different entrances for each area may be needed.

Live Music Clubs

Similar to a dance club, live music clubs are venues for bands to play. Some nightclubs with careful layout can have live music on some days of the week, and have a DJ for others. Live music clubs can be divided into rock, country-western, jazz, or blues. Some live music clubs, depending on the music choices, may have a dance floor, a mosh pit, or simply chairs and tables for the patrons to sit and enjoy the evening's selections. The music is the primary draw for the clientele, thus determining the demographics of the listening group. Some nightclubs will book and stage different bands on different nights. For example, Wednesday is country-western while Friday is rock and roll. Other nightclubs will focus on one type of music, such as a jazz club. Nightclubs that book the same type of music on a regular basis will have an easier time marketing future events to the clientele than clubs that change musical selections. Live music clubs will also need to invest in visuals and sound equipment in the main area and will need equipment case storage and changing rooms for the talent.

Live music clubs normally need entertainment licenses. They need to work extensively with local band agents and managers to book groups. Paying the band can become complicated as the costs of advertising may be divided between the club and the band. Popular bands with a following may demand a percentage of the cover charge or sales of drinks. Well-known regional and national bands will want long booking leads, six months or more, with an advertising commitment from the club.

Comedy Clubs

Open-mike nights are becoming a popular route to comedic fame: Chris Rock and Jay Leno were both discovered in comedy clubs on amateur nights. Comedy clubs are managed similarly to live music clubs, but with a microphone and spotlights instead. Some nightclubs that have already invested in the lighting and sound systems for music can feature a comedy night or open-mike nights on slower nights of the week.

Since audiences at a comedy club are seated, tables and chairs will be needed for the customers. Smart clubs can also add wireless "applause meters" that register approval (or disapproval) for jokes. Like a music club, the clientele will mostly reflect the appeal of the comedian. For the club, finding comedians may be an issue. Open-mike nights may not draw in enough clientele. Other clubs will deal with agents who will book regionally and nationally known talent for an operation. As with booking known talent, you face long booking times and heavy advertising expenses.

For clubs that focus on amateur talent, set up a series of contests where comedians "face off," and the winner continues to the next round. At the end of the quarter or year, a final week of contests can be held during a slow week for maximum sales effect.

Adult Clubs

With pretty women (and the occasional man), scantily dressed, slithering across a stage removing clothes, adult clubs are the naughty older sister of the bar industry. Adult clubs focus on entertaining mostly men, and may add other entertainment between the performances. Other adult clubs will add pool and karaoke for entertainment. Adult clubs can be extremely profitable for an owner, but are not without some risks.

Adult clubs usually face extensive zoning and licensure requirements beyond those of a regular nightclub. Most cities either prohibit this type of establishment or limit it to a certain area within the town. An adult nightclub will need special entertainment licenses specific to this type of entertainment. The first adult club in a city will also face significant public scrutiny concerning offerings and the dress levels of the entertainers. Adult clubs are watched carefully by local law enforcement for public decency violations, which includes what can be shown, how much and what touching is legal, and for signs of prostitution.

Differences Between Bars and Nightclubs

While most basic bar management is the same for nightclubs, there are some important differences between the two that affect how they operate. The following section discusses the major differences.

Licenses

In addition to a regular alcohol service license, nightclubs generally require additional entertainment licenses, especially if they offer bands or adult entertainment. These licenses are different from the regular licenses and may be granted on a yearly or as-needed basis. Entertainment licenses are very specific for what is allowed, and a nightclub may need additional permits for events that they do not normally hold. Since local governments grant licenses, anyone thinking of opening a nightclub is wise to seek legal council concerning regulations and permissions.

Location

Nightclubs are categorized by size. Small nightclubs hold about 250 patrons and range from 3,000 to 4,000 square feet. Medium-size nightclubs range from 4,000 to 15,000 square feet and can hold roughly 2,500 patrons. Massive nightclubs can serve more than 2,500 patrons and are usually more than 15,000 square feet. Remember, the square footage for the establishment includes the customer areas, public lobbies, public restrooms, and all of the back-of-the-house areas such as kitchens, storerooms, and dressing areas.

For most nightclub owners, finding large spaces that are relatively affordable can be a challenge. Usually the further from the main city area, the better the chances of finding reasonable rental rates. As nightclubs tend to be destinations, an out-of-town spot is feasible, as long as it is easy to find or not too expensive to reach via a cab. Other owners may decide to make a square footage/number-of-stories trade-off by renting a building and spreading the operations over several floors. This has the advantage of a compact footprint, yet employees, customers, and product will be going up and down flights on a nightly basis. For owners who want an inner-city location, this may be their only alternative.

Finding so much space under one roof can be tricky. Given the cost of modern construction, it may be cheaper to renovate. Other possibilities include warehouses, theaters, and strip malls. Another alternative is converting an old building, such as a factory, prison, or school that may be eligible for local and state grants or tax abatements, as an owner is renovating a building that would otherwise be demolished and off the tax rolls for several years. Several huge mansions have been successfully converted into multi-story nightclubs in the last few years.

Interior Costs

Because of their size, fixed costs such as rent, utilities, and taxes will be higher. Decorating costs will be higher as well. Nightclubs will also need more guest-related equipment such as tables, chairs, and glasses. All of these costs need to be carefully budgeted by management.

Visual Elements

A good nightclub will have a wide assortment of visual elements available for use by the band or DJ. Visual elements include the following:

- Strobe lights

- Spot lighting

- Smoke machines

- Pyrotechnics

- UV paints and black lights

- Laser light shows

- Psychedelic patterns

- Image projectors

- Beacons

- Bubble machines

- Rain or water misters

- Pin-beam spotlights

- Fog machines

- Disco mirror ball

Having a good visual light show is a key component of nightclubs, and patrons expect a certain level of "wow" on a nightly basis. Good visual effects are constantly changing and are patterned to match the beat and feel of the music. During breaks, lighting may still "play" until the music is back on.

None of this is cheap, however, but the visual elements equipment can last for years with careful use. Nightclub managers should hire a lighting consultant for maximum output with minimal equipment. As different visual effects components may not be compatible with items from other companies, the lighting consultant can help bridge those hardware issues. Finally, most component systems can be pre-programmed on a computer for the DJ to have "one-key" access to popular show combinations.

When the lighting plan is finished, have an experienced, licensed electrician install all of the pieces as well as check the electrical circuitry. This is one area not to skimp on, as the electrical draw of these items may compromise other pieces of equipment in the nightclub. Try to avoid situations where the bartender cannot run the dishwasher during certain light shows, as the power consumption will overload the circuits. A good electrician can adjust electrical loads and draws in such a way as to keep the business moving.

For pyrotechnics, check with the local fire marshal to make sure they are allowed in your area. If allowed, work with the fire department to check that the area is free from flammable materials such as drapes, wallboards, wall coverings, or furniture. If they are not allowed, make sure that traveling bands do not use them during their shows.

Sound Elements

Because hearing the music is an important part of the nightclub experience, managers need to invest in quality sound equipment. Depending on the layout of the nightclub, certain areas will be more "dead" or "flat" than others and will need careful speaker placement to even out the sound issues. Acoustical issues are found when the club is filled, as music can be absorbed or bounce off patrons, walls, and flooring. A wise nightclub manager will hire an acoustical expert to visit and get a feel for the room and its unique sound properties.

Sound components include speakers, amplifiers, mixers (soundboards), equalizers, compressors, music players (turntables, CD players), microphones, and cable/wiring components. As the music is a key attraction for customers, aim for heavy-duty commercial components that can handle the loud volumes and heavy use. Sound systems can be bought as a system or as components that are assembled at the nightclub. Again, hire a good electrician to run the cables and wires, and check to make sure that the wires can withstand the use. Keep a backup amplifier handy incase the main one blows out; a DJ should be able to swap it out quickly to keep the music going.

A sound system is one of those areas where "you get what you paid for." Buy the best system that the budget can handle, and keep it in good working order.

Video Feeds/TV

With flat-screen TV and computer monitors getting larger every day, nightclubs can easily invest in them to add visual excitement to the club. Using a feed from the cable or satellite TV stations, patrons can watch sporting events while dancing on the floor. When not being used for shows, a digital camera or video recorder can scan the crowd and feed the live images to the screens. With simple presentation programs, the screens can also show promos for upcoming events, the night's activities, and drink and food specials, right on the screen for customers to see.

Other options for video feeds include tables and bars with wireless programming. They are sturdy, waterproof computer monitors mounted horizontally with a computer program that senses movement from patrons and glasses. These tables can be programmed to show TV programs, menus, or nightclub events. They can also be programmed to have random or directed patterns when guests move their glasses. The customers can interact with the table during the evening and play games or trivia while it is running.

Again, this is not cheap technology, but it is easy to hook up and get running. Use the video feeds as backup entertainment in case the music goes down or talent is running late to the stage. Video feeds can also serve as eyes for patrons in the back of the room, helping to alleviate the inevitable push for the front that happens with live bands.

Layout

Nightclubs usually divide the actual building into two sections: front-of-the-house, where the customers are, and back-of-the-house, where only employees can go. Nightclubs, compared to other bars, will need a greater percentage of floor space for the back-of-the-house for liquor storage, music storage, band equipment storage, dressing rooms, employee break and restrooms, and central switching stations for all of the electronics. Front-of-the-house may require multiple bars setups, stages, dance floors, and décor that enhance the sound and lights rather than distract from them.

Layout starts with identifying the target customer and their desires. If needed, stages, DJ areas, and dance floors will be laid out first. Customer restrooms, lobbies, and the bars are added next. If an owner is starting with a blank slate, layout will be much easier. If it is a renovation, the layout may have to be retrofitted to existing utility setups to avoid extensive remodeling costs. Back-of-the-house rooms are blocked out after the front-of-the-house, using extras space as needed.

Layout is affected by local codes concerning fire exits and maximum capacity laws. An astute owner will involve the building inspectors when the club is still on the drawing board to avoid expensive changes later on. Since several nightclubs have been in the news recently for evacuation problems that caused patron deaths, this is one area to concentrate on as early as possible.

After the main elements are in, the sound and visual elements will need to be wired. Because of the amount of wiring and electrical draw from these devices, they will need to be placed in the rooms as early as possible. While speakers and TV can be moved later, planning all possible locations early means that electrical work can be done at this time for later use. Keeping options open is always a wise idea for layout.

Finally, layout needs to be reviewed for flow of customers, employees, and product. The quicker and easier it is for customers to get a drink or get on the dance floor, the more popular and profitable the club will be. The faster employees can get stock and serve customers, the easier their jobs are. Good layout means that everything flows around the rooms with ease.

Layer design on after the layout is done. Design is the theme—tropical, country-western, subway, or outer space—that identifies the nightclub and unifies every element. For example, two nightclubs may have the same visual and sound components, but design is what sets them apart. One nightclub may have a tropical theme using bamboo; the other may have a subway theme using metal gratings to cover speakers.

Design in a nightclub flows from the target customer and the unique needs of the establishment. Design elements includes the following:

- Wall coverings

- Ceiling treatments

- Floor treatments

- Style of table and chairs

- Bar style

- Columns

- Signs

- Room dividers

Good design in a nightclub helps to pull all of the various elements together to deliver the "wow" factor necessary to impress guests. Design also helps sound by amplifying or muting noise from speakers and highlights the visual elements of the nightclub. Good design is also classic; that is, what is installed now, will still look good with only minor tweaking in a few years.

Designers can employ some innovative tricks in nightclubs. Foam sculptures and elements can be created to absorb noise and lend to the theme. Wall coverings can help to absorb sound and create a sense of warmth. Colors used can help to convey a mood. Well-designed nightclubs will create an ambiance that increase profits by making the clientele comfortable.

Finding Talent

Nightclubs that rely on bands, comedians, and adult entertainers for the evening's activities will soon become very familiar with booking talent. Talent is divided into two categories: 1) amateurs who are not paid (except prize money) and are doing it for fun, and 2) professionals who expect a check at the end of the night. Some nightclubs will run amateur or open-mike nights as a cost-effective promotional program, but relying on unpaid talent to build a customer base, especially for dance club, comedy club, or music hall, will not ensure customers over the long run.

Whether looking for a DJ, comedian, band, or adult entertainer, the process for hiring entertainment is the same. For this example, a band will be used, but the others are handled in similar fashion. Most nightclubs will have one entertainment manager whose primary job it is to book, handle, and pay the entertainment after the evening is over, but all managers in a nightclub should be familiar with how it is done.

Most entertainers have a manager whose job it is to promote the talent to every possible venue. The managers will contact the nightclub directly and set up appointments to sell their group. Once a date is confirmed, the band manager will send the following items to the nightclub:

- Promotional kit for the band, including reproducible photos, bios, and standard flyers.

- Stage plot with where various electrical and acoustical equipment needs to be.

- Line chart explaining the electrical connections needed by the band's equipment.

- Song list for the band.

- Sample promotional items, such as T-shirts, CDs, and other items that the band wants to sell.

For the nightclub, having the promotional items as soon as possible means the advertising can start right away.

Some nightclubs will work with an entertainment bureau that is a "middleman" booking agency with a large roster of bands. Since a particular band may have an exclusive relationship with one entertainment bureau, nightclubs may have to work with several of them get all desired performers. When a nightclub works with an entertainment bureau, they normally work with one booking agent at that company, and the nightclub will pay the entertainment bureau in advance for the bookings. While working with a middleman may be more expensive, the nightclub will have some protection if the band breaks up before the appearance or the talent is sick; the bureau can usually find a last-minute replacement. Entertainment bureaus also make their money on successful promotions, so they can usually help with the extensive advertising needed to promote the event. Some entertainment bureaus are generalists, representing all types of talent. Other bureaus are specialists, only representing one type of talent, such as comedians, or even as specific as only country-western bands, making them a good source for similar talent pools.

Other nightclubs will have "house" talent—the DJ or band that play on a regular schedule at that nightclub only. This group of talent is employed by the nightclub and report directly to the entertainment manager. The nightclub is responsible for their equipment and possibly instruments. A good house band or DJ can be a marketing draw; a bad one will drive customers away. Some nightclubs employ both strategies by having a house DJ during the week and hiring a live band for the weekends.

Bar Management for Nightclubs

Controls

Controls are a very important component of the nightclub business. With the huge number of patrons and employees, keeping careful track of what is going on becomes an important part of the day-to-day operations. Most profitable nightclubs have extensive controls in place to make sure that all money and product is accounted for at the end of the evening.

One of the most important controls in a nightclub is creating standard drink recipes and standard pour amounts of liquor. If a nightclub has 1,000 patrons who all drink three drinks each in the course of an evening, and each of those drinks were over-poured by ½ ounce, then the nightclub went through 50 additional liter bottles of alcohol in one night. If the average bottle has a profit of $40 per bottle, the nightclub has $2,000 in lost profits. To combat this, a good nightclub owner will install point-of-sale (POS) cash registers and computerized pour systems to make sure the right amount is dispensed. If a computerized pour system cannot keep up with demand, then the nightclub will need to adjust their price of drinks upward to address the loss of profits.

Cash controls are another crucial area. Expanding on the previous example, 3,000 drinks at an average price of $10 per drink is $30,000 in revenue in one evening. Depending upon the clientele, this $30,000 may be mostly cash with some credit cards mixed in. Nightclubs need to make sure that all of the revenues are accounted for and can be traced back to each server or bartender. One practice for a nightclub is to issue small cash banks to each server, and then have the servers or bartenders hand back their total sales at the end of the night; whatever is left is their tip. Another alternative includes having several POS registers installed around the rooms, with multiple servers on each one, but it may prove difficult to determine who is responsible when money is short.

Ordering and inventory controls is another crucial area for nightclub managers. Due to the amount of alcohol needed, it may be physically impossible to store more than a day or two of stock on the premises. Nightclubs may be ordering and receiving deliveries on an almost-daily basis to meet demand. Keeping careful track of what is on order, what has arrived, and what invoices need to be paid may need an additional bookkeeper for the paperwork.

Inventory control is another critical area. Once the liquor has been received, it needs to be stored and issued to the bartenders as needed. Due to the high volume of drink orders, simple requisition forms are impossible to maintain. Managers need to set up a requisition system based on the physical layout of the bar that ensures alcohol is nearby yet countable at the end of the evening. Some suggestions include issuing an overabundance of liquor and requiring bartenders to stow the empties for counting after the evening is over. The empty bottle count should match the number of drinks served or the revenue from those bartenders.

Security

Security issues are usually more problematic in a nightclub than in a bar. If the nightclub has multiple floors or venues, security is responsible for making sure that guests are guided to their desired area and are safe while in the building. Because demographics are different depending on what is playing, there could be a situation where one floor is playing jazz, for example, while another floor is playing hip-hop, with two different groups within the building. Make sure that there are no conflicts between the different groups. Security needs to be well trained in monitoring customer behavior and watching for developing situations. Having bartenders and servers linked to security personnel via walkie-talkies or headsets will also help in the long run. Check out:

- GLK Corporation provides high-quality headsets for both original equipment manufacturers and for replacement markets. **ReplacementHeadsets. com**™ provides virtually all types of replacement headsets to many industries, including entertainment and nightclubs. Visit **www.replacement-headsets.com** for more information or call 262-784-8560.

Security also includes watching for and dealing with minors. If the nightclub allows minors and of-age patrons in the same room or area, door personnel need to check identification and mark the underage patrons, possibly with wristbands. If the nightclub does not allow minors, then the doormen need to carefully check IDs and prohibit minors from entering. The same is implied for dealing with intoxicated individuals: doormen need to prevent their entry for liability issues and escort out and arrange rides for those who overindulge within the club.

Security costs and number of personnel can be quite high. A nightclub serving about 1,000 patrons will need roughly 15 to 20 bartenders, and 12 to 15 security personnel in the room, with 4 to 6 doormen at the entrances of the club. After paying for the liquor, labor will be one of the highest costs for the nightclub.

Marketing

Marketing will begin before opening by defining target customers and designing the nightclub around their needs. Marketing will influence the layout and design and will affect which alcoholic beverages are sold. Promotions are the advertising that tells potential customers what is available and when bands are playing.

Most nightclubs will soon find that customers will migrate night by night to different places. A hip-hop lover will go to one club on Monday night, a different club on Tuesday, a third on Wednesday, and so on, all the way through the week. For the club, that would mean Monday night is salsa lovers, Tuesday is jazz fans, Wednesday is the hip-hop crowd, and then different groups on Thursday, Friday, Saturday, and Sunday. This means that a nightclub could conceivably have six or seven different groups, each with their own demographic and needs. Matching the different groups' desires will become a main part of the promotional plans.

Hiring the different groups means booking different bands, DJs, or adult entertainment to match that night's clientele. It may also mean different liquor selections need to be available for the customers. Finally, it may mean differences in the physical aspect—removing chairs and tables or muting or boosting certain speakers to create the proper ambiance for this particular set of customers.

Promotions are the supporting piece of the marketing effort. Promotions tell clientele who is playing at the establishment on what days. Getting the word out is the focus of the promotional activity and starts just after the talent is booked. Using the band example in the "Finding Talent" section, a promotional plan may look like the following:

PROMOTIONAL PLAN	
Group:	"No Name" band—a very popular regional band is booked to play in nightclub four months from now.
Goal:	Maximize customer revenue on that night.
After Booking:	Determine cover charge for the evening.
Promotional Pieces:	1. Post band photo, bio, and dates on club Web site and customer e-mail newsletter.
	2. Place ads in all nightlife papers and magazines highlighting who is playing in the club in the upcoming week and month. For "No Name" band, plan on a small blurb immediately and then major space in the appropriate publications, as the night grows closer.
	3. Have a radio spot on radio stations that "No Name" band fans listen to, mentioning their appearance at your club in a few weeks.
	4. Send out a press release (PR) to the local radio stations and general newspapers at least two months in advance, highlighting the appearance and the club's name. Send out reminder notices two weeks and then one week prior to the event.
	5. Send a notice to the "events" sections of general newspapers and nightlife magazines for low-cost advertising.
	6. Make sure that the club's Web site and newsletter are updated with information on "No Name" band. Use the promotional materials that the band sent as information for the site.
	7. Send information to all nightclub Web sites in your area—make sure that they have updated information and a link to your Web site for more information.

Nightclubs need to be constantly marketing and promoting their establishment. The more information that is sent out to the target markets, the more likely people will find out about the nightclub and visit.

Conclusion

Nightclubs are a fascinating part of the bar industry and can be very profitable. To make money, nightclub managers need to be looking for new ideas, new promotions, and new talent for their club. As the glamorous big sister of bars, they are the fun place to work and enjoy in this industry.

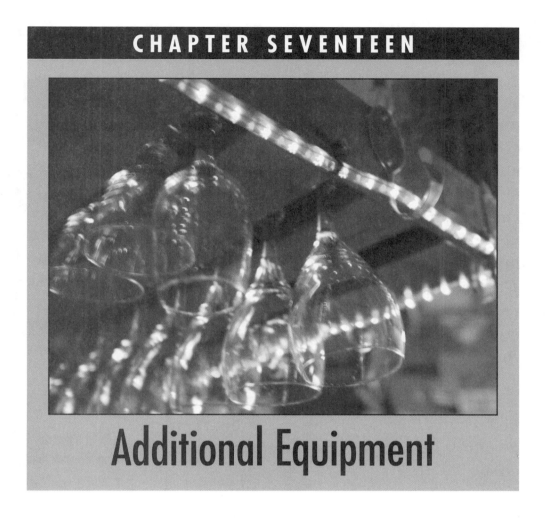

CHAPTER SEVENTEEN

Additional Equipment

The equipment in your bar will vary greatly, depending on the type of operation you are running. Some, such as glassware, are common to all bars. Others, such as walk-in refrigeration units, may only apply to certain establishments.

This chapter provides an overview of sources for general equipment, as well as specific types of specialty equipment offered by certain manufacturers. In addition, at the end of this chapter you will find a comprehensive alphabetized list of supplies. Note: See *Chapter 7: Preparing and Serving Beverages* for information on wine service and storage. See *Chapter 9: Bar Controls* for information regarding inventory, pouring, and liquor control systems.

Smallware and General Equipment

You may want to consider one source for all your smallware needs. Here are some sources:

- **Royal Industries, Inc.** has been an innovative leader in the food service industry for over 60 years. Specializing in, among other things, bar stools and chairs, table tops and bases, waitress stations, back bar units, and podiums, Royal Industries, Inc. services a nationwide market as furniture manufacturers and as importers of commercial food service products for restaurant, bar, hospitality, and institutional industries. They are a one-stop-shop for wholesale restaurant supply, food service products, and manufactured restaurant and hospitality furniture. To see a full line of products and locate a sales rep or distributor in your area, visit **www.royalindustriesinc.com**.

Royal Industries, Inc. double-ring bar stool, black with back.

- **Franklin Machine Products** also specializes in parts and accessories for the food service industry. With over 10,000 items, they offer kitchen accessories, kitchen equipment, maintenance products, office supplies, serving accessories, thermometers, and more. To view the complete online catalog, visit **www.fmponline.com**.

- **Browne-Halco** is a prime supplier of smallwares in the United States, offering in excess of 3,000 smallwares products including buffetware, flatware, tabletop essentials, barware, cookware, steam table pans, bakeware, food preparation, and kitchen essentials. For further details and to view the Browne-Halco product line, visit **www.halco.com**.

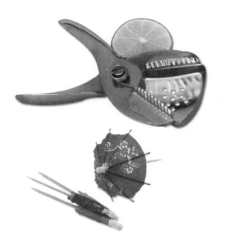

From professional corkscrews to stainless cocktail shakers, SureShot® pourers to overhead glass racks, Browne-Halco has a wide selection quality bar supplies.

Kitchen Equipment

If you decide to add food to your bar operation, you are going to need a properly equipped kitchen. Kitchens must have the appropriate amount of space for food production and appropriate traffic flow patterns to make everyone's work easier.

A restaurant designer or consultant may be brought in to analyze your existing setup. Kitchens will be based on how and where food products are received, stored, prepared, served, cleaned up, and disposed of. A basic kitchen will need the following:

- Separate work surfaces for food-contact and non-food-contact areas.

- Work sinks for preparation and cleanup.

- Enough cutting surfaces to prevent cross-contamination.

- Storage for:

  - Utensils and small equipment.

  - Cooking equipment.

  - Food products that have been prepared for service.

  - Unused food products.

- Adequate refrigeration and freezer storage.

- Garbage facilities.

You may need to make some adjustments before you begin. Before you design your kitchen and choose equipment, be sure to find out whether the location and layout meet with local zoning laws. Check the zoning laws and the local board of health to determine if additional permits are needed.

Ranges and Ovens

Commercial kitchens generally favor gas stoves, which may be expensive, but they can be purchased at second-hand stores or auctions. It is quite possible to manage without a range for a long time. One low-cost solution is to be licensed as a "cold" kitchen. You could also start with a half-size convection oven. Convection ovens are light, portable, and very convenient. Be aware that domestic ovens are not allowed in commercial kitchens by the board of health.

If you are buying a regular commercial oven, you can purchase a range oven combination, or there are stackable ovens as well. Stack ovens are good because you can buy one at a time and add more if your food business increases. They also take up less floor space.

Henny Penny is a manufacturer of food service equipment including pressure fryers, open fryers, rotisseries, heated merchandisers, island merchandisers, display counter warmers, SmartHold humidified holding cabinets, heated holding cabinets for floor or countertop, bun warmers, SmartCooking Systems™, combis, blast chillers/freezers, and breading systems. Visit www.hennypenny.com for more information or call 800-417-8417.

Flat-top stoves are useful because you can fit any size pan on the burners. They come with four or six burners in the standards sizes. These stoves provide fast, high heat needed for items like omelets and for sautéing.

Griddle stoves are good for quickly sautéing small amounts of food, such as diced onions. These stoves can also be used to keep foods warm and as a griddle for items such as burgers.

One of the latest trends in ovens is induction cooking. The induction cooktop is becoming increasingly popular with caterers. They come in a variety of forms, from full-size ranges to portable hot plates. They cook food quickly, are easy to use, and easy to clean. Induction cooktops can be used with any type of food and will cook as thoroughly and evenly as any electric or gas range. Induction cooking can be used with any type of cookware, from frying pans to woks. However, it only works when used with magnetic-based materials, such as iron and steel, that will allow an induced current to flow within them.

Combi ovens, also known as steamers, combine the browning capacity of a regular oven with convection steam cooking, keeping meats moist and preventing cooking loss. They also cook 30 to 40 percent faster than conventional convection ovens. Roasting in

SmartCooking System™ from Henny Penny. Cooking a complete menu is simple. Press the SmartCooking Control™ key, and select the type of food. It cooks everything from roasts to fish to casseroles to pies, literally at the touch of a button. For greater control, simply press the moist heat or dry heat mode keys and set time, temperature, and special functions.

Blodett's Gas Boilerless Combination Oven/Steamer. To see a complete selection of Blodett's combi ovens, visit www.blodgett.com or call 800-331-5842.

combi mode reduces shrinkage 20 to 30 percent (and food cost), yielding a juicier product. Shellfish cook rapidly in steam mode without washing out flavors or dealing with heavy stockpots. Hot-air mode operates as a normal convection oven for baking. High-sugar recipes are less likely to scorch when using combi mode.

Other oven options include:

- **Deck ovens.** These horizontal ovens can be used for baking and roasting and usually have one shelf each.

- **Rotating ovens** have rotating shelves and are used as high-production ovens.

- **Conveyor ovens** are useful for fast, continuous production such as pizzas or steaks for large parties.

- **Roll-in ovens** are constructed so you can roll racks of food directly into the oven. These are great ovens for large events. Roll-in ovens designed for baking have steam injectors and some come equipped with automatic thermostats to keep the food at a desired temperature.

- **Low-temperature ovens** cook at a temperature so that a hood is not required. Like the combi oven, meat cooked in a low-temperature oven stays moist and shrinkage is minimal.

Restaurant shows and food service magazines are the best places to look for the announcement and review of new equipment. You can also visit manufacturers' Web sites or other sites that let you compare brands and prices, such as:

- **www.amanacommerical.com**

- **www.hennypenny.com**

- **http://Web1.panasonic.com/food_service/cmo**

- **www.ckitchen.com**

- **www.abestkitchen.com**

- www.bevles.com

- www.horizonfoodequipment.com

- www.restaurantequipment.net

- www.hatcocorp.com

- www.blodgett.com

- www.business.com/directory/food_and_beverage/restaurants_
  and_foodservice/equipment_and_supplies/cooking_and_baking/
  ovens

Grills, Smokers, and Rotisseries

Grills provide a cooking source that gives food an attractive appearance. The grill marks on steaks or vegetables add to a winning plate presentation. For most catering operations, grills are used to mark food and to pre-cook it. Then the food is finished in the oven.

You can find gas, charcoal, and electric grills. Gas grills have lava stones. The fat dripping onto the stones gives flavor to the meat.

If you will be serving specialty items, such as barbecue, you may be interested in a grill or rotisseries. There are numerous types and many manufacturers from which to choose. Check out the following:

- **Big John Grills & Rotisseries** has designed, manufactured, packaged, and distributed outdoor cooking equipment for over 42 years. The extensive product line includes gas grills, portable gas grills, smokers, roasters, portable griddles, steam tables, gas towables, utility stoves, smokers, portable fryers, countertop fryers, ovens, and ranges, as well as countertop griddles, broilers, and fryers. For more information, visit **www.bigjohngrills.com** or call 800-326-9575.

- **Belson Outdoors** also has a wide selection of portable grills including the PORTA-GRILL® Mobile Trailer-Mounted Barbecue Grills, Pig Roaster Rotisserie for PORTA-GRILL® Commercial Barbecue Grills, Chicken & Rib Roaster Rotisserie for PORTA-

GRILL®, and PORTA-GRILL® Corn & Potato Roaster Barbecue Grills. Visit **www.belson.com** or call 800-323-5664.

- **Holstein Manufacturing.** Offering custom-built products, Holstein Manufacturing has numerous products including a six-foot towable barbecue grill, a corn roaster, a deep-fat fryer, and portable concession trailer. For more information, visit **www.holsteinmfg.com** or call 800-368-4342.

- **Cookshack** offers state-of-the-art electric smoker ovens, such as the SmartSmoker with electronic controls, pre-programmed for brisket, ribs, and chicken. It is available in four sizes and eight models to fit your needs. For more information, **visit www.cookshack.com** or call 800-423-0698.

The E-Z Way Roaster is a product of Big John Grills & Rotisseries. You simply open the hood, place a pig inside, fill the smoking trough with wood chips, start the fuel-efficient 80,000 Btu gas burner, and walk away. Come back hours later to enjoy a delicious pig-pickin' party. The entire process of preparing a moist, tender, flavorful pig roast is that easy.

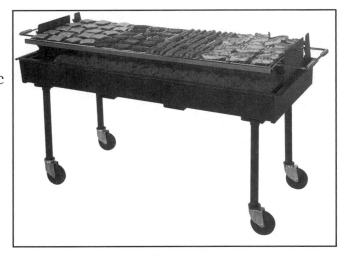

Belson's PORTA-GRILL® I Commercial Barbecue Grill. This charcoal-fired model is big enough to feed large gatherings, yet light enough to be transported without a trailer. It has casters for short trips and removable legs for long trips. With a sanitary nickel-plated cooking grate made from round steel bars, it easily adjusts to four different cooking heights. Patented flip-back grill feature allows for easy charcoal servicing and cleaning.

Refrigerators and Freezers

At least one separate refrigerator and one large freezer are essential. You'll need refrigerated space for deliveries such as dairy items, salads, vegetables, meats, fish, and poultry. In general, a large commercial refrigerator will accommodate all these requirements.

Walk-in freezers and refrigerators are used by most commercial kitchens. These allow plenty of room to roll in carts of food as well as providing shelf space. Leer Limited Partnership manufactures stock and custom walk-in coolers and freezers. They offer standard nominal sizes to special configurations. Visit **www.leerlp.com** to see their product line.

Dishwashers

Consider a commercial dishwasher with more than two racks. It saves time when storing glasses on dishwasher trays. Heat generated by dishwashers can be a problem. Solve the problem by installing a condenser over the dishwasher. Choose a dishwashing system that is engineered to meet your kitchen and bar's requirements. Base your decision on such factors as the space available, layout, traffic flow, amount and type of food soil, and the hardness of the water.

Pots and Pans

The type, number, and size of pots and pans you'll need is highly dependant on the menu you offer. Following are some sources for pots and pans:

- **Regal Ware Food Service**, a division of Regal Ware Worldwide™, specializes in providing top-quality beverage

Elegance Stainless Steel Cookware
by Regal Ware.

and food preparation products to the food service industry. With craftsmanship dating back to 1945, Regal Ware Food Service offers a variety of products. Visit **www.regalwarefoodservice.com** or call 262-626-2121 for more information.

- **Sitram Cookware.** For more than 40 years, Sitram has supplied chefs across Europe with a comprehensive range of heavy-duty "catering" cookware. Sitram's success is the result of the heavy copper bottom sandwiched between two layers of stainless steel. Copper is a good conductor of heat and guarantees fast, uniform heat distribution. Extremely durable, the cookware is also impervious to acidic foods: won't pit, discolor, or alter the flavors of foods. It's dishwasher safe and carries a lifetime limited warranty. Visit **www.sitramcookware.com/catering** or call 800-515-8585 for more information.

Sitram's Catering (Inox) Collection.

- **Browne-Halco** offers an extensive line of high-quality cookware that is both durable and reliable. Eagleware® Cookware is their premier line of professional aluminum cookware. It features a thick bottom construction for even heat distribution as well as a heavy top with smooth rim. The beadless rim eliminates food traps and makes cleaning easier. Other product lines include Futura Stainless Steel Professional Cookware and Thermalloy Aluminum Cookware. To view their online catalog, visit **www.halco.com** or call 888-289-1005 for more information.

- **Polar Ware Company.** Polar Ware has a wide selection of food preparation, serving, and storage products—from heavy-duty mixing bowls to kitchen utensils and storage canisters. They also offer a wide variety of stainless steel and tri-ply stainless steel stock pots and matching covers. The aluminum cookware line is manufactured using deep draw techniques perfected by Polar Ware. Visit **www .polarware.com** or call 800-237-3655 for more information.

Polar Ware Aluminum Cookware.

Additional Food Preparation Equipment

Depending on your menu, you may want to consider purchasing the following items to use for food prep:

Knives

Invest in the best chef's knife (sometimes called a French knife), carving knife (slicer), large serrated knife, and several smaller paring knives that your budget will allow. Complete the collection with a knife sharpener and a sharpening stone. For special purposes, you may also need a boner and a fillet knife. Learn how to sharpen and hone your knives. Hone them regularly and sharpen them about once a year.

Cutting Boards

Have at least two small and two large cutting boards. Look for HDP (plastic) cutting boards as opposed to wooden ones, as any odor or stain on polyethylene boards can easily be removed with a chlorine soak.

Scales

Have at least three scales: one so sensitive that it can weigh a cinnamon stick accurately; one less accurate that can weigh anything from 3 to 10 pounds; and a third larger scale that can weigh at least 25 pounds. They should also be used to help you accurately measure portions.

6" Portion-Control Scale from Browne-Halco.

Thermometers

Thermometers are critical to food safety. You will need to check temperature frequently to make sure you are preparing and holding food properly. There are a wide variety of thermometers available. Visit **www.atlantic-pub.com** to see a complete selection specifically for food service.

Busboxes

These are used to carry dirty dishware from the dining room to the back kitchen area for washing. They are usually made of plastic and measure 12 by 18 inches to 18 by 24 inches.

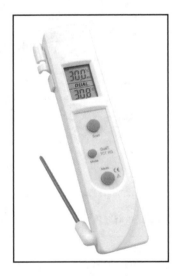

The ThermaTwin Infrared Thermometer, available from Atlantic Publishing.

Specialty Beverage Equipment

To make beverage service easier, or for specialty items such as blended drinks, you may want to invest in specialized beverage equipment, such as the following.

Frozen Beverage Dispensers

For high-margin specialty drinks such as smoothies, frozen cocktails, and other drinks, a frozen beverage dispenser can be a good solution. The Stowaway Countertop Frozen Beverage Dispenser from Stoelting has an eye-catching design with illuminated product allows the customer to see the frozen beverage. Cooling air enters the front and exhausts from the rear of the unit so it requires less counter space than other models. With front-to-back airflow, units can be placed side-by-side for multiple flavor applications. The high production capacity will allow up to seven gallons of drinks to be served per hour. Perfect for frozen cocktails, slush, lemonade, and frozen cappuccino. For more information, visit **www.stoelting.com** or call 800-558-5807.

Juicers and Garnish Equipment

Fresh fruit is used frequently for juice and garnishes. You can make your own juice with the Sunkist Commercial Juicer. It operates at 1,725 rpm, making it extremely easy for an operator to extract 10 to 12 gallons of juice per hour using precut citrus. It has a unique strainer that oscillates 3,450 times per minute to help separate the juice from the pulp. It's quiet yet heavy-duty motor is housed in gleaming chrome-plated steel and looks great with any décor. The Sunkist Commercial Juicer comes with three different-size extracting bulbs (one each for lemon/lime, orange, and grapefruit). Removable parts can go in a commercial dishwasher for quick and easy sanitizing.

Sunkist Commercial Juicer.

The Sunkist Sectionizer will save you many hours in kitchen/bar prep time. It makes quick work of slicing, halving, and wedging a wide variety of fruits and vegetables. In addition to sectionizing citrus fruit, it can core and wedge apples and pears. It will also slice firm tomatoes and mushrooms for sandwiches and pizzas or wedge them for salads. The sectionizer can slice and/or wedge hardboiled eggs, kiwi fruit, small to medium potatoes, strawberries; just about any firm (not hard) fruit or vegetable without pits that will fit through the blade cup. It is as simple to use as pulling a handle and is much safer than cutting fruits and vegetables with a knife. The Sunkist Sectionizer has seven interchange-able blade cups to choose from, making it one of the most versatile manual food cutters on the market. Blade cups and plungers are commercial dishwasher safe.

Sunkist Sectionizer.

Purchase Sunkist Foodservice Equipment from your dealer or order direct by calling the company toll free at 800-383-7141. More information can be found on the Sunkist Web site at **www.sunkistfs.com/equipment**.

Additional Resources to Find Equipment

Now that you know what you need for your operation, how do you find it? We have listed many manufacturers in this chapter from which you can purchase directly. There are also many other avenues to try when searching for equipment. Make sure you're creative when looking for the larger items; you are likely to save some money.

- **Restaurant equipment stores** are a good place to start. Make sure to check the Yellow Pages for second-hand stores. It may also be worth a trip to the National Restaurant Show held each May in Chicago. Major areas of focus include food, beverage, equipment, apparel, furnishings, and design. You can get information about the show from the National Restaurant Association.

- **Retail stores** such as Homegoods and T.J. Maxx are a good option for dishware and pans. These types of stores are often hit or miss, but if you can find what you are looking for, the price is usually right.

- **Networking** is also a way to find equipment. You should talk to friends in the business.

- **Restaurant equipment auctions** are a good place to look for the large and small items. You can find everything from ovens to rolling racks to boxes of flatware. Since these are usually going-out-of-business sales, the prices tend to be pretty attractive.

Here are some additional ideas for where to find equipment:

- These aren't the most cost-effective sources for equipment and uniforms, but they are convenient: **www.chefscatalog.com** and **www.chefswear.com**.

- **Online auctions.** This is another hit-or-miss source, but it's worth pursuing. Log on and register at **www.ebay.com**.

Equipment is an area where you don't want to scrimp. Spend the money up front for quality items and avoid the hassle and expense of having to replace pieces only months later.

Comprehensive Equipment List

The following is an alphabetized list of bar and beverage equipment. While you may not need everything on this list, it is a good source to review for necessary supplies.

A

accounting & financial services

advertising services,
  materials & electronic catalogs

air cleaners/purifiers

air-conditioning & heating eqt. sales

air curtains

air pollution control systems

air screens/air curtains
  for entranceways

alcoholic beverages

aluminum foil

antioxidants for
  fruits & vegetables

apparel

appetizers

appliances: food service machines

aprons

artificial flowers & plants

ashtrays & stands

associations, trade

ATMs—automated teller machines

attorney at law

audiovisual eqt. & systems

awards, plaques & certificates

awnings, canopies & poles

B

bacon

badges/name badges

bags & covers: paper, plastic,
  cheesecloth

bags, cooking

bags, food: paper & plastic

bains marie

bakers eqt. & supplies

baking ingredients

baking supplies

balers

banners & flags

banquet service eqt.

bar codes/uniform product codes

bar eqt. & supplies

barbeque pits, machines,
  eqt. & supplies

bars, liquor service

bars, portable
  & folding bases
  & legs, tables
  & booths

baskets, bread & roll

bathroom accessories
  & eqt.

beer & ale

beer brewing eqt.

beer service eqt.

beverage service eqt.

beverage/coffee servers

beverages, concentrated fruit

beverages, nonalcoholic

beverages: beer/ale/wine

beverages, carbonated
    & noncarbonated

beverages: liquors/liqueurs

bibs, adult & child

bins, ingredient

bins, silverware

bins, storage

blackboards

blenders

bookkeeping systems

books, educational
    & technical

books, reservation

booths & chairs, tables,
    bases & legs

bowls: mixing, salad & serving

brass fittings & tubing

breadings & batters:
    seafood & poultry

brochures & postcards

broilers, electric & gas

broilers, infrared

broilers, charcoal & conveyor

broilers, charcoal, electric & gas

brooms

brushes, cleaning

buffalo products

buffet products: chafers, fuel, etc.

bulletin boards

bulletin boards: changeable letters

butchers eqt. & supplies

butter, margarine & cooking oils

C

cabinets: food warming & conveying

cabinets: miscellaneous

cafeteria eqt.

can openers: electric & hand-
    operated

candelabra & candle holders

candle light, nonflammable

candle warmers for food & beverages

candles & tapers

canned foods: fish, fruits &
    vegetables, meat & poultry

canopies: ventilation

cappuccino coffee eqt.

carbon dioxide

carbonators

carbonic gas/bulk CO_2

carpet sweepers

carpets & rugs

carriers, food & beverage insulated

carts, espresso & coffee

carts, food service

carts, transport

carts, storage & serving

cash register supplies: tape, ribbon, etc.

cash registers & control systems

casters

catalogues & directories

ceilings: acoustical, tin, wood, etc.

ceramic dinnerware

ceramics

chafing dishes

chairs, folding or stacking

chairs, restaurant

check recovery services

cheese

chillers

china, table

choppers: electric for food & meat

chopping blocks

cigars, cigarettes, tobacco products: display & storage systems

citrus products/citrus syrups

cleaners for grills, griddles, pans, etc.

cleaners, hand

cleaners, multipurpose

cleaners, ovens

cleaners, rug & upholstery

cleaners, window

cleaning eqt., materials, services & supplies

cleaning systems, pressurized

cleaning: exhaust maintenance

clocks, electric

coasters, beverage

coat & hat checking eqt.

cocktail mixes

cocktail stirrers

cocoa

coffee

coffee-brewers, glass & filters

coffee mills

coffee urns & makers

coin sorters & handling eqt.

cold plates

communication systems, services & eqt.

compactors, waste

computer aided design (CAD) systems

computer furniture

computer software: accounting, administrative, hospitality, cost control, etc.

computer supplies

computerized food service systems

computerized restaurant management systems

computerized systems, wireless

computers/internet

concession eqt. & supplies

condiments & condiment holders

connectors: gas/water/steam

construction: materials/renovation

consulting services

containers, food

containers, microwave

containers, ovenable paperboard

containers: aluminum,
    plastic & glass

conveyors & subveyors

conveyors, belt

cooking computers or timers

cooking eqt., electric & gas

cooking eqt., induction

cooking eqt., outdoor

cooking heat/warmers

cooking wines & marinades

cookware, induction

cookware: pots, pans & microwave

coolers, beverage

copperware

counters & tabletops

counters, cafeteria

covers, rack

crackers

creamers

credit cards: card
    processing/authorization

croutons

crushers, can & bottle, electric

cups: disposable,
    portion, thermal, etc.

cutlery: chef's eqt. & supplies

cutlery, disposable

cutlery, silver-plated & stainless
    steel

cutters, food

cutting boards

D

dairy substitutes

dance floors, portable

data processing eqt.,
services & supplies

decaffeinated beverages

decor & display materials

decorations: holiday,
    party favors,
    balloons, etc.

degreasers & nonslip
    treatment products

deli products

deodorizers

designers/decorators

dessert products

dicers, hand-operated

dicers, vegetable-cutting, power

dinnerware, heat-resistant, glass

dinnerware, metal

dinnerware: china,
    stainless steel,
    plastic or disposable

disco equipment

dish tables

dishwashers/ware:
  washer eqt. & supplies

dishwashing compounds

disinfectants & cleaning supplies

dispensers for concentrates

dispensers, carbonated beverage

dispensers, condiment

dispensers: controls & timers

dispensers, cup

dispensers, custom

dispensers, french fries

dispensers, glove

dispensers, ice

dispensers, ice cream

dispensers: liquor, beer
  & wine

dispensers, napkins

dispensers, noncarbonated
  beverage dispensers,

dispensers, salad dressing

dispensers: self-leveling
  for dishes & trays

dispensers, snack

dispensers, soap
  & detergent

dispensers, straw

dispensers, toilet paper

dispensers, water:
  hot and/or cold

dispensers, wine

dispensers: liquids,
  beverages, cream/milk,
  syrup & dressings

display cases

distributor, food & beverage

distributor, food eqt.

doors: cold storage &
  freezer

doors: hinged, revolving & swinging

dough dividers/rounders

dough: prepared, frozen & canned

doughnut mix

drain cleaners/line maintenance

draperies, curtains & hangings

draperies, stage

drapery & curtain hardware

drug testing

dry grocery items: staples

dry ice

dryers, clothes

dryers, dish/tray

E

eggs/egg products/egg substitutes/
  boilers & timers

electric utility services/
  energy conservation

electronic data capture

electronic funds transfer

embroidered apparel

employee benefit services

employee scheduling & services

employment agencies,
    services & leasing

energy cost analysts

entertainment, sports-
    themed

entertainment/
    entertainment systems

entrées, fresh & frozen

environmental products

equipment, cook/chill

equipment, dish handling

equipment, drain cleaning

equipment, food forming

equipment, front office

equipment, heating:
    boilers, furnaces,
    radiators, etc.

equipment, leasing

equipment, marinade

equipment: preventive
    maintenance programs

equipment: repairs/parts/
    installation

equipment, rug cleaning

equipment, sales & service

equipment, under-bar

equipment, upholstery
    cleaning & shampooing

espresso coffee & coffee eqt.

ethnic foods

exhaust fans

exhaust maintenance cleaning

extractors, fruit juice

extracts, flavoring

F

---

fabrication, wood

fans, electric & ventilating

fats & oils, cooking

fats & oils: systems & supplies eqt.

faucets

filters, air-conditioning

filters: coffee makers

filters, cooking oil

filters, exhaust systems

filters, grease extracting

filters, water

financial services/
    financial consultants

financial: tax & legal planning

fire alarm systems

fire protection systems:
    extinguishers/
    suppression/sales/service

first-aid eqt. & supplies

fish: canned, fresh,
    frozen, pre-portioned & smoked

flatware carts & trays
for storage & dispensing

flatware, disposable

flatware: recovery machines

flatware: silver/gold
plated, stainless
& disposable

floor cleaning & maintenance eqt.

floor drain treatment

flooring: floor treatments, nonslip
preparations & coating

flour & flour sifters

flowers, foliage & plants

food containers: aluminum, plastic
& glass

food covers

food, dehydrated

food delivery & catering eqt.

food eqt.: service & parts

food: frozen:
cooked/precooked

food portioning eqt.

food processors:
grinders & slicers,
electric & manual

food products: deli/ethnic,
import/export

food products: prepared, canned
& frozen

food reproduction
& replication/props

food safety training

food thawing device

food waste disposers

food, processed

forms: guest checks
& business forms

fountain syrups & flavors

fountains, beverage

fountains, ornamental & display

franchise consultants

freezers/refrigeration
eqt.: service & parts

freezers, portable

frequent dining programs/clubs

frozen cocktail machines

frozen food reconstitutor

fruit juices: canned,
concentrated, fresh & frozen

fruit syrups

fruits & vegetables:
candied, brandied & pickled

fruits & vegetables:
canned, fresh & frozen

fryers, convection

fryers, deep fat & pressure

fryers, oil-less

fuel: synthetic/alternative

furniture design

furniture, health care

furniture: fiberglass,
metal, plastic, upholstered & wood

furniture, portable/folding

G

games

garbage can liners

garbage containers: metal, plastic or concrete; waste receptacles & compactors

gas, propane

gas: service/supplier & natural

gelatin

glass replacement service

glass washers

glass, beveled & tempered

glass, decorative

glassware chiller & froster

glassware, service

glazes

gloves: cloth or synthetic

gourmet foods

grease exhaust systems: cleaning & maintenance

grease traps: cleaning, maintenance, elimination & analysis

griddles & grills

guest checks

guest questionnaires, comment cards & boxes

H

HACCP training

hair dryers

hand dryers

hand trucks

handicapped: aids & accessories

hangers, clothes

health care products & eqt.

health foods

heat lamps

heaters, water

hors d'oeuvres

hoses: flexible gas connectors

hot chocolate mix

hot dog grills/cookers

hot food tables

hot plates, electric & gas

I

ice bins, buckets, carts & containers

ice cream

ice cream cabinets

ice cream dishes

ice cream freezers

ice cream makers & soft serve machines

ice cream, toppings, syrups

ice crushers, cubers & shavers

ice eqt. & supplies

ice machine repairs, service
   & maintenance

ice makers, bins,
   dispensers, crushers & cubers

ice transport systems

incentive programs

information service

infrared ovens, ranges & broilers

insect traps

insecticides

inserts, steam table

insulation materials: hot & cold

insurance

interior décor/interior design

international
   marketer/distributor: food eqt.

inventory control eqt.

inventory systems: eqt.
   & supplies

investigative services

J

janitorial: cleaning/sanitizing

janitorial supplies

juice fountains

juicers/extractors

K

kettles, steam

key & lock systems

key tags

kitchen accessories

kitchen fabrication

kitchen layout & design

knife sharpeners

L

ladles

laminated plastic for counters, etc.

laminating services & products

lamps: floor, table,
   electric, battery,
   candle, infrared & oil

lampshades

laundry eqt. & supplies

laundry machinery

LED message displays

legal services

legumes

lighting fixtures

lighting systems, emergency

lighting, fluorescent & neon

lights: flood, spot, etc.

linen products

linen products, rental

liquor substitutes

liquor supplies & liqueurs

lockers

M

management services

marinades

marketing materials & services

marketing research

marketing: promotional items
& public relations

matches/matchbooks

mats, floor

mats, rubber & composition

mattresses & bedsprings

meat analogs

meat cookers

meats: fresh, frozen,
canned, pre-portioned
& processed

menu accessories

menu covers & holders

menu display

menu planning
& development

menu price changers

menus, menu boards &
menu card systems

mesquite wood

metal polish

metal work: kitchen eqt.

microwave accessories

microwave ovens & cookware

mini bars

mirrors, murals & wall decorations

mixers, drink

mixers, food: electric

mixes, cocktail

mixes, food

mixes: prepared flour/dough

mobile restaurants

money counters

mops & mopping eqt.

motivational incentives,
employee contests & games

mushrooms

music & sound systems

music licensing:
organizations & copyright law

music systems

music videos

musical instruments

N

name badges/tags

napkin rings

napkins, disposable

napkins, fabric

nondairy creamers

nutrition services & information

nuts: specialty nut meats

O

office machines

office supplies

oils, cooking: fats & oils

olives

onion rings

onions, dehydrated

online services

ordering systems

organizers: calendars,
notebooks & seating charts

ovens & ranges: cooking
eqt., parts & service

ovens, baking & roasting

ovens, brick

ovens, combination
convection/steam

ovens: convection,
conveyor, infrared,
low temperature,
microwave, quartz,
vapor & wood burning

ovenware: china or glass

P

packaging & wrap: foil,
plastic & paper

packaging materials: wrapping

packaging, take-out

paging systems
& employee call systems

paint markers or strippers

pan liners & coatings

paneling & partitions,
acoustical

paper goods & disposable
tabletop items

parking lot maintenance

pasta cookers

pasta: fresh, frozen,
flavored, homemade
& processed

payroll companies

payroll processing services

peanut butter

pepper mills

personnel services:
recruitment, leasing & consultants

pest control services & products

photographic services & eqt.

pickles & pickled products

pitchers

pizza eqt. & supplies

pizza products

placemats

plants, flowers & greenery

plastic signs

plasticware, disposable
& nondisposable

plasticware, disposable,
molded

plates, disposable

platforms & risers, portable

platters

plumbing fixtures & eqt.

point-of-sale eqt.,
materials & supplies

polishes & waxes, floor

popcorn equipment

posters & poster systems

pot & pan washing eqt.

potato products

potatoes, processed

pots & pans

poultry information

poultry: fresh, frozen,
canned & pre-portioned

powders, fry-kettle

precooked frozen food

pre-portioned foods:
jam, cheese, salt,
pepper, etc.

pre-portioned meat, fish
& poultry

pre-washing machines

premiums & incentives

pressure cookers

pressure fryers

pretzels

printing & design

printing forms, notices, etc.

produce: fruits & vegetables

property management systems

prosciutto

public address systems

public cold storage

R

racks, coat & hat

racks, dish & glass

racks, dishwashing

racks, drying

racks, luggage

racks, shelving & storage

railings: brass, chrome,
stainless steel, wood, etc.

ranges, electric & gas

real estate: analysis,
brokerage & financing

recipe card indexers

recycling containers,
eqt. & services

refinishing services:
tableware

refrigeration eqt.: display

refrigeration eqt.: reach-in

refrigeration eqt.:
   repair & service

refrigeration eqt.: walk-ins

relishes, chutneys, etc.

rendering services

rental: supplies & eqt.

rentals & leasing: cars
   & trucks

rentals & leasing party supplies

reservation services

responsible vendor training

restaurant consultants

restaurant eqt. & supplies

restoration

rice/rice products

rotisseries

S

---

safes & vaults

safety products

sandwich & salad
   units, refrigerated

sandwiches

sanitation eqt. & supplies

sauces & sauce bases

sausage

saws, meat cutting: power

scales, food

scouring pads

seafood & seafood products

seafood steaming eqt.

seasonings & spices

seating systems: charts
   & wait lists

seating, auditorium
   & theater

seating, food court

secret shopper service

security eqt. systems
   & services

septic tank cleaning,
   repairs & maintenance

serving dishes

sharpening services:
   knives & eqt.

shelf liners

shellfish tools/mesh
   steaming bags

shelving, plastic

shelving, steel & wood

shortening

signs, changeable
   letter

signs, electrical & electronic

signs, painted

signs, tabletop

signs, wooden

signs: engraved, led, & neon

silver burnishers,
cleaners & compounds

sinks, kitchen

sinks, under-bar

slicers, food: electric

slicers, mechanical/
hand-operated

slush machines

smoked meats & sausage:
manufacturer

snack bar units

snack foods: candies,
chips & nuts

sneeze guards

soap, toilet & bath

soaps: detergents &
cleaning compounds

soda fountain supplies

soda fountains & eqt.

soft serve eqt. & products

sorbet

sound systems

souvenirs, novelties
& party favors

specialty foods

stages, mobile & fold-
ing; dance floors

stainless steel

stanchions
& decorative rope

staples

starch, cooking

steam cleaning services

steam cookers

steam tables

sterilizers

stirrers: wood or plastic

straws

strip doors

sugar & sugar products

supplies: electronic
machines: paper, rolls
& ribbon

sweetening products

syrups & toppings

systems, intercom

T

table covers, disposable

table padding

table toys & table games

table: skirting, linens, napkins, etc.

tables, banquet room
& folding

tables & counters, restaurant

tables, kitchen

tables, pedestal

tables: hot/cold food;
serving & folding

tableware, disposable

takeout service/

delivery service

tea making
   & dispensing eqt.

tea & iced tea

technical research

telecommunication
   services

telephone pay

telephone systems,
   sales & service

television, closed
   circuit

television, satellite

tenderizers

testing & evaluation
   services: safety
   & sanitation

theme party supplies

thermo delivery pouches

thermometers

tiling

tilting skillets

time keeping eqt. & supplies

time recorders

tissues, disposable

toasters, automatic:
   gas or electric

tobacco products

toilet paper

toilet seat covers

tomato products

tools: garnishing,
   ice carving, etc.

toothpicks & party picks

toppings

tortilla press

tortilla products

touch screens

towels: cotton or linen

towels, paper

trade publications

training films
   & filmstrips

training materials

tray covers

tray stands

tray washers

trays, foam

trays, paper

trays, plastic

trays, restaurant

trays: storage, serving
   & display

trucks for folding
   tables, chairs

U

uniform emblems: imprinted
   or embroidered

uniforms: clothing

uniforms: hats & caps

uniforms: protective
    apparel

upholstery cleaners

utensils, cooking/kitchen

utility, analysis, con-
    trol & distributions

vacuum cleaner

V

vacuum-packed/vacuum-
    sealed bags & pouches

vegetable cutters & peelers

vegetable juice

vehicles, maintenance

vehicles, personnel

vending machines

vending products

vending vehicles

ventilating systems,
    kitchen

ventilators
    & ventilating eqt.

vinegars

W

waitstaff call system

walk-in coolers & freezers

wall covering

wall panels, tile, wallboard, etc.

wall cleaners & maintenance

walls, movable

warehousing

warmers, beverage

warmers, dish/plate

warmers, food

wash cloths

waste disposal systems

waste grease collection

waste reduction eqt.
    & services

waste reduction/waste disposal

wastebaskets & receptacles

water conditioner
    & softener eqt. & supplies

water machines:
    heating & cooling

water purification/filtration

water vacuums/brooms

water, bottled

water, mineral

water & water dispensers

whipping eqt.: cream,
    sour cream & toppings

whipping eqt.: accessories

wholesale club

windows

wine accessories

wine cellars

wine consultants
   & distributors

wine service eqt.

wines

wipes

wire accessories

woks, electric & nonelectric

woodenware, bowls
   & kitchen utensils

work tables, kitchen

wraps: lemon, stem, etc.

Y

---

yogurt eqt.

yogurt: frozen, fresh
   & soft-serve

CHAPTER EIGHTEEN

Laws by State

One of the most important aspects of being a bar owner is serving alcohol responsibly. You and your employees must be knowledgeable of and follow all local and state laws. In addition, you should have a documented program in place to train employees to serve responsibly. We recommend *The Responsible Serving of Alcoholic Beverages: A Complete Staff Training Course for Bars, Restaurant, and Caterers*. It is available from Atlantic Publishing for $49.95. To order, call 800-814-1132 or visit **www .atlantic-pub.com**.

This chapter has a summary of the serving laws of each state along with notes on training and contact for each state.

ALABAMA

Dram Shop State?	Yes
BAC Level	0.08
Age—Pour	21
Age—Sell	21 (19–20 restaurant license only)
Age—Serve	21 (restaurants with Responsible Vendor Certification can serve at 19–20)
Happy Hour Laws	No two-for-one promotions; same price, all day long.
Number of Drinks	Not regulated.
Max Alcohol per Drink	No established limit, but amount of alcohol in each drink must be posted.
Mandatory Server Training	Yes
Mandatory topics?	Yes

Notes on Training: The Responsible Vendor Program is voluntary for licensees. It costs $35 per license, per year. Licensees can complete an approved independent program and become registered with the state as a Responsible Vendor. Participation is voluntary, but suggested. The cost and length of time required for training varies.

Web/Contact for State	Alabama Alcoholic Beverage Control Board 334-271-3840 www.abcboard.state.al.us
Hours	On-Premise Drinking: 24 hours, except after 2 a.m. on Sunday; local regulations apply.

ALASKA

Dram Shop State?	Yes
BAC Level	0.08
Age—Pour	21
Age—Sell	21 (19–20 restaurant license only)
Age—Serve	21 (restaurants with Responsible Vendor Certification can serve at 19–20)
Happy Hour Laws	No single-priced, unlimited-service drink specials, free drinks for patrons, or two-for-one drink specials. Cannot encourage or promote any organized game that awards alcohol as a prize or promotes excessive drinking. May offer a food and drink combination for a special price only if the special is equal to or greater than the normal price of the drink.
Number of Drinks	2
Max Alcohol per Drink	Not regulated.
Mandatory Server Training	Yes
Mandatory topics?	Yes

Notes on Training: Requires all employees who serve or sell alcohol to complete an approved server-training program within 30 days of hiring and to be able to produce a certification card. The state approves programs.

Web/Contact for State	Alaska Alcoholic Beverage Control Board 907-269-0350
Hours	On-Premise Drinking Monday–Saturday: 8 a.m. to 5 a.m., Sunday: 8 a.m. to 5 a.m.

ARIZONA

Dram Shop State?	Yes
BAC Level	0.08
Age—Pour	19
Age—Sell	19
Age—Serve	19
Happy Hour Laws	No free drinks to patrons. Licensees may give away free drinks; may offer a food and drink combo for a special price. No difference between "happy hour," "drink specials," and/or "promotions."
Number of Drinks	Cannot serve more drinks than legal volume.
Max Alcohol per Drink	32-oz. beer; 1-liter wine; 4-oz. distilled spirits
Mandatory Server Training	No, but does have guidelines.

Notes on Training: Does not require server training, nor does the state provide a training program for licensees. However, the state does certify trainers of private programs to train Arizona Liquor Law. If a state-certified trainer in an approved program trains a licensee, fines and penalties for violations can sometimes be mitigated. Trainers in Arizona are required to use the Arizona Supplement as part of the training program and all servers must receive a certification of completed alcohol training programs form. Trainers can obtain this form from the Arizona Department of Liquor Licenses and Control. A basic and management-approved training class is now required for the person responsible for the day-to-day operations of the business. This requirement is only for new managers or for a new licensee application.

Web/Contact for State	Arizona Department of Liquor Licenses & Control, 602-542-5141, www.azll.com
Hours	On-Premise Drinking: Monday–Saturday: 6 a.m. to 1 a.m., Sunday: 10 a.m. to 1 a.m.

ARKANSAS

Dram Shop State?	Yes
BAC Level	0.08
Age—Pour	21
Age—Sell	21
Age—Serve	21
Happy Hour Laws	Licensees may not give patrons free drinks.
Number of Drinks	Not regulated.
Max Alcohol per Drink	Not regulated.
Mandatory Server Training	Yes
Notes on Training: Responsible Permittee Regulation: The maximum a trainer can charge for training is $25. Length of the program is up to the program provider.	
Web/Contact for State	Arkansas Alcoholic Beverage Control Board 501-682-8174, ABCAdmin@dfa.state.ar.us
Hours	On-Premise Drinking: Private Clubs: Class A: 7 a.m. to 2 a.m.; Class B: 10 a.m. to 5 a.m.; Restaurants: 7 a.m. to 1 a.m.; Sunday: Prohibited (local option possible)

CALIFORNIA	
Dram Shop State?	Yes
BAC Level	0.08
Age—Pour	21
Age—Sell	21
Age—Serve	21 for bartenders and cocktail servers, 18 to serve alcohol in a bona fide eating place, if working in an area primarily designed and used for the sale and service of food and as an incidental part of a server's overall duties.
Happy Hour Laws	No free drinks, two-for-one drink specials, or anything of value in conjunction with the sale of an alcoholic beverage. Permitted to offer a food and drink combo for a special price as long as the drink is not free or complimentary. The price paid for a meal alone must be less than the price for a meal and an alcoholic beverage together. No difference between "happy hour," "drink specials," and/or "promotions" as these are generic terms used to describe reduced rates for drinks and are permitted as long as the retailer charges a price for the drink that does not undercut the wholesale price paid.
Number of Drinks	Not regulated.
Max Alcohol per Drink	Not regulated.
Mandatory Server Training	No

CALIFORNIA

Notes on Training: No state laws regulating server training. Some cities or counties may require server training as part of their Conditional Use Permit process (for example, City of Dana Point in Orange County). The Department of Alcoholic Beverage Control offers a voluntary training program for licensees called LEAD (Licensee Education on Alcohol and Drugs). This program focuses its training efforts on new license applicants, licensees located in high-crime areas, licensees who have violated ABC laws, major special events and county fairs. This program is, however, open to all persons.

Web/Contact for State	California Department of Alcoholic Beverage Control, cust.serv@abc.ca.gov
Hours	On-Premise Drinking: Monday–Sunday: 6 a.m. to 2 a.m.

COLORADO

Dram Shop State?	Yes
BAC Level	0.08
Age—Pour	18
Age—Sell	18
Age—Serve	18 [Note: To pour/serve must be supervised by someone who is 21—only in places where full meals are regularly served. Tavern employees must be 21 unless the tavern regularly serves meals.]
Happy Hour Laws	Not regulated.
Number of Drinks	Not regulated.
Max Alcohol per Drink	Not regulated.
Mandatory Server Training	Yes
Notes on Training: Colorado's Responsible Vendor Program went into effect on April 1, 2005. This program offers mitigating benefits to any licensee found to have served a minor during an established sting operation by the state and/or local licensing authority.	
Web/Contact for State	Colorado Dept of Revenue Liquor Enforcement Division, 303-205-2306, www.revenue.state.co.us/liquor_dir/home .asp
Hours	On-Premise Drinking: Monday–Sunday: 7 a.m. to 2 a.m.; no restrictions for on-premise sales on Sundays.

CONNECTICUT

Dram Shop State?	Yes
BAC Level	0.08
Age—Pour	18
Age—Sell	18
Age—Serve	18
Happy Hour Laws	No single-priced, unlimited-service drink specials or encourage/promote any organized game that awards alcohol as a prize or promotes excessive drinking.
Number of Drinks	One
Max Alcohol per Drink	Not regulated.
Mandatory Server Training	No
Web/Contact for State	Dept. of Consumer Protection, 860-713-6210, www.ct.gov/dcp/cwp
Hours	On-Premise Drinking: Monday–Thursday: 9 a.m. to 1 a.m.; Friday–Saturday: 9 a.m. to 2 a.m.; Sundays: 11 a.m. to 1 a.m. on-premises, unless changed by local ordinance.

DELAWARE

Dram Shop State?	No
BAC Level	0.08
Age—Pour	21
Age—Sell	21
Age—Serve	19
Happy Hour Laws	No two-for-one drinks, drinks sold below cost, or given away free. May offer a food and drink combo for a special price. No difference between "happy hour," "drink specials," and/or "promotions."
Number of Drinks	No more than one alcoholic beverage may be sold to a person less than 15 minutes prior to closing each day that a license is open.
Max Alcohol per Drink	Not regulated.
Mandatory Server Training	Yes
Notes on Training: All who sell or serve alcohol, supervisors, and licensees if directly involved in the management of the premises to complete a mandatory server-training course. Servers must complete a course within 30 days of employment. An ID card is issued upon completion of the course and must be presented on request by an OABCC agent or employer; otherwise, the employee will be cited for a violation. The legislature passed a server training law for package stores slated to begin on January 1, 1998.	
Web/Contact for State	Delaware Div. of Alcoholic Beverage Control, 302-577-5222, www.state.de.us/dabc
Hours	On-Premise Drinking: Everyday: 9 a.m. to 1 a.m.; Sundays: 9 a.m. to 1 a.m. for restaurants.

DISTRICT OF COLUMBIA

Dram Shop State?	No
BAC Level	0.08
Age—Pour	21
Age—Sell	18
Age—Serve	18
Happy Hour Laws	Licensees may not offer two-for-one specials.
Number of Drinks	One per regulations, backup drinks include second drinks served as part of a "two-for-one" promotion, second drinks served just prior to last call and second drinks provided complimentary by the licensee or purchased by other patrons. Except as provided above, backup drinks do not include two different drinks served together, such as a beer and a shot or any other industry drink that can be considered a shot and a mixer. The prohibition against backup drinks also does not apply to the service of wine with a meal where the patron has not finished a previously served cocktail.
Max Alcohol per Drink	Not regulated.
Mandatory Server Training	Yes
Notes on Training: Effective September 30, 2004, the District of Columbia has a mandatory training program for managers of on-premise establishments.	
Web/Contact for State	Dept. of Consumer & Regulatory Affairs, Alcohol Beverage Div., 202-442-4445, http://dcra.dc.gov/dcra
Hours	Monday–Friday: 8 a.m. to 2 a.m.; Saturday: 8 a.m. to 3 a.m.; Sunday: 10 a.m. to 3 a.m.

FLORIDA

Dram Shop State?	No
BAC Level	0.08
Age—Pour	18
Age—Sell	18
Age—Serve	18
Happy Hour Laws	May offer food and drink combinations for a special price.
Number of Drinks	Not regulated.
Max Alcohol per Drink	Not regulated.
Mandatory Server Training	No

Notes on Training: Florida does not mandate training, approve programs, or offer a state program. Florida has a Responsible Vendor Act that sets standards for licensees to meet in order to be considered a responsible vendor. Licensees who obtain this status can present it as a mitigating factor against penalties for violations by employees.

Web/Contact for State	Florida Division of Alcoholic Beverages & Tobacco, 850-488-3227, www.state.fl.us/dbpr/abt
Hours	Local option 7 days a week.

GEORGIA

Dram Shop State?	Yes
BAC Level	0.08
Age—Pour	18
Age—Sell	18
Age—Serve	18
Happy Hour Laws	Regulated by local ordinances.
Number of Drinks	Not regulated.
Max Alcohol per Drink	Not regulated.
Mandatory Server Training	No
Notes on Training: Does not currently regulate server training. However, the State Revenue Department does have a training program for wholesale dealers, retail dealers, and consumption-on-premises dealers.	
Web/Contact for State	Georgia Alcohol & Tobacco Division, 404-417-4900
Hours	Local communities set laws on hours.

HAWAII	
Dram Shop State?	Yes
BAC Level	0.08
Age—Pour	18
Age—Sell	18
Age—Serve	18
Happy Hour Laws	No free drinks when connected to the sale of other merchandise. Encouraging or promoting any organized game that awards alcohol as a prize or promotes excessive drinking is prohibited. Food and drink combos may be offered as long as the liquor is not used as an inducement. No food with the liquor offered "free" if the food item is purchased. No differentiation between "happy hour," "drink specials," and "promotions." Laws vary by locality; contact county liquor commission for further details.
Number of Drinks	No information available at this time.
Max Alcohol per Drink	No information available at this time.
Mandatory Server Training	Server training regulations are enforced at the local level in Hawaii.
Notes on Training: No information available at this time.	
Web/Contact for State	Liquor Commission of the City and County of Honolulu, 808-523-4458; Hawaii: 808-961-8218; Kauai: 808-241-6580; Maui: 808-243-7753; www.co.honolulu.hi.us/liq
Hours	Monday–Saturday: 6 a.m. to 2 a.m.; 6 a.m. to 4 a.m. for hotels; 8 a.m. to 4 a.m. for cabarets; Sundays: 6 a.m. to 2 a.m.

IDAHO

Dram Shop State?	Yes
BAC Level	0.08
Age—Pour	19
Age—Sell	19
Age—Serve	19
Happy Hour Laws	No official "happy hour" laws. May offer a food and drink combo for a special price.
Number of Drinks	Not regulated.
Max Alcohol per Drink	Not regulated.
Mandatory Server Training	No

Notes on Training: Idaho currently does not regulate server training. The ABC does provide a training program for licensees.

Web/Contact for State	State Liquor Dispensary, 208-947-9400, www2.state.id.us/isld
Hours	On-Premise Drinking: Monday–Saturday: 10 a.m. to 1 a.m. (local ordinances can extend or limit); Sunday: Permitted only through local option.

ILLINOIS

Dram Shop State?	Yes
BAC Level	0.08
Age—Pour	18 (unless regulated by local ordinance)
Age—Sell	21 (unless regulated by local ordinance)
Age—Serve	18 (unless regulated by local ordinance)
Happy Hour Laws	No single-priced or unlimited-service drink specials. No free drinks or advertise any of the aforementioned practices. May offer a food and drink combo (meal package) for a special price.
Number of Drinks	One
Max Alcohol per Drink	Not regulated.
Mandatory Server Training	At local level.
Notes on Training: Local government authorities may enact ordinances with requirements that mandate server training programs, ranging from who is required to participate to who may provide the training. The Illinois Liquor Control Act states that if BASSET training is mandated, an Illinois BASSET licensee must perform it.	
Web/Contact for State	Illinois Liquor Control Commission, 312-814-2206, www.state.il.us/lcc
Hours	Local option, but no liquor sales on Sunday unless provided by local ordinance.

INDIANA

Dram Shop State?	Yes
BAC Level	0.08
Age—Pour	21
Age—Sell	18 for drug/grocery; 21 everywhere else
Age—Serve	21
Happy Hour Laws	No two-for-one drink specials. Drink specials must last for the entire business day.
Number of Drinks	No more than one drink per order for one.
Max Alcohol per Drink	Not regulated.
Mandatory Server Training	Yes
Notes on Training: Effective July 1, 2005, all servers, sellers, and some managers will be required to receive training. Affected employees will have until July 1, 2008, to complete training.	
Web/Contact for State	Alcohol & Tobacco Commission, 317-232-2469, www.in.gov/atc or comments@atc.in.gov
Hours	Monday–Saturday: 7 a.m. to 3 a.m.; Sunday: Noon to 12:30 a.m.

IOWA

Dram Shop State?	Yes
BAC Level	0.08
Age—Pour	18
Age—Sell	16
Age—Serve	18
Happy Hour Laws	Iowa does not have laws regulating "happy hours" or promotions, but local ordinance may apply. May offer a food and drink combination for a special price. "Happy hour," "drink special," and "promotions" are not regulated.
Number of Drinks	Local ordinance may apply.
Max Alcohol per Drink	Not regulated.
Mandatory Server Training	No
Notes on Training: Iowa currently does not regulate server training, nor does the state provide a training program for licensees. However, server training is recommended.	
Web/Contact for State	Alcoholic Beverages Division, 866-469-2223, www.iowaabd.com
Hours	Monday–Saturday: 6 a.m. to 2 a.m.; Sunday: 8 a.m. to 2 a.m.

KANSAS	
Dram Shop State?	No
BAC Level	0.08
Age—Pour	21 to mix or dispense
Age—Sell	21
Age—Serve	18 to serve, if no less than 50% of gross receipts are derived from the sale of food; otherwise 21.
Happy Hour Laws	No single-priced, unlimited-service drink specials or free drinks for patrons. May not encourage or promote any organized game that awards alcohol as a prize or promotes excessive drinking. May offer a food and drink combo for a special price dependent upon the licensee being able to articulate how much of that price was for the drink versus the food. The same drink would have to be offered for that same price as a solo purchase for the entire day. Regardless of the terms used, "happy hour," "drink special," and/or "promotion," all drinks have to have the same price throughout the same day/evening.
Number of Drinks	Not regulated.
Max Alcohol per Drink	Not regulated.
Mandatory Server Training	No
Notes on Training: Kansas currently does not regulate server training; however, the state does provide a training program for licensees who opt to take it in lieu of serving a suspension upon first violation (available only for underage violations).	
Web/Contact for State	Dept. of Revenue, 785-296-7015, www.ksrevenue.org/abc.htm
Hours	Monday–Saturday: 9 a.m. to 2 a.m.; Sunday: 9 a.m. to 2 a.m.

KENTUCKY

Dram Shop State?	No
BAC Level	0.08
Age—Pour	20
Age—Sell	20
Age—Serve	20
Happy Hour Laws	Licensees may not offer patrons free or complimentary drinks. The law does allow a licensee to offer a food and drink combination for a special price.
Number of Drinks	Not regulated.
Max Alcohol per Drink	Not regulated.
Mandatory Server Training	No

Notes on Training: Kentucky currently does not regulate server training. The state offers a program called STAR that covers Kentucky laws.

Web/Contact for State	Alcoholic Beverage Control, 502-564-4850, abc.info@ky.gov
Hours	Monday–Saturday: Local option can set hours between 6 a.m. to midnight; Sunday: local ordinance may vote to permit Sunday sales.

LOUISIANA

Dram Shop State?	No
BAC Level	0.08
Age—Pour	18
Age—Sell	18
Age—Serve	18
Happy Hour Laws	All-you-can-drink limitations. Licensees may offer single-priced, unlimited-drink specials. All-you-can-drink must end before 10 p.m.
Number of Drinks	Not regulated.
Max Alcohol per Drink	Not regulated.
Mandatory Server Training	Yes
Notes on Training: Responsible Vendor Act is mandatory and all servers have to be certified every two years. Some cities do regulate server training and offer their own training.	
Web/Contact for State	Louisiana Office of Alcohol & Tobacco Control, 225-925-4041, www.atc.rev.state.la.us
Hours	Local option; Sunday sales: governed by local ordinance.

	MAINE	
Dram Shop State?	Yes	
BAC Level	0.08	
Age—Pour	17 [Note: All require supervisor on duty who is at least 21.]	
Age—Sell	17 [Note: All require supervisor on duty who is at least 21.]	
Age—Serve	17 [Note: All require supervisor on duty who is at least 21.]	
Happy Hour Laws	No free drinks or encourage or promote any organized game that awards alcohol as a prize or promotes excessive drinking. May offer a food and drink combo for a special price. Maine distinguishes between "happy hour," "drink special," and/or "promotions."	
Number of Drinks	Two	
Max Alcohol per Drink	Not regulated.	
Mandatory Server Training	Yes	

Notes on Training: State-established criteria for server training programs, approved courses, and monitored training. Server training not mandatory. The state offers two training programs through its liquor offices.

Web/Contact for State	Maine Bureau of Alcoholic Beverages, 1-800-452-4663, Ext. 2555, www.maineliquor.com	
Hours	Monday–Saturday: 6 a.m. to 1 a.m.; Sundays: 9 a.m. to 1 a.m.	

MARYLAND

Dram Shop State?	No
BAC Level	0.08
Age—Pour	18 for beer/wine licensees, 21 for beer/wine/liquor licensee
Age—Sell	18 for beer/light wine, 21 for Class D licensees
Age—Serve	18 for beer/wine licensees, 21 for beer/wine/liquor licensees
Happy Hour Laws	City/County liquor control boards regulate "happy hours" on a local level. All alcohol beverages consumed on a retail premise must be purchased from that retail premise. May restrict free snacks/food during "happy hours."
Number of Drinks	Subject to local regulations.
Max Alcohol per Drink	Varies by city and county; generally not more than 2 oz. per drink; however, this is not regulated by the state.
Mandatory Server Training	Yes

Notes on Training: State approves server training programs. Certification must be completed every four years. A permit is needed for both the program and the trainer. Program providers and trainers must re-register with the state every year by October 31. Retail establishments must have a minimum of one employee trained in a server training program in order to renew or apply for a new license. The holder of a Statewide Caterer's (SCAT) license shall have at least one individual on-site during a catered event that has been certified by an alcohol-awareness program licensed by the State Comptroller's Office.

Web/Contact for State	Comptroller of Maryland, 410-260-7314, www.comp.state.md.us
Hours	Local option on sales time.

MASSACHUSETTS

Dram Shop State?	Yes
BAC Level	0.08
Age—Pour	18
Age—Sell	18
Age—Serve	18
Happy Hour Laws	No offering single-priced, unlimited-service drink specials; free drinks to patrons; encouraging any organized game that awards alcohol as a prize; or promoting excessive drinking.
Number of Drinks	Two
Max Alcohol per Drink	Not regulated.
Mandatory Server Training	No
Notes on Training: None available.	
Web/Contact for State	Massachusetts Alcoholic Beverages Control Commission, 617-727-3040, www.mass.gov/abcc
Hours	On-Premise Drinking: No official hours; Sundays: complex law; local licensing boards may regulate hours. See state statutes.

MICHIGAN

Dram Shop State?	Yes
BAC Level	0.08
Age—Pour	18
Age—Sell	18
Age—Serve	18
Happy Hour Laws	No offering single-priced, unlimited-service drink specials, free drinks to patrons, or two-for-one drink specials.
Number of Drinks	Not regulated.
Max Alcohol per Drink	Not regulated.
Mandatory Server Training	Yes—under certain circumstances.

Notes on Training: A licensee obtaining a new on-premise license or transferring more than 50% interest in an existing on-premise license is required to have server-trained supervisory personnel employed during all hours alcoholic beverages are served.

Web/Contact for State	Michigan Liquor Control Commission, 517-322-1345, www.michigan.gov/cis
Hours	Monday–Saturday: 7 a.m. to 2 a.m.; Sunday: Noon to 2 a.m. with Sunday sales permit.

"

MINNESOTA

Dram Shop State?	Yes
BAC Level	0.1
Age—Pour	18
Age—Sell	18
Age—Serve	Under 17 not permitted to work in areas where alcohol is served or consumed.
Happy Hour Laws	No current statutes/rules governing "happy hours." Rules Chapter 7515/0740(L) does not allow premiums or inducements to encourage alcoholic purchases and consumption. There is a difference between "happy hour," "drink specials," and/or "promotions." "Happy hour" and "drink specials" for the most part would be considered one and the same. Drink promos may or may not be legal depending on the terms and conditions of the promotion. Recommends that if interested in running drink promos, submit them for review by the state agency.
Number of Drinks	Not regulated.
Max Alcohol per Drink	Not regulated.
Mandatory Server Training	No
Notes on Training: Does not regulate server training, nor does the state provide a training program for licensees.	
Web/Contact for State	Dept. of Public Safety Alcohol & Gambling Enforcement, 651-296-6979, www.dps.state.mn.us
Hours	Monday–Saturday: 8 a.m. to 2 a.m.; Sunday: Noon to 2 a.m.; may restrict on-premises alcohol sales on holidays.

MISSISSIPPI	
Dram Shop State?	Yes
BAC Level	0.08
Age—Pour	21
Age—Sell	21
Age—Serve	18
Happy Hour Laws	No promotion may require proof of purchase of an alcohol beverage. All drinks must be served to the customer. Bottle sales, except for wines and champagnes, are prohibited. Allowance to offer a food and drink combo for a special price.
Number of Drinks	Not regulated.
Max Alcohol per Drink	Not regulated.
Mandatory Server Training	No
Notes on Training: Does not regulate server training, nor do they offer server training programs through the state. However, a one-hour education program on ABC laws is offered free of charge by ABC Enforcement Agents.	
Web/Contact for State	Office of Alcoholic Beverage Control, 601-856-1301, www.mstc.state.ms.us
Hours	Monday–Saturday: 10 a.m. to midnight; Sunday: prohibited. May be allowed/limited by the commission upon request by local jurisdiction.

MISSOURI	
Dram Shop State?	Yes
BAC Level	0.08
Age—Pour	21
Age—Sell	21; 18 to serve with permission in some establishments
Age—Serve	18 to serve with permission in some establishments
Happy Hour Laws	May give free drinks, have two-for-one specials, etc. Prohibited from advertising these specials; allows, under certain conditions, offering of a food and drink combo for a special price.
Number of Drinks	Not regulated.
Max Alcohol per Drink	Not regulated.
Mandatory Server Training	No
Notes on Training: Does not regulate server training. However, a licensee can request a session with an enforcement agent to review the laws and information regarding preventing intoxication and recognizing intoxicated patrons.	
Web/Contact for State	Liquor Control Division, 573-751-2333, www.mdlc.state.mo.us
Hours	Monday–Saturday: 6 a.m. to 1:30 a.m.; Sunday: 9 a.m. to midnight; designated convention site: Monday–Saturday till 3 a.m.

MONTANA

Dram Shop State?	Yes
BAC Level	0.08
Age—Pour	18
Age—Sell	As allowed by state and federal labor laws.
Age—Serve	As allowed by state and federal labor laws.
Happy Hour Laws	May not sell "liquor" for less than the posted price. No regulations regarding food and drink combos. Promos are considered items such as neck hangers, coupons, rebates, etc. Every promo must have prior approval from the state prior. No definitions in the state statute for "happy hour" and drink specials.
Number of Drinks	Not regulated.
Max Alcohol per Drink	Not regulated.
Mandatory Server Training	No
Notes on Training: Does not regulate server training, nor does the state provide a training program for licensees.	
Web/Contact for State	Montana Liquor Licensing, 406-444-6900, www.mt.gov/revenue/forbusinesses
Hours	Monday–Saturday: 8 a.m. to 2 a.m.; Sunday: 8 a.m. to 2 a.m.; sales may be further restricted by local ordinances.

Dram Shop State?	No
BAC Level	0.08
Age—Pour	19
Age—Sell	19
Age—Serve	19
Happy Hour Laws	May not offer single-priced, unlimited-service drink specials or two-for-one drink specials. Allowance to offer a food and drink combo for a special price. Differentiates between "happy hour," "drink specials," and/or "promotions."
Number of Drinks	One
Max Alcohol per Drink	Not regulated.
Mandatory Server Training	No
Notes on Training: Does not regulate server training, nor does the state provide a training program for licensees. Does require training for new license applicants who do not have experience or training in the sales or serving of alcoholic beverages.	
Web/Contact for State	Liquor Control Commission, 402-471-2571, www.nol.org/home/NLCC
Hours	Monday–Saturday: 6 a.m. to 1 a.m.; Sunday: check local ordinances.

NEVADA

Dram Shop State?	No
BAC Level	0.08
Age—Pour	Regulated at the city and county level.
Age—Sell	Regulated at the city and county level.
Age—Serve	Regulated at the city and county level.
Happy Hour Laws	"Happy hour" laws vary by city and county. Contact local agency for further information.
Number of Drinks	Regulated at the city and county level.
Max Alcohol per Drink	Regulated at the city and county level.
Mandatory Server Training	A new statewide mandatory training law will become effective on July 1, 2007. Las Vegas and Clark County have mandatory training ordinances. Reno has a limited training ordinance for sellers, mandatory for only a part of downtown Reno.

Notes on Training: Training for sellers, servers, and security staff in Nevada will become mandatory statewide on July 1, 2007. Regulations have not yet been drafted. Currently Clark County and Las Vegas have mandatory training ordinances. Reno has a limited training ordinance, mandatory only for a part of downtown Reno.

Web/Contact for State	Dept. of Taxation, 775-684-2000, tax.state.nv.us
Hours	Regulated by local governments only.

NEW HAMPSHIRE

Dram Shop State?	Yes
BAC Level	0.08
Age—Pour	18
Age—Sell	16 to run a register in an off-premise situation (with 18-year-old supervision)
Age—Serve	18
Happy Hour Laws	No free drinks to patrons. No special drink prices may be advertised off the licensed premises. Per RSA 179.42, may offer a food and drink combo for a special price.
Number of Drinks	No more than one drink in the food/drink combo.
Max Alcohol per Drink	Not regulated.
Mandatory Server Training	Yes—under certain circumstances.
Notes on Training: It is mandatory for any new licensee or his/her designee to attend a management training seminar, developed and provided by the State Liquor Commission within 45 days of issuance of the license. This requirement applies to both on-premise and off-premise licensees. This requirement does not apply to anyone holding a license as of the effective date (September 9, 2001).	
Web/Contact for State	State Liquor Commission, 603-271-3134, info@ liquor.state.nh.us
Hours	Monday–Saturday: 6 a.m. to 1 a.m.; Sunday: 6 a.m. to 1 a.m.

NEW JERSEY

Dram Shop State?	Yes
BAC Level	0.08
Age—Pour	18
Age—Sell	18
Age—Serve	18
Happy Hour Laws	No single-priced, unlimited-service or two-for-one drink specials. May not encourage or promote any organized game that awards alcohol as a prize or promotes excessive drinking. Allowance to offer a food and drink combo for a special price.
Number of Drinks	Not regulated.
Max Alcohol per Drink	Not regulated.
Mandatory Server Training	No
Notes on Training: New Jersey currently does not regulate server training.	
Web/Contact for State	Division of Alcoholic Beverage Control, 609-984-2830, www.state.nj.us/lps/abc/index.html
Hours	Determined by city ordinance.

NEW MEXICO

Dram Shop State?	Yes
BAC Level	0.08
Age—Pour	21
Age—Sell	19 (in an establishment where the primary source of revenue is food)
Age—Serve	19 (in an establishment where the primary source of revenue is food)
Happy Hour Laws	No single-priced, unlimited-service, free drinks for patrons or two-for-one drink specials.
Number of Drinks	Two
Max Alcohol per Drink	Not regulated.
Mandatory Server Training	Yes
	Notes on Training: State certification program using state-provided curriculum.
Web/Contact for State	Alcohol and Gaming Division, 505-476-4875, rld.state.nm.us
Hours	Monday–Saturday: 7 a.m. to 2 a.m.; Sunday: Noon to midnight (Sunday sales permit required)

NEW YORK

Dram Shop State?	Yes
BAC Level	0.08
Age—Pour	18
Age—Sell	18
Age—Serve	18
Happy Hour Laws	No unlimited drink offerings; for example, "all you can drink."
Number of Drinks	Not regulated.
Max Alcohol per Drink	Not regulated.
Mandatory Server Training	No
Notes on Training: A voluntary Responsible Vendor Program sets standards in order to be considered a responsible vendor. Status can be presented as a mitigating factor against penalties for violations by employees. Consult the New York State Liquor Authority for more details.	
Web/Contact for State	Division of Alcoholic Beverage Control, 518-474-0810, www.abc.state.ny.us
Hours	Monday–Saturday: 8 a.m. to midnight. Differs by county.

NORTH CAROLINA

Dram Shop State?	Yes
BAC Level	0.08
Age—Pour	21 to pour distilled spirits, 18 to pour beer and wine
Age—Sell	18
Age—Serve	18
Happy Hour Laws	"Happy hours" or drink specials must be offered for the entire business day. No free drinks or offer two-for-one drink specials. No allowance to offer a food and drink combo for a special price. No difference between "happy hour," "drink specials," and/or "promotions."
Number of Drinks	One
Max Alcohol per Drink	Not regulated.
Mandatory Server Training	No, but ABC provides free Responsible Alcohol Seller Program training provided by their education specialists.

Notes on Training: Does not regulate server training. However, does offer the BARS program (Be A Responsible Server), taught by alcohol law enforcement agents. BARS is a one- to two-hour program and is provided at no cost to the retailer.

Web/Contact for State	Alcoholic Beverage Commission, 919-779-0700, www.ncabc.com or ContactUs@ncabc.com
Hours	Monday–Saturday: 7 a.m. to 2 a.m.; Sunday: Noon to 2 a.m. with a mixed beverage or brown bagging permit. Election Day: no restrictions.

NORTH DAKOTA

Dram Shop State?	Yes
BAC Level	0.08
Age—Pour	21
Age—Sell	19 to collect money (see "Serve" conditions below)
Age—Serve	19 to serve if in dining area separate from bar and gross food sales are at least equal to gross alcohol sales and done under direct supervision of someone 21 or older.
Happy Hour Laws	Subject to local regulations.
Number of Drinks	Not regulated.
Max Alcohol per Drink	Not regulated.
Mandatory Server Training	No
Notes on Training: None available	
Web/Contact for State	Office of the State Tax Commissioner, 701-328-4576, www.wineinstitute.org /shipwine/state_abcz/abcz.htm#mstates
Hours	Monday–Saturday: 8 a.m. to 1 a.m.; Sunday: Noon to 1 a.m.

OHIO

Dram Shop State?	Yes
BAC Level	0.08
Age—Pour	21 to serve liquor across the bar, 19 to serve beer and wine across the bar
Age—Sell	19 as server, 21 to sell across the bar
Age—Serve	19
Happy Hour Laws	No single-priced, unlimited-service, free drinks for patrons, or two-for-one drink specials. May not encourage or promote any organized game that awards alcohol as a prize or promotes excessive drinking. "Happy hour" drink specials must end before 9 p.m.
Number of Drinks	Not regulated.
Max Alcohol per Drink	Not regulated.
Mandatory Server Training	No

Notes on Training: No. The Department of Public Safety offers a server education program to retail permit holders. Call 614-644-2415 for details.

Web/Contact for State	Div. of Liquor Control, 614-644-2411, www.liquorcontrol.ohio.gov/liquor.htm
Hours	Monday–Saturday: 5:30 a.m. to 1 a.m.; Nightclubs: 5:30 a.m. to 2:30 a.m.; Sunday sales permit required: 11 a.m., 1 p.m., or 10 a.m. to midnight based on local option.

OKLAHOMA

Dram Shop State?	No
BAC Level	0.08
Age—Pour	21
Age—Sell	21
Age—Serve	18, if server works outside separate bar area
Happy Hour Laws	No difference between "happy hour," "drink specials," and/or "promotions." "Happy hours" are illegal—no reduced drink prices. Drink specials must occur for an entire calendar week (Sunday–Saturday). Promos are allowed if they follow the same calendar week schedule. No allowance to offer a food and drink combo for a special price.
Number of Drinks	Two
Max Alcohol per Drink	Not regulated.
Mandatory Server Training	No
Notes on Training: None available.	
Web/Contact for State	ABLE Commission, 405-521-3484, www.able.state.ok.us
Hours	Monday–Saturday: 10 a.m. to 2 a.m.; set by county. Sundays: check local ordinances.

OREGON

Dram Shop State?	Yes
BAC Level	0.08
Age—Pour	18 with a service permit, restrictions apply to 18–20 year olds
Age—Sell	18
Age—Serve	18 with a service permit, restrictions apply to 18–20 year olds
Happy Hour Laws	May not be advertised outside the licensed business. Same rule applies to a licensee who wishes to offer a food and drink combo for a special price if the price includes a temporary price reduction on the alcohol. Does not distinguish between "happy hour," "drink specials," and/or "promotions."
Number of Drinks	Not regulated.
Max Alcohol per Drink	Not regulated.
Mandatory Server Training	Yes

Notes on Training: There is a mandatory alcohol server education program managed by the Oregon Liquor Control Commission (OLCC). It is for owners, managers, and servers of alcohol at businesses licensed for on-premises consumption.

Web/Contact for State	Liquor Control Commission, 800-452-6522, 503-872-5000, www.olcc.state.or.us
Hours	Monday–Saturday 7 a.m. to 2:30 a.m.; Sunday: 7 a.m. to 2:30 a.m.

PENNSYLVANIA

Dram Shop State?	Yes
BAC Level	0.08
Age—Pour	18
Age—Sell	18
Age—Serve	18
Happy Hour Laws	May not offer single-priced, unlimited-service or two-for-one drink specials. "Happy hour" specials may only be two consecutive hours long and must occur before 12:00 a.m. Drinks of an increased size must be accompanied by a corresponding increased price. One daily drink special may be offered as long as it ends by 12 a.m. Does allow offering of a food and drink combo for a special price as long as it does not violate Section 13.102 of the Board's regulations on the licensee's ability to discount the price of alcoholic beverages.
Number of Drinks	Unlimited as long as there is no discount for multiple purchases and the person is not visibly intoxicated.
Max Alcohol per Drink	Not regulated.
Mandatory Server Training	No
	**Notes on Training:** No required server training. However, the state does offer a voluntary "Responsible Alcohol Management Program" (RAMP). Licensees' compliance with the Responsible Alcohol Management provisions can be a mitigating factor in a subsequent citation for sales to minors or visibly intoxicated persons. While the program is otherwise voluntary, a judge may order a licensee to comply with the Responsible Alcohol Management provisions for up to a year, if the licensee has been found to have sold alcohol to minors or to a visibly intoxicated person.
Web/Contact for State	Liquor Control Board, 717-783-9454, www.lcb.state.pa.us
Hours	Monday–Saturday: 7 a.m. to 2 a.m.; Sunday: 11 a.m. to 2 a.m. (with permit).

RHODE ISLAND

Dram Shop State?	Yes
BAC Level	0.08
Age—Pour	18
Age—Sell	18
Age—Serve	18
Happy Hour Laws	May not offer single-priced, unlimited-service or encourage or promote any organized game which awards alcohol as a prize or promotes excessive drinking.
Number of Drinks	One
Max Alcohol per Drink	1.0 to 1.5 oz.
Mandatory Server Training	Yes
Notes on Training: The law became effective January 1, 2006.	
Web/Contact for State	Department of Business Regulation, Liquor Control Administration, 401-222-2562, www.dbr.state.ri.us/liquor_comp.html
Hours	Monday–Saturday: 6 a.m. to 1 a.m.; Sunday: 6 a.m. to 1 a.m.

SOUTH CAROLINA

Dram Shop State?	Yes
BAC Level	0.08
Age—Pour	21
Age—Sell	No minimum age if sold in sealed containers.
Age—Serve	18
Happy Hour Laws	No two-or-more-for-the-price-of-one drink specials and may not give free mixed drinks, beer, or wine. Regular drink prices may be reduced between 4:00 p.m. and 8:00 p.m. only. The State General Assembly issued new regulation for the use of standard-size bottles during the 2005 legislative session.
Number of Drinks	Not regulated.
Max Alcohol per Drink	Not regulated.
Mandatory Server Training	Yes
Notes on Training: Server training is voluntary.	
Web/Contact for State	Dept. of Revenue & Taxation, 803-898-5864, www.sctax.org/default.htm
Hours	Monday–Saturday: 24 hours for beer and wine, 10 a.m. to 2 a.m. for liquor, cease at midnight Saturdays; Sunday: local option.

SOUTH DAKOTA

Dram Shop State?	No
BAC Level	0.08
Age—Pour	21
Age—Sell	If 50% of retail is transacted from the sale of food, persons 18–20 may wait tables, no bartending.
Age—Serve	If 50% of retail is transacted from the sale of food, persons 18–20 may wait tables, no bartending.
Happy Hour Laws	Does not specifically address "happy hour." May offer a food and drink combo for a special price under the circumstances that the licensee cannot sell below wholesale cost (drink). No difference between "happy hour," "drink specials," and/or "promotion," as the statute only refers to selling below wholesale cost.
Number of Drinks	Not regulated.
Max Alcohol per Drink	Not regulated.
Mandatory Server Training	No
Mandatory Topics, Language, or Questions	Yes
Notes on Training: Done on a voluntary basis. Approved training cuts civil penalties in half for licensees whose clerks sell alcohol to teenagers.	
Web/Contact for State	Dept. of Revenue & Regulation, 605-773-3311, www.state.sd.us/drr2/revenue.html
Hours	On-Premise Drinking: Monday–Saturday: 7 a.m. to 2 a.m.; Sunday: if granted Sunday sales by local option—11 a.m. to midnight; local ordinances may be stricter.

TENNESSEE

Dram Shop State?	Yes
BAC Level	0.08
Age—Pour	18
Age—Sell	18
Age—Serve	18
Happy Hour Laws	May not offer single-priced, unlimited-service, give free drinks to patrons, or encourage or promote any organized game that awards alcohol as a prize or promotes excessive drinking. May not offer "happy hour" specials after 10 p.m.
Number of Drinks	No limit until 10 p.m., then one drink at a time.
Max Alcohol per Drink	Not regulated.
Mandatory Server Training	Yes
Notes on Training: Regulating law established May 1995 (effective July 1996). Does not apply to beer-only establishments. They are regulated by county beer boards. Employees in establishments regulated by beer boards are not required to have state server permits.	
Web/Contact for State	Alcoholic Beverage Commission, 615-741-1602, www.state.tn.us/abc
Hours	Monday–Saturday: 8 a.m. to 3 a.m.; Sunday: 10 a.m. to 3 a.m.; unless municipality has opted out; if so, noon to 3 a.m.

TEXAS

Dram Shop State?	Yes
BAC Level	0.08
Age—Pour	18
Age—Sell	18
Age—Serve	18
Happy Hour Laws	No single-priced, unlimited-service, or two-for-one drink specials. May not encourage or promote any organized game that awards alcohol as a prize or promotes excessive drinking. "Happy hour" specials must end before 11:00 p.m. May offer a food and drink combo for a special price. No difference in the law between "happy hour," "drink specials," and "promotions."
Number of Drinks	Two
Max Alcohol per Drink	Not regulated.
Mandatory Server Training	Yes

Notes on Training: Has laws regulating server training for all people who sell, serve, dispense, or deliver alcohol. They establish which entities are eligible as providers for the training and set the minimum requirements for a training curriculum. The Texas Alcoholic Beverage Commission offers the Stop Alcohol Violations Early (SAVE) program, developed by the commission for retailers at no cost. Program is approximately one hour in length and discusses the laws concerning sales to minors, intoxicated customers, the consequences of such illegal sales, and regulatory matters. SAVE does not meet the requirements for seller/server certification.

TEXAS	
Web/Contact for State	Alcoholic Beverage Commission, 1-888-THE-TABC, 512-206-3333, www.tabc.state.tx.us
Hours	Monday–Saturday: 7 a.m. to midnight—late-hours permit/license available in certain areas extends hours of sale to 2 a.m.; Sunday: with food service or at a "sporting venue" may start at 10 a.m. to midnight. Other permits may start at noon and serve until 2 a.m. with late-hours permit.

Dram Shop State?	Yes
BAC Level	0.08
Age—Pour	21
Age—Sell	21
Age—Serve	21
Happy Hour Laws	Prohibited from engaging in discounting practices that encourage over-consumption of alcohol (for example, "happy hours," "two-for-ones," "all you can drink" for a set price, free alcohol, selling at less than cost, etc.). May not buy a patron a drink. Ads may not encourage over-consumption or intoxication, promote the intoxicating effects of alcohol, or overtly promote increased consumption of alcoholic products. No food and drink combos for a special price.
Number of Drinks	Patrons of restaurants may have no more than one spirituous liquor beverage before them at a time. Patrons of restaurants, limited restaurants, and private clubs may have no more than two alcoholic beverages (of any kind) before them at a time.
Max Alcohol per Drink	1 oz. of primary liquor per drink. Beer may be sold to an individual patron only in a container that does not exceed 1 liter. Beer may be sold by the pitcher (up to 2 liters) to two or more patrons.
Mandatory Server Training	Yes

UTAH

Notes on Training: Required server training for all who sell or furnish alcoholic beverages for consumption on the premises. Employees, including managers and supervisors, are required to be server trained within 30 days of hire. The state has approved training programs to be provided by private entities. Trainers are required to register each server who successfully completes their course with the state.

Web/Contact for State	Dept. of Alcoholic Beverage Control, 801-977-6800, hotline@utah.gov or www.alcbev.state.ut.us
Hours	Monday–Saturday: 10 a.m. to 1 a.m.; Sunday: 10 a.m. to 1 a.m.

VERMONT

Dram Shop State?	Yes
BAC Level	0.08
Age—Pour	18
Age—Sell	16 for off-premise, 18 for on-premise
Age—Serve	18
Happy Hour Laws	No alcohol at reduced prices for any period less than a full day. Cannot encourage or promote any organized game that awards alcohol as a prize or promotes excessive drinking. May allow food and drink combination for a special price as long as they do not use the words "complimentary" or "free."
Number of Drinks	Two
Max Alcohol per Drink	32 oz. of beer; 4 oz. of spirits
Mandatory Server Training	Yes

Notes on Training: Requires all licensees (both on- and off-premise) to complete a Licensee Education and Server training course. Offers a four-hour course called ASAP (Alcohol Servers Awareness Program) at no cost to the retailer. Recertification is required every three years or licenses will not be renewed and no new license will be issued without training. Employees are required to be trained before they can sell or serve alcohol. Can be done by either attending a seminar put on by the DLC or trained by their employer using materials provided by the DLC. Employees must be trained once every two years.

VERMONT	
Web/Contact for State	Dept. of Liquor Control, 802-828-2345, www.state.vt.us/dlc
Hours	Monday–Saturday: 8 a.m. 2 a.m.; Sunday: 8 a.m. to 2 a.m.

VIRGINIA

Dram Shop State?	No
BAC Level	0.08
Age—Pour	21
Age—Sell	18
Age—Serve	18
Happy Hour Laws	No single-priced, unlimited-service, free drinks for patrons or two-for-one drink specials. The hours that "happy hour" can be conducted are from 6 a.m. to 9 p.m. No "happy hour" drink specials between 9 p.m. and 2 a.m. of the following day. Cannot advertise "happy hour" in the media or on the exterior of the premises. Cannot increase the amount of the alcoholic beverages in a drink without charging a higher price. Cannot sell pitchers of mixed beverages.
Number of Drinks	Two
Max Alcohol per Drink	Not more than 24 oz per drink; cannot serve one customer an entire bottle of spirits.
Mandatory Server Training	No
Notes on Training: Does not regulate server training. However, ABC agents provide both trainer workshops and server sessions throughout the state.	
Web/Contact for State	Dept. of Alcoholic Beverage Control, 804-213-4400, www.abc.state.va.us
Hours	Monday–Saturday: 6 a.m. to 2 a.m.; Sunday: 6 a.m. to 2 a.m.

WASHINGTON

Dram Shop State?	No
BAC Level	0.08
Age—Pour	21
Age—Sell	18
Age—Serve	18
Happy Hour Laws	No two-for-one drink specials or encourage any activity that promotes excessive drinking. May offer a food and drink combo for a special price as long as no liquor is sold below the cost of acquisition. The law differentiates between "happy hour," "drink specials," and/ or "promotions." "Happy hour" is a specific time of day; "drink specials" can be by house policy but cannot be sold below cost of acquisition; "promotions" must be approved by the Advertising Coordinator at the LCB. The board can take action against any licensee who promotes over-consumption or consumption by persons under 21.
Number of Drinks	Not regulated.
Max Alcohol per Drink	Not regulated.
Mandatory Server Training	Yes

Notes on Training: Mandatory server training program for on-premise establishments became effective January 1, 1997. Requires servers to have either a Class 12 or Class 13 permit. Permits are valid for five years. A list of approved programs and trainers is available from the liquor control board. As of January 1, 2005, trainers must use the standardized exam.

WASHINGTON

Web/Contact for State	State Liquor Control Board, 360-664-1600, wslcb@liq.wa.gov or www.liq.wa.gov/default.asp
Hours	Monday–Saturday: 6 a.m. to 2 a.m.; Sunday: 6 a.m. to 2 a.m.

WEST VIRGINIA

Dram Shop State?	No
BAC Level	0.08
Age—Pour	18 (supervised by person over 21 at all times).
Age—Sell	18
Age—Serve	18
Happy Hour Laws	Not covered by West Virginia law.
Number of Drinks	Not regulated.
Max Alcohol per Drink	Not regulated.
Mandatory Server Training	No
Notes on Training: Not regulated.	
Web/Contact for State	Alcohol Beverage Control Administration, 800-642-8208, www.wvabca.com
Hours	Monday–Saturday: 7 a.m. to 3:30 a.m.; Sunday: Noon to 3 a.m.

WISCONSIN

Dram Shop State?	No
BAC Level	0.08
Age—Pour	18
Age—Sell	18
Age—Serve	18
Happy Hour Laws	No laws specifically addressing "happy hours" or promotions. Does not address whether a licensee is allowed to offer food and drink combos for a special price; therefore, it is permitted. No differentiation between "happy hour," "drink specials," and/or "promotions."
Number of Drinks	Not regulated.
Max Alcohol per Drink	Not regulated.
Mandatory Server Training	Yes
Notes on Training: Requires licensees and servers to obtain alcohol awareness training if they are licensed to have a job selling or serving alcoholic beverages and the city or county requires a permit. In such cases, training is mandatory as a condition of obtaining a license.	
Web/Contact for State	Dept. of Revenue, 608-266-3969, www.dor.state.wi.us
Hours	On-Premise Drinking: Monday–Friday: 6 a.m. to 2 a.m.; Saturday–Sunday: 6 a.m. to 2:30 a.m.

WYOMING

Dram Shop State?	Yes, with qualifications
BAC Level	0.08
Age—Pour	18
Age—Sell	18
Age—Serve	21 (18 in dining-only areas)
Happy Hour Laws	No laws specifically addressing "happy hours" or promotions. Allows offering of food and drink combs for a special price.
Number of Drinks	Not regulated.
Max Alcohol per Drink	Not regulated.
Mandatory Server Training	Yes

Notes on Training: Has a Voluntary Responsible Vendor Program. The Wyoming Department of Revenue Liquor Division must approve all alcohol server training programs. All providers (trainers) must be certified per rules and regulations. Training is mandatory in Cheyenne for all servers, on-site managers, and staff involved in "physical security" (bouncers, doorkeepers, etc.). Training is mandatory in Douglas for all owners, managers, and supervisory personnel.

Web/Contact for State	Dept. of Revenue, 307-777-7961, revenue.state.wy.us
Hours	Monday–Saturday: 6 a.m. to 2 a.m. (maximum); Sunday: 6 a.m. to 2 a.m. (maximum). Note: Municipalities may be more restrictive on Sunday hours.

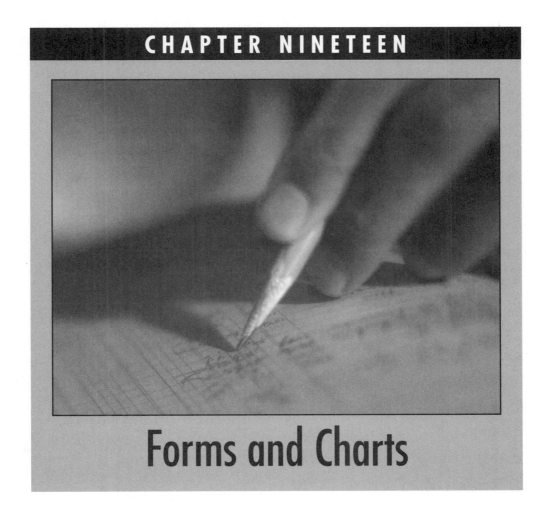

CHAPTER NINETEEN

Forms and Charts

This chapter contains useful forms and charts that can improve the efficiency and productivity of your bar. You will find a PDF version of all of the material in this chapter on the accompanying CD-ROM as well as Word documents that you can revise and customize specifically for your establishment.

Table of Contents

Wine Pronunciation & Food Accompaniment

WINE PRONUNCIATION

Cabernet Sauvignon
Cah-bear-nay So-veen-yohn

Chardonnay
Shar-done-nay

Chenin Blanc
Chen-nahn Blohn

Fume Blanc
Foo-may Blohn

Johannisberg Riesling
Yo-han-iss-bairg Reez-ling

Merlot
Mare-low

Pinot Noir
Pea-no Nwar

Sauvignon Blanc
So-veen-yohn Blohn

FOOD ACCOMPANIMENT

To achieve the best match of food and wine, it is necessary to analyze the basic components in both the wine and the food. Neither the food nor the wine should overpower the other. The main elements to consider are:

- Flavor, Intensity, and Characteristic
- Weight
- Acidity
- Salt
- Sweetness

White Wines
Serve with: Seafood, Fish, Poultry, Creamed Soups, Cream Sauces

- Chardonnay
- Semillon
- Sauvignon Blanc
- Riesling
- Chenin Blanc

Blush Wines
Serve with: Desserts, Fruit, Ham, Pork, Salads

- White Zinfandel

Red Wines
Serve with: Steak, Roasts, Game, Pasta, Cheese, Ham, Veal, Pork

- Cabernet Sauvignon
- Merlot
- Pinot Noir
- Zinfandel

Wine Stocking Guidelines

RED WINE	NUMBER TO STOCK
Light-bodied—RED MEATS	4
Full-bodied—ALL RED MEATS, DUCK	4
Semi-sweet—DESSERT. Never before dinner, as the sweetness will spoil the customer's appetite.	4
WHITE WINE	**NUMBER TO STOCK**
Dry light-bodied—SHELLFISH, SOME SEAFOOD	2
Full-bodied—WHITE MEATS, SEAFOOD	4
Semi-sweet—SEAFOOD	4
ROSÉ	**NUMBER TO STOCK**
Dry light-bodied—Can be served in place of either dry white or red wines.	1
SPARKLING WINES	**NUMBER TO STOCK**
Dry—May be served in place of dry white wines.	1
Semi-sweet—May be served in place of semi-sweet whites.	1
CHAMPAGNE	**NUMBER TO STOCK**
Dry—WITH ANY ITEM	1
Extra-dry (Brut)—WITH ANY ITEM	1

Beverage-Specific Garnishes & Drink Recipe Card

GARNISH GUIDELINES

- For alcoholic beverages, one straw for every drink with ice.

- Kiddie Cocktails – an orange flag or two cherries.

- Three cocktail onions per sword – in drink.

- Two olives per sword – in drink.

- Cherries – no sword.

- Twist – lemon peel used to flavor rim of glass, then dropped in drink.

DRINK GARNISHES

Manhattans: cherry

Gibson: cocktail onions

Martini: olives or a twist (ask customer's preference)

Collins and Sours: orange speared with a cherry

Tonic Drinks: lime wedge

Rob Roy: cherry

Old-Fashioned: cherry

Coffee Drinks: whipped cream, cherry

Drinks with Bloody Mary Mix: lime wedge or wheel and celery or pickle

All Coolers: lime wheel or wedge

Pineapple Juice Drinks: pineapple wedge speared with a cherry

Orange Juice Drinks: orange speared with a cherry

Margaritas/Daiquiris: lime wheel or wedge

ITEM _____

INGREDIENTS:	PROCEDURE:	GLASS:
_____	_____	_____
_____	_____	_____
_____	_____	_____
_____	_____	GARNISH:
_____	_____	_____
_____	_____	_____
_____	_____	_____
_____	_____	_____
_____	_____	_____
_____	_____	_____

Alcohol Awareness Summary

BLOOD ALCOHOL LEVELS

Alcohol is is a mood-altering drug. It may appear to be a stimulant, but it is actually a depressant, limiting bodily functions. As it is absorbed into the bloodstream, behavioral changes can occur. As the the liver oxidizes the alcohol and removes it from the body, the person's behavior returns to normal. This is often called "sobering up."

Only the passage of time rids the body of the effects of alcohol. Unfortunately, remedies such as black coffee, cold showers, and exercise are not effective.

When you consume more alcohol than your liver can oxidize, the amount of alcohol in your blood increases. Blood Alcohol Concentration (BAC) is the amount of alcohol in the bloodstream. It is measured in percentages. For instance, having a BAC of 0.10 percent means that a person has 1 part alcohol per 1,000 parts blood in the body. BAC is the legal standard frequently used to indicate when a person is "driving under the influence" (DUI) or "driving while intoxicated" (DWI). BAC can be measured by breath, blood, or urine tests.

Visible changes occur as a person's BAC increases. Their behavior changes visibly. Responsible servers are aware of the the progressive affects of alcohol and alert to the signs of over-indulgence. Although any one particular behavior may not indicate intoxication, a combination of several behaviors is a definite warning signal.

INTOXICATION VS. IMPAIRMENT

Impairment and intoxication are not the same thing. Impairment starts at the first drink. Impairment is the point where a person's intake of alcohol affects their ability to perform appropriately. Judgement, coordination, and reaction time may be affected. Intoxication is a **legal** term defining the level of alcohol in the blood where impairment is so severe that criminal actions may

be taken for driving or other activities. The level of legal intoxication is .08 in most states. Several states have additional definitions for people under age 21 (.00-.02). Some states also have mandatory jail time for drinking and driving while intoxicated.

CHECKING IDS

Serving alcohol to a minor can have very serious consequences. In fact, it is advisable to check the ID of any patron under who appears to be under 30, unless you are certain of a guest's age. In some cases, you could even be held accountable for serving someone with a fake ID, so be careful.

- Look for state seals or holograms.

- Look for any alterations, such as a cut around year of birth or typesets that don't match.

- Make sure it's not someone else's ID. Carefully examine the picture/description to make sure it matches the person using it.

- Look for groups that "pool" cash to an older person in the party.

In most states an acceptable ID is:
- A valid state driver's license or a valid state identification for non-drivers.

- A valid passport.

- A valid United States Uniformed Service Identification (your employer should provide you with an example).

All IDs should have a picture, signature, birth date, and description. Expired IDs are not acceptable.

Alcohol Awareness Summary

GUIDELINES TO DETERMINE THE SYMPTOMS OF INTOXICATION

Service Guidelines

- Before serving a guest, determine his or her condition.

- If you think a customer is already intoxicated, offer snacks and get them a menu quickly.

- Keep track of drinks served. The service order is a ready reference of how many drinks each person consumed.

- Watch for changes in the customer's behavior. Don't hesitate to decline further service, if you think the customer is becoming intoxicated.

- If you have any doubts about a customer's condition, refuse service.

Intoxication Indicators

- Ordering more than one drink at a time.

- Buying drinks for others.

- Concentration problems, losing train of thought (especially when ordering).

- Drinking very fast.

- Careless with money on the bar or can't pick up change.

- Complaining about drink strength, preparation, or prices.

- Overly friendly with customers or employees.

- Loud behavior: talking or laughing and annoying other patrons or making too many comments about others in the establishment.

- Brooding, remaining very quiet, detached from others, continually drinking.

- Mood swings: happy to sad or vice versa.

- Use of foul language.

- Lighting the wrong end of a cigarette.

DEALING WITH INTOXICATED PATRONS

If you notice someone appears to be intoxicated:

- Do not offer alcohol. Refill water, nonalcoholic beverages, and bread. Offer dessert.

- Alert your supervisor immediately. He or she may arrange for a safe ride home for the guest or refuse service.

Employer Responsibilities

- Employers should record incidences of refusal of sales in your manager's log. It serves as a legal record of your responsible alcohol practices in the event of a liability claim.

- Signs should be posted within guests' view with policies on alcohol consumption and responsible hospitality.

- All employees are trained in alcohol awareness and attendance has been documented.

Alcohol Awareness Test

1. Drinkingand driving is the number-two killer of Americans between the ages of 17–24, second only to cancer.
   a. True
   b. False

2. Statistically, in the United States, one person is killed in drunk driving accidents every:
   a. 24 hours
   b. 72 hours
   c. 90 minutes
   d. 22 minutes

3. A bartender sells a pitcher of beer with four glasses to a customer who is over 21 years of age. The customer takes the beer and glasses to a table. Later, police officers determine two of the four at the table are only 18. The bartender is not at fault.
   a. True
   b. False

4. The legal drinking age in your area is:
   a. 18
   b 20
   c. 21

5. If a customer appears to be over the legal drinking age, you do not have to request an ID in order to serve them an alcoholic beverage.
   a. True
   b. False

6. Due to their bodies' fat distribution and a decreased amount of alcohol-metabolizing enzymes, women may respond more quickly to alcohol:
   a. True
   b. False

7. Intoxication is a legal term that establishes a certain level of alcohol in the blood as the point of impairment severe enough that criminal sanctions may be enforced for driving and other actions. You can be impaired without being intoxicated.
   a. True
   b. False

8. To counter the effects of alcohol, people should drink coffee or take a cold shower to "sober up."
   a. True
   b. False

9. Which of the following are acceptable IDs to determine the age of a guest who is requesting an alcoholic beverage:
   a. A valid state driver's license, a valid state identification with a photograph and date of birth for those who don't drive, a valid passport, a valid United States Uniformed Service Identification.
   b. A valid state driver's license, a birth certificate and credit card with the same name listed in combination, a school ID from a valid university with a birth date listed next to the picture, a valid passport.
   c. A valid state driver's license, a school ID from a valid university with a birth date listed next to the picture, a valid passport, a valid United States Uniformed Service Identification.

10. One drink is the equivalent of a 12-oz. glass of beer, a 5-oz. pour of wine, or a mixed drink with about 1 oz. of alcohol. Approximately how long does it take the liver to eliminate the alcohol in one drink from the body?
    a. 15 minutes
    b. 30 minutes
    c. One hour
    d. Two hours

11. Blood Alcohol Concentration charts are the only way of determining the amount of alcohol circulating in a person's bloodstream.
    a. True
    b. False

12. Everyone metabolizes alcohol at the same rate.
    a. True
    b. False

13. Beer and wine have less alcohol than tequila.
    a. True
    b. False

14. Offering low- or nonalcoholic beverages, appetizers, bread, and water are good ways of promoting responsible alcohol consumption.
    a. True
    b. False

Alcohol Awareness Test

15. Which of the following behaviors are possible signs that a customer may be intoxicated? (Check all that apply.)
    - ❑ He or she is overly friendly and annoying other customers.
    - ❑ Eyes are glassy, the pupils are somewhat dilated, unfocused, sleepy-looking.
    - ❑ Trying to light a cigarette but is unable to do so upon the first try.
    - ❑ Purse is open and items are falling out but doesn't notice.
    - ❑ Spilling drinks.
    - ❑ Speech is slurred.
    - ❑ Loses his train of thought while trying to communicate order to you.
    - ❑ Sways and staggers a little and appears to lose balance only for a quick moment.

16. Once you have determined that a customer entering the establishment is intoxicated, what is the proper course of action?
    a. The customer should be served no more than one drink. Since he or she drank more elsewhere, if you serve them only one drink, you will not be liable and won't make him or her angry.
    b. The customer should be asked to leave.
    c. The customer should not be served any additional alcoholic beverages, and arrangements should be made so the customer is not driving.

17. Restaurant patrons' dining experience can be enhanced by enjoying wine and alcohol with their meal in a responsible manner.
    a. True
    b. False

18. As a special promotion for a certain brands of alcohol, it is legal to have "super cheap and super double shooter nights" if you count the number of "super cheap and super double shooters" each customer consumes.
    a. True
    b. False

19. The best way to inform someone that they have had their quota of drinks is by:
    a. Communicating with him or her in a friendly, caring, and non-threatening manner and alerting a manager if necessary.
    b. Pretending not to hear his or her requests for additional drinks.
    c. Asking the patron to leave.

20. Food and water may slow the onset of alcohol into the bloodstream, so it's important that water and appetizers are offered, and bread is served right away. As long as a customer is eating, you can serve him or her as much alcohol as he or she would like.
    a. True
    b. False

21. If you serve alcohol to someone who is intoxicated, you may be personally liable for any damages that incur from their drunken behavior and may have to pay monetary damages.
    a. True
    b. False

22. Statistically, how many Americans do NOT drink alcohol?
    a. One in ten
    b. One in twenty
    c. One in three

23. Serving alcohol in a responsible manner protects you, your friends, your family, and your employer's or your business.
    a. True
    b. False

24. Intoxication is the point where one's intake of alcohol affects their ability to perform appropriately.
    a. True
    b. False

25. Blood Alcohol Concentration, or BAC, measures the number of grams of alcohol in 100 milliliters of blood. The level of legal intoxication is .20 in most states.
    a. True
    b. False

Alcohol Awareness Test Answer Key

1. Drinkingand driving is the number two killer of Americans between the ages of 17–24, second only to cancer.
   a. True
   b. **False–it is the number-one killer.**

2. Statistically, in the United States, one person is killed in drunk driving accidents every:
   a. 24 hours
   b. 72 hours
   c. 90 minutes
   d. **22 minutes**

3. A bartender sells a pitcher of beer with four glasses to a customer who is over 21 years of age. The customer takes the beer and glasses to a table. Later, police officers determine two of the four at the table are only 18. The bartender is not at fault.
   a. True
   b. **False**

4. The legal drinking age in your area is:
   a. 18
   b. 20
   c. **21–in most states.**

5. If a customer appears to be over the legal drinking age, you do not have to request an ID in order to serve them an alcoholic beverage.
   a. True
   b. **False**

6. Due to their bodies' fat distribution and a decreased amount of alcohol-metabolizing enzymes, women may respond more quickly to alcohol:
   a. **True**
   b. False

7. Intoxication is a legal term that establishes a certain level of alcohol in the blood as the point of impairment severe enough that criminal sanctions may be enforced for driving and other actions. You can be impaired without being intoxicated.
   a. **True**
   b. False

8. To counter the effects of alcohol, people should drink coffee or take a cold shower to "sober up."
   a. True
   b. **False–Only removal of alcohol from the body via the liver sobers people**

9. Which of the following are acceptable IDs to determine the age of a guest who is requesting an alcoholic beverage:
   a. **A valid state driver's license, a valid state identification with a photograph and date of birth for those who don't drive, a valid passport, a valid United States Uniformed Service Identification.**
   b. A valid state driver's license, a birth certificate and credit card with the same name listed in combination, a school ID from a valid university with a birth date listed next to the picture, a valid passport.
   c. A valid state driver's license, a school ID from a valid university with a birth date listed next to the picture, a valid passport, a valid United States Uniformed Service Identification.

10. One drink is the equivalent of a 12-oz. glass of beer, a 5-oz. pour of wine, or a mixed drink with about 1 oz. of alcohol. Approximately how long does it take the liver to eliminate the alcohol in one drink from the body?
    a. 15 minutes
    b. 30 minutes
    c. **One hour**
    d. Two hours

11. Blood Alcohol Concentration charts are the only way of determining the amount of alcohol circulating in a person's bloodstream.
    a. True
    b. **False**

12. Everyone metabolizes alcohol at the same rate.
    a. True
    b. **False**

13. Beer and wine have less alcohol than tequila.
    a. True
    b. **False**

14. Offering low- or nonalcoholic beverages, appetizers, bread, and water are good ways of promoting responsible alcohol consumption.
    a. **True**
    b. False

Alcohol Awareness Test Answer Key

15. Which of the following behaviors are possible signs that a customer may be intoxicated? (Check all that apply.)
    - ☑ **He or she is overly friendly and annoying other customers.**
    - ☑ **Eyes are glassy, the pupils are somewhat dilated, unfocused, sleepy-looking.**
    - ☑ **Trying to light a cigarette but is unable to do so upon the first try.**
    - ☑ **Purse is open and items are falling out but doesn't notice.**
    - ☑ **Spilling drinks.**
    - ☑ **Speech is slurred.**
    - ☑ **Loses his train of thought while trying to communicate order to you.**
    - ☑ **Sways and staggers a little and appears to lose balance only for a quick moment.**

16. Once you have determined that a customer entering the establishment is intoxicated, what is the proper course of action?
    - a. The customer should be served no more than one drink. Since he or she drank more elsewhere, if you serve them only one drink, you will not be liable and won't make him or her angry.
    - b. The customer should be asked to leave.
    - c. **The customer should not be served any additional alcoholic beverages, and arrangements should be made so the customer is not driving.**

17. Restaurant patrons' dining experience can be enhanced by enjoying wine and alcohol with their meal in a responsible manner.
    - a. **True**
    - b. False

18. As a special promotion for a certain brands of alcohol, it is legal to have "super cheap and super double shooter nights" if you count the number of "super cheap and super double shooters" each customer consumes.
    - a. True
    - b. **False**

19. The best way to inform someone that they have had their quota of drinks is by:
    - a. **Communicating with him or her in a friendly, caring, and non-threatening manner and alerting a manager if necessary.**
    - b. Pretending not to hear his or her requests for additional drinks.
    - c. Asking the patron to leave.

20. Food and water may slow the onset of alcohol into the bloodstream, so it's important that water and appetizers are offered, and bread is served right away. As long as a customer is eating, you can serve him or her as much alcohol as he or she would like.
    - a. True
    - b. **False**

21. If you serve alcohol to someone who is intoxicated, you may be personally liable for any damages that incur from their drunken behavior and may have to pay monetary damages.
    - a. **True**
    - b. False

22. Statistically, how many Americans do NOT drink alcohol?
    - a. One in ten
    - b. One in twenty
    - c. **One in three**

23. Serving alcohol in a responsible manner protects you, your friends, your family, and your employer's or your business.
    - a. **True**
    - b. False

24. Intoxication is the point where one's intake of alcohol affects their ability to perform appropriately.
    - a. True
    - b. **False–that is the definition of impairment.**

25. Blood Alcohol Concentration, or BAC, measures the number of grams of alcohol in 100 milliliters of blood. The level of legal intoxication is .20 in most states.
    - a. True
    - b. **False–the level of legal intoxication is between .08 and .10 in most states.**

Blood Alcohol Content Chart

ONE DRINK EQUALS

12 ounces of beer
(5% alcohol content)

3 ounces of wine
(12% alcohol content)

1 ounce of spirits
(80 proof)

BAC CHARTS ARE ONLY A GUIDELINE.
THERE ARE NUMEROUS VARIABLES THAT DETERMINE HOW ALCOHOL AFFECTS INDIVIDUALS

MALE

Percentage of alcohol in bloodstream based on weight and consumption.

Weight	NUMBER OF DRINKS CONSUMED IN ONE HOUR OF TIME								
	1	2	3	4	5	6	7	8	9
100	.04	.08	.11	.15	.19	.23	.26	.30	.34
120	.03	.06	.09	.12	.16	.19	.22	.25	.28
140	.03	.05	.08	.11	.13	.16	.19	.21	.24
160	.02	.05	.07	.09	.12	.14	.16	.19	.21
180	.02	.04	.06	.08	.11	.13	.15	.17	.19
200	.02	.04	.06	.08	.09	.11	.13	.15	.17
220	.02	.03	.05	.07	.09	.10	.12	.14	.15
240	.02	.03	.05	.06	.08	.09	.11	.13	.14

FEMALE

Percentage of alcohol in bloodstream based on weight and consumption.

Weight	NUMBER OF DRINKS CONSUMED IN ONE HOUR OF TIME								
	1	2	3	4	5	6	7	8	9
100	.05	.09	.14	.18	.23	.27	.32	.36	.41
120	.04	.08	.11	.15	.19	.23	.27	.30	.34
140	.03	.07	.10	.13	.16	.19	.23	.26	.29
160	.03	.06	.09	.11	.14	.17	.20	.23	.26
180	.03	.05	.08	.10	.13	.15	.18	.20	.23
200	.02	.05	.07	.09	.11	.14	.16	.18	.20
220	.02	.04	.06	.08	.10	.12	.14	.17	.19
240	.02	.04	.06	.08	.09	.11	.13	.15	.17

Alcohol's Effect on Driving Skills

ONE DRINK EQUALS

 **12 ounces of beer (5% alcohol content)** =  **3 ounces of wine (12% alcohol content)** = **1 ounce of spirits (80 proof)**

Blood Alcohol Content .02%
Tracking ability diminishing. The ability to focus on tasks and pay attention may suffer.

Blood Alcohol Content .05%
Vision is impaired. Judgment and restraint slacken. Steering errors increase.

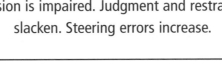

 3-4 drinks

Blood Alcohol Content .08%
(legally drunk in most states)
Reaction times noticeably slower. You're 3 to 4 times more likely to have an accident than a sober driver.

 2-4 drinks

 3-5 drinks

Blood Alcohol Content .10%
Reaction time slows even more. Movements are clumsy and uncoordinated. You are 6 times more likely to have an accident.

 2-5 drinks

 4-7 drinks

Blood Alcohol Content .15%
Reaction time increasingly affected. Your field of vision narrows. You are 25 times more likely to have an accident.

 3-7 drinks

Employee Alcohol Policy Notification Agreement

Date: _____ Employee: _____

As a server of alcoholic beverages, I understand that I have a legal responsibility to refuse service to anyone under the legal drinking age or to anyone who is already intoxicated.

I will immediately stop serving alcoholic beverages to any person who exhibits signs of intoxication, such as the following:

- ❏ He or she is overly friendly and annoying other customers.
- ❏ His or her eyes are glassy, the pupils are somewhat dilated, unfocused, and sleepy-looking.
- ❏ He or she is trying to light a cigarette but is unable to do so upon the first try.
- ❏ Her purse is open and items are falling out but she doesn't notice.
- ❏ He or she is spilling drinks.
- ❏ His or her speech is slurred.
- ❏ He or she loses train of thought while trying to communicate.
- ❏ He or she sways and staggers and appears to lose balance.

I agree to follow the policies established by management for the responsible service of alcoholic beverages.

_____

Signature

Service Refusal Form

If, at any time, you feel a patron is intoxicated and should not be served any more alcohol, notify your supervisor immediately. Then fill out the form below to the best of your ability.

Date: _____

Name of Employee Refusing Service: _____
_____

Please write a short description of why you felt the individual should not have been served alcohol or when the decision was made to discontinue further service. _____
_____
_____
_____
_____
_____
_____

Did the patron exhibit signs of intoxication, such as the following? Check all that apply.

- ❑ Slurred speech
- ❑ Difficulty lighting a cigarette
- ❑ Arguing with or annoying other guests
- ❑ Tearfulness
- ❑ Drowsiness
- ❑ Difficulty focusing eyes
- ❑ Memory loss
- ❑ Spilling drinks
- ❑ Falling or stumbling
- ❑ Difficulty picking up change

Please provide specific information about the customer.

Customer's Name (if known): _____

Sex: ○ M ○ F   Height: _____   Weight: _____

Hair: _____   Eyes: _____   Age: _____

Approximately how long was the customer on the premises?
_____

Please list, if known, the time the customer entered, left, and was denied service:

Arrival	_____	a.m./p.m
Departure	_____	a.m./p.m.
Time Service Denied	_____	a.m./p.m.

How many drinks did the customer have on the premises?
○ 1-2   ○ 3-4   ○ 5-6   ○ 7-10   ○ _____

What was the customer drinking? _____
_____

How much money did the patron spend? _____
_____

What was the customer's reaction to being refused service?
_____
_____
_____
_____

Was a cab called for the customer? ○ Yes   ○ No

Was an alternate method of transportation offered?
○ Yes (please list) _____   ○ No

Were the police called? ○ Yes   ○ No

Did anyone witness the refusal of service? ○ Yes   ○ No
If so, please list their names.
_____
_____
_____
_____

_____   _____   _____
Signature of Employee   **Print Name**   **Position**

_____   _____
Signature of Manager on Duty   **Print Name**

Liquid Measure Conversion Chart & Bar Supplies

CONVERSION CHART FOR LIQUID MEASURES

METRIC SIZE	FLUID OUNCES	U.S. MEASURE	FLUID OUNCES
50 ml	1.7	Miniature	1.6
200 ml	6.8	½ Pint	8.0
500 ml	16.9	1 Pint	16.0
750 ml	25.4	⅘ Quart	25.6
1 Liter	33.8	1 Quart	32.0
1.75 Liters	59.2	½ Gallon	64.0

SOME COMMONLY USED BAR MIXERS, JUICES & GARNISHES

JUICES

Orange juice

Cranberry juice

Pineapple juice

Grapefruit juice

Tomato juice

Lime juice

Lemon juice

FRESH FRUIT

Oranges

Limes

Bananas

Cherries

Strawberries

Lemon peels

Lemons

Pineapple

SODA & WATER

Coke or Pepsi

Diet Coke or Diet Pepsi

Sprite or 7-Up

Ginger ale

Tonic water

Soda water

Sparkling or mineral water

Purified water

GARNISHES

Cherries

Stuffed olives

Cocktail onions

Kosher salt

Celery salt

MIXERS, MISC.

Sweet-and-sour bar mix

Coconut cream concentrate

Grenadine

Bitters

Orgeat syrup

Worcestershire sauce

Tabasco sauce

Sugar-saturated water

Liquor Requisition

DATE:	SERVICE AREA:		SHIFT:	

ITEM	# EMPTIES	BOTTLE SIZE	BAR	MANAGEMENT

Beverage Requisition Form

DATE:	ISSUED FROM:			ISSUED TO:		

BRAND & KIND OF BEVERAGE	Size	Ordered	Delivered	Perpetual Marked	Cost	Extension

Beverage Perpetual Inventory

Product: _____ Distributor: _____

Size: _____ Case Cost: $_____ Bottle Cost: $ _____

Date	Requisitioned Inventory/Size	Purchases/ Size	On-Hand Inventory/Size	Manager's Initials

NOTES/COMMENTS:

Bar Inventory & Requisition

Date: _____ Inventory Taken By: _____

Issued By: _____ Received By: _____

Description	List #	Size	Par Stock	On Hand		Qty.	Unit Cost	Total Cost	Unit Sale Value	Total Sale Value		Unit Cost	Total Cost

Where the **REQUISITION** columns are: Qty., Unit Cost, Total Cost, Unit Sale Value, Total Sale Value; and the **INVENTORY** columns are: Unit Cost, Total Cost.

Wine Cellar Issue

Date: _____

Product	Vintage	# of Bottles	Guest Check #	Removed By

NOTES/COMMENTS:

BIN CARD

Date: _____ Product: _____

Balance Brought Forward: _____ Bottle Size: _____

DATE	IN	OUT	TOTAL ON HAND

BIN CARD

Date: _____ Product: _____

Balance Brought Forward: _____ Bottle Size: _____

DATE	IN	OUT	TOTAL ON HAND

Bottled Beer Count Form

Date: _____   Employee: _____

Brand	Begin Inventory	Bar Req.	Adjust. Inventory	End Inventory	Depletion	Sales Price	Est. Sales
	+	=	-	=	x	$	$
	+	=	-	=	x	$	$
	+	=	-	=	x	$	$
	+	=	-	=	x	$	$
	+	=	-	=	x	$	$
	+	=	-	=	x	$	$
	+	=	-	=	x	$	$
	+	=	-	=	x	$	$
	+	=	-	=	x	$	$
	+	=	-	=	x	$	$
	+	=	-	=	x	$	$
	+	=	-	=	x	$	$
	+	=	-	=	x	$	$
	+	=	-	=	x	$	$
	+	=	-	=	x	$	$
	+	=	-	=	x	$	$
	+	=	-	=	x	$	$

Total Estimated Sales	$
(subtract) Complimentary Sales @ Retail	$
(subtract) Waste & Spillage @ Retail	$
(EQUALS) Adjusted Estimated Sales	$
(subtract) Cash Register Sales	$
EXTENSION TOTAL	$

Bartender's Report

BARTENDER _____   **BARTENDER** _____

MANAGER _____   **MANAGER** _____

BOOKKEEPER _____   **BOOKKEEPER** _____

CASH IN

$100.00 _____	$1.00 _____
$50.00 _____	$0.50 _____
$20.00 _____	$0.25 _____
$10.00 _____	$0.10 _____
$5.00 _____	$0.05 _____
$1.00 _____	$0.01 _____
TOTAL	TOTAL

CASH OUT

$100.00 _____	$1.00 _____
$50.00 _____	$0.50 _____
$20.00 _____	$0.25 _____
$10.00 _____	$0.10 _____
$5.00 _____	$0.05 _____
$1.00 _____	$0.01 _____
TOTAL	TOTAL

CHARGES

1. _____
2. _____
3. _____
4. _____
5. _____
6. _____

TOTAL

SALES SUMMARY

LIQUOR SALES _____

FOOD SALES _____

WINE SALES _____

MISC. SALES _____

TOTAL _____

SALES TAX _____

VOID SALES _____

Note: Itemize checks separately on back.
Enter figure in sale and sales breakdown.

ITEM	LIQUOR	WINE
Housed	_____	_____
Manager	_____	_____
Comp	_____	_____

EMPLOYEE _____
Total # _____   #__# _____   Initial _____
Return _____   Verify _____

EMPLOYEE _____
Total # _____   #__# _____   Initial _____
Return _____   Verify _____

EMPLOYEE _____
Total # _____   #__# _____   Initial _____
Return _____   Verify _____

Liquor Order Form

ITEM	BUILD TO AMT.	DATE									

Liquor/Wine Inventory Form

ITEM	SIZE	QUANTITY				TOTAL	COST	EXTENSION

Inventory Form

Date: _____   Total Liquor: _____

Inventory By: _____   Total Beer: _____

Extension By: _____   Total Wine: _____

Examined By: _____

Product	Size	Open Bottles	Full Bottles	Store-room	Total	Cost	Extension

EXTENSION [   ]

Liquor Used & Restocked Form

LIQUOR	USED	RESTOCKED	LIQUOR	USED	RESTOCKED

Bar & Inventory Control Report

Date: _____ Time: _____

Inventory By: _____ Approved By: _____

ITEM _____ Unit _____

Opening Inventory _____

+ Requisitions: _____

TOTAL Inventory: _____

Closing Inventory: _____

TOTAL OF AMOUNT SOLD: _____
(subtract Closing Inventory from Total Inventory)

TOTAL OF AMOUNT SOLD: _____

x Price _____

Cost of Goods Sold: _____
(multiply the Total of Amount Sold by the Price)

# of Drinks Sold: _____

x Sales Price _____

TOTAL RETAIL VALUE: _____
(multiply the Number of Drinks Sold by the Sales Price)

LIQUOR COST PERCENTAGE: _____
(divide the Cost of Goods Sold by the Total Retail Value)

ITEM _____ Unit _____

Opening Inventory _____

+ Requisitions: _____

TOTAL Inventory: _____

Closing Inventory: _____

TOTAL OF AMOUNT SOLD: _____
(subtract Closing Inventory from Total Inventory)

TOTAL OF AMOUNT SOLD: _____

x Price _____

Cost of Goods Sold: _____
(multiply the Total of Amount Sold by the Price)

# of Drinks Sold: _____

x Sales Price _____

TOTAL RETAIL VALUE: _____
(multiply the Number of Drinks Sold by the Sales Price)

LIQUOR COST PERCENTAGE: _____
(divide the Cost of Goods Sold by the Total Retail Value)

ITEM _____ Unit _____

Opening Inventory _____

+ Requisitions: _____

TOTAL Inventory: _____

Closing Inventory: _____

TOTAL OF AMOUNT SOLD: _____
(subtract Closing Inventory from Total Inventory)

TOTAL OF AMOUNT SOLD: _____

x Price _____

Cost of Goods Sold: _____
(multiply the Total of Amount Sold by the Price)

# of Drinks Sold: _____

x Sales Price _____

TOTAL RETAIL VALUE: _____
(multiply the Number of Drinks Sold by the Sales Price)

LIQUOR COST PERCENTAGE: _____
(divide the Cost of Goods Sold by the Total Retail Value)

Liquor Storeroom Inventory Report

Date: _____   Time: _____

Inventory By: _____   Approved By: _____

Item	Unit	Opening Invent.	Purchases	Totals (A)	Requisitions by day of period month:							Totals (B)	Balance (A less B)	Closing Invent.	+/-	Price	Extension

Beverage Consumption Report

Date: _____   Event: _____

Beverage Type	Beginning Amount	Additions	Total Avail.	End Amount	Total Usage	Unit Cost	Total Cost
BEER							
1.							
2.							
3.							
4.							
LIQUOR							
1.							
2.							
3.							
4.							
5.							
6.							
WINE							
1.							
2.							
3							
OTHER							
1.							
2.							

TOTAL PRODUCT COST

Total Product Cost: _____   Cost Per Guest: _____   # Guests Served: _____

Liquor Waste Tracking Sheet

DATE	ITEM WASTED	AMOUNT	UNIT	REASON	COST
				TOTAL WASTE	

Drink Spill Sheet

DATE	SERVER NAME	DRINK	REASON	INITIALS

Cost of Beverage Consumed

Accounting Period

_____ to _____

Beginning Inventory $ _____

   (+)

Purchases $ _____

Goods Available $ _____

   (-)

Ending Inventory $ _____

   (-) $ _____

Transfers from Bar $ _____

   (+) $ _____

Transfers to Bar $ _____

Cost of Beverage Consumed $ _____

Beverage Cost Estimate

DATE	ISSUES		SALES		BEV. COST ESTIMATE	
	TODAY	TO DATE	TODAY	TO DATE	TODAY	TO DATE
Subtotal						
+ / -						
TOTAL						

Beverage Cost Report

Prepared By: _____ **Date:** _____

DATE	DAY		SALES
	SUNDAY	1st shift	
		2nd shift	
	MONDAY	1st shift	
		2nd shift	
	TUESDAY	1st shift	
		2nd shift	
	WEDNESDAY	1st shift	
		2nd shift	
	THURSDAY	1st shift	
		2nd shift	
	FRIDAY	1st shift	
		2nd shift	
	SATURDAY	1st shift	
		2nd shift	
		TOTAL	$

Cost of Goods Sold ($ _____)

Total Beverage Sales ($ _____)   = Beverage Cost Percentage (x 100 =   %)

Beverage Cost Report II

Prepared By: _____ **Date:** _____

	SUN	MON	TUE	WED	THUR	FRI	SAT	TOTAL
1st Shift Sales								
LIQUOR								
WINE								
BEER								
SHIFT TOTAL								
2nd Shift Sales								
LIQUOR								
WINE								
BEER								
SHIFT TOTAL								
DAILY TOTAL								

PERIOD BEVERAGE COST BREAKDOWN — SALES MANAGEMENT ANALYSIS						
	Cost of Goods Sold	Sales (Shift Totals)	Beverage Cost %	Sales	Retail Value	Over (Short)
Item						
LIQUOR						
WINE						
BEER						
TOTAL						

Cost Per Ounce — 750ML

The table below shows the cost per ounce for 750ml bottles ranging in price between $1.02 and $25.65. To figure the cost per ounce for 750ml bottles that cost more than $25.65, divide the bottle cost by 25.4 oz.

750ml Cost	$/oz.	750ml Cost	$/oz.	750ml Cost	$/oz.	750ml Cost	$/oz.
$1.02 – $1.26	.04	$7.37 – $7.61	.29	$13.73 – $13.97	.54	$20.07 – $20.31	.79
$1.27 – $1.52	.05	$7.62 – $7.87	.30	$13.98 – $14.22	.55	$20.32 – $20.57	.80
$1.53 – $1.77	.06	$7.88 – $8.12	.31	$14.23 – $14.47	.56	$20.58 – $20.82	.81
$1.78 – $2.03	.07	$8.13 – $8.38	.32	$14.48 – $14.73	.57	$20.83 – $21.08	.82
$2.04 – $2.28	.08	$8.39 – $8.63	.33	$14.74 – $14.98	.58	$21.09 – $21.33	.83
$2.29 – $2.53	.09	$8.64 – $8.88	.34	$14.99 – $15.23	.59	$21.34 – $21.58	.84
$2.54 – $2.79	.10	$8.89 – $9.14	.35	$15.24 – $15.49	.60	$21.59 – $21.84	.85
$2.80 – $3.04	.11	$9.15 – $9.39	.36	$15.50 – $15.74	.61	$21.85 – $22.09	.86
$3.05 – $3.30	.12	$9.40 – $9.65	.37	$15.75 – $16.00	.62	$22.10 – $22.35	.87
$3.31 – $3.55	.13	$9.66 – $9.90	.38	$16.01 – $16.25	.63	$22.36 – $22.60	.88
$3.56 – $3.80	.14	$9.91 – $10.15	.39	$16.26 – $16.50	.64	$22.61 – $22.85	.89
$3.81 – $4.06	.15	$10.16 – $10.41	.40	$16.51 – $16.75	.65	$22.86 – $23.11	.90
$4.07 – $4.31	.16	$10.42 – $10.66	.41	$16.76 – $17.01	.66	$23.12 – $23.36	.91
$4.32 – $4.57	.17	$10.67 – $10.92	.42	$17.02 – $17.27	.67	$23.37 – $23.62	.92
$4.58 – $4.82	.18	$10.93 – $11.17	.43	$17.28 – $17.52	.68	$23.63 – $23.87	.93
$4.83 – $5.07	.19	$11.18 – $11.42	.44	$17.53 – $17.77	.69	$23.88 – $24.12	.94
$5.08 – $5.33	.20	$11.43 – $11.68	.45	$17.78 – $18.03	.70	$24.13 – $24.38	.95
$5.34 – $5.58	.21	$11.69 – $11.93	.46	$18.04 – $18.28	.71	$24.39 – $24.63	.96
$5.59 – $5.84	.22	$11.94 – $12.19	.47	$18.29 – $18.54	.72	$24.64 – $24.89	.97
$5.85 – $6.09	.23	$12.20 – $12.44	.48	$18.55 – $18.79	.73	$24.90 – $25.14	.98
$6.10 – $6.34	.24	$12.45 – $12.69	.49	$18.80 – $19.04	.74	$25.15 – $25.39	.99
$6.35 – $6.60	.25	$12.70 – $12.95	.50	$19.05 – $19.30	.75	$25.40 – $25.65	1.00
$6.61 – $6.85	.26	$12.96 – $13.20	.51	$19.31 – $19.55	.76		
$6.86 – $7.11	.27	$13.21 – $13.46	.52	$19.56 – $19.81	.77		
$7.12 – $7.36	.28	$13.47 – $13.72	.53	$19.82 – $20.06	.78		

Cost Per Ounce — Liters

The table below shows the cost per ounce for liter bottles ranging in price between $1.00 and $34.13. To figure the cost per ounce for liters that cost more than $34.13, divide the bottle cost by 33.8 oz.

Liter Cost	$/oz.	Liter Cost	$/oz.	Liter Cost	$/oz.	Liter Cost	$/oz.
$1.00 – $1.35	.03	$9.47 – $9.80	.28	$17.92 – $18.25	.53	$26.37 – $26.70	.78
$1.36 – $1.68	.04	$9.81 – $10.13	.29	$18.26 – $18.58	.54	$26.71 – $27.03	.79
$1.69 – $2.02	.05	$10.14 – $10.47	.30	$18.59 – $18.92	.55	$27.04 – $27.37	.80
$2.03 – $2.36	.06	$10.48 – $10.81	.31	$18.93 – $19.26	.56	$27.38 – $27.71	.81
$2.37 – $2.70	.07	$10.82 – $11.15	.32	$19.27 – $19.60	.57	$27.72 – $28.05	.82
$2.71 – $3.04	.08	$11.16 – $11.49	.33	$19.61 – $19.94	.58	$28.06 – $28.39	.83
$3.05 – $3.37	.09	$11.50 – $11.82	.34	$19.95 – $20.27	.59	$28.40 – $28.72	.84
$3.38 – $3.71	.10	$11.83 – $12.16	.35	$20.28 – $20.61	.60	$28.73 – $29.06	.85
$3.72 – $4.05	.11	$12.17 – $12.50	.36	$20.62 – $20.95	.61	$29.07 – $29.40	.86
$4.06 – $4.39	.12	$12.51 – $12.84	.37	$20.96 – $21.29	.62	$29.41 – $29.74	.87
$4.40 – $4.73	.13	$12.85 – $13.18	.38	$21.30 – $21.63	.63	$29.75 – $30.08	.88
$4.74 – $5.06	.14	$13.19 – $13.51	.39	$21.64 – $21.96	.64	$30.09 – $30.41	.89
$5.07 – $5.40	.15	$13.52 – $13.85	.40	$21.97 – $22.30	.65	$30.42 – $30.75	.90
$5.41 – $5.74	.16	$13.86 – $14.19	.41	$22.31 – $22.64	.66	$30.76 – $31.09	.91
$5.75 – $6.08	.17	$14.20 – $14.53	.42	$22.65 – $22.98	.67	$31.10 – $31.43	.92
$6.09 – $6.42	.18	$14.54 – $14.87	.43	$22.99 – $23.32	.68	$31.44 – $31.77	.93
$6.43 – $6.75	.19	$14.88 – $15.20	.44	$23.33 – $23.65	.69	$31.78 – $32.10	.94
$6.76 – $7.09	.20	$15.21 – $15.54	.45	$23.66 – $23.99	.70	$32.11 – $32.44	.95
$7.10 – $7.43	.21	$15.55 – $15.88	.46	$24.00 – $24.33	.71	$32.45 – $32.78	.96
$7.44 – $7.77	.22	$15.89 – $16.22	.47	$24.34 – $24.67	.72	$32.79 – $33.12	.97
$7.78 – $8.11	.23	$16.23 – $16.56	.48	$24.68 – $25.01	.73	$33.13 – $33.46	.98
$8.12 – $8.44	.24	$16.57 – $16.89	.49	$25.02 – $25.34	.74	$33.47 – $33.79	.99
$8.45 – $8.78	.25	$16.90 – $17.23	.50	$25.35 – $25.68	.75	$33.80 – $34.13	1.00
$8.79 – $9.12	.26	$17.24 – $17.57	.51	$25.69 – $26.02	.76		
$9.13 – $9.46	.27	$17.58 – $17.91	.52	$26.03 – $26.36	.77		

Pour Cost Chart

Drink: _____ Priced By: _____ Date: _____

UNIT	ITEM	PRICE/OZ	TOTAL
Subtotal			
Loss			
TOTAL			

To-Do List

DATE: DAY:

HIGH PRIORITY:

- ❑ _____
- ❑ _____
- ❑ _____
- ❑ _____
- ❑ _____
- ❑ _____

MEDIUM PRIORITY:

- ❑ _____
- ❑ _____
- ❑ _____
- ❑ _____
- ❑ _____
- ❑ _____

LOW PRIORITY:

- ❑ _____
- ❑ _____
- ❑ _____
- ❑ _____
- ❑ _____
- ❑ _____

ON HOLD:

- ❑ _____
- ❑ _____
- ❑ _____
- ❑ _____

NOTES:

Daily Planner

DATE:	DAY:

DAILY SCHEDULE & APPOINTMENTS

Time	
7:00	
7:30	
8:00	
8:30	
9:00	
9:30	
10:00	
10:30	
11:00	
11:30	
12:00	
12:30	
1:00	
1:30	
2:00	
2:30	
3:00	
3:30	
4:00	
4:30	
5:00	
5:30	
6:00	
6:30	

DAILY TO-DO LIST:

- ❑ _____
- ❑ _____
- ❑ _____
- ❑ _____
- ❑ _____
- ❑ _____
- ❑ _____
- ❑ _____
- ❑ _____

EXPENSES:

- ❑ _____
- ❑ _____
- ❑ _____
- ❑ _____
- ❑ _____
- ❑ _____

CONTACTS:

- ❑ _____
- ❑ _____
- ❑ _____
- ❑ _____
- ❑ _____
- ❑ _____

NOTES:

Cashier's Report Form

Prepared By: _____

Date: _____ **Day:** _____ **Shift:** _____

		BAR REGISTER		SERVICE REGISTER		TOTAL
		Day	Night	Day	Night	All Shifts
1	**BANK DEPOSIT** Part I					
2	Currency					
3	Silver					
4	Checks					
5	**SUB TOTAL**					
6	**CREDIT CARDS:**					
7	MasterCard/Visa					
8	American Express					
9	Diners Club					
10	Other					
11	**OTHER RECEIPTS:**					
12	**TOTAL BANK DEPOSIT**					
13	**CASH SUMMARY** Part II					
14	Sales per Register					
15	Sales Tax per Register					
16	**ADJUSTMENTS:**					
17	Over/Under Rings					
18	Other: Complimentaries					
19	Other					
20	**TOTAL ADJUSTMENTS**					
21	Sales to Be Accounted For					
22	Sales Tax to Be Acctd. For					
23	Accounts Collected					
24	Other Receipts:					
25						
26						
27	**TIPS CHARGED:**					
28	MasterCard/Visa					
29	American Express					
30	Diners Club					
31	Other					
32	House Accounts-Tips					
33	**TOTAL RECEIPTS**					
34	**DEDUCT: PAID OUTS**					
35	Tips Paid Out					
36	House Charges					
37	Total Deductions					
38	**NET CASH RECEIPTS**					
39	**BANK DEPOSIT** (Line 12)					
40	**OVER or SHORT**					

Important Phone Numbers

UPDATED ON:

NAME	PHONE NUMBER	EXTENSION	PURPOSE/COMPANY

Emergency Contacts

AMBULANCE: _____

FIRE-RESCUE: _____

HOSPITAL: _____

PHYSICIAN: _____

POLICE: _____

POISON CONTROL: _____

LOCAL OSHA OFFICE: _____

Our address is:

_____

_____

Purchase Ledger

COMPANY _____ MONTH _____

DATE	INV #	AMT $	INV #	AMT $	INV #	AMT $	PAID OUTS
GRAND TOTAL							

PAGE TOTAL | |

Purveyor Information

Prepared By: _____   **Date:** _____

PURVEYOR	PHONE NUMBER	PRODUCTS SUPPLIED	SALES REP.	DELIVERY DAYS

Detailed Incident Report

RESTAURANT INFORMATION

Restaurant Name: _____ Date complaint reported:____ /____ /____

Address: _____

City: _____ State:_____ Zip Code: _____

Phone Number:_____

CLAIMANT INFORMATION

Name: _____ Date of visit: ____ /____ /____

Address: _____

City: _____ State:_____ Zip Code: _____

Phone Number:_____

Number of guests in your party? 1 2 3 4 5 6 7 8 9 10+

WITNESS INFORMATION

Name: _____ Date of visit: ____ /____ /____

Address: _____

City: _____ State:_____ Zip Code: _____

Phone Number:_____

Name: _____ Date of visit: ____ /____ /____

Address: _____

City: _____ State:_____ Zip Code: _____

Phone Number:_____

INCIDENT INFORMATION

Describe incident: _____

_____

_____

_____

Specific area where incident occurred: _____

Condition of area where incident occurred: _____

Employee involved: _____

Items involved: _____

Actions taken: _____

Manager on Duty: _____ Signature:_____

Customer Comment Form

Day: SU M T W TH F S **Date:** _____ **Shift:** _____ **Manager:** _____

Prepared By: _____ **Position:** _____

Comments heard about service:

_____

_____

_____

_____

_____

_____

Guest's name (if known): _____

Overall, service comments were: ❑ positive ❑ negative ❑ neutral

---

Comments heard about food:

_____

_____

_____

_____

_____

_____

Guest's name (if known): _____

Overall, food comments were: ❑ positive ❑ negative ❑ neutral

Comments heard about physical facility:

_____

_____

_____

_____

_____

_____

Guest's name (if known): _____

Overall, facility comments were: ❑ positive ❑ negative ❑ neutral

Robbery Description Facial Form

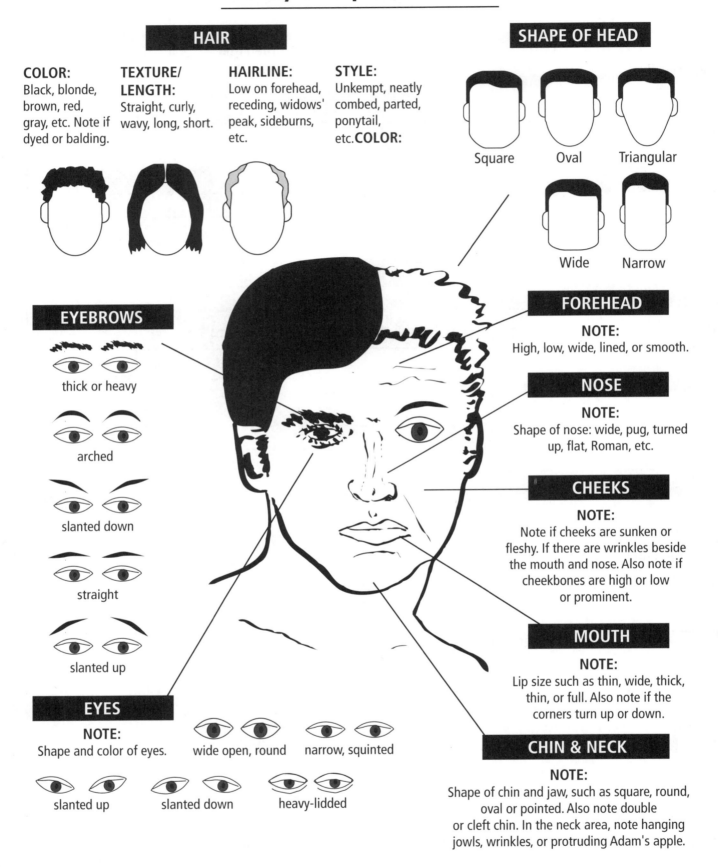

HAIR

COLOR:
Black, blonde, brown, red, gray, etc. Note if dyed or balding.

TEXTURE/ LENGTH:
Straight, curly, wavy, long, short.

HAIRLINE:
Low on forehead, receding, widows' peak, sideburns, etc.

STYLE:
Unkempt, neatly combed, parted, ponytail, etc. **COLOR:**

SHAPE OF HEAD

Square

Oval

Triangular

Wide

Narrow

EYEBROWS

thick or heavy

arched

slanted down

straight

slanted up

FOREHEAD

NOTE:
High, low, wide, lined, or smooth.

NOSE

NOTE:
Shape of nose: wide, pug, turned up, flat, Roman, etc.

CHEEKS

NOTE:
Note if cheeks are sunken or fleshy. If there are wrinkles beside the mouth and nose. Also note if cheekbones are high or low or prominent.

MOUTH

NOTE:
Lip size such as thin, wide, thick, thin, or full. Also note if the corners turn up or down.

EYES

NOTE:
Shape and color of eyes.

wide open, round

narrow, squinted

slanted up

slanted down

heavy-lidded

CHIN & NECK

NOTE:
Shape of chin and jaw, such as square, round, oval or pointed. Also note double or cleft chin. In the neck area, note hanging jowls, wrinkles, or protruding Adam's apple.

Robbery Description Physical Characteristics Form

PHYSICAL DESCRIPTION

Sex _____

Age _____

Race _____

Height _____

Weight _____

Hair _____

Eyes _____

Facial Hair _____

Identifying Marks (scars/tattoos) _____

_____

Complexion _____

Glasses _____

Hat _____

Shirt _____

Coat _____

Pants _____

Shoes _____

Additional Details _____

_____

_____

_____

_____

_____

_____

_____

_____

WEAPONS

❏ Knife

❏ Revolver

❏ Automatic

❏ Rifle

❏ Shotgun

❏ Other (describe)

_____

_____

_____

PISTOL

AUTOMATIC

RIFLE

SHOTGUN

Receiving Checklist

SUPPLIER: **TIME OF DELIVERY:**   a.m./p.m.

- ❏ Y   ❏ N   Frozen products arrive frozen solid
- ❏ Y   ❏ N   Refrigerated products arrive at a temperature below 41°F
- ❏ Y   ❏ N   Frozen products put away within 15 minutes of delivery

- ❏ Y   ❏ N   Refrigerated products put away within 30 minutes of delivery
- ❏ Y   ❏ N   Refrigerated and frozen products dated and stored for FIFO usage
- ❏ Y   ❏ N   Damaged products rejected

EMPLOYEE CHECKING IN PRODUCTS: **DATE:**

SUPPLIER: **TIME OF DELIVERY:**   a.m./p.m.

- ❏ Y   ❏ N   Frozen products arrive frozen solid
- ❏ Y   ❏ N   Refrigerated products arrive at a temperature below 41°F
- ❏ Y   ❏ N   Frozen products put away within 15 minutes of delivery

- ❏ Y   ❏ N   Refrigerated products put away within 30 minutes of delivery
- ❏ Y   ❏ N   Refrigerated and frozen products dated and stored for FIFO usage
- ❏ Y   ❏ N   Damaged products rejected

EMPLOYEE CHECKING IN PRODUCTS: **DATE:**

SUPPLIER: **TIME OF DELIVERY:**   a.m./p.m.

- ❏ Y   ❏ N   Frozen products arrive frozen solid
- ❏ Y   ❏ N   Refrigerated products arrive at a temperature below 41°F
- ❏ Y   ❏ N   Frozen products put away within 15 minutes of delivery

- ❏ Y   ❏ N   Refrigerated products put away within 30 minutes of delivery
- ❏ Y   ❏ N   Refrigerated and frozen products dated and stored for FIFO usage
- ❏ Y   ❏ N   Damaged products rejected

EMPLOYEE CHECKING IN PRODUCTS: **DATE:**

NOTES/CONCERNS:

Kitchen Safety Inspection Form

Date Completed: _____ Shift: _____

Prepared By: _____ Manager on Duty: _____

EQUIPMENT

Is all kitchen equipment clean, well-maintained, and in proper working order? ❏ Yes ❏ No

Are grease traps cleaned regularly? ❏ Yes ❏ No

Are the fryers in a separate location, away from grills, griddles, and open flames? ❏ Yes ❏ No

Is all refrigeration equipment free from dust and grease? ❏ Yes ❏ No

Comments or Corrective Actions Needed: _____

_____

_____

_____

_____

FIRE PREVENTION

Is there a fire-prevention system installed and in good working order? ❏ Yes ❏ No

Has the system been inspection by a professional and been marked with a valid inspection tag? ❏ Yes ❏ No

Are all cooking areas adequately covered by the fire-suppression system? ❏ Yes ❏ No

Are the fire-prevention nozzles aimed correction? ❏ Yes ❏ No

Are fire extinguishers easily accessible? ❏ Yes ❏ No

Are fire extinguishers charged and inspected yearly? ❏ Yes ❏ No

Has the automatic sprinkler system been inspected yearly and tagged? ❏ Yes ❏ No

Is the sprinkler system valve open and in good condition? ❏ Yes ❏ No

Comments or Corrective Actions Needed: _____

_____

_____

_____

_____

VENTILATION SYSTEMS

Are exhaust vents and fans clean and inspected on a regular basis? ❏ Yes ❏ No

Does the exhaust hood adequately cover all cooking areas? ❏ Yes ❏ No

Are all the exhaust hood filters clean, well-maintained, and free of grease? ❏ Yes ❏ No

Comments or Corrective Actions Needed: _____

_____

_____

_____

_____

ELECTRICAL

Is the electrical room also used for storage? ❏ Yes ❏ No

Is the fuse box or fuse panels easily accessible? ❏ Yes ❏ No

In the fuse box, are all the breakers labeled clearly? ❏ Yes ❏ No

Are any of the breaker switches covered with tape? ❏ Yes ❏ No

Are all electrical switches covered? ❏ Yes ❏ No

Are all electrical outlets covered? ❏ Yes ❏ No

Are all electrical junction boxes and fittings covered? ❏ Yes ❏ No

Are there any extension cords in use? ❏ Yes ❏ No

Are all exposed electrical cords untangled, properly insulated, and in good condition? ❏ Yes ❏ No

Comments or Corrective Actions Needed: _____

_____

_____

_____

_____

Daily Sales Report Form

	DAY	DATE	FOOD SALES		LIQUOR SALES		WINE SALES		TOTAL SALES	MONTH-TO-DATE	
			AMT $	INV #	AMT $	INV #	AMT $	INV #		ACTUAL	BUDGET
1											
2											
3											
4											
5											
6											
7											
7-DAY TOTAL											
8											
9											
10											
11											
12											
13											
14											
14-DAY TOTAL											
15											
16											
17											
18											
19											
20											
21											
21-DAY TOTAL											
22											
23											
24											
25											
26											
27											
28											
28-DAY TOTAL											
29											
30											
31											
TOTAL											

Daily Sales Report Form

OVER UNDER	# DINERS	PER HEAD	CASH OV/U	MANAGERIAL			HOUSED			COMPLIMENTARY		
				FOOD	LIQR	WINE	FOOD	LIQR	WINE	FOOD	LIQR	WINE

Labor Analysis Form

	DAY	DATE	DAILY SALES	DAILY PAYROLL BUDGET	ACT	OV/UND	%	MONTH TO DATE	MONTH-TO-DATE PAYROLL BUDGET	ACT	OV/UND	%
1												
2												
3												
4												
5												
6												
7												
7-DAY TOTAL												
8												
9												
10												
11												
12												
13												
14												
14-DAY TOTAL												
15												
16												
17												
18												
19												
20												
21												
21-DAY TOTAL												
22												
23												
24												
25												
26												
27												
28												
28-DAY TOTAL												
29												
30												
31												
TOTAL												

Conclusion

At this point, you have plenty of facts, tips, and ideas for managing your bar. Whether your bar is a dance bar, sports bar, or one of the other varieties mentioned here, you now know enough about your customers, staff, supplies, and finances to make a success of your establishment. You will want to refer to this book again and again to refresh your ideas and to look up specifics. You may even want to suggest this book to your staff, especially if they need to learn the basics about bar operation.

Whether you are starting your own bar or already managing an established bar, you now have the tools needed to:

- Hire and train employees

- Develop a budget

- Develop a menu and drink menu

- Establish controls

- Lure in the Right customers

- Deal with problems

- Manage your bar's money

- Keep your bar safe

- Deal with customers

- Ensure high customer satisfaction

- Add the touches that will bring success to your bar

- Maximize profits

There is a whole world out there to feed and entertain, so start today in managing your bar to success!

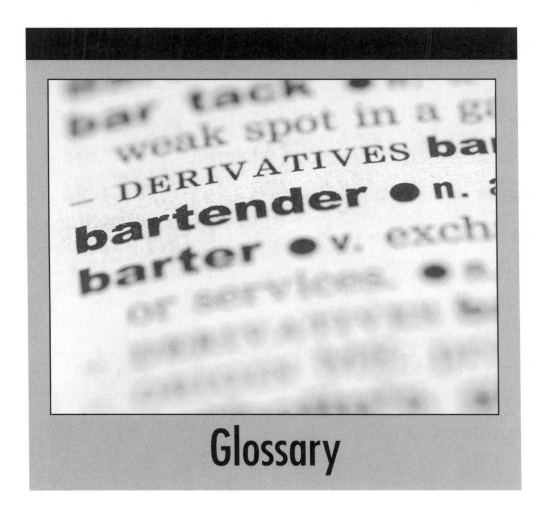

Glossary

A

A LA CARTE – A list of individually priced and sold items.

ACETALDEHYDE – Colorless, flammable liquid that is formed during ethanol metabolism.

ADDITIVES – A small amount of a substance added to something else to improve it.

ADJUNCT – Substance used instead of grains to make beer cheaper.

AGE – Used as a measure of quality with alcohol.

AIRLOCK – A chamber that allows carbon dioxide to escape during fermentation.

ALCOHOL – A colorless, intoxicating liquid produced by distilling fermented fruits, vegetables and grains.

ALE – Alcoholic beverage brewed from

malt and hops.

APERITIF – An alcoholic drink taken before a meal to stimulate appetite.

B

BAC – Blood alcohol concentration.

BACK BAR – The shelves that hold the liquor behind the bar.

BAKING SODA – A leavening agent used in baking.

BANK – Money with which bartenders or servers start their shift.

BAR ACCESSORIES – Any item that is used in a bar.

BAR BACK – A bartender's assistant that does not serve drinks.

BAR BOTTLES – A decorative bottle intended to be refilled for dispensing various types of liquor.

BAR HEIGHT – The dimension of a bar measured from its top to its bottom.

BARTENDER – A person who mixes and serves drinks at a bar.

BEER – An alcoholic beverage brewed from a mash of malted barley and other cereals, flavored with hops and fermented with yeast.

BISTRO SET – Used for casual dining, a bistro set consists of a round table with two matching chairs.

BITTERS – A bitter or bittersweet flavoring agent.

BOTTLE CONDITIONING – Maturing of the bottle to develop the nuances of many wines.

C

CALL – Liquor that a customer specifically asks for by name.

CARAFE – A pot or bottle used for serving water, coffee, or wine.

CARBON DIOXIDE – A by-product of fermentation that causes carbonation.

CASK – Barrel-shaped container used to store beer or wine.

CHASER – A beverage usually drunk immediately after drinking another beverage.

COCKTAIL – Any alcoholic beverage that mixes two or more ingredients.

COD – Cash Bar.

COMPS – Management-authorized free drinks; complimentary drinks.

CONDITIONING TANK – A tank where the beer matures, clarifies and is naturally carbonated through secondary fermentation.

CONTEMPORARY – Modern furniture.

CONVERTIBLE BAR – Open or folding bar.

D

DEXTRIN – Un-fermentable carbohydrate.

DISTILLATION – Purifying liquids through boiling so that the steam or vapors condense to a pure form.

DRAFT – Keg beer served on tap.

E

ESTER – Compound formed during fermentation giving beer a spicy taste.

F

FERMENTATION – Changing sugar into ethyl alcohol and carbon dioxide.

FERMENTER – A closed and sterile container used for fermentation.

FRAPPES – The combination of many types of liquor served over crushed ice; usually an after-dinner drink.

FREE POUR – Pouring alcohol without using a measuring device.

G

GRENADINE – Nonalcoholic syrup used to sweeten and color drinks.

GUN – Used to measure and pour soda.

H

HAND PUMP – Used to serve draft beer.

HEAD – The foam on top of beer.

HIGHBALLS – A simple mixture of whiskey and club soda served in a tall glass.

HOPS – Flowers used to flavor beer and ale.

ingredients and a spirit.

J

JIGGER – Used to calculate an exact amount of liquid; also called a shot glass.

K

KEG – One-half barrel that holds approximately 15.5 gallons.

L

LACE – The last ingredient in a recipe.

LAGER – Beer stored in a cask or vat for a period of one to three months.

LIGHT BEER – Low-calorie beer.

LIGHT-STRUCK – Having a skunk-like smell due to light exposure.

LIQUEUR – Alcoholic beverage with a sweet taste made by flavored

M

MALT LIQUOR – Higher alcohol content than standard beer.

METALLIC – Over-aged beer.

MINOR – Guest under the age of 21.

MIST – Filling a glass with crushed ice and then pouring undiluted spirits on top.

MUDDLE – To mash or crush ingredients together.

MUSTY – Moldy flavor and aroma due to cork or brew spillage.

N

NEAT – A drink without ice, water, or mixers.

NIGHTCAP – A drink taken at the end of an evening.

NIP – A small drink; to drink in small sips.

NONALCOHOLIC – A beverage containing less than 0.5 percent alcohol by volume.

O

OCCUPANCY CAPACITY – Number of people allowed in one area determined by the fire and building codes.

ON THE ROCKS – Alcohol poured over ice cubes.

P

PAR LEVEL – Level set to prevent running out of something.

PAR STOCK – The level to which inventory is restored each time an order is placed.

PHYSICAL INVENTORY – Exact amount of alcohol.

POURING COST – The cost determined by dividing consumption by sales.

PROOF – Measures the strength of alcohol.

PUBLICAN – Pub owner or manager.

R

RACKING – Siphoning off the clear juice that has fallen to the bottom of a container.

S

SHOT – A small amount of liquor; usually one to two ounces.

SHRINKAGE – Inventory loss not affiliated with sales.

T

TOP SHELF – Liquor that is the most expensive.

TOT – Liquor in small amounts.

V

VIRGIN – Nonalcoholic drink.

W

WELL – House liquor.

WINE BAR – Wine holding bar.

Z

ZYMURGY – The science of brewing beer.

Manufacturers Reference

The following manufacturers submitted photos and/or information to be used as references in *The Professional Bar & Beverage Manager's Handbook*.

Accardis Systems, Inc.
20061 Doolittle Street
Montgomery Village, MD 20886
1-800-852-1992
www.accardis.com

Accubar
9457 S University Blvd
#261
Highlands Ranch, CO 80126
1-800-806-3922
www.accubar.com

Amana Commercial Products
2800 220th Trail
Amana, IA 52204
1-888-262-6271
www.amanacommercial.com

Aprons, Etc.
PO Box 1132
9 Ellwood Court
Mauldin, SC 29662
1-800-460-7836
www.apronsetc.com

Belson Outdoors, Inc.
111 North River Rd
North Aurora, IL 60542
1-630-897-8489
www.belson.com

Big John Grills & Rotisseries
770 W College Ave
Pleasant Gap, PA 16823
1-800-326-9575
www.bigjohngrills.com

Blodgett
44 Lakeside Avenue
Burlington, VT 05401
1-800-331-5842
www.blodgett.com

Browne-Halco, Inc.
2840 Morris Ave
Union, NJ 07083
1-888-289-1005
www.halco.com

CommLog
2509 E Darrel Rd
Phoenix, AZ 85042
1-800-962-6564
www.commlog.com

Cookshack, Inc.
2304 N Ash St
Ponca City, OK 74601
1-800-423-0698
www.cookshack.com

DayMark Safety Systems
12830 South Dixie Highway
Bowling Green, OH 43402
1-800-847-0101
www.daymark.biz

Duncan Industries
PO Box 802822
Santa Clarita, CA 91380
1-800-785-4449
www.kitchengrips.com

EasyBar Beverage Management Systems
19799 SW 95th Ave, Suite A
Tualatin, OR 97062
1-503-624-6744
www.easybar.com

Exadign, Inc.
2871 Pullman Street
Santa Ana, CA 92705
1-949-486-0320
www.exadigm.com

Franklin Machine Products
101 Mt. Holly Bypass
Lumberton, NJ 08048
1-800-257-7737
www.fmponline.com

General Espresso Equipment Corporation
7912 Industrial Village Road
Greensboro, NC 27409
1-336-393-0224
www.geec.com

Henny Penny Corporation
1219 U.S. 35 West
Eaton, OH 45320
1-800-417-8417
www.hennypenny.com

Holstein Manufacturing
5368 110th St
Holstein, IA 51025
1-800-368-4342
www.holsteinmfg.com

InTouch POS
1601 N California Blvd
Walnut Creeek, CA 94596
925-939-0888
www.intouchpos.com

Loyal Rewards
812 W Chestnut St
Perkasie, PA 18944
1-800-309-7228
www.loyalrewards.com

Matrix Engineering, Inc.
3434 Industrial 33rd St
Ft. Pierce, FL 34946
1-800-926-0528
www.griprock.com

Microframe Corporation
604 S 12th St
Broken Arrow, OK 74012
1-918-258-4839
www.restaurantpager.com

Motoman Inc.
805 Liberty Lane
West Carrollton, OH 45449
1-937-847-6200
www.motoman.com

Moving Targets
812 W Chestnut St
Perkasie, PA 18944
1-800-926-2451
www.movingtargets.com

Nuvo Technologies, Inc.
6060 East Thomas Road
Scottsdale, AZ 85251
1-480-222-6000
www.barvision.com

OZEM Corp.
832 Harvard Dr
Holland, MI 49423
1-866-617-3345
www.ozwinebars.com

Polar Ware Company
2806 North 15th St
Sheboygan, WI 53083

1-800-237-3655
www.polarware.com

Precision Pours, Inc.
12837 Industrial Park Blvd
Plymouth, MN 55441
1-800-549-4491
www.precisionpours.com

Regal Ware, Inc.
1675 Reigle Dr
Kewaskum, WI 53040
1-262-626-2121
www.regalwarefoodservice.
com

Replacement Headsets
A Division of GLK
Corporation
2385 S 179th St, Suite B
New Berlin, WI 53146
1-262-784-8560
www.replacementheadsets.
com

Royal Industries
4100 W Victoria Street
Chicago, IL 60646
1-773-478-6300
www.royalindustries.com

Scannabar
101 Federal St, Suite 1900
Boston, MA 02110
1-888-666-0736
www.scannabar.com

Sitram USA
4081 Calle Tesoro, Ste G
Camarillo, CA 93012
1-800-515-8585
www.sitramcookware.com

Slecta Corp dba Dickies
Chef
13780 Benchmark Dr
Farmers Branch, TX 75234
1-866-262-6288
www.dickiechef.com

Stoelting, LLC
502 HWY 67
Kiel, WI 53042
1-800-558-5807
www.stoelting.com

Sunkist Foodservice Eq.
720 E Sunkist St
Ontario, CA 91761
1-800-383-7141
www.sunkistfs.com/
equipment

Tucel Industries
2014 Forestdale Road
Forestdale, VT 05745
1-800-558-8235
www.tucel.com

Vinotemp International
17621 S Susanna Rd
Rancho Dominguez, CA
90221
1-310-886-3332
www.vinotemp.com

Vital Link POS
8567 Vinup Road
Lynden, WA 98264
1-360-318-9946
www.vitallinkpos.com

Winekeeper
625 E Haley St
Santa Barbabra, CA 93103
1-805-963-3451
www.winekeeper.com

WNA Comet
6 Stuart Road
Chelmsford, MA 01824
1-888-962-2877
www.wna-inc.com

Zing Zang Inc
950 Milwaukee Ave
Glenview, IL 60025
1-888-891-7489
www.zingzang.com

Index

G

Galliano 150

garbage 396

garnishes 111, 221, 333, 405

gas stove 396

gin 146, 182

glassware 62, 120, 224

gloves 271

grand opening 70

grappa 148

grills 399

guidebooks 30

H

HACCP 243

happy hour 69, 305

heat 65

hiring 76, 92

holidays 336

hors d'oeuvres 237

hostess 79

hours 326

hygiene 225

I

ice 120

IDs 47

incentives 108, 135, 300

insects 268

insurance 34, 41, 62

Internal Revenue Service 40

Internet 134, 328, 359

intoxication 41

inventory 51, 65, 107, 282, 308

investors 35

J

Jagermeister 151

juice 111, 222, 280, 405

jukebox 350

K

Kahlua 151

karaoke 345

kegs 280

Kirsch 147

kitchen 395

knives 118, 273

L

labeling 114

laundry 63

lawyer 41

layout 385

liability insurance 55

license 38, 381

lighting 330, 340, 382

linens 63

liquor license 18

loans 34

location 25, 35, 381

DID YOU BORROW THIS COPY?

Have you been borrowing a copy of *The Professional Bar & Beverage Manager's Handbook* from a friend, colleague, or library? Don't you wish you had your own copy for quick and easy reference? To make it easy for you to order, please photocopy the order form below and send to:
Atlantic Publishing Company • 1210 SW 23 Place • Ocala, FL 34474-7014

YES! Send me_____copy(ies) of THE PROFESSIONAL BAR & BEVERAGE MANAGER'S HANDBOOK (Item # PBB-01) for $79.95 + $5.00 for shipping and handling.

Atlantic Publishing Company
1210 SW 23 Place
Ocala, FL 34474-7014

Add $5.00 for USPS shipping and handling. For Florida residents PLEASE add the appropriate sales tax for your county.

Please Print

_____
Name

_____
Organization Name

_____
Address

_____
City, State, Zip

Order toll-free
800-814-1132
FAX 352-622-5836

❑ My check or money order is enclosed. *Please make checks payable to Atlantic Publishing Company.*

❑ My purchase order is attached. *PO #_____*

www.atlantic-pub.com • e-mail: sales@atlantic-pub.com

DID YOU BORROW THIS COPY?

Have you been borrowing a copy of *The Professional Bar & Beverage Manager's Handbook* from a friend, colleague, or library? Don't you wish you had your own copy for quick and easy reference? To make it easy for you to order, please photocopy the order form below and send to:
Atlantic Publishing Company • 1210 SW 23 Place • Ocala, FL 34474-7014

YES! Send me_____copy(ies) of THE PROFESSIONAL BAR & BEVERAGE MANAGER'S HANDBOOK (Item # PBB-01) for $79.95 + $5.00 for shipping and handling.

Atlantic Publishing Company
1210 SW 23 Place
Ocala, FL 34474-7014

Add $5.00 for USPS shipping and handling. For Florida residents PLEASE add the appropriate sales tax for your county.

Please Print

_____
Name

_____
Organization Name

_____
Address

_____
City, State, Zip

Order toll-free
800-814-1132
FAX 352-622-5836

❑ My check or money order is enclosed. *Please make checks payable to Atlantic Publishing Company.*

❑ My purchase order is attached. *PO #_____*

www.atlantic-pub.com • e-mail: sales@atlantic-pub.com

ALCOHOL SERVICE POSTERS

Decorative and instructional, these full-color posters will be popular with both your employees and customers. Containing essential information, drink photos, recipes, and more, they will help increase sales and grab attention. Posters are laminated to reduce wear and tear and measure 11" x 17".

12 Classic Cocktails
with Recipes
Item # CC-PS

12 Popular Cocktails
with Recipes
Item # PC-PS

Types of Beer • Item # TOB-PS

Categories of Liquor
Item # COL-PS

10 Types of Martinis
Item # TOM-PS

Drink Garnishes
Item # DG-PS

Common Bar
Abbreviations
Item # CBA-PS

Series of 7 Posters • Item # ASP-PS • ONLY $59.95!

To order, call 1-800-814-1132 or visit www.atlantic-pub.com

WINE SERVICE POSTERS

These five color posters cover all the wine basics—from service to pronunciation. Essential information for anyone serving, pouring, or selling wine, yet attractive enough to display in your dining room. Posters are laminated to reduce wear and tear and measure 11" x 17".

$9.95 EACH

Wine Pronunciation Guide
Item # WPG-PS • $9.95

Red Wine
Item # RWP-PS • $9.95

Sparkling Wine & Champagne
Item # SWC-PS • $9.95

Proper Wine Service
Item # PWS-PS • $9.95

White Wine
Item # WWP-PS • $9.95

Series of 5 Posters • Item # WPS-PS • ONLY $39.95!

To order, call 1-800-814-1132 or visit www.atlantic-pub.com

ALCOHOL AWARENESS POSTERS

Alcohol awareness is an important issue. This new poster series covers ten fundamental topics and should be posted in any establishment that serves alcohol. Posters are in full color and laminated to reduce wear. They measure 11" x 17".

$9.95 EACH

Right to Refuse Service
Item # RTR-PS • $9.95

One Drink Equals
Item # ODE-PS • $9.95

Spotting a Fake ID
Item # FID-PS • $9.95

Symptoms of Intoxication
Item # SIO-PS • $9.95

We Check IDs
Item # CID-PS • $9.95

Drinking & Pregnancy
Item # D&P-PS • $9.95

Blood Alcohol Content Chart—Female Item # BACF-PS • $9.95

Blood Alcohol Content Chart—Male Item # BACM-PS • $9.95

Don't Drink & Drive
Item # DDD-PS • $9.95

Alcohol Slows Reaction Times
Item # ASR-PS • $9.95

Series of 10 Posters • Item # AAP-PS • ONLY $89.95!

To order, call 1-800-814-1132 or visit www.atlantic-pub.com

ORDER THE COMPLETE 3-BOOK REFERENCE SET FOR YOUR FOOD SERVICE OPERATION!

These three titles are the ultimate reference for running a restaurant or food service operation! Each comes with a companion CD-ROM.

The Encyclopedia of Restaurant Training: A Complete Ready-to-Use Training Program for All Positions in the Food Service Industry From orientating the new employee and maintaining performance standards to detailed training outlines and checklists for all positions, this book will show you how to train your employees in the shortest amount of time. The companion CD-ROM contains the training outline for all positions in MS Word, to customize for your own use.

The Restaurant Manager's Handbook: How to Set Up, Operate, and Manage a Financially Successful Food Service Operation
This comprehensive manual will show you step by step how to set up, operate, and manage a financially successful food service operation. It shows the logical progression from dream to reality, from concept to finding a "market gap" to operating an eating establishment. Also covers menu planning, employee training, equipping the kitchen, food protection, sanitation, and more. This knowledge is ready to apply immediately, whether you are planning a new restaurant or have an established successful one. There are literally hundreds of ways demonstrated to streamline your restaurant business. To make the kitchen, bars, dining room, and front office run smoother and increase performance. The CD-ROM has 118 forms, charts, diagrams, and checklists, all ready to use.

The Encyclopedia of Restaurant Forms: A Complete Kit of Ready-to-Use Checklists, Worksheets, and Training Aids for a Successful Food Service Operation For the new and veteran food service operators alike, this book is essentially a unique "survival kit" packed with tested advice, practical guidelines, and ready-to-use materials for all aspects of your job. The book and companion CD-ROM focuses on the issues, situations, and tasks that you face daily. Included in this book are hundreds of easy-to-implement tools, forms, checklists, posters, templates, and training aids to help you get your operation organized and easier to manage while building your bottom line! The material may be used as is or readily adapted for any food service application.

To order, call 1-800-814-1132 or visit www.atlantic-pub.com